MW01595852

Markets, Morals and Policy-Making

Economic theory emerged out of the Scottish Enlightenment as a social science with relevance for public issues. Over the past century or so, however, economics retreated into the vapid mechanics of optimization. In this imaginative and creative book, Enrico Colombatto presents a wide-ranging restatement of the moral and social foundations of economics as a publicly-relevant discipline.

Richard Wagner, *George Mason University, USA.*

Free-market economics has attempted to combine efficiency and freedom by emphasizing the need for neutral rules and meta-rules. These efforts have only been partly successful, for they have failed to address the deeper, normative arguments justifying – and limiting – coercion. This failure has thus left most advocates of free-market economics vulnerable to formulae which either emphasize expediency or which rely upon optimal social engineering to foster different notions of the common will and of the common good. This book offers the reader a new perspective, one in which the defence of markets is no longer based upon the utilitarian claim that free markets are more efficient; rather, the defence of markets rests upon the moral argument that top-down coercive policy-making is necessarily in tension with the rights-based notion of justice typical of the Western tradition.

In arguing for a consistent moral basis for the free-market view, we depart from both the Austrian and neoclassical traditions by acknowledging that rationality is not a satisfactory starting point. This rejection of rationality as the complete motivator for human economic behaviour throws constitutional economics and the law-and-economics tradition into new relief, revealing these approaches as governed by considerations derived by various notions of social efficiency, rather than by principles consistent with individual freedom, including freedom to choose.

This book shows that the solution is in fact a better understanding of the lessons taught by the Scottish Enlightenment: the role of the political context is to ensure that the individual can pursue his own ends, free from coercion. This also implies individual responsibility, respect for somebody else's preferences and for his entrepreneurial instincts. Social virtue is not absent from this understanding of politics, but rather than being defined through the priorities of policy-makers, it emerges as the outcome of interaction among self-determining individuals. The strongest and most consistent case for free-market economics, therefore, rests on moral philosophy, not on some version of static-efficiency theorizing.

This book should be of interest to students and researchers focussing on economic theory, political economics and the philosophy of economic thought, but is also written in a non-technical style making it accessible to an audience of non-economists.

Enrico Colombatto is Professor of Economics at the University of Turin (Italy) and Director of the International Centre for Economic Research.

Routledge foundations of the market economy
Edited by Mario J. Rizzo
New York University
and
Lawrence H. White
University of Missouri at St Louis

A central theme in this series is the importance of understanding and assessing the market economy from a perspective broader than the static economics of perfect competition and Pareto optimality. Such a perspective sees markets as causal processes generated by the preferences, expectations and beliefs of Economic agents. The creative acts of entrepreneurship that uncover new information about preferences, prices and technology are central to these processes with respect to their ability to promote the discovery and use of knowledge in society.

The market economy consists of a set of institutions that facilitate voluntary cooperation and exchange among individuals. These institutions include the legal and ethical framework as well as more narrowly "economic" patterns of social interaction. Thus the law, legal institutions and cultural and ethical norms, as well as ordinary business practices and monetary phenomena, fall within the analytical domain of the economist.

Previous books in this series include:

Markets, Morals and Policy-Making

A new defence of free-market economics

Enrico Colombatto

Routledge
Taylor & Francis Group

LONDON AND NEW YORK

First published 2011
by Routledge
2 Park Square, Milton Park, Abingdon, Oxon OX14 4RN

Simultaneously published in the USA and Canada
by Routledge
711 Third Avenue, New York, NY 10017

Routledge is an imprint of the Taylor & Francis Group, an informa business

British Library Cataloguing in Publication Data
A catalogue record for this book is available from the British Library

Library of Congress Cataloging in Publication Data
Colombatto, Enrico.
    Markets, morals, and policy-making : a new defense of free-market
    economics / by Enrico Colombatto.
    p. cm.
    Includes bibliographical references and index.
    1. Free enterprise. 2. Liberty. 3. Civil rights. 4. Economics–Moral and
    ethical aspects. I. Title.
    HB95.C65 2011
    330.12'2–dc22
    2011002037

ISBN: 978-0-415-58854-6 (hbk)
ISBN: 978-0-203-80835-1 (ebk)

Typeset in Times
by Wearset Ltd, Boldon, Tyne and Wear

Contents

Acknowledgements

I am grateful to many friends and colleagues for having read parts of this book while the various chapters were being written. In particular, Stefano Adamo, Sergio Beraldo, Hardy Bouillon, David Gay, Randall Holcombe, Jean-Michel Josselin, Gary Libecap, Alain Marciano, Arie Melnik, Fabio Mendez, Giovanni Pavanelli, Pavel Pelikán, Moshe Syrquin, Simon Teitel and Zhang Xue helped me a lot in discussions as well as in offering ideas, criticism and questions. Special thanks to Christine Henderson, who read every word of this book with great patience and whose thoughtful advice saved me from many errors, linguistic and otherwise.

I am also indebted to the Stanford University's Hoover Institution, directed by David Brady and the Northwestern University's Searle Center, directed by Henry Butler. Most of this work was carried out during my stay in those two great establishments, where I took advantage of the outstanding scholarly environment David and Henry created.

Last, but not least, I should express my gratitude to a number of other institutions where I discussed parts of my work during the past two years: the Liberty Fund (Indianapolis), the Northwestern University School of Law, the Transatlantic Law Forum at the American Enterprise Institute, the University of Arkansas, the University Paul Cézanne (Aix-en-Provence), the University of Hamburg, the Federico II University of Naples, the University of Paris II (Panthéon-Assas), the University of Economics (Prague), the University of Rennes.[1]

1 Introduction

1.1 Lessons from a crisis

When the so-called subprime crisis reached its zenith at the beginning of 2009, the opponents of free-market economics thought they finally had an opportunity to make the headlines again. After having been silenced by the 1989 collapse of central planning, their hopes for an intellectual comeback were not misplaced. Certainly, the 2007/2009 crash created many losers: tax payers, unemployed, investors, fixed-income earners, all those more or less close to retirement who suddenly saw a consistent part of their wealth vanish or their expected pension reduced. Yet, there was also one category of clear winners: politicians and rule-makers in general, that is those for whom state intervention is essential and for whom justifications in favour of public expenditure and regulation are always welcome. As a matter of fact, after a few days of panic in September 2008, politicians and rule-makers quickly perceived the possibility of transforming a crisis into a pretext to expand state intervention and to enhance their status.[1] While the financial meltdown was unfolding, they swiftly announced their willingness to step in, support and/or simply bail out companies whose failure (and rescue) would be large enough to make headlines, set up appropriate agencies in charge of comprehensive international supervision, design and enforce better rules and harsher sanctions to rein in alleged speculators and even partially nationalize large chunks of the banking industry.

Yet, in those months it would have been intellectually easy to set the record straight and argue the case for free-market economics once again. Contrary to many impassioned evaluations, the 2007/2009 crash was the reaction of the free-market mechanism to years of attempts carried out by "government" to deceive individuals and regulate prices. It was the market, not the regulator, who had signalled that something was rotten[2] and that a fresh start was needed. The market had not misled anyone; rather, the government had deceived public opinion by proclaiming that the banking system was healthy and reliable, since it was complying with the precautionary regulations imposed by the government itself or by international agencies jointly created by several governments. As for price regulation, there is no doubt that if both the Federal Reserve and the European Central Bank had not increased the money supply at about 8 per cent a year for several years, interest rates would have not been artificially depressed, borrowers would have abstained from signing themselves into unsustainable debt and lenders would have not given away resources to low-quality debtors. The bubble in the housing market is perhaps the best known effect (Holcombe and Powell 2008; Norberg 2009), but it is surely not the only one.

Put differently, the crisis was generated by sustained bad monetary policy, questionable risk-taking by incompetent, greedy and sometimes dishonest managers, and ineffective supervision by rating and monitoring agencies. Of course, the fact that these phenomena characterized both sides of the Atlantic offers no ground to conclude that the cause and explanation are a matter of "globalization", as some authors have recently suggested.[3] Rather, the broad nature of the crisis should have stimulated considerations of the role of the state on both sides of the ocean and also of the shortcomings of the judiciary, which should have hunted down fraudulent behaviour[4] and let competition take care of unprofitable companies, especially if led by inept leaders. Yet, despite its simplicity, the essence of the story was probably exceedingly embarrassing for too many people, for whom forgetting the past and regulating the future seemed a much more comfortable and rewarding solution. As often happens after major social catastrophes in which both the victims and the culprits are numerous and dispersed, there are lots of good reasons not to explore in great detail the origins of events. Ignorance, a self-serving notion of fairness and the unwillingness to admit that greed and superficiality have driven individual action might not constitute satisfactory and rigorous explanations, but they contribute to weakening the sense of individual responsibility. As a result, the blame tends to fall on abstract notions (e.g. market failure and excesses, or collective irrationality) or third parties,[5] and the case for redistributing the losses strengthens. In retrospect, it is clear that opinion leaders and the public at large were eager to turn an uncomfortable page and ask the rule-makers to promise and ensure that the crash would never happen again. The pursuit of the culprits never really began in earnest, as if what had happened had been deplorable, but nonetheless consistent with the social rules of the game agreed upon earlier and therefore legally acceptable.

Economists were also more than willing to play the game and promptly stepped in line with the shared attitude mentioned above. They admitted – albeit some of them only grudgingly – that optimally-designed regulations were not that optimal, after all, and swiftly suggested proposals for institutional reforms: new restrictions on individual behaviour and enhanced discretionary powers of the policy-makers, nationally and internationally. Different schools of thought varied in the details: how the crisis should have been tackled and what kind of new rules should be designed and enforced in the future. Yet, all the basic "lessons" drawn from the crisis have seemed to share a belief in some underlying social contract that legitimizes coercion for the sake of the common good. Such a contract would need no confirmation, but its scope should be extended and made more credible.

By contrast, the essence of this book lies in demonstrating that free-market economics is first and foremost the denial of a social contract characterized by compulsory solidarity and social rationality and that the foundations of free-market thinking originate from moral philosophy, rather than from political expediency. In other words, free-market supporters believe that state intervention and other forms of centrally-defined common good are objectionable because they violate a principle of justice, not because they violate a criterion of social welfare maximization. Likewise, free-market ideas do not deserve recognition because they perform well. We do not deny that respect for the free-market values – freedom from coercion, private property and freedom of contract – might also produce efficient outcomes and prosperity. We insist, however, on the fact that efficiency and economic performance are not the core argument in support of the free-market vision; and that advocating better rules, smaller government, honest politicians and hard-working bureaucrats is not enough to qualify as a free-market supporter. Put differently, a free-market approach built on consequentialism or wishful thinking will falter whenever a crisis strikes, and necessarily force its advocates to acquiesce to some version of the third way.

1.2 What's wrong with today's economics

Widespread opportunism, consequentialism and wishful thinking are not the only problems, though. In this book, we also argue that the economic way of reasoning prevailing today is mostly inadequate for understanding the nature and legitimacy of policy-making. Economic activities take place in environments that are not merely systems of mechanical exchanges carried out by rational individuals, regulated by contracts and characterized by enforcement procedures aiming at reducing the so-called transaction costs. These environments are also social contexts, in which the rules of the game reflect historically-determined shared values. Regrettably, economists have too often neglected the implications of such shared values, either by ignoring them altogether, or by ascribing them to the residual category of "culture", where the term "residual" designates what the economic profession is unwilling or unable to analyse, let alone explain. In particular, if one excludes the attempts to rationalize economic performance as a result of good politics,[6] the orthodox approach to economic events – the last crisis being of course one of them – falls victim to two methodological weaknesses that mainstream scholarship has all but avoided discussing for the last 50 years.[7] These flaws are the post-Keynesian drive towards holism and the late nineteenth-century claim in favour of hedonistic rationality. As discussed in the next chapter, taken together, holism and hedonistic rationality have sustained – and have been sustained by – ongoing efforts to pursue "hard" scientific status, thereby giving in to inductivist temptations and indulging the illusory search for quantitative and predictive accuracy.

1.2.1 Holism and the quest for normality

To be fair, the mainstream view does recognize that individuals are the basic actors characterizing an economic event. But it also considers that a science should result in the formulation of general, precise and constant laws and that one cannot conceive of such laws for each human being, especially if each human being changes his features more or less continuously. Thus, it concludes that in order to acquire scientific status, economics must necessarily create a typical individual, articulate theories that apply to this fictitious player, and finally test the validity of the theories with respect to this hypothetical representative agent. The quest for quantitative empirical confirmation and the temptation to draw policy implications have provided additional momentum in this direction and – unfortunately – eased the way towards forgetting that the typical-individual assumption should remain just a textbook hypothesis, as Alfred Marshall underscored about a century ago. Unfortunately, however, the mainstream approach has cast the typical individual into the centre of the real world by boldly transforming him into a fraction of the whole. Put differently, clones are regarded as purposeful agents and aggregates of clones are ascribed purposes and personalities (holism). As a result, and despite the lesson by Condorcet and Arrow, today's economists frequently feel thereby entitled to formulate and rank preferences for the aggregate, investigate the behaviour of a community by considering its fraction (the clone), and put forward recommendations about how to reach desirable, pre-assigned (social) objectives.

Not surprisingly, holism opened the way to policy-making, in order to pursue the common interest and correct deviations from normality, with normality being the expected condition of the typical agent. By focusing on aggregates, however, the economic profession has lost sight of the fact that economic activities are necessarily performed by humans, not clones. Likewise, the focus on normality has led most scholars to ignore individual preferences or to consider deviations sometimes as irksome exceptions, or sometimes as the result of systematic misperceptions by irrational agents, thereby requiring corrections by the enlightened technocrat and the well-meaning politician.

1.2.2 Rationality and institutionalism

The role of "normality" can hardly be overestimated, especially when one considers that the notion of "normal preferences" has been very close to that of "rational behaviour". In particular, and consistent with J.S. Mill's *Homo Oeconomicus* as well as with Walras's concept of general equilibrium, until the early 1970s mainstream economics considered that economic agents were pursuing material, quantifiable goals expressed in terms of costs and benefits in a world characterized by negligible transaction costs and perfectly designed contracts. Thus, they could be considered "rational".[8]

Granted, during the past decades, the mainstream (neoclassical) approach has strived to amend this rather mechanistic vision. Yet, on the one hand it did not always succeed in coming to grips with such notions as rationality, consciousness and altruism. On the other hand, its extensive research efforts to incorporate the contributions offered by the so-called (new) institutional economists have remained far from conclusive.[9] Although the institutionalists deserve credit for developing the economics of contracts and underscoring the role of transaction costs, which are far from negligible, some crucial shortcomings remained. In particular, the institutional school lacked (and lacks) an explanation of how institutions evolve and interact with the agents. Absent a satisfactory evolutionary and interaction theory, either one assumes that preferences are exogenous, acknowledging that economics has little or nothing to say about individual behaviour and moving on to psychology; or one transforms economics into an inductive science, within which forecasting techniques play the major role and theories are developed *ex post*. As mentioned earlier, both scholarly agendas are well represented on the economic scene right now. On the one hand, experimental economics and the economics of complexity strive to model psychological patterns by taking into account and formalizing emotional refinements into what is de facto a hedonistic game. On the other hand, a-theoretical quantitative methods have transformed economic investigation into the development and application of increasingly sophisticated statistical techniques.

In the end, we feel that the fascination with rationality or the institutional extensions have not offered much help in understanding what has happened to economic performance in the past decades. Rather, we are persuaded that the economics profession needs to reconsider the basic elements of collective interaction and to accept a deeper, critical examination of the foundations and implications of the lines of reasoning that have contributed to weakening individual responsibility, one of the very touchstones of the free-market vision.

1.3 The Scottish lesson and its demise

The alternative to the drift towards economic statistics and policy-making in the name of the common good is of course rooted in the Scottish legacy, which defined the nature and boundaries of scholarly work in the social sciences. Francis Hutcheson, David Hume, Adam Ferguson and their followers suggested that a society is indeed part of the natural order, which one might call "divine" (Hutcheson 1726: I,V). But although it was admitted that godly design is beyond human reach, the Scots urged men to use reason in order to understand the mechanisms driving the interaction among God's children: the way spontaneous interaction develops and the nature of its consequences. In particular, economics turned out to be the science studying the unintended consequences of voluntary individual action in contexts characterized by scarce resources.[10] And since it dealt with the system of interaction, cooperation and coordination made possible by social contexts defined within a political framework, it was in fact named "political economy".

As we have mentioned earlier, in the recent past this vision has been often disregarded by economists, both in academia and in the real world. In particular, the Scottish research programme came under attack on two fronts, one levelled towards the end of the nineteenth century, another one developed during the second half of the twentieth century. The first criticism was originally articulated by Thorstein Veblen and Carl Menger (Langlois 1989), despite their very substantial disagreements on almost everything else and their emphasis on different aspects of this very question. They both started from the classical-liberal claim according to which individuals are shaped by experience and by institutions, which also operate as some kind of constraint. If that is true, however, in their view a full account of the economic process cannot ignore the possibility that the routines and mechanisms characterizing it are not constant, but always evolving as social interaction unfolds. As a result, unless it is assumed that institutions are constant, economic analysis requires that one formulate a dynamic theory about the way individuals change their perceptions vis-à-vis the outside stimuli, and about the way these changes translate into reactions and eventually provoke transformations of the institutional framework. Unfortunately, Veblen, Menger and their followers did not go much further than that and ultimately failed to answer the very question they had raised. Consistent with their views, therefore, Veblen ended up arguing in favour of the end of economics as a social science. Menger, instead, contented himself with situational analysis, which mirrors partial equilibrium, except that the "other-things-being-constant" assumption was replaced by a "given-constant-institutions" hypothesis.

The second set of criticisms has been of greater consequence. Its proponents have claimed that if we accept that economics is about processes driven by human purposeful behaviour – a statement that only staunch behaviouralists would reject – then economic analysis necessarily requires a clear definition of the target(s) pursued by the agents. Hence, by extending Mill's original and fateful emphasis on wealth, the idea of purposeful action has become the Trojan horse by means of which economics has been gradually and successfully transformed into an excuse for engaging in "what-if" exercises. Once this teleological view became the backbone of economic thinking – which is what actually happened to economic science in the twentieth century, despite some isolated efforts in the opposite direction[11] – the late nineteenth century doubts were simply shelved among the curiosities in the history of economic thought. For once the individual or the social goal is identified, the meaningful actor becomes the policy-maker, as in public choice; or the judge, as in Posnerian Law and Economics (L&E). As a result, institutions become the tool of economic policy, rather than the pragmatic or the organic constraint, in Menger's terminology.[12]

1.4 A solution to the institutional deadlock

Despite appearances, we believe that the institutional concerns put forward by Veblen, Menger and Hayek are less devastating than meets the eye and that much of the Scottish lesson retains its validity today, especially if one reconsiders some key concepts that are blindly accepted by the economics profession. We will focus on these assumption in the first block of chapters, tackling a number of methodological issues that are usually taken for granted in the literature: in Chapter 2 we discuss the notion of equilibrium in the history of economic thinking and, more generally, how the economics profession veered towards constructivism; Chapter 3 is devoted to the concepts of time, rationality, consciousness and altruism, while Chapter 4 deals with the nature and legitimacy of formal institutions. The second part (Chapters 5–7) explores the two main theoretical bodies that traditional (consequentialist) free-market supporters usually articulate: constitutional economics and transaction-cost economics. The final set of chapters turns to the real world and reassesses standard analyses of growth (Chapter 8) and of poverty and transition (Chapter 9). Common to all these analyses, however, are two critical sets of assumptions, which are briefly outlined below and will repeatedly appear throughout the book.

The first set of assumptions regards individual behaviour and introduces the notion of uncertainty. In contrast with the traditional view, individuals in the free-market world vision do not maximize anything. Except for the very short run, they ignore or are unable to define their targets with sufficient accuracy. Moreover, most decisions are at least partly subject to ongoing revision, as a result of the changing world, of the agents' changing perception of the world and of the system of social interactions. More realistically, this analysis claims that human beings try to improve their satisfaction both by imitating (a cheap substitute for information) and by trial-and-error.

The second set of assumptions deals with pragmatic and historical institutions and defines the terms of social interaction, with reference to which the Scottish legacy is accepted or rejected. Pragmatic institutions are the cognizant results of the actions of selected groups. These groups pursue common goals and strive to restrain the behaviour of the other members of their community so as to generate privileges and appropriate rents. Pragmatic institutions evolve relatively rapidly[13] and follow one of two patterns. One tracks technological progress: institutions adjust in response to the features of the problem that the rules were and are supposed to address or in response to the modifications in the balance of power among coalitions. For instance, the relative strength of the sub-groups that form the elite might be altered, or their interests and needs modified. Another example is related to progress in military technology, which has frequently changed the amount of resources required to preserve authority and power. Of course, in all these cases the desirability of the outcomes has to be assessed on a case-by-case basis. Nothing guarantees that institutions systematically evolve for the better. The other pattern affecting pragmatic institutions is generated by ideologies, the success and impact of which also depend on luck, economic contingencies, media manipulation and major mistakes by the incumbent rulers (including war, of course). In contrast with most of the current literature, it is here maintained that pragmatic institutions exhibit modest path-dependence. Of course, the fact that events at time $(t+1)$ depend on the context at time (t) is not contested. But we deny that what we observe at $(t+1)$ is the only possible event which could have followed from (t). And it is equally denied that failure to predict such an event is merely due to the lack of a satisfactory theory (as positivistic determinism would have it) or to our inability to read the past and let the data speak for themselves (the historicist position).

Historical institutions (the definition is ours) characterize the moral and political foundations of a collective body:[14] the shared traits of a large community, the eventual implicit covenant that keeps it together and the rules of the game that govern its functioning and its ultimate goals, as understood or perceived by the overwhelming majority of its components. For example, feelings of envy and unfairness play important roles in this context (Schoeck 1966), with consequences for the role of policy-making – redistribution and violations of private property rights. Put differently, historical institutions shape the grand situational context within which pragmatic institutions are created and subsequently modified. Historical institutions change very rarely in time, show no path dependence and have deep effects on the nature of social interaction, as well as on the role of the authorities. When an overwhelming majority sharing the same system of values is in place, the historically-institutional grid is wide enough to absorb political changes and economic shocks.[15] Absent an overwhelming majority sharing the same system of values, a society loses its legitimacy and breaks apart, sometimes violently (e.g. civil war), other times relatively smoothly, as subgroups strive to define historical institutions that might allow collective agreements. The obvious examples are peaceful secession or political fragmentation.

1.5 The economic implications

This conceptual framework definitely remains within the realm of the Scottish approach, according to which individual economic action is shaped by experience (Marciano 2006) as well as by man's own feelings about conduct (Stein 1980: 9–10). Past events affect both the way agents perceive reality and the meaning of the term well-being (thereby justifying a relativistic view of ethics). The outcomes are sets of "behavioural routines", which define how agents act, given their "psychological patterns" and the normative constraints to which they are subject.[16]

Put differently, the principle of sufficient reason (conscious choice) applies to psychological patterns, for these truly reflect preferences, instincts and propensities. Behavioural routines, by contrast, also include the efficient-cause mechanisms (predictable reactions to exogenous incentives). The result is that economics should indeed study efficient-cause relations, but it should also study sufficient reason derived from the historical-institutional framework. Lack of attention to the latter prevents a proper understanding of the former.

With regard to the scope for policy-making, the following chapters will argue that there is very little room for compromise between the natural rights typical of the free-market vision as defined in Section 1.1 and appropriate super-laws. In this vein, two categories of constitutions can be identified. One category consists of attempts to formalize the historical institutional context of the time, in order to galvanize consensus and enhance concord or collusion among political factions. The outcome is usually a list of desirable outcomes, apparently of little use: either they are redundant, since the real constitution is the historical institutional set, or they are necessarily ambiguous, since each faction tends to interpret them according to the circumstances. In practice, however, such constitutions serve the purpose of justifying an elite, especially when its hold on power is insecure and legitimacy is badly needed. Consistent with our earlier argument, historical conditions will determine to which extent these efforts are going to be successful.

The second category of constitutions deals with political procedures, that is with the rules of the game with which competing rule-makers must comply. Contrary to a large part of the recent literature, which often suggests that appropriate constitutional design can provide effective restrain to abuse, we maintain that constitutional engineering can hardly prevent change when the historical institutional setting has modified. Sometimes, it doesn't even provide adequate restraint in the existing setting. Designing constitutions in order to fix the boundaries of policy-making is also illusive. As the history of constitutional interpretation proves, super-laws characterized by substantial moral content are no exception.

1.6 Final remarks

To summarize our argument, we do not deny that the process of efficient cause led (or pushed) by the invisible hand or by evolutionary forces holds true, but we add that they explain only part of the story. In particular, the real challenge is not only to figure out how the invisible hand works, or what kind of evolutionary process is operating, but also to understand how these mechanisms evolve and how they affect purposeful action. The answer given here is that (*a*) sufficient reason remains unaffected unless the historical setting is transformed and (*b*) although economic interaction over the centuries changes in accordance with the evolution in the technological constraints, the perceived system of natural rights as defined earlier (see Section 1.4) remains basically constant. Two consequences follow. Pragmatic institutions are either the instruments through which society solves collective-action problems in compliance with the historical and technological framework, or they are ways of developing privileges (rents) for selected interest groups. Moreover, it appears that different historical settings might develop different attitudes towards free-market values. For instance, when the (shared) fundamental principles characterizing a historical institutional setting imply that in a number of cases the individual is subject to the will of the community or of its representatives, the free-market approach is by definition senseless. At most, the challenge for the political philosopher and the economist is to work out feasible and legitimate solutions for dissenting minorities.

In other words, wondering whether free-market economics is "better" than economic socialism turns out to be a (pointless) exercise in rhetoric, unless one specifies the evaluation criteria. To repeat our earlier contention, efficiency – as measured by wealth or GDP – won't do. Efficiency describes outcomes, not moral principles or ideas. The alternative thus consists in abandoning the standard of efficiency ("it is good because it works") and replacing it with that of justice ("it is good because it does not violate natural rights", in accord with the definition of this expression offered earlier). If so, it may well happen that policy-making is neither a socialist must, nor a free-market taboo. Rather, policy-making would be a realistic prospect for those who explicitly accept coercion *ex ante*, or a threat that anybody can avoid by opting out at a low cost. Granted, framed in these terms, the debate on policy-making is much harder to model and thus possibly less than appealing to mainstream scholars. Yet, we believe it is the only way of ensuring that normative economics belongs to the realm of the social sciences, rather than to the drawers of self-referential technocrats.

2 On the nature and scope of economic reasoning

2.1 Setting the stage

As mentioned in the introductory chapter, this book is about the foundations of normative economics, an area that during the twentieth century has gradually become a medley of policy measures dictated by expedience, often times driven by short term goals and heavily influenced by political constraints. Almost invariably, such measures are presented as social imperatives (e.g. fairness) and/or as necessary means to obtain shared goals (the common good), with little regard for logical or moral consistency. The economics profession has not done much to clarify the foundations and legitimacy of those social imperatives and shared goals. Instead, it has preferred to concentrate on exercises aiming at quantifying the consequences of policy action, or designing centralized agencies capable of attaining desirable objectives that individuals would be unable to reach through spontaneous cooperation. As a result, research agendas in economic policy have increasingly been characterized by a persistent drift towards undiscerning consequentialism and mechanical induction. Regrettably, nowadays the desirability of policy-goals seems to justify most kinds of intervention, the effectiveness of the tools employed tends to rest on past experience, theoretical and methodological questions are often sidestepped, as if the solutions were to be revealed by sophisticated statistics.

Although both consequentialism and induction have some merit when taken with a grain of salt, economics has not always been limited to social engineering and what-if simulations. Even today, introductory textbooks often refer to a definition that indeed leaves the door open to positivism, but is neither normative, nor characterized by number crunching. That definition dates back to the 1930s, when Lionel Robbins (1932) developed an earlier insight by Ludwig von Mises and offered the well-known portrayal that seemed to settle the issue once and for all: "Economics is the science which studies human behaviour as a relationship between ends and scarce means which have alternative uses" (ibid.: 15). These words can hardly be criticised. Surely, even today few would dispute that economics is about human action and that it is also about the production, employment and consumption of scarce goods and services.

Sometimes, however, simple stories conceal more complicated issues. As will be explained in the following pages, upon closer inspection Robbins's statement turned out to be somewhat deceptive. It did not take adequate account of where economics was coming from and failed to provide adequate methodological guidance to many generations that followed. Despite its apparent clarity, it left (and leaves) several aspects in the dark and ultimately generated considerable confusion. Hence, the ongoing unease about the nature and scope of economics (Buchanan 1979), which continues to raise important questions and to which only partial answers have been offered.

Put differently, by focusing too narrowly on Robbins's definition, many have ended up neglecting that for several centuries economics meant something different than what we believe it does today. Failure to realize and consider the reasons that occasioned changes of attitude over the centuries has had consequences, since it has frequently induced both the layman and the researcher to take for granted moral and axiomatic statements – if not visions of the world – that are not necessarily self-evident, but that can nevertheless bear dramatically upon the nature of scholarly work and policy action.[1]

In this light, this chapter sets out to examine why economics evolved from being almost a non-issue, into becoming a social science and finally into being characterized by dubious attempts to make it join the league of the hard disciplines. Thus, it will be shown that today's state of confusion owes a great deal to the economists' ambition to move away from analysing human action and interaction and follow the lead of Auguste Comte (1798–1857), Léon Walras (1834–1910) and Gustav Schmoller (1838–1917) to pin down universal and exact mathematical laws that allegedly typify human behaviour under scarcity conditions. The following pages develop two main trains of arguments, related to each other. They both concern the essence of economic reasoning and insist on the notions of human action on the one hand, of equilibrium on the other. We maintain that economics began as the study of human action and interaction in a world characterized by scarcity and impersonal exchange, but also inscribed within a more general design of divine harmony, Providence. Human action was thus conceived of as an effort to realize the role of man within this context of natural (God-given) equilibrium. We shall further claim that such early view started to evolve when natural harmony was gradually superseded by the concept of man-made equilibrium, within which human action was no longer the search for virtue and compliance with God's design, but rather the search for efficient (rational) decisions aimed at obtaining the common good (artificial equilibrium). This was a critical step, since it did away with moral judgements of human behaviour. Instead, action became subject to evaluation according to its "social rationality", i.e. its compliance with the collective interest. As a consequence, the notions of rationality and equilibrium turned out to be the same thing.[2] Despite some opposition, this last perspective is today prevailing: it assimilates and develops Lord Robbins's insight, it makes the idea of the common good explicit and de facto transforms economics into a technical exercise in optimization.

With this vision in mind, the next section aims at explaining the limited perception of economics as a social science until some three centuries ago. Sections 2.3 and 2.4 focus on the nature of economics before the marginalist revolution by emphasizing the importance of holism and the notion of natural equilibrium in the classical tradition. Section 2.5 explains what occasioned change in the 1870s, the replacement of the notion of natural equilibrium by that of man-made equilibrium, and what the economics profession made of it. The survey on the history of an idea – equilibrium – is further pursued in Section 2.6, in which it is explained why in the aftermath of the great depression/stagnation in the 1930s, the economics profession found it convenient to follow Keynes's lifeline, which was actually less disruptive than usually maintained. Section 2.7 summarizes the pivotal steps in the transition of economics towards its constructivist ambitions, from the classical natural approach to the marginalist turn and eventually to Keynes's assumptions about human behaviour and the macro-solutions they required. Finally, Sections 2.8 and 2.9 present the state of the current debate, which is essentially articulated around the contrast between the positivist and the praxeological approaches, the former relying on induction and consequentialism, the latter on a priori theorizing.

2.2 When economics was not a social science

As mentioned above, it took millennia before the systematic study of economics made any scholarly sense. Surely, as early as the fourth century BC Xenophon had already observed the importance of good management driven by profit and directed towards the production of wealth. Both in *Cyropaedia* and in *Oeconomicus* he had considered "economics" as a "branch of knowledge" and even dignified enough to absorb the time of a monarch on a daily basis: the importance of rational production techniques, effective human resource management, careful bookkeeping and organization was widely acknowledged. He even grasped very clearly the difference between price and value, the critical linchpin of modern economics (*Oeconomicus*: chapter 1). And equally valuable are the author's repeated efforts to clarify economic concepts and actions, such as the division of labour and the connection between specialization and productivity. Yet, those attempts and analyses refrained from considering choice and exchange as essential features of a community and abstained from developing systematic theories of societal interaction under scarcity constraints.[3] As a matter of fact, in the Greek world the purpose of a social community was to promote virtue, not wealth:[4]

> It is not the end of the city to provide an alliance for mutual defence against all injury, nor does it exist for the purpose of exchange or [commercial] dealing ... [A]ny city which is truly so called, and is not merely one in name, must devote itself to the end of encouraging goodness ... to make the citizens good and just.
>
> (Aristotle, *Politics*: III.9)

Things did not change for a long time and Aristotle probably had some responsibility for that.[5] Although the Romans understood economic phenomena very well – including the functioning of capital and credit markets, as mentioned in Temin (2006) – in the Christian era, economic activities were not an object of investigation in their own right, but rather an important source of sinful behaviour. For instance, Saint Augustine (354–430) has been considered as the most imposing forefather of subjectivism and entrepreneurship (Stark 2006: 78–80), but condemned trade. Some 900 years later Saint Thomas (1224–1274) discussed at length the notion of property and the moral foundations of private property, key elements that have characterized the economic profession until this day; but eventually concluded that the main role of private property is to avoid social conflicts. More generally, if one excludes the frequent aspiration to boost tax revenues so as to increase the size of the army or to build magnificent monuments, in the Middle Ages political and social arrangements were not usually conceived of by taking into account their effects upon economic activities. Even less were economic activities deemed relevant for designing or explaining institutional arrangements.[6] In fact, despite evidence pointing in other directions as well, once the individual's compliance with Christian religion had replaced the search for pagan virtue, for centuries it was generally accepted that communities are formed and kept together by the need to cooperate against aggressions or in dealing with natural disasters. In other words, the social covenant that replaced the polis was supposed to be founded on defence, rather than on trade and industry.[7] The authority was of course aware of the fact that people engaged in economic activities. But this encouraged monitoring in order to ensure that such activities would not run against spiritual orthodoxy (religion and thus morality).

A middle class made of traders and little artisans started to surface in the eleventh century in several Western European areas. This was accompanied by a new attitude towards labour, no longer a sign of shame, but of merit (i.e. merit would legitimize monetary rewards). As mentioned above, however, merchants continued to be regarded with mistrust. This attitude started to change only during the fifteenth and sixteenth centuries, when the emphasis moved from indiscriminate attack towards mercantile activities to criticism levelled against misbehaviour by bad merchants, either because inclined to greed and neglect of charity or, more generally, because inclined to disrupt the divine order in this world: "As the merchants be one of the best members in our common weal, so they be the very worst if their doings be not looked unto in time; and forced to keep good order" (Thomas Gresham 1560, quoted in Heckscher 1994, vol. II: 320). This was true both for the Catholic Church and for the leaders of Reformation.[8]

Until the Calvinist and – more importantly – the Puritan ideas spread out, there was also little incentive to adopt an economic orientation to life. Living was a rather static experience, even in eschatological terms, since life was often regarded as the time span the individual was given to prepare for death and achieve salvation, much less as an opportunity to realize one's own ambitions. As pointed out in Tawney (1926: 22), "The gross facts of the social order are accepted, in all their harshness and brutality. They are accepted with astonishing docility and, except on rare occasions, there is no question of reconstruction".[9]

At most, and even after the Middle Ages were past, "a man's expectations in life were determined by the position in society in which he happened to be born" (Knights 1937: 27). Economic activities were necessary to survive, both as an individual and as a member of the community (insofar as wealth often implied defence capabilities). But they were based on small-scale local trade, or sometimes on family-based and family-wide "firms", whose functioning had to conform to the general rules of the community, which were more inclined to stability than efficiency. Moreover, for the vast majority of the population, the prospects and the opportunities for self-improvement were limited: during 1500–1820 Western Europe grew at an average yearly rate of 0.14 per cent (in terms of GDP per capita), which means that an individual would experience an increase in his living standard of about 4 per cent over 30 years (Maddison 2005). Trying to do something different and possibly better was thus likely to bear only very minor rewards, while the cost of getting it wrong could be very high (starvation).

All this denies neither the existence of impersonal trade, nor of capitalist spirits. History abounds with examples from the Italian and Flemish Middle Ages (twelfth and fourteenth centuries, respectively), not to mention the rise of the Netherlands and England in the seventeenth century. These examples reveal that capitalism and economic activity were well alive even when a community-oriented culture was prevailing. Nevertheless, it was commonly held that the duties of the individual towards the community came before his own preferences and that production and exchange beyond what needed for personal subsistence could be appropriate only if consistent with the goals of the community. It is not by chance that economic activities came to the surface with greater ease in geographic areas in which power was decentralized, mobility harder to restrain and fixed hierarchical structures more difficult to maintain. Tolerance was the principle that summarized all these features, promoted first by the Low Countries towards the end of the sixteenth century, to be imitated by England a few decades later. In a word, uniformity and homogeneity were highly praised: "Fyrste walke in thy vocation, and do not seke thy lotte to change; For through wicked ambition, many mens fortune hath ben straynge."[10] Thus, compliance with pre-ordained cosmic order was all but imperative. It did not matter whether such order was too complex to apprehend. But it was important not to act in ways that might disrupt it. Tillyard (1943, especially chapters 2–4) documents that this concern for divine harmony was also typical of late sixteenth-century England, where

> The part of Christianity that was paramount was not the life of Christ but the orthodox scheme of the revolt of the bad angels, the creation, the temptation and fall of man, the incarnation, the atonement, the regeneration through Christ.
>
> (Ibid.: 26)

Put differently, and arguably with the notable exception of the Spanish Scholastics on the continent and of Thomas Mun and Edward Misselden in England, until the end of the seventeenth century economic issues did not call for systematic in-depth scrutiny and proper understanding.[11] Economic action was taken as given: its nature and consequences did merit investigation, but only for purposes of moral approval or political control. Those who dealt with economic phenomena saw no need to explore systematically the causal connections through which individuals would be induced to exchange and find ways to increase their wealth (or satisfy their needs, as we would say today). Instead, individual activities to improve material conditions were analysed with some apprehension, as if they could be the source of potential turmoil or social change. This is not surprising. As Appleby (2004 [1978]: 258) has explained in a broader context,

> Treating economic relations as part of a natural order involved the assumption of certain basic regularities which made possible explanations and predictions. ... As long as human beings appeared, as they did in Shakespearean literature, as creatures driven by reason and passion or, as in Reformation writings, as struggling between their "fallen" and "redeemable" natures, they offered no firm basis for constructing a natural social order.[12]

If anything, more "technical" analyses were confined to – and motivated by – the interest of the state or of the prince in finding ways to boost tax revenues and in tampering with monetary issues to increase seigniorage while enforcing legal tender. Typical examples are the experiments carried out by Jean-Baptiste Colbert and John Law under Louis XIV and Louis XV, respectively.

As we know, after Westphalia (1648) it became increasingly clear that international relations among princes were being replaced by relations among nation states and those wars and military technologies required the commitment of the whole realm, not only the personal treasury of the incumbent monarch. Similarly, it gradually became evident that the power to conquer and to control domestic trouble depended on the wealth of the country, and that the wealth of the country did not depend solely upon the quantity of land available. This awareness also coincided with a period of systematic financial crisis that hit Europe, and France in particular, towards the end of the seventeenth century: the rulers were no longer able to counteract by forced borrowing and confiscation. Hence, studying the laws that determined the activities and transactions pertaining to the production and distribution of income among the categories of owners of resources – land, raw materials, labour, fixed capital – started to become more interesting and, not surprisingly, economic enquiries began to be appreciated.

2.3 Economics before the marginalists: natural law meets production

In the eighteenth century, the legacy of natural law met with the need to produce more riches. As a matter of fact, although religion was clearly denied any moral influence on economic matters, most "economists" were essentially in agreement with the fact that the science of political economy[13] was an instrument to understand how Providence and Nature had given man resources that would enable policy-makers to pursue the common interest, understood in both material and moral terms. Adam Smith made further progress, by elaborating on Tucker's claim that commercial activities are part of godly design;[14] and by emphasizing the connection between individual instincts, actions, national security and virtuous policy-making: "Political economy, considered as a branch of the science of a statesman or a legislator, proposes ... to enrich both the people and the sovereign" (Smith 1981 [1776]: 428).

Although this view does not seem far away from how contemporary normative economics sees its own goal – the attainment of common desirable objectives – during the eighteenth century it became apparent that in order to help the prince to increase his wealth and power, efforts were to be directed towards the discovery of the eternal (objective) laws of exchange, production and distribution, defined by – or similar to – natural phenomena. At the same time, speculation about virtuous instincts (the modern version of the natural law) would assist in determining and subsequently approximating the "just" state of affairs, so as to recognize when human irrationality prevents nature from running its course and attaining desirable results. Religious guidance would show the appropriate route:

> The natural course of things cannot be entirely controlled by the impotent endeavours of man ..., religion enforces the natural sense of duty: and hence it is, that mankind are generally disposed to place great confidence in the probity of those who seem deeply impressed with religious sentiments.
>
> (Smith 1982 [1759]: 168)

This attitude explains why the classical tradition could not consider sub-disciplines:[15] all economic problems were necessarily defined in terms of general (natural) equilibrium, for only a general approach would allow one to frame conclusions in terms of natural phenomena. In addition, the search for general laws implied the understanding of the logics/mechanism of agricultural production (action) and trade (interaction), with no need for further specialization. In fact, sub-disciplines come to the surface when the study of action and interaction is applied to different fields, each of them characterized by its own peculiarities, often times of a normative nature.

The eighteenth-century view also sheds light on the role played by laissez-faire, which owes less to Thomas Le Gendre's reaction to Colbert's interventionism and more to De Gournay's urging to let nature do its course.[16] Finally, and perhaps more importantly, it explains why during the nineteenth century economics retained the notion of equilibrium – allegedly the ideal state of nature – and why policy-making was progressively accepted as a necessary and legitimate way of restoring "stability", insofar as deviations from a known, ideal state of affairs called for action to contain, amend and punish. Put differently, equilibrium originally referred to the underlying natural condition of human societies, for which the rules were similar to those of the natural world (e.g. mechanics) and all attempts to alter them were frowned upon. Applied to economic matters, natural order (equilibrium) was thus perceived as a long-term issue, so that investigation necessarily became focused on the long-term features of prices and production, with an emphasis on the distribution of income. We still bear the consequences today, of course. For instance, the classical and neoclassical definitions of competition insist on a static, welfare-maximizing idea of equilibrium, according to which nobody actually competes, but merely survives by avoiding losses, and innovates following instinct rather than profit opportunities.[17] It also rejects the idea of rival producers striving to meet somebody's needs (e.g. buyers' demand). In fact, this static notion of equilibrium is the very principle that today inspires the action of anti-trust authorities as regulators, judges, enforcers.

To sum up, since the late seventeenth century until the so-called marginalist revolution of the 1870s, the nature and content of economic science presented a rather standardized landscape, in that economists were homogeneous and consistent in understanding the subject matter of their discipline. The ultimate purpose of economics was to understand the rules and consequences of individuals' interaction and learn how to obtain the orderly working of a society:[18] the stability of communities characterized and kept together by the "pleasure of mutual sympathy" on the one hand[19] and the interest, wealth and power of a political body (the prince or the state) on the other. Not surprisingly, for many centuries that was the accepted notion of equilibrium in the social sciences. In particular, economics showed only occasional concern for individual behaviour, and even less attention to individual consumption. Instead, production continued to occupy the centre of the stage well into the mid-nineteenth century:

> Political Economy ... has nothing to do with the consumption of wealth, further than as the consideration of it is inseparable from that of production, or from that of distribution. We know not any of the laws of the consumption of wealth as a subject of a distinct science: they can be not other than the laws of human enjoyment. Political economists have never treated of consumption on its own account, but always for the purpose of the inquiry in what manner different kinds of consumption affect the production and distribution of wealth.[20]

Differences were present, of course; and so were disagreements. For instance, James Steuart and Adam Smith proposed a (mistaken) theory of value against the positions held by Ferdinando Galiani, Étienne de Condillac and Anne Robert Turgot. David Hume's views on money were not the same as those maintained by Richard Cantillon. Supporters of free trade frequently opposed mercantilist theses and ad hoc, country-specific solutions. Adam Smith and David Ricardo considered growth was valuable; for others, such as John Stuart Mill, it was an evil to bear. Similarly, various authors also drew different conclusions about the future of the world: Jean Antoine Condorcet was rather optimistic, David Ricardo offered a gloomier perspective, while Adam Smith and later Thomas Malthus were often ambiguous, if not contradictory.[21]

More importantly for our purposes, however, these discrepancies were usually akin to personal divergences and more or less pronounced differences in opinion, rather than the result of diverse schools of thought or of altogether conflicting visions regarding human nature and society.[22] Put differently, the general purpose of economic investigation was essentially taken for granted and evolved gradually, almost unconsciously, with little open disagreement.

The main reason for the lack of conflict among economists was probably due to the fact that for a long time economics was hardly regarded as a discipline in its own right, as already mentioned in the previous section. True enough, during all ages men have been interested in finding ways of promoting their well-being and interests – or merely ensure survival – by transforming labour and natural resources into goods and services, either to be consumed by the producers themselves, or to be exchanged against other goods and services. Especially before the Enlightenment, however, economic activities tended to be considered phenomena generated by spontaneous human action and interaction requiring (*a*) investigation and ultimately approval by the "philosophers" (i.e. the spiritual authorities, possibly under the pretext of preserving the virtue of the soul tempted by greed and luxury); (*b*) institutional monitoring – when not resolute intervention – by the prince or the religious hierarchies; (*c*) practical solutions (e.g. contract enforcement) for the lawyer to solve. There was relatively little interest in studying how a community could peacefully increase its wealth, whether there were limits to growth, whether it made any sense to investigate the meaning of communal welfare as opposed to the well-being of those who composed the social body. Growth was not neglected altogether, of course, but it was sometimes regarded as a temporary phenomenon, sometimes as the inevitable product of "industrial progress", almost always an element to take into account when assessing and steering the evolution of the social bodies towards other desirable ends.[23]

2.4 The classical view in perspective: holism, interdisciplinarity, statics

At the time when classical economics saw the light (more or less when the Wealth of Nations was published) and during its glory days almost until the end of the nineteenth century, the legacy of the past was not altogether discarded or forgotten. Holism, interdisciplinarity and the deductive approach were pervasive. Yet, these very features proved to be the soft spot of the classical approach, once it became apparent that classical theorizing was unable to explain what was happening in the real world.

2.4.1 Holism and its deceptions

The holistic vision typical of the classical-liberal world originated from the understanding that while the economic context was the result of individual action, most engagements were the result of instincts, to be controlled and in some cases repressed for the sake of virtue (morality). Instincts were supposed to be common to any human being, but were not supposed to be disciplined in the same way in all communities or even within a single community. In contrast with the Middle Ages, it is far more debatable whether these "expectations" entertained by the ruling class were actually shared by the population. Not unlike the Middle Ages, however, each player was supposed to comply with some sort of pre-assigned role, following class/birth condition – as a worker, a merchant, a land-owner, a capitalist. Talents were to be exploited only within the given social and cultural context, which also established to which extent instincts, including those of economic relevance such as entrepreneurship and aspirations to better living standards, had to be repressed, moderated, guided. In other words, behavioural patterns were established by the rules of the game, i.e. the formal and informal norms characterizing the community and the sub-community (the family, the guild) to which the individual belonged. It was indeed recognized that men try to improve their conditions all the time, but as Adam Smith pointed out, self-betterment mainly referred to the individual's ambitions to climb the social ladder and to obtain public esteem and approbation within a community. In a word, all was ultimately rooted in the (morally acceptable) desire for distinction:

> From whence, then, arises that emulation which runs through all the different ranks of men, and what are the advantages which we propose by that great purpose of human life which we call bettering our condition? To be observed, to be attended to, to be taken notice of with sympathy, complacency and approbation, are all the advantages which we can propose to derive from it. It is the vanity, not the ease, or the pleasure, which interests us. But vanity is always founded upon the belief of our being the object of attention and approbation.
>
> (Smith 1982 [1759]: 50)

This attitude was not without consequences. For instance, by attributing exchange to the human instinctive propensity to trade, rather than to differences in individual preferences and therefore to the potential gains people could obtain from trade, Adam Smith and the classical tradition failed to perceive that exchange is beneficial not only because it allows specialization, but also because goods and services are thus transferred from those who value them relatively little to those who appreciate them relatively more. Of course, one mistake could easily lead to another. And it did. By not seeing that exchange is also based on differences in subjective values,[24] the classical economists failed to perceive the weakness of the labour theory of value and ultimately confused prices with values.[25]

More generally, the classical school combined natural law with production in an effort to preserve holism and thereby succeeded in opposing the argument in favour of political interference: as noted by Appleby (2004 [1978]: 103), "When Adam Smith freighted the full burden of automatic, self-sustaining economic laws upon the basic human qualities of a love to 'truck and barter' and a cease-less urge to 'self-improvement', he was standing in a long line of thinkers'' dating back to the very beginning of the seventeenth century. But this mix also made some gross theoretical mistakes inevitable. As a result, and with the important exception of the so-called "old historical school" headed by Wilhelm Roscher, until the end of the nineteenth century, many thinkers preferred to focus on a fairly static vision of the economic system, in which innovation and progress play a minor role (Ricossa 1986: 77), entrepreneurship is virtually absent and even the market system tends to be conceived as the product of an enlightened social engineer, rather than following the vision of spontaneous interaction among individuals popularized by Adam Smith.[26] One might specu-late that a more accurate observation of the fundamental features of Western civ-ilization would have helped.[27] After all, and consistent with Bouckaert (2007), when Western civilization came to the surface in the High Middle Ages, society could hardly be defined as static or sleepy. Although the existing social order was widely accepted, in several regions communities strived to trade, acquire independence, revolt against abuse and exploitation. Economic growth was indeed low in per-capita terms, but not negligible overall. Why did the classical thinkers ignore some 800 years of tensions, both in individuals and in the social bodies? Why were they misled and therefore induced to miss the major implica-tions of subjectivism: entrepreneurship and price theory (demand)? A satisfac-tory reply to these questions would require a book entirely devoted to this very subject. It is possible that economists were misled by the modest material results of those strains (negligible improvements in living standards) and blindly fol-lowed the medieval labour theory of value, according to which a price is fair when it remunerates the producer's efforts. This meant that the seller should be paid enough to survive (in the case of workers and peasants) or to live with dignity (in the case of the land-owning aristocrat), with the commercial bour-geoisie left in a limbo.[28] More importantly, for our purposes, it also meant that the notion of individual preferences was more or less irrelevant.

Or perhaps economists fell victim to bad historians and questionable ideo-logical fashions long accepted at face value: Among such dubious histories were the eighteenth-century Enlightenment creations of the myth of medieval obscu-rantism to discredit the Church, and – later – the reaction of nineteenth-century German Romanticism to the Enlightenment through the invention of the legend of the medieval organic community, ruled by love, kinship, harmony and altru-ism (the so-called *Gemeinschaft* described, for instance, by Tönnies 2001 [1887]).

2.4.2 The inductivist temptation

During the nineteenth century, interest towards inductive techniques increased, prompted by the spectacular developments in the hard sciences, in which sys-tematic observation had allowed perceiving regularities, detecting causal mech-anisms and explaining phenomena by formulating exact laws. With the passing of time the temptation to look for mechanical regularities in the social sciences proved irresistible. True, lack of computing equipment and of large enough data sets prevented satisfactory testing. Yet, the economists' quest for the perfect model had begun. As of the beginning of the nineteenth century, mathematics was then added to economics in order to transform economic phenomena and propensities into laws, to articulate the theoretical existence and properties of equilibrium, to explore the consequences of policy-making. Surely, most early economics texts did not include anything close to today's formalization, but the search for mathematical laws to describe social behaviours and interactions pioneered by Nicolas-François Canard (1750–1838) and Augustin Cournot (1801–1877) was nonetheless marked and heedlessly accepted (Ingrao and Israel 1987).

In the end, it is not a coincidence that when the clench of Romanticism weakened and rationalism turned into scientism, economics started to acquire those very constructivist ambitions and traits that Adam Smith had once rejected in clear terms:

> The man of system … seems to imagine that he can arrange the different members of a great society with as much ease as the hand arranges the different pieces upon a chess-board. He does not consider that the pieces upon the chess-board have no other principle of motion besides that which the hand impresses upon them; but that, in the great chess-board of human society, every single piece has a principle of motion of its own, altogether different from that which the legislature might chuse to impress upon it. If those two principles coincide and act in the same direction, the game of human society will go on easily and harmoniously, and is very likely to be happy and successful. If they are opposite or different, the game will go on miserably, and the society must be at all times in the highest degree of disorder.
>
> (Smith 1982 [1759]: 233–234)

2.5 The subjectivist revolutions: one missed, one failed

To be fair, the classical crisis that detonated in the 1870s could have been averted if more attention had been paid to the work by Jean-Baptiste Say (1767–1832), who conceived of economics as a consistent set of explanations of individual actions and social interactions. Typical examples are his treatment and critique of Adam Smith with regard to the role of labour, his re-introduction of the entrepreneur (after Cantillon's *Essai sur la nature du commerce en général*), his insight into the production process as dependent on the ongoing acquisition of knowledge (Say 2006 [1852]: tome I, chapter VI). Unfortunately, Say's departure from objectivism[29] and his introduction of a theory of entrepreneurship failed to revolutionize economic thinking. It is not easy to explain why. Possibly, under the influence of Adam Smith, most of Say's readers were persuaded that the industrial revolution was the result of greater fixed investment and extended markets, with little scope for entrepreneurship and technological advances (except for the improvements connected with the learning-by-doing allowed by the division of labour). If so, Say's entrepreneur would be no more than the instrument through which the existing technological opportunities could be exploited, rather than the originator or the promoter of new opportunities (as Menger and Mises would clarify several decades later).

From a different angle, in order for the new theory of value to change economic science, the very notion of equilibrium would have had to come under attack. But this was not the main, explicit message conveyed by Say or his immediate followers.[30]

Other attempts to break away from the classical holistic and rather static foundations also went unnoticed, possibly because those attempts denied constructivism, as in the case of Claude-Frédéric Bastiat (1801–1850), the best known champion of the virtues of entrepreneurial growth and the outstanding warden against state promises of fair and welfare-enhancing intervention in economic affairs. Or because nobody paid attention, as happened to Hermann Heinrich Gossen (1810–1858), who formulated the laws of consumers' behaviour in the goods market in 1854. Be that as it may, an early opportunity to jettison the old economic paradigm went lost and for much of the nineteenth century, therefore, economics remained the analysis of the long-run equilibrium conditions based on the labour theory of value.[31]

A second chance to formulate a new approach to economics surfaced towards the end of the nineteenth century, when societies began to be considered the product of human action, rather than the design of divine will. In the realm of economics, the search for natural equilibrium was thus replaced by attempts to obtain a "scientific" (i.e. mathematical) definition of general equilibrium in terms of prices and quantities determined by the agent's choices. This was made possible by the marginalists, who defined scarcity the proper way and introduced demand; and by the Walrasian marginalists in particular, who created the perfect economy by defining the properties of a hypothetical static, "efficient" equilibrium. Marginalism's truly revolutionary aspect, in fact, was that equilibrium lost its earlier, natural connotations and rapidly acquired man-made contents: from natural equilibrium to artefactual equilibrium, from a quasi-divine order to man-made societies, from human action driven by instincts and propensities to behaviour governed by rationality. Hence, it should not surprise that the most appealing elements of marginalism – Walras's insistence on the use of mathematics[32] and, to a lesser extent, Jevons's rediscovery of Gossen – turned out to be those related to their potential for technocratic, constructivist developments; while other and equally significant innovative contributions – the Mengerian notions of dynamics, entrepreneurship, uncertainty, as well as a number of methodological insights, including subjectivism – went all but unnoticed. Resistance was not altogether absent, but it was not enough to reverse the tide, and weakened further during the second half of the century.

In other words, marginalism won over the classical vision not only because it finally developed a theory of demand, but also because it promised to make economic investigation similar to physics; and to convert economists into social engineers. Hence, rather than drawing the methodological lessons implied by this subjectivist turn, economists took pleasure in the illusion they were about to acquire the key that would allow them to crown their quest for scientism and solve the equilibrium problem once demand was no longer exogenous (and ultimately an issue to be assessed by demographers).[33] Subjectivism was not absent, but its implications were de facto nullified by applying it to the typical individual we have already mentioned in the previous chapter. By no means was it considered the touchstone of a fundamentally new way of thinking:

> Walras did not come into possession of his concept of marginal utility and his method of using it to derive a theoretical demand curve until after he had clearly outlined his mathematical theory of a network of interrelated markets.... What Léon Walras was after was the completion of his competitive market model, and *not* the elaboration of a theory of subjective valuation in consumption.
>
> (Jaffé 1976: 513 and 515)

2.6 Keynes's synthesis and the Keynesians: from the long run to the short run

Walras and Menger offered two different versions of marginalism. Walras's version was surely consistent with the classical tradition in that it kept focusing on long-run issues: his analysis concentrated on the (static) general equilibrium obtained under allegedly perfect and constant conditions with zero transaction costs. Instead, Menger's version was a break with the tradition, in that he actually denied both the existence of equilibrium (other than as an expression to describe situations where markets clear) and the relevance of the long run. In particular, from the Mengerian perspective, the long run should be understood as a succession of short run situations in which economic agents continuously adjust their preferences and revise their choices. Or, it could be characterized as the time span over which the economic agents formulate their informed guesses in order to estimate the streams of costs and benefits provoked by their current actions.

As mentioned above, Menger lost the intellectual fight to the constructivist ambition to transform economics into a hard science that would create scientific happiness and welfare. Yet, the real world was soon to offer a challenge that took the Walrasian supporters wrong-footed. In an effort to explain unemployment and stagnation in the 1920s (mainly in Europe) and in the 1930s (all over the world), the economics profession chose a different tack by offering a four-point diagnosis, here articulated by Keynes:

1   growth during the 50-year-long pre-war period had been unique, "a happy age, ... an extraordinary episode in the economic progress of man". That episode built on the accumulation of capital, which had been made possible

by the inequality in the distribution of wealth, by a once-and-for-all increase in the supply of raw materials and agricultural goods[34] and by the fact that investment decisions had been dominated by a limited number of knowledgeable and professionally competent individuals who had taken advantage of exceptional conditions.

2   Furthermore,

This remarkable system depended for its growth on a double bluff or deception. On the one hand the laboring classes accepted ... a situation in which they could call their own very little of the cake that they and nature and the capitalists were co-operating to produce. And on the other hand the capitalist classes were allowed to call the best part of the cake theirs and were theoretically free to consume it, on the tacit underlying condition that they consumed very little of it in practice;

3   The system collapsed with the First World War:

The war has disclosed the possibility of consumption to all and the vanity of abstinence to many. Thus the bluff is discovered; the laboring classes may be no longer willing to forgo so largely, and the capitalist classes, no longer confident of the future, may seek to enjoy more fully their liberties of consumption so long as they last.

4   The final step was the materialization of the class struggle:

By combining a popular hatred of the class of entrepreneurs with the blow already given to social security by the violent and arbitrary disturbance of contract and of the established equilibrium of wealth which is the inevitable result of inflation, these governments are fast rendering impossible a continuance of the social and economic order of the nineteenth century.

(Keynes 1920: chapters 2 and 6)

Schumpeter's reading of Keynes's pages adds a further element in the same vein:

The conditions were rapidly passing in which entrepreneurial leadership was able to secure success after success, propelled as it had been by rapid growth of populations and by abundant opportunities to invest that were incessantly recreated by technological improvements.... But now (1920) those impulses were giving out, the spirit of private enterprise was flagging, investment opportunities were vanishing.

(Schumpeter 1946: 500–501)

In other words, Keynes's analysis led the profession to perceive pre-war growth as an exception, stagnation as the rule and crisis as the consequence of demagoguery and bad government policies (money printing in particular). The "psychology of society" would explain behaviour during the crisis and the difficulties met by spontaneous recovery. Put differently, according to Keynes's vision, capitalism is affected by inherent breakdown possibilities because its own success has made the capital market accessible to the ignorant and voluble mass, and the economy has therefore become vulnerable to the "instability of human nature", to wavering and unpredictable instincts (the animal spirits), to perceptions and expectations about the "political and social atmosphere".

To summarize, Keynes's economics was about equilibrium. By blaming the agents' emotional behaviour, he did not deny the foundations of the Walrasian (and neoclassical in general) penchant for optimal, efficiency-enhancing regulation, and also justified discretionary intervention by the state in order to offset "the outcome of the mass psychology of a large number of ignorant individuals … liable to … a sudden fluctuation of opinion due to factors which do not really make much difference to the prospective yield" (Keynes 1973 [1936]: 154).[35]

Surely, Keynes's foundations could be questioned, but his a prioris were clear and his theorizing consistent. The same could not be said for most Keynesians, who transformed Keynes's theorizing based on the mass-psychotic business cycle into normative instructions for policy-making in the presence of structural rigidities. Not surprisingly, these efforts gradually became analyses of the features and consequences of such rigidities (a quasi neoclassical agenda, except for the fact that in the Keynesian framework man-made constraints/rigidities replace alleged market failures), studies in the methodology of aggregation, exercises in applied econometrics: all in all, today's policy-making owes much more to the various families of Keynesians than to Keynes himself, who was actually rather cautious about modelling and opposed quantitative analysis (Patinkin 1976; Lachmann 1983: 374–375).

2.7 Preliminary conclusions: from natural to general equilibrium

To sum up the argument so far, this chapter has tried to show that notwithstanding a limited number of noteworthy dissident voices, throughout its history, the economics profession has been characterized by the focus on equilibrium. During the early classical period natural equilibrium meant "harmony" and defined the social rules of the game. Later on, equilibrium became equivalent to an iron law dictated by scarcity and market clearing. More recently, it turned into the quest for an ideal mix combining static efficiency, rational decision-making, social objectives; in short it became a synonym for optimality.

Of course, this emphasis on equilibrium has not been an economists' invention, for it in fact reflects the legacy of universalism that theism and perhaps Plato's idealism transferred to the West: this world is the creation of God and therefore cannot be less than perfect. If there exist imperfections, these are entirely man's fault, for God could only design perfection. Equilibrium and perfection were thus considered synonymous with two important implications, which are still with us today. First, equilibrium is necessarily a desirable condition and must therefore be identified and pursued. Second, equilibrium cannot change its features, since perfection is by definition timeless.[36] Yet, these two elements would justify social rules to protect and encourage compliance with moral standards, not policy-making. In order to legitimize policy-making as we understand it today, equilibrium needed to be transformed into a set of guidelines to evaluate the features of future, expected human action. This was obtained by moving away from the classical concept with the emphasis on coordinated, predictable actions, to the present (neoclassical) view that encourages the creation of incentives to induce agents to behave in the desired way. To repeat, in the classical context, equilibrium served as a reference to understand why and when agents would deviate from their (God-given) nature. In today's context, it has reproduced Pareto's imaging and become a blueprint for "optimal" policy-making.[37] Certainly, by identifying the extent to which the market fails to attain desirable results, more and more attention has been devoted to conceiving not only the necessary remedial measures, but also the political structures that are more likely to create and effectively enforce them.

The Keynesian experience strengthened this approach. Not denying the (static) notion of long-run equilibrium, it drew attention to the alleged damages of popular capitalism and opened a new research programme, which focused on the macro conditions to obtain equilibrium in the presence of speculative drives provoked by irrational bursts of mass optimism or pessimism – the former generally self-correcting, the latter often leading to permanent traps. It described human action as the result of instincts, "nerves and hysteria", rather than of conscious choice. Innovation and technical progress were not altogether neglected, but they were considered the consequences of human nature, which encourages some individuals to take chances. Entrepreneurship as we understand it today (Shane 2003; Holcombe 2007) was totally ignored.

As hinted earlier, the alternative would have been (and would be) to forget about equilibrium and instead analyse the consequences of conscious choice under scarcity constraints. Lachmann (1986: 4) neatly called attention to the key question: "No market process has a determinate outcome. It is this property, more than any other, that distinguishes market processes as ongoing processes from those which appear in equilibrium models in which determinism is of the essence of the matter." Although this research programme is much more consistent with the essence of the Western mind than the holistic classical and neoclassical approaches, it presents a dramatic break with respect to the standard views. Furthermore, it raised/raises at least two sets of problems which might imply serious limitations to the scope of economic study. First, if exchange is the instrument through which individuals improve their condition, then the interesting question is whether individuals really do what they believe they are doing, i.e. whether they are rational. Experimental economists investigate these questions and their work inevitably leads to studying psychology, be it cognitive or evolutionary (more on this in the next chapter). Following this approach, however, one might wonder whether economics and psychology are the same discipline, or whether economics is in fact a branch of psychology. Second, it often happens that the institutional framework effectively constrains or alters individuals' choices, so that man's economic actions become subject to incentive systems and do not necessarily follow individual preferences as they would appear in a free context. In this case, then, economics becomes a rather mechanical what-if exercise (how institutions affect economic behaviour). Or it becomes a question regarding the legitimacy of man-made incentives (rules): are rules legitimate because they increase individual welfare despite the individuals' revealed preferences? or because the individual is no longer considered the key agent in economic matters? Be that as it may, one suspects that political philosophy might offer better answers than economics.

These are embarrassing questions, which probably contribute to explaining why over the past 50 years the vast majority of the economics profession has preferred to stay away from psychological and moral issues. Studies in the former area have usually been interpreted as evidence in favour of human irrationality and masochism, thereby further justifying technocratic design and intrusion. Research in the institutional context has met a different fate. Yet, its political-philosophical roots have been ignored and substituted by the planning of optimal incentive systems designed by the regulator.

2.8 Mainstream economics today

The bottom line is that today's mainstream view consists of an enlarged version of the original Keynesian proposal, according to which the technocrat has explicitly replaced the politician.[38] In particular, two different research strategies have prevailed, and de facto defined the orthodox approach to economics nowadays. According to a first reading, economics is a positive science that predicts future phenomena. More generally, the task of the social scholar is to conceive of parsimonious, accurate and consistent descriptions of the real world (selection and logical layout of knowledge), which can then be extrapolated for predictive or normative purposes. Competing theories are thus accepted or discarded according to their "realism", i.e. to their different abilities to forecast given classes of events. Neoclassical model-making definitely belongs to this tradition. For instance, it consciously sidesteps several issues regarding individual behaviour and institutional incentives by making ad hoc and admittedly debatable simplifying assumptions. These assumptions are nevertheless let pass and sometimes even encouraged as long as the model remains mathematically tractable and its foretelling power is satisfying. With this understanding, the quality of economic analysis

> is to be judged by the precision, scope, and conformity with experience of the predictions it yields. In short, positive economics is, or can be, an "objective" science, in precisely the same sense as any of the physical sciences … to be judged by its predictive power for the class of phenomena which it is intended to "explain".
>
> (Friedman 1953: 4 and 8)[39]

On the other hand, a second approach insists on the importance of assessing the quantitative significance and the statistical properties of more or less complex phenomena, e.g. when two or more causal mechanisms are operating at the same time, possibly in opposite directions, so that the outcome is uncertain. According to this view, which was originally formulated in Condorcet's efforts to create a *mathématique sociale* and was further proposed again by Pareto,[40] the economist is supposed to look for interesting empirical questions and make use of his quantitative skills in order to obtain fitting answers, which then become theories.

Far from being mutually exclusive, the descriptive and the quantitative approaches outlined above both depend on the acknowledgement of an implicit benchmark. The positivists need it in order to elaborate predictive models that on average reproduce reality. The quantitatives need it in order to test the quality – accuracy and reliability – of their statistical exercises. In general, this benchmark is provided by some notion of equilibrium. The core of the matter, therefore, is to understand the features of such equilibrium and the nature of the actors who are supposed to bring it about. The economist usually stops in front of such a question, without much justification. Yet, this is clearly no deterrent to the policy-maker, despite the inadequacies mentioned at the very beginning of this chapter.

2.9 The Austrian challenge to the value paradigm

To be fair, the mainstream approach has not gone unchallenged. For instance, the Austrians have seriously questioned the significance of equilibrium in economic analysis: because individuals do not have the relevant information in order to assess what would generate equilibrium; because even if one knew what equilibrium requires at time t, that information would be obsolete at time $t+1$; because agents never operate in equilibrium and even if they did, individuals would always strive to break away from an equilibrium condition, to make a profit, to acquire power, to win fame and prestige. In addition, the Austrians have also downplayed the importance of empirical research, arguing instead in favour of a priori speculation, the idea being that a theory can only be the result of deductive reasoning and therefore ultimately truistic, as Friedman would have critically pointed out. Thus, according to this vantage point, the merit of all economic investigations would depend on the nature and logical consistency of the axioms formulated *ex ante*. So much for logical positivism, whereby economic laws are assessed by comparing predictions and empirical observations; and for induction as a whole, which should be left to economic history, defined as "the collection and systematic arrangement of all the data of experience concerning human action" (Mises 1963 [1949]: 30). Surely, statistics and data mining are a welcome addition; but not really necessary and potentially dangerous: when a good theory does not match the data, according to this view the researcher should question the quality of the data. A poor data fit would not be enough to disqualify a theory; nor would a good data fit demonstrate the opposite.

According to Mises, Rothbard, Lachmann and their followers, therefore, once equilibrium and inductions are discarded, economics becomes the analysis of the logical mechanisms that power human action. This is the essence of the so-called "praxeological" approach, according to which the individual is sovereign and his freedom of action can never be encroached upon, except when it results in physical violence or fraud.[41] Clearly, determinism should be rejected in all its versions, while the nature and features of policy action ought to be founded on moral philosophy rather than on collective/social efficiency, let alone hermeneutics.[42]

The list of disagreements and challenges could continue. But there is no doubt that over the past few decades the positivist/quantitative view has prevailed and has become mainstream. Most contributions to economics are now based on modelling some sort of optimizing behaviour, the actors being sets of individuals or political communities. Of course, that also implies that equilibrium – in fact, a particular notion of equilibrium, as we have shown in the previous sections – occupies the centre of the stage in economic analysis. Over a century after the *Methodenstreit*,[43] the (old) historicist side seems to have overpowered the relatively small groups of praxeological opponents and won the war. Granted, some keep arguing that economics is about the application of a given set of analytical tools (e.g. cost–benefit analysis, constrained maximization) to all areas of human behaviour, while others insist on identifying economics by the subject matter (for instance, the motivations of acting individuals, the rules and arrangements that make exchange easy and mutually profitable).[44] Yet, a cursory look at the contemporary literature shows that the academic profession is focused on "looking for interesting empirical questions" and carrying out empirical investigation to provide answers. In short, the dispute about the inductive/deductive nature of economic theorizing is virtually over and the exchange paradigm has been all but confined to the history of economic thought.

Be that as it may, this is no reason to give up and concede defeat to an allegedly a-theoretical and value-free technocracy. Despite the importance the mainstream views have acquired, assessment of the firmness of their methodological foundations remains generally and perhaps opportunely neglected; and too many statements end up being accepted at face value. Put differently, such lack of knowledge and of interest explains the easy, almost credulous acceptance of the positivist encompassing claims, the mistreatment of areas of investigation that deserve to be explored more thoroughly, the evaluation of policy measures according to their ability to enhance some notion of social efficiency and to strengthen consensus, rather than to their intrinsic consistency. In a word, there remain plenty of reasons to keep waging war or to start fighting anew.

It is of course undeniable that the classic static, natural-equilibrium vision was inadequate. But the modern static, man-made-equilibrium alternative does not carry us much further. It is then plausible to suggest that those interested in understanding the nature and foundations of policy-making look back to some of the basic questions that the history of thought has offered us to ponder upon and that the prevailing technocratic resolve – whatever its origin – has induced us to disregard or simply take for granted. This is the purpose of the chapters that follow, which aim at offering new food for thought and new answers to key questions: How important is the assumption about rational behaviour? What are the alternatives and what are their implications for economic analysis? What are the foundations and the limits of individual liberty and how do these foundations and limits affect such notions as fairness, common good and social contract? How come that despite the weak philosophical legitimacy of a large share of policy-making, public opinion in the West accepts and sometimes even requires widespread encroachment upon individual freedom as well as extensive rent-seeking by the policy-makers?

3   Time, rationality, cooperation

3.1 Equilibrium alone won't do

In the introductory chapter we have argued that policy-making is founded on a fairly peculiar notion of economics, one which does not consider real individuals, but rather typical agents or broadly defined groups of people, including latent and active coalitions. This kind of economics shows a relatively modest interest in explaining what actors in fact think and do and is usually satisfied with articulating simplified working hypotheses that are subsequently exploited in order to track down fundamental statistical patterns. As clearly spelled out by Milton Friedman some 60 years ago, these hypotheses are then accepted or discarded according to their predictive power. Although lip service is sometimes paid to analysing preferences – which are admittedly hard to define or generalize – most economists are also inclined to proceed as if individuals enjoyed being in equilibrium, strived to reach it, and knew when they had attained it. All other elements are not ignored completely, but are de facto excluded from the realm of economic investigation and attributed to other disciplines, such as psychology or anthropology. Not surprisingly, this attitude has led to the construction of models and sets of equations that describe actions and interactions by quasi-robots, either in equilibrium or in their endeavours to obtain equilibrium. During the past decades, the search for – and the definition of – these equilibrium features has represented the core of the positivist view and thus of the mainstream drive to qualify economics as a hard science.

Yet, the notion of "equilibrium" per se does not lead the prospective policy-maker very far. Taken literally, this term merely refers to a situation in which each agent has no incentives to change his behaviour and engage in a different course of action. Coherence would then imply that policy-making for equilibrium consists in helping the individual in his search for happiness constrained by scarcity; that is, in his efforts to make the most out of the resources available to him. This should amount to little more than ensuring the protection of physical integrity, property rights, freedom of contract and possibly the enforcement of voluntary agreements. Briefly put, policies should aim at easing the search for equilibrium and then ensuring that such equilibrium is not molested. A similar comment would apply to the notion of "social equilibrium", which identifies a situation in which the agents are supposed to be happy with what they do, as long as their behaviour remains consistent – or is amended in accordance – with the collective interest marked out by a political elite.[1]

Thus, from a normative standpoint, equilibrium is either a tautology or a pretext for arbitrariness. If the emphasis is on the fact that each agent always acts the way he does because he thinks that no better alternative is available, then he is always in equilibrium, by definition. Nothing needs to be done, other than the minimal guarantees mentioned above. By contrast, if equilibrium is a pre-defined collective goal hidden behind a veil of uncertainty or ignorance, a veil which is luckily and mysteriously pierced through by the politician and/or the technocrat,[2] then characterizing the goal becomes a matter of arbitrariness by the chosen few, rather than the object of scholarly investigation.

In order to become operationally useful, the idea of equilibrium needs to be enriched by two lines of theorizing. One regards the notion of time, the other of rationality. These concepts and their implications highlight one of the two pillars of policy-making[3] and make it logically possible for skilful, concerned planners to develop strategies to pursue desirable goals (constructivism), or to accelerate what otherwise would be the result of attractive, but exceedingly slow evolutionary processes (the spontaneous-order approach). The analysis of these aspects forms the main part of this chapter (Sections 3.2 and 3.3), in which we try to examine the foundations of individual behaviour and evaluate to which extent individual action justifies external intervention, to correct mistakes and/or enhance cooperation. With this purpose in mind, the consequences are then assessed against different backdrops in the fourth section, devoted to free riding, altruism, culture and custom.

3.2 The delusion of timeless economics

Many years ago, Alchian (1950) observed that the analysis and planning of equilibrium makes sense only if one is willing to do without the notion of time, that is, if one pays no attention to the fact that human action in the future differs from that in the present on two accounts. First, because preferences and opportunities change as a consequence of acquired knowledge,[4] technological progress, institutional evolution and new psychological patterns.[5] Second, because uncertainty ensures that such change is at least partly unpredictable.[6] Put differently, when time is present, the future is to some extent unknown, since we are unaware of what is going to happen around us, we can't foresee how we are going to react to new incentive systems, we don't even know whether the stimuli already experienced in the past will elicit the same responses. Hence, when the presence of time is taken into account and extrapolation is netted out, prediction necessarily turns into guessing, or informed guessing at best. Within this context, the notion of equilibrium is perhaps relevant for descriptive analyses, as in the field of economic history; but its appeal for explanatory or normative purposes is limited.[7]

By contrast, in an economy without time, the future is the repetition of the present, augmented by the results or the projection of today's actions. In other words, what we shall be doing tomorrow is the predictable combination of what we are at present and the new constraints generated by our current behaviour. As noted earlier, models and statistical techniques are developed in order to describe these combinations. Somewhat paradoxically, therefore, nowadays good economic model-makers are those who offer a good description of the past and happen to deal with an area that has not been affected by new events. In short, successful scholarship requires that the future should not arrive before credit for the good statistical fit is reaped. This is hardly surprising: when nothing new occurs, extrapolation and prediction necessarily coincide.

3.2.1 The absence of time and the nature of countercyclical policy-making

To be fair, a timeless approach is good enough to carry out exercises in simulation. But it plays a critical and problematic role when justifying policy-making for stabilization. Granted, the profession does not deny the existence of uncertainty. Even the staunchest positivist knows that his crystal ball is not totally transparent and is indeed ready to acknowledge that uncertainty-induced changes might weaken his claim to normative, time-invariant perfection. A cursory look at most dynamic models suffices to realize that their designers do warn readers against the presence of potential "shocks", which identify the moment when the model applies and/or expires.

Nonetheless, the policy-maker also believes that the present is undesirable, that it needs to be corrected through some sort of enlightened dirigisme and that there is little hope for spontaneous and sufficiently fast improvements. Despite his awareness of the technocratic challenges ahead, he trusts that benevolent planning will eventually get it right, or almost right. Indeed, according to the followers of mainstream positivism, even an opaque crystal ball is adequate to validate intervention, and the assumption about timelessness is acceptable, at least within the time spans defined by the shocks. If problems arise, "optimal" adjustment will be the name of the game. For instance, if the policy-maker aims at enhancing aggregate production and possibly the demand for labour in the economy, and if the selected tool is a lax monetary and credit policy, doubts about the side effects of such measures will be downplayed. Or, those doubts will be assuaged by prompting further measures at a later stage, to reduce the damage inflicted by possibly undesirable results and with little concern for the interaction between the two packages, e.g. in terms of expectations. By keeping to our example, we know that the time problem forces the decision-maker to periodically appraise whether the current features of the credit and monetary policy are effective in achieving the desired targets – high growth and employment. When one of these two variables produces unwelcome figures, more money is pumped in. When the economy overheats (inflation), liquidity is withdrawn. Two consequences follow. On the one hand, agents will have to take into account the time lag between the moment policy action is deliberated and the moment policy action affects the economy. As frequently pointed out in the literature, this is going to be far from easy, not least because the reasons that prompted intervention might no longer be in place when the measures become effective. On the other hand, the nature of the correction required might not be clear-cut, especially when policy goals generate potential conflicts. The obvious examples are inflation versus growth; the expansionary effects of governmental expenditure versus the contractionary effects of present or future taxation; the temptation to grant social guarantees (privileges) versus the reduced opportunities for the unemployed and protectionism.

In the end, all this shows that a particular kind of policy-making is likely to emerge from opaque crystal balls. Consistent with the ongoing-tuning requirements mentioned above, and given that the inability to take into account uncertainty becomes of less consequence with the shortening of the time horizon, faith in policy-making implies that sensible intervention necessarily tends to apply to the short run. The long run is transformed into a succession of short-run undertakings, subject to frequent revisions and updating. The upshot, of course, is that by ignoring uncertainty, policy-making turns into an unavoidable source of uncertainty in itself.[8]

3.2.2 A digression: old wine in new bottles

To be fair, all this is not entirely new. In fact, the effort to found a timeless social science reproduces a rather simplified version of an old story: the conception of man's time horizon.[9] In the Christian Middle Ages, the future was the End of the world, the time of the Last Judgement.[10] Since the End was assumed to be fixed, the passing of time became known as the "shortening of time". In those days, it implied that man should forget about material welfare and devote his energies to becoming spiritually ready to enter eternity among the chosen few.

In the seventeenth century, the Thirty Years War made the shortening of time a medieval fantasy, to be replaced by the opposite view: the acceleration and humanization of time, according to which the passing of time was no longer measured as the distance separating society from the Last Judgement, but as the time available to the individual to realize himself – to improve his condition and to make progress. Thus, the new goal was no longer the accomplishment of religious unity in view of the Last Judgement, but the promotion of religious tolerance in order to avoid conflicts and grief on earth. A goal-minded universal body was gradually replaced by open-minded individuals.[11]

In today's parlance, one can thus posit that timeless economics is equivalent to the acceptance of a time-shortening approach, whereby societies must reach an end-goal characterized by an ideal – say, social fairness, stabilization, sustainable growth or stagnation – which lies at least in part outside the purpose of man's action and which could be missed or betrayed, if individuals were left free to pursue their own "selfish" material ambitions. Not unexpectedly, this view contrasts with the time-acceleration version, according to which the future is the unknown result of man's efforts and creativity, and by definition beyond the planner's and social designer's horizons.[12]

Unfortunately, one is tempted to conclude that during recent decades, mainstream economics and policy-making have been following a vision of the world that had already become obsolete 350 years ago. Sometimes the contradiction between a time-shortening vision and expectations for ever higher living standards has been successfully swept under the rug by fast, self-propelled technological progress, especially when social engineering has not interfered too much with entrepreneurial activities. Sometimes the contradiction has become manifest and has led to crises. For instance, it happened at the end of the 1920s and once again in 2007/2009, when shocks elicited populist reactions by the politicians and social, time-shortening options prevailed. In both cases the choice was Martin Luther, rather than David Hume. Surely, the horizon was no longer defined by the allegedly imminent End of the world, but the urgent need to promise social fairness and safeguards – the modern version of the end of time – was unmistakable.

3.3 From methodological individualism to rationality and consciousness

As a partial response to these inconsistencies, two different lines of reasoning have been developed over the past decades. They are both ostensibly value free and thus claim to be subject neither to moral scrutiny, nor to eschatological constraints. One goes under the heading of rationality and will be examined momentarily. The other discusses some issues related to cooperation and will be the object of Section 3.4.

The relevance of the rationality question is associated with what is usually defined as methodological individualism. Briefly put, methodological individualism claims that all explanations of social phenomena start from the individual, for the subject of any purposeful action is necessarily an individual. One can of course debate whether individual action is based on selfish, cold-blooded reasoning, on instincts and passions, on replicating or opposing what somebody else is doing, on the position of the stars, or on all these components at the same time. Be that as it may, according to this approach, the primary engine of an action remains the human being, who can act as a single player in isolation, such as Robinson Crusoe (little or no exchange); or follow ascetic patterns (little or no production). But he can also – and most frequently does – choose to exchange by trading the goods or services he produces; decide to cooperate with others by engaging in agreed-upon procedures (coordination); or opt to delegate to others the task of acting on his behalf. Many individuals taken together can generate a collective action. In a similar vein, the interactions among the individuals that form a social body produce what can be defined as "aggregate behaviour".

Thus, methodological individualism does not deny that the social environment (institutions) influences individual preferences and behaviours. Even if one posits that preferences are not the subject matter of economic investigation,[13] individuals' actions are indeed interdependent. And since interdependence unfolds following given sets of rules, there is no doubt that methodological individualism necessarily attributes a central role to the institutional picture, both in a static and in a dynamic context.

To conclude, it is hard to disagree with the essence of the individualist position.[14] But once it is accepted, the methodological dispute necessarily moves on to the next step, which is the core of the rationality debate: does the individual actually do what he would like to do? Does he really act in order to pursue his best interest?

3.3.1 Rationality and policy action

If the answer is in the positive, then policy-makers should stay put and possibly concentrate on economic constitutions, on making it easier for the individual to act purposefully and to interact with potential counterparts. As we know, this is the Austrian position. If the answer is in the negative, then the scope of policy-action is to intervene in order to make the agent happier, despite his own myopia and inconsistencies[15] or, according to the economist's jargon, despite his lack of rationality.[16] This view clearly differs from the two justifications for policy-making presented in the previous chapter.[17] For in this case intervention is targeted at doing what the individual would be doing if he acted consistent with his material preferences. Put differently, the reason for intruding and possibly violating the agent's freedom in a timeless economy is the agent's deviation from an ideal Walrasian equilibrium, in which the acquisition of knowledge is ruled out (there is nothing new to know) and uncertainty is prevented from disrupting individual plans. Thus, by calling upon (ir)rationality, the policy-makers appeals to the individual's pursuit of happiness, the implicit rationalization – almost an implicit contract – being that nobody in his right mind could possibly object to outside interferences that clearly make him better off.

In truth, several authors have maintained that much of the debate on rationality is almost a useless discussion on terminological issues.[18] After all, it is claimed, there is no doubt that the individual always tries to enhance his satisfaction (utility). Thus, there is no need to introduce the term "rationality" (or utility) to describe the fact that a happy condition is preferable to a not-so-happy situation.[19] Although we do not deny that this position has merit, we argue that it misses the point. Once it is recognized that individuals cannot always see or choose in order to maximize their pay off (i.e. they are not rational), and once it is accepted that irrational actions are a potential nuisance which frequently run against man's interests and will be regretted in a long-run perspective,[20] then the decision about what is rational (and what is not) is indeed critical. In particular, it creates a purpose and a motivation for policy-making, which allegedly aims at neutralizing irrational and presumably undesirable behaviour. Clearly, in this case this argument is not just a matter of terminology and is further reinforced when the goal is a social issue: for instance, redistribution or production of "merit goods".[21]

To sum up, the debate on rationality can be split into two parts. The first block consists in clarifying whether decisions consciously taken by agents always aim at improving their material, observable well-being, even if one might subsequently regret or revise earlier choices. The second block depends on the answer to the previous question. If it is in the positive, then rationality defines the criterion according to which one can test consistency between ends and means, between what the agent wants to achieve and how he does it (individual rationality).[22] Within this context, "optimal" policy-making is thus justified as an instrument to help individuals to avoid mistakes. If the answer is in the negative and individuals follow a wider notion of well-being, which is not necessarily observable by third parties, then rationality can only provide a guideline to describe and interpret the dynamics of a social aggregate. This is all one can make of the notion of "social rationality": it identifies the features and desirability of the evolutionary process through which some actions tend to be repeated and others discarded. Put differently, in this latter case, the rationality criterion filters the development of the real world with respect to a given benchmark defined by a more or less legitimized ruler. Of course, under such circumstances the ambitions to obtain a psychology-free, amoral and operationally useful concept of (social) rationality turn into wishful thinking.[23]

3.3.2 Consciousness

The above takes for granted that human behaviour can be categorized as rational or irrational and that judgement on irrational acts can offer useful insights to lay out guidelines for normative economics or economic history. However, this is not the only way to frame the relevant question.

Although it took them some time, economists eventually recognized that men strive to improve their own condition and loosen the scarcity constraint; that they do their best to create and exploit opportunities to become different from what they are, by changing their behaviour and finding new ways of adapting to the surrounding environment and/or by modifying the environment itself.

Contrary to the Darwinian perspective, this very effort to be different distinguishes human beings from the other living creatures:

> a central difference between my dog and any one of us lies in his lack of any sense of becoming different from what he is. ... we, as human beings, also know that we can, within limits, shape the form of being that we shall be between now and the time of death, even when we fully reckon on the stochastic pattern of life expectancy.
>
> (Buchanan 1979: 94)

Thus, the attribute of "consciousness", as opposed to unconsciousness, unawareness, instinct-driven behavioural mechanisms, marks the difference between humans and other species.[24] It is built upon a process of perception and categorization of the outside world, learning from experience, memorizing;[25] it is driven by the desire to improve one's material or emotional well-being; and it is ultimately constrained by internal or external moral assessments.[26] Put differently, when making a choice, individuals are not simple machines run by genetics or chemistry. They are aware of what they are doing and can decide not to do it. As mentioned earlier, choice may be the result of consistent, cost–benefit reasoning (synonymous with rationality), but also of emotions, established routines, deontic principles. These provide stimuli and suggest courses of action that are sometimes deliberately preferred to the use of cold-blooded, self-interested calculus, and they contribute to articulating decisions on whether and with whom to exchange, whether and to what extent to acquire information and knowledge, whether and where to apply talents to create new knowledge (innovation and technological progress) or exploit new opportunities (entrepreneurship).

Surely, consciousness covers a broader set of actions than rationality and probably does a better job in marking the difference between man and the other living creatures on earth. Granted, mainstream economics does not deny the limits of rationality. Nevertheless, it claims that rationality is easier to grapple with and that it should therefore be preferred. On the one hand – the argument goes – it is difficult enough to articulate formal models (behavioural routines) by referring to the rationality paradigm. The leap into consciousness would be all but impossible to handle. On the other hand, the positivist claim insists on formal elegance, simplicity and predictive power. As long as the rational paradigm meets these requirements – or promises to do so – consciousness can be quietly ignored or simply considered a (convenient) residual.

Still, we believe that these objections are not enough to set aside the concept of consciousness, which in fact can contribute significantly to our assessment of the foundations of policy-making. First, and contrary to the argument put forward in the post-marginalist literature, the move from the rationality to the consciousness paradigm would not kill economics as a social science. It would, however, weaken its ambition to be a "hard" discipline and would force economists to become interdisciplinary, rather than colonizers. Second, the rationality principle offers firm ground to develop a case in favour of policy-making, the main purpose of which would be to make up for irrational behaviour (faulty or anti-social appreciation of a given payoff matrix). By contrast, consciousness would be a rather fragile justification for coercive intervention. Unconscious behaviour is much more difficult to demonstrate: it would require ad hoc investigation and would probably lead to persuasion, education and psychological attention, rather than to straight rule-making. Yet, we believe that the emergence of the need for a different approach to normative economics is not per se a good enough reason to ignore what creates such need. Third, by appreciating consciousness, one necessarily raises the issue of individual responsibility, in that the wider the boundaries of legitimate individual action, the sharper the notion of individual liberty and the greater implications for personal accountability. If one accepts that consciousness is the distinctive feature of man, it follows that all kinds of conscious behaviour must be accepted, unless they violate other distinctive features and entitlements of the individual (freedom of expression and, in general, freedom from coercion and possibly the right to self-preservation). Instead, if the rationality paradigm is assumed to be the benchmark, a gap between rational action and human action broadly understood opens up. The gap may consist of socially irrelevant events (Mr Green irrationally forgets to look at the weather forecasts, gets soaked in the rain and catches a cold), but may also consist of allegedly undesirable undertakings (e.g. refusal to cooperate with selected categories of people or to acquire insurance against catastrophic events, willingness to buy cheap but possibly dangerous products). Such a gap is clearly the ideal area for regulators to intervene and apply their (rational) wisdom.

3.3.3 Is the individual-rationality criterion useful?

The previous paragraphs have made clear that we are inclined to believe that the essence of human action is consciousness, rather than rationality. Moreover, we tend to believe that this analytical a priori should apply to all *Sciences de l'Homme*, as the French have aptly defined the realm of the social sciences.[27] Of course, this also pertains to economics, which refers to individual behaviour in a framework characterized by scarcity. We do not deny that human action is frequently driven by a principle of cost–benefit consistency. When individuals take a decision, they do rank the various alternatives and they often try to develop something similar to a pay-off matrix associated to the various events and outcomes. Nonetheless, we are persuaded that this is not the whole story, that human actions can have economic consequences also when non-rational elements come into the picture and that, therefore, it makes little sense to claim that non-rational behaviour falls outside the domain of economics. For instance, nationalism or religious fundamentalism might lead an individual not to buy some goods because they come from a foreign or an "infidel" supplier, even if the latter offers the desired merchandise at a lower price. From a different angle, one can also think of the boycotting of South African goods in the 1980s, to protest apartheid. In all these cases, exchange is not the result of a maximizing exercise about the value and price of the goods (the mainstream perspective). Instead, it includes psychological/ideological elements outside much of the post-marginalist tradition, which would thus be flawed: the mainstream, neoclassical vantage point would de facto preclude economic investigation, while sticking to an Austrian perspective would be equivalent to advocating the role of a methodological watchdog.

Can one thus conclude that the economist would do a better job by forgetting rationality, a source of terminological problems, but a solution to none? Not quite, because there are situations in which the role of conscious, non-rational behaviour (emotions, moral imperatives) is minimal[28] and determinism prevails (or ought to prevail). For instance, this applies when action is delegated to loyal intermediaries, who are supposed to enhance cooperation by enforcing contracts or reducing the cost of exchanging; or are required to obtain specific targets, as in the case of a company manager or a personal wealth manager. Under such circumstances, however, the individual-rationality paradigm is no longer an analytical tool, but rather a benchmark for testing.

To sum up, individual rationality can be retained when designing empirical exercises to examine whether agents behave as expected (i.e. according to the incentives created by the rules of the game), or whether they deviate – either because it pays not to behave rationally, which reveals poorly designed rules, or because agents remain unable to behave rationally despite the social scientist's wishes. In this light, the post-marginalist ambition to explain individual behaviour is actually an effort to simulate what people would do if they followed a more or less arbitrarily-defined utility function and, even more importantly, had a permanent inclination to ignore fairness, deontic principles, trust and cooperation. But of course, this is also the limit of this methodological choice.

Perhaps it is no accident that when mainstream economists take themselves too seriously and design policy-making structures to compensate for non-rational behaviour and thus obtain "optimal" outcomes, in fact they undermine key and priceless components of the human person, such as trust and honesty. This does not deny that breach of trust and lying lead to damages and that these can often be quantified. It does mean, however, that when trust and honesty are derived from a moral code, it makes no sense to conceive of a price at which such behavioural rules can be violated. Yet, once the policy-maker introduces a regulatory framework (formal rules buttressed by credible sanctions), breach of trust and immoral behaviour acquire a price (the sanction) and are de facto accepted, as long as one knows there might be a price to pay.[29] Put differently, in the absence of policy-making, there are situations in which there is no trade off between a rational act and a deontic principle: "you should not lie because lying is bad, no matter what". In the presence of policy-making, however, lying is no longer out of the question: it simply becomes an expensive option. In such cases, choosing between lying and telling the truth becomes a mere matter of rational choice and the gap between consciousness and rationality shrinks. In short, and somewhat paradoxically, the breach between consciousness and rationality makes policy-making hardly acceptable. But once enforced, policy-making contributes to closing the gap and thus to justifying its existence.

3.3.4 Social and group rationality

If rationality is not a satisfactory explanatory or normative paradigm in dealing with the economic issues raised by individual behaviour, what about its relevance for social interaction? Can we accept *conscious* behaviour for individuals and nevertheless make an argument in favour of *rational* interaction within a community?

Once again, the answer to this question ultimately depends on our understanding of human nature. Today economists estimate that individuals are generally selfish. As noted earlier, the mainstream view does acknowledge that selfishness may be abandoned either for strategic reasons,[30] or because genetic interests prevail and priority goes to enhancing the welfare and reproductive chances of one's genes.[31] Still, by and large the economics profession continues to stick to the "me-first" assumption and to make use of these strategic and genetic options to offer residual explanations. In this vein, ad hoc strategic models are developed in order to shed light on phenomena that fail to be explained by simpler games, while genetic references tend to be bundled together into "error terms", together with instincts, erratic psychological drives and animal spirits. Be that as it may, in this context the expression "social rationality" is all but meaningless.

Yet, there is also another way of looking at social rationality. The alternative argument would underscore the role of the hereditary component and maintain that individuals are the product of an evolutionary process that has become part and parcel of our genetic heritage and is possibly supplemented by educational experiences.[32] Such genetic heritage includes several elements, but for our purposes three of them deserve to be stressed: (*a*) individuals tend to enhance their chances to prosper by living with a group (as opposed to living in isolation), (*b*) groups are founded on cooperation, which may be strengthened by formal and informal rules, (*c*) it usually pays to take chances as long as the goal is approved by the group. If the counterpart reacts as expected, new wealth is created; but even if the deal falls through as a consequence of the counterpart's bad faith, cheating or negligence, the actor's reputation within the group is enhanced and group solidarity might partly compensate for the losses incurred.

In this light, the notion of social rationality is no longer empty. In fact, it can take three different meanings, according to which one can attribute different contents to policy-making. One may follow orthodoxy and posit that the purpose of social interaction is to obtain a given set of outcomes, so that social rationality actually implies instrumental rationality in the pursuit of a socially desirable goal. Policy-making would then take on the traditional socialist function. Second, one may favour an evolutionary interpretation, given that the primary and secondary purposes of interaction remain survival and wealth creation, respectively. In this case, the role for policy-making becomes ambiguous. It can be claimed that the strength of the group ultimately depends on the entrepreneurial abilities of its members, on their willingness to take chances, bear responsibilities, respect property rights and refrain from violence. That would define a free-market system, but it would also allow for the rise of a minimal state, or possibly a paternalist state in charge of selecting the winning actors and industries and of supporting them for the sake of the group. On the other hand, the emphasis might be on cohesion. If so, policy-making should enforce some kind of compulsory solidarity, in order to avoid "social tensions", to ensure the smooth flowing of economic activities and to create a homogenous front against external aggressors: invaders in the past, effective competitors today. Third, one might opt for a more radical vision, by making a distinction between social rationality and group rationality and eventually dropping the latter notion altogether. In particular, social (economic) rationality defines productive exchange among voluntarily-interacting individuals. Such interaction can fall through if institutional costs are high,[33] if reputational costs are low, or if the genetic drive to take chances and risk cooperation within a poorly defined formal context is weak. By contrast, group rationality focuses on the process through which the collective outcome is obtained, rather than on the process through which exchange is carried out. Dropping the concept of group rationality amounts to agreeing to institutional competition, so that institutions are no longer designed and enforced in order to pursue a collective goal or to comply with a closed social contract.[34] This last option would obviously be again consistent with the free-market view, according to which the notion of social rationality refers to the reduction of the cost of voluntary interaction.

3.4 On the consequences of individual and social rationality

The upshot of our argument so far is simply put. Policy-making implies the pursuit of collective goals independent of voluntary exchange among individuals. Such goals can only be conceived and realized by assuming away uncertainty. Moreover, they can be justified as long as they are founded on some kind of group rationality, either because it is assumed a priori that social choice takes deontic priority over individual rationality, or because it is acknowledged that since individuals are subject to contradictory if not self-defeating behaviour, appropriate intervention is necessary. The notions of bounded rationality, free riding, altruism and culture can certainly be considered in this perspective and will be discussed in the next sub-sections.

3.4.1 On bounded rationality

We have noted that rationality requires that individuals choose when they know what the options are and have fairly clear ideas about the effects of their actions. The real world offers a different picture, though, for in most situations individuals prefer not to acquire and/or process all the data they need in order to formulate a fully-informed decision. This applies when information is expensive, time-consuming, or when the data are too rich for easy/fast processing and action cannot be put off. In these cases, individuals resort to rule of thumb and experimented routines as substitute criteria to obtain quick assessments and act accordingly.[35] Since "clarity" is the standard criterion stemming from evolutionary selection,[36] these rules and routines are usually simple: don't spend more than a given amount of money and time in acquiring potentially relevant information, or follow the crowd, or trust the experts, especially if filtered or blessed by the media.

This is the essence of the notion of bounded rationality, which describes why it is efficient not to be fully rational. Although it is obvious that an informed decision frequently leads to better results than groping in the dark, in fact bounded rationality is a way of claiming that individuals are unable to lay out and evaluate their payoff matrix; and that rather than following alternative decision-making procedures such as emotions, deontic constraints, genetically determined impulses, they are better off by making "rational mistakes". Sometimes rational mistakes are randomly distributed, sometimes they are systematic (especially in the case of herd behaviour induced by the media or the authorities). More importantly for our discussion, however, bounded rationality represents the terminological twist by means of which individuals are included within the rationality paradigm despite their propensity to err. In particular, bounded rationality allows individuals to deviate from the expected solution, but they are not supposed to question its wisdom.[37] Last, but not least, bounded rationality creates opportunities for the authority not only to persuade and disseminate information, but also to produce the right kind of information, to give new shape to the payoff matrices available (avoid mistakes), and to develop ad hoc agencies and institutions that help the agents to behave as if they were fully rational.

Not unexpectedly, the above is hardly compatible with the subjectivist standpoint, according to which the distinction between rational and bounded-rational behaviour is simply irrelevant. In the subjectivist context the critical concept is in fact consciousness, supplemented by the "satisficing" criterion, which drives human action and implies a trial-and-error discovery process. This is the true origin of mistakes – not irrationality or bounded rationality. Surely, individuals have limited abilities to acquire and process information and they sometimes reach what *ex post* turn out to be "wrong" decisions. Still, the introduction of simplified utility functions and optimization procedures justified by such limits does not really explain human behaviour: at best, it "describes", as Paul Samuelson's revealed-preference approach documents. Let us now examine how these considerations affect our understanding of free riding, altruism and culture.

3.4.2 Free riding

Free riding is also utilized to justify intervention. In this case it is for the sake of fairness. Simply put, free riding defines a situation in which A enjoys benefits produced by B without paying any fee to B or without sharing proportionately in the production cost (Breton 1996). This occurs whenever B engages in activities that could indeed enhance A's welfare, but when A's readiness to pay is irrelevant to B's decision to act: either because B does not care about A's welfare, or because A and B fail to agree on a contract (and thus A cannot be required to pay). This is what happens when A walks by the façade of a beautifully designed fifteenth-century palace and enjoys looking at it; or when he casually enters a showroom to admire a Ferrari that he will never afford to buy.[38] By and large, the economic relevance of these situations can be analysed from two different standpoints, depending upon whether the observer emphasizes the notions of scarcity or of rationality.

From the vantage point of scarcity, free riding involves zero marginal costs for the giver and should simply be ignored by normative economics and economic analysis in general: zero-marginal-cost gifts do not affect scarcity. The fact that it is an involuntary gift is irrelevant. After all, free riding does not encroach upon any individual right.[39] Surely, B might be unhappy about A's free ride, but envy or frustration is hardly a source of rights or moral standards.[40]

The picture changes if one neglects to realize that rationality is merely a teaching tool or a working hypothesis for predictive modelling, and instead transforms it into the crucial assumption behind man's economic action. Under such circumstances, since the natural right to freedom applies to rational human beings only, irrational behaviour implies that the actor is no longer "human" and thus loses his natural claim to freedom. In this light, the key question is of course whether a free rider can qualify as irrational. The answer is usually in the negative from an individual-rationality perspective: consistent behaviour does not imply compliance with a specific notion of individual fairness: A cannot become irrational simply because B envies him. The answer is however in the positive if group rationality is the relevant benchmark in order to evaluate the human nature of individual behaviour. According to the collectivist tenet, people must thus cooperate even when they don't want to, either for their own good, or for the sake of the common interest. In other words, since free riding involves the underproduction of desirable goods and services (Ferrari showrooms, in our case), partial-equilibrium consequentialism makes sure that free riders be forced to pay for what they are supposed to enjoy, until the socially optimal quantity of output is obtained.[41] Should they refuse to "cooperate" (pay) spontaneously, they lose their human features and may thus become the objects of legitimate coercion.

In the end, it appears that the whole debate on the relevance of free riding boils down to deciding what comes first: individual liberty or the planner's assessment of the common interest? Individual fairness or the ruler's idea of social fairness? Agent B can surely feel ill at ease with the idea that A improves his well-being, while he (B) carries the cost. If the moral code regards the principles governing the community, then B might well feel legitimized in taking action accordingly. But if ethics regards individual behaviour, then B will have to come to terms with his envy and be content with the sympathy he might obtain from the other members of the community.

Two further points deserve to be briefly mentioned within this group-rational context, one from a moral and one from a consequentialist standpoint. First, nobody would deny that free riding is ultimately about the notion of surplus. Indeed, aversion to free riders is usually motivated by the fact that they are enjoying benefits – a surplus – they do not "deserve".[42] However, the very concept of well-being implies that we have free rides all the time: There would be no well-being if everything we do and obtain is exactly offset by the sacrifices we incur and the goods we have to give up. In fact, the absence of a free lunch would imply that we are indifferent between living a miserable existence, committing suicide (religious prohibitions aside) and making $1 million a year. There would be nothing to redistribute if nobody had a free lunch. As a corollary, all rulings regarding unfair, "anticompetitive" pricing are the outcome of a political, necessarily arbitrary decision about the redistribution of free lunches among individuals.

It then follows that policy-making against free riding is not about promoting an abstract notion of fairness or about fighting anti-social behaviour. It does differ from plain redistribution, in that in the free-riding case the victim of policies inspired by an alleged principle of social fairness is required to give up (or pay for) goods and services he has acquired for free. But there is no a priori reason to believe that the net benefit enjoyed by a (free-riding) passerby who admires a fifteenth-century façade and is taxed to finance its upkeep, is larger than that of an internet user who pays $20 a month to surf the web and is molested no further by the taxman. More generally, it is hard to formulate moral principles to obtain a fair redistribution of the property rights on surpluses that nobody allegedly "deserves". Furthermore, one wonders whether it is just that B is rewarded for the benefits others enjoy even if the author/producer did nothing to that effect and never meant to be of advantage to A.[43]

By contrast, policies to internalize free riding clearly rest on more solid ground when based on consequentialist foundations, since it is undeniable that once an appropriate collective utility function is defined, utilities are measured and eventually compared, then the social planner can indeed assess whether too much or too little of a given good is being produced. However, it should also be noted that consistency requires outright planning, not just a utilitarian approach. For whenever the free rider (or, more generally, the beneficiary of a surplus) is asked to pay for the sake of efficiency, he is actually forced to reduce his consumption of his typical basket of goods and services. In addition, it is assumed that he is consuming some units of the public good and is forced to pay and justify production, even if he consumes little or nothing of it.[44] In other words, the policy-maker cannot restrict himself to measuring how much the individual benefits from a positive externality and forcing him to pay. The social planner must also detail the optimal quantity to be produced for each good, so that social welfare is maximized independent of individual utilities; and then use a utilitarian criterion to gather the necessary funds to subsidize production.

To conclude, the debate on free riding proves that consistency allows no third way. At one extreme, you have human action founded on individual consciousness, which is the bedrock of free-market economics. When flaunted or highly visible, free riding may elicit envy and social outcry. It can have sociological implications and affect interaction (the potential for cooperation), but it hardly justifies coercion. At the opposite extreme, you have the rationality-based approach, which however acquires an operational meaning only if rationality actually means "group rationality". But then policy-making turns into a command system ruled by more or less sophisticated versions of the general will.

3.4.3 Altruism, spurious and pure

Altruism is usually considered another critical quality of a creature worthy of respect and freedom. Taken literally, altruism finds little room within economics, unless it is associated with the idea of rationality. No one denies that an individual may intentionally act in order to benefit other people, even when it is likely or certain that the beneficiary will never reciprocate the favour, let alone pay for it. Anonymous charity is the obvious example. Nonetheless, many among the theses put forward in order to explain deviations from material self-interest eventually acknowledge that altruistic behaviour does benefit the actor as well. For instance, the "impartial spectator" portrayed by the Scottish Enlightenment encourages the individual to behave properly towards other human beings even when there is no formal sanction for not doing so.[45] But of course, this view implies that failure to behave properly brings about punishment (guilt and/or shame). Hence, altruism is in fact a way of avoiding the psychological pain generated by "selfish" or unfair conduct.

In other cases one might be altruistic because one likes the idea of making someone else better off (generosity) or one likes receiving gratitude (vanity).[46] Still, it is hard to deny that generous and vain individuals experience pleasure when observing the results of their actions. Thus, under such circumstances, altruism makes them better off, too. The fact that generosity usually meets social approval while vanity brings about some frowning makes no difference from a consciousness/rationality standpoint.[47]

A different perspective underscores the role of evolutionary components: individuals are aware of the importance of reputation and know that "altruistic" behaviour is one way of enhancing one's standing and credibility within a community. This may be the result of conscious, rational behaviour (as it happens in the case of vanity); but it could also be an instinct, an automatic response originated and filtered by a selective evolutionary process.[48] Margolis (1982: 11, 15, 21) defined this instinct the "fair-share" a priori, which in his view should be included into a new rationality paradigm that reflects man's sense of "social responsibility". This fair-share hypothesis is then applied to explain the spontaneous production of public goods and even the birth of the state, which in the author's view relieves the individual from the burden of deciding how to deploy his altruistic drive and obtain the best outcome (Margolis 1982: 123). In a similar vein – and in many ways similar to what happens in the voter's paradox[49] – altruism can also be perceived as a way through which an individual takes pride in asserting his membership to a group and confirms to himself his close attachment to the community.

All the above standpoints seem to suggest that intentional, pure altruism does not exist: either it produces satisfaction for the individual or it is genetic (i.e. all but involuntary). In other words, the literature does not deny that people can consciously and willingly choose to help and do good to other people.[50] But it takes it for granted that the various explanations of altruism stem from an inner drive that rests either on rational calculus or on an instinct produced by evolution. We call this type of (self-centred) altruism "spurious altruism".

Although the presence of these components is well taken, we dare suggest that other factors are at work and that a different kind of altruism – "pure altruism" – is also possible. Unlike the spurious version, we posit that pure altruism originates from motivations created by ideology which, once accepted, become part of the individual's psychological pattern.[51] In particular, ideology affects what people understand by deontic duty and social legitimacy: what a human being is supposed to do in order to fulfil his nature, and the bonds that keep individuals together in a community, including solidarity without reciprocity. In this perspective, pure altruism refers to situations that are not characterized by significant genetic or sentimental relationships between the giver and the beneficiary;

and in which the giver is nonetheless willing to act for the sole or prevailing purpose of complying with his own ethical code, his notion of justice and fairness.

The general idea is rather simple and includes two points. First, all individuals are born with instincts and psychological patterns. These are filtered through time and transferred from one generation to the other according to selective evolutionary processes.[52] Perhaps they even account for the role and features of the inner judge, although the very notion of consciousness implies that we do not always follow our instincts and psychological impulses. Instead, we often amend our urges, we adapt to the circumstances; and we subsequently transmit such adapted behavioural routines to our friends and to our children. Second, psychological patterns can be affected by ideas: Not only do these change the way people develop their preferences, but – and more importantly – they also have an impact on their value judgements, on the notions of good/evil, just/unjust, fair/unfair (their inner judge).

Pure altruism derives from the second set of phenomena. It is not an uncontrolled instinct, but the result of a psychological pattern which creates an urge to contribute to the common weal because we perceive that that is our nature and our role in society. Under such circumstances, failure to be altruistic is not sanctioned, nor does it provoke pain. Instead, it is perceived as the betrayal of one's own nature.[53]

This has consequences, both when an action takes place within a community and when interacting with other communities. Three examples may help clarify our point. The first considers individuals' attitudes towards tax evasion or tax avoidance in institutional contexts where the expected return to illegal behaviour is clearly positive.[54] When collective solidarity is thought to be part and parcel of the (implicit) social contract and the state is recognized as the neutral intermediary that transfers resources in accordance with that contract, tax evasion is perceived as a shameful offense. On the other hand, when one of these two elements is missing, tax evasion is regarded as the legitimate protection of private property against an act of violence. It is no accident that the general attitude towards tax evasion in Sweden is different from that in Italy or France.

The second example regards immigrants. When landing in a new country, they have two possibilities: either they form an enclave and create a community within a larger society; or they try to integrate into the larger society of destination.[55] In the first case, spurious altruism is likely to prevail and characterize the set of relationships within the enclave, but not between the members of the enclave and the outside world. In the second case (integration), altruism might be a way of accelerating integration. However, the latter mechanism succeeds only when pure altruism of the right kind is at work, i.e. where altruism is part of the local culture (ideology), which is in turn absorbed by the immigrants. When that happens, the immigrant considers free riding (including petty illegal behaviour and crime in general) an offense per se, not a potentially unfair behaviour directed towards a third party nobody cares much about.[56] That explains why integration is easier for second- or third-generation immigrants or when migrants are more or less isolated. In the former case, the ideological climate of the receiving country is more likely to have made an impact. In the latter case, a virtuous filtering process might have taken place, according to which selected small migrating groups were already characterized by suitable psychological patterns.

The third example regards situations in which social relations come under stress. Once again, the presence and different roles of spurious and pure altruism can make the difference; but more articulated results may now come to the surface. Of course, unless it degenerates into heavy paternalism, spurious altruism is generally instrumental in softening social tensions. Nonetheless, spurious altruism might crowd out pure altruism. This happens, for instance, when the population believes in a social contract according to which the state takes care of solidarity, both directly (outright redistribution) and indirectly (e.g. by producing merit goods that are subsequently sold at prices below costs). Surely, spurious altruism ensures that the taxpayer complies with his civic duties, either because he is afraid of the stigma associated with tax evasion, or because his paying taxes is a way of feeling part of the community, of acquiring the right to fair treatment and gaining access to merit goods and solidarity when in need. Under such circumstances, however, one may also observe that the individual believes that his moral duty is towards the social contract that binds him to the state, rather than towards other individuals. Put differently, the behavioural routine imposed by the state, reinforced by spurious altruism and supported by effective ideological sway, might bring about an attitude of neglect towards other individuals and trust in the state, which is ultimately perceived as the instrument through which altruistic desires come true. If that applies, the social fabric ultimately weakens, as the state acquires a life of its own, forgets about its origins and principled obligations and disaffection creeps in.

In the end, spurious altruism turns into short-term opportunism, with consequences: crony capitalism or socialist nomenclatures, fragmentation into associations kept together by habit, racial or geographic prejudice, sectarian devotion or simply the need to cooperate in order to obtain a specific goal. As individuals learn to behave within such restricted groups, their external observers,[57] their sense of vanity and generosity, their understanding of social membership are shaped accordingly. Pure altruism is out of the question and the social structure progressively slides into chaos, as the restricted groups break down and new, similar groups fail to replace them.

3.4.4 Culture and beliefs

According to the core argument articulated in this chapter, although there is little excuse for advancing normative suggestions in the quest for equilibrium in a timeless context, standard economics has developed a rich set of conceptual and technical instruments based on the double assumption of rational behaviour and exogenous, ever-lasting preferences. Within this context, the policy-maker intervenes, either to prevent irrational deviations by individuals, or to pursue a rationally-designed common goal.

The free-market view takes a different approach. First, by drawing attention to the role of conscious behaviour, it casts doubts on the "compelling desirability" of the individual's rational behaviour: emotions, established routines and deontic principles matter. Second, it empties the term "social rationality" of much of its operational content and explains voluntary cooperation in terms of rational self interest supplemented by two categories of altruism. In accord with the recent literature, we define the ingredients of these two categories as "culture".[58] Thus, culture identifies a set of elements shared by the psychological patterns of most members of a community, rather than just "tastes and styles" as Jardine (2008: xviii) put it. These patterns affect the way interaction unfolds and generate behavioural routines. Custom and tradition ensure that after a while these routines become expected routines, which sometimes acquire the status of informal rules and sometimes are included in sets of formal rules. Hence, a "strong culture" includes individuals for whom the external observer does not conflict with the inner judge and these two "actors" are fairly similar across the population.

There is no doubt that from a free-market standpoint the role of culture in economics is critical. One can debate about the ways cultures emerge, evolve and possibly vanish. Nonetheless, as we have argued in the last sections, culture does affect choice, exchange and interaction. Culture may lead to behaviours that run against what rationality suggests, it may even weaken consciousness to the extent that it creates sets of automatic responses based on habit and tradition;[59] and last, but not least, it can influence the newcomers' psychological patterns.

It has been maintained that the above has lost importance in today's globalized world. After all – some authors claim – culture matters only in closed societies, in which the absence of competition ensures that tradition consolidates and that different communities end up with different cultures (Jones 2006). As a result, when opening up to the world, societies that developed institutional frameworks geared to specific cultural patterns may enter a period of crisis, since pressure for change may clash with engrained behavioural routines. That is particularly acute when psychological patterns are rigid, so that change is irrationally but consciously resisted.

Should one then agree with the orthodox economist and neglect cultural matters, other than a source of tensions during transition to a more open environment? Should one accept that cultural divides are the legacy of a past characterized by clustered societies and that they are bound to disappear as globalization spreads out, while new psychological patterns emerge? And will the bearers of these new psychological patterns necessarily be less inclined to take tradition for granted and ready to experiment with trial-and-error processes, possibly supplemented by opportunistic conformism to occasional groups kept together by short-run interests?

Our earlier considerations offer a perspective that in fact amends the notion of culture rightly questioned by Jones (2006) by introducing a different set of concepts. We have observed that the essence of altruism is the ability to interact with others in matters of economic relevance. This ability and willingness are influenced by several variables. Some lead to spurious altruism, other to pure altruism. We posit that culture is germane to spurious altruism, in that whenever the external observer is present and shares a set of common features across a group of people for an extended period of time, those features can be called "culture". The observer does not command what ought to be done, but rather offers a grid of rules regarding what the individual is expected to do when others are in need and what the individual is expected not to do, so as to guarantee the cohesion of the group. This pressure can be strengthened or weakened by the inner judge, the deontic principles of the individual (the origin of pure altruism). Surely, in a perfectly globalized world, beliefs migrate and individuals would shop for those they prefer. Hence, culture would lack a solid geographic connotation. But this is not a perfectly globalized world. Mobility across countries is often limited, institutions do differ and so do languages. Thus, the notion of national sovereignty acquires important practical implications and shapes people mindsets – even in Jones's "globalized" world.

Two possible scenarios result, with implications regarding our appreciation of policy-making. On the one hand, when the accepted social contract legitimizes the role of the state, beliefs frequently have strong inertial features, since the state itself ensures that the current ideology is preserved and ideological competition stifled. It usually takes a major shock to disrupt inertia, but with different consequences. Since human nature often tempts individuals to blame others for their own mistakes, in the aftermath of a general crisis, policy-measures aiming at regulating the alleged aggressor are usually welcome. These are carried out in the name of rationality, while deviations from the "common wisdom" are regarded with suspicion. By contrast, a crisis in the regulatory culture does not necessarily bring about a change in beliefs, but just a desire for improvement. Thus, the change will affect institutions, not the nature or the attitude of the inner judge and of the external observer. People may adjust the way they act responding to the new sets of incentives, but their beliefs and principles will evolve at a much slower pace. Put differently, culture stays the same even if institutions evolve.

On the other hand, it may happen that repeated interaction within a new institutional context affects how individuals perceive the institutional context and the moral foundations of their role in society. For instance, if the state is no longer perceived as an instrument through which rents are created and distributed, but as a credible solution to a number of coordination problems (the cost of enforcing desirable cooperation), then the judge and the observer evolve and so does culture.

To conclude, consciousness is critical to those who expect economic analysis to offer explanations, even if the ambitions to acquire hard-science status must be abandoned. In particular, consciousness implies discretionary choice, which also depends on deontic principles. When principles are shared with many other individuals, and create routines refined by interaction with these individuals, they form a culture. We feel at ease with those who share our culture because we know that we share the same external observer, the same moral standards; and because we know that these elements lead our counterpart to sets of semi-automatic, predictable acts and reactions. However, culture and institutions remain two different concepts. Culture is about perceptions and judgement, legitimacy and morality. As we shall argue in the next chapter, institutions are about the rules of the game, sometimes even expediency and consequentialism.

4 Institutions

4.1 Rational individuals and institutions

The previous chapters focused on the implications, requirements and weaknesses of the meta-background typical of a large portion of the current economic way of thinking: equilibrium in its various forms, the alleged rational nature of economic actors and the role of conscious decision-making in society. In particular, in Chapter 2 we have pointed out that the gradual shift, from a conception of the world ruled by divine will, to one characterized by human design, transformed economic analysis from an investigation within the realm of moral philosophy – the evaluation of certain categories of actions and interactions with respect to some general principles – into an enquiry regarding the properties of an alleged optimal, man-made ideal order. Furthermore, in Chapter 3 we have observed that the concept of consciousness has been gradually replaced by that of rationality, while deontic principles and emotions have been conveniently set aside and ascribed to philosophy, psychology and possibly social psychology. In a similar vein, the rationality assumption has been instrumental in introducing the "typical individual". From an analytical perspective, this has generated increasing attention towards macro-phenomena. From a normative standpoint, it also justified the replacement of the notion of conscious cooperation with that of social rationality, thereby giving new meanings to concepts such as free riding and altruism.

These changes led to a number of problems. First, economic behaviour has been mistakenly characterized as the outcome of inadequately informed[1] cost–benefit maximizers, with given welfare and production functions. As a result, economics has virtually lost its dynamic connotation, since time makes sense only if understood as the domain in which ignorance and uncertainty become knowledge; in which luck, efforts, trial and error lead to discovery; and in which new ignorance and uncertainty are generated as new technological and institutional possibilities unveil. Moreover, many scholars have been encouraged to neglect that although the analysis of non-rational behaviour might lie outside the subject matter of economics, such behaviour does have economic consequences, since it influences how human beings perceive scarcity and act/cooperate to reduce its effects. Finally – and perhaps most importantly – the term "rationality" has ceased to be used as a descriptive tool and has slowly justified prescriptive conclusions, thereby sidestepping moral issues or drastically reshaping their contours.

In particular, "rational" has become a synonym for "advantageous", with "social" advantage emerging as the default criterion when evaluating the indirect consequences of voluntary interaction. Not surprisingly, however, closer scrutiny reveals that this is not satisfactory. The notion of social fairness is vague[2] and can hardly be reconciled with the static and dynamic versions of equilibrium, let alone their allegedly scientific features, which would require precise answers and thus equally precise pictures of the ideal world. Furthermore, it is in sharp contrast with the very principle of voluntary interaction, according to which the default solution in case of disagreement is aborted exchange, and indirect consequences are simply ignored unless the property rights of third parties are encroached upon.

The obvious alternative would have been to abandon positivist temptations, focus on a priori theorizing, possibly engage in closer interaction with psychology so as to obtain a better understanding of the irrational origins of a large set of economically relevant phenomena and let the moral and political philosophers deal with the normative questions. This is indeed the approach favoured in these pages. Yet, economists have preferred to model rational behaviour and to concentrate on the divergences between the real world and the model, or between the real world and the ideal goal, as if these divergences were some sort of residual to be minimized through policy-making. Regrettably, this choice has opened the way to further questions.

One of these questions concerns the criterion to adopt when modelling refers to the rational behaviour of a (typical) agent who does not exist in reality. Indeed, even if one tries to simulate how a purely rational individual is going to act, rules out by definition the presence of (irrational) emotions, ignores the existence of diversified individual preferences and assumes perfect information,[3] a significant share of the agents' knowledge would still regard the likelihood that future events might occur (as opposed to the nature of the events themselves). Action would thus depend on the different perceptions and judgements regarding the various probability distributions (complex effects), as well as on how the other actors react to risk and thus alter the relevant environment (strategic behavioural components). True, the positivist vision has turned these problematic shortcomings on their head by emphasizing the predictive ambitions of the model: "why bother, if the coefficients are significant?". Nevertheless, this implies that "rational" has almost become synonymous with "average", and that a good model is one that minimizes deviations from the average. As a result, the scholarly challenge moves from explaining human action to explaining deviations from average. This is unfortunate, since in the social sciences deviations from the average should not necessarily be a source of discomfort. Individuals are not clones and communities follow different rules for a variety of reasons, some of which will be explored shortly. Thus, efforts to minimize deviations often end up sweeping under the rug the very object of social research.

A second set of difficulties resulting from yielding to positivism's temptations regards the environmental conditions within which individuals make their choices. This is the focus of this chapter. The essence of the problem is straightforward. The notion of rationality involves reactions to incentives which are generated by the external environment. Thus, given sets of individual actions and interactions acquire rational or irrational connotations depending upon the environment in which the individual operates: stealing can be rational if the probability of being detected is negligible and the love for risk not very high, but much less so otherwise. Likewise, rent-seeking makes sense when the role of the state is considerable and its pervasive normative intervention is more or less tolerated, if not encouraged, by public opinion. But the quest for privileges can be a waste of time or can generate negative returns (bad reputation) in small, open economies operating under widely shared free-market principles. This explains why the need to identify the nature of the gaps between the ideal world and the real context has encouraged research into institutional economics – the nature and dynamics of the rules of the game designed and possibly enforced by men – with the purpose of bridging those gaps.

The economics of institutions presents an apparently persuasive and deceptively simple story. When interacting, individuals benefit from being able to predict their counterparts' behaviour. Therefore, rules (institutions) develop spontaneously or are deliberately introduced in order to reduce uncertainty and to provide constraints that ensure consistency and long-term planning. This applies to situations in which habit and tradition have created recognized behavioural routines or informal rules, as well as to situations in which it pays to undertake credible strong commitments, for instance when the absence of formal constraints would generate opportunities for fraudulent or otherwise undesirable actions.[4] In this context, institutionalists have taken different paths: the so-called "old institutional school" focuses on how exogenous incentive systems of formal and informal rules shape individual and collective behaviours, while the so-called "new institutional school" focuses on how individuals strive to obtain the institutional context that better suits their interests.[5]

Of course, the fact that institutions affect human behaviour is obvious. Similarly, nobody doubts that individuals or groups of individuals are often seduced by the possibility of shaping the rules of the game in order to favour their own advantages, even at the expense of somebody else's and even if these rules might violate shared principles (e.g. property rights, freedom of choice, fairness). As a matter of fact, this is what rent-seeking and much of the public-choice research programme are about. Institutional economics differs from public choice, however, in that while the latter focuses on the connection between policymakers and king-makers (in most cases more or less extended interest groups), the former aims at understanding the causal relations between rules and individuals, i.e. under what circumstances formal rules are exogenous and under what circumstances they are the result of human interaction. From an institutional standpoint, therefore, the study of the rule-making process evolves from articulating an analysis of the costs and benefits of political action accruing to selected groups, given the preferences of the electoral body broadly understood, into developing more refined investigations into the dynamics of such preferences and thus into the consequences of these dynamics on the institutional context and economic performance.

Unfortunately, the general conclusions of this ambitious research agenda are mixed and perhaps slightly disappointing despite – or perhaps because of – its intuitive simplicity. According to some authors (e.g. North 1990), formal rules of the game tend to be rather stable for fairly long periods of time, but feature a drift (path dependence), so as to reduce transaction costs or to strengthen rent-seeking positions. Falling transaction costs characterize good institutions; rising rent-seeking characterizes bad institutions. Other authors suggest that the rules are exogenous in the short run and endogenous in the long run (Setterfield 1993). However, even during the periods characterized by marginal and slow adaptation, external contingencies may exercise latent strains. If so, sometimes pressure reaches a tipping point and the context evolves, smoothly or more abruptly, depending on the circumstances (Fiori 2002). On other occasions, those external contingencies may be absorbed and ultimately nullified by the existing institutional context, which would act as some kind of shock-absorber (Greif 2001).

In the end, it seems that each situation has its own features and its own *ex post* rationalization (Poirot 1993). One may even venture to say that there is no general theory of institutional change, but merely ways of reading and systematizing the observed evolution and features of contracts, agencies and organizations, both informal and formal. Yet, the enormous institutional literature that has been flourishing for more than a century underscores a general point: rules are desirable as long as they are stable, reliable and reduce uncertainty about other people's behaviour. That explains why good formal rules enhance impersonal trade and why they cannot be in conflict with the informal institutions: tensions would follow and the whole social structure would be destabilized (Pejovich 1999).[6] Reliability and stability have actually occupied the centre stage of the institutional normative agenda and have also justified the need for shared (meta-) rules, in order to shore up credibility and constancy, to check the arbitrary temptations of the rule-making authorities: encroaching upon such shared meta-rules would imply the loss of authority, and the use of violence would elicit lawful refusal to obey, if not insurrection. These shared meta-rules play a critical role especially in the classical-liberal and social democratic perspectives: in the former case they should ultimately ensure the rule of law, in the latter they should guarantee fairness.

In spite of the difficulties in articulating a theory of institutions and of institutional dynamics, it is hard to overestimate the relevance of the institutional perspective for several areas of economic investigation. One can surely conceive of many ways the rules of the game can alter the cost of exchanging and affect cooperation. As sketched above, the interaction between formal and informal (spontaneous) institutions is also critical, and so is the role of the meta constraints. From a free-market vantage point, however, we believe that the key question is a very simple one: It regards whether the institutional context is characterized by competing systems of formal rules or whether one set of rules should prevail, to the exclusion of other sets of rules – even if imposed coercively. In particular, the free-market approach maintains that economic institutions are acceptable only if they are consistent with the notions of human dignity (individual preferences should not be imposed), freedom from coercion (no violence is admitted, except for self-defence) and freedom of contract (full enjoyment of property rights). When these conditions are met, economic institutions can be regarded as default behavioural routines that the agents are free to accept, thereby saving the cost of drafting a new contract. Of course, when such default rules are deemed inappropriate, agents within a free-market context should be free to amend them, or to reject them altogether and possibly opt for alternatives. By contrast, a general question about legitimacy emerges when the rules cannot be discarded or circumvented. The traditional view would maintain that a criterion of social efficiency would be enough to provide the answer. But that would of course be hardly satisfactory to an observer aware of, and receptive to, the free-market perspective.[7]

It is important to bear in mind that, from a free-market vantage point, not all formal rules are the same. To illustrate this line of reasoning, the next sections of this chapter examine two categories of formal institutions: optional rules and coercive rules.[8] This way of framing the institutional debate presents two advantages. First, it shows that the double problem of interaction – how people shape the rules of the game and how formal and informal rules reinforce or undermine each other – assumes different features according to the category under scrutiny. Second, our investigation into these matters shows that the judgement on the normative role of institutions is actually closely connected with one's understanding of the nature and legitimacy of the state, which is generally defined as a hierarchically organized group endowed with the power to create rules, to enforce them and to veto (outlaw) at its own discretion rules created by others (Block 2007).

4.2 The nature of optional institutions

Like other formal institutions, optional rules consist of clearly defined arrangements, written or otherwise widely publicized. They also imply the existence of an authority in charge of enforcement, e.g. the judiciary and a police force. Their distinctiveness, however, consists in the fact that violations are punishable only after the rules are accepted by the individual, explicitly or by default. Simply put, optional institutions are characterized by the fact that agents can reject them at a negligible cost.

Ideally, optional institutions are born when an institutional entrepreneur sees unexploited opportunities for mutually profitable exchange and cooperation and puts forward proposals in order to make exchange attractive enough for the transaction to be completed. For instance, this applies when a tennis club is founded and the rules for the club members are specified; or when a builder transforms a construction into a condominium and the regulations for residents are issued; and also when the terms of buying and selling are established at the initiative of the partners involved or of an intermediary. Those interested in playing tennis or buying a flat or doing business within an organized setting, are informed about the rules, evaluate their credibility and are of course also free to reject them. If the rules are considered unacceptable or obsolete, in the absence of barriers to entry new rules, new rule-makers or new tennis clubs will probably emerge and offer more desirable alternatives.

When rules come into force following explicit consent – joining an association or taking part in an event – the institutional element is in fact equivalent to a contractual agreement. As we pointed out in the previous section, however, one can also imagine optional institutions in contexts in which individuals are subject to rules by default, e.g. by right (or duty) of birth or of residence. If so, under an optional institutional context, the rule-maker – let us call him "the weak state" – can only put forward proposals, rational social devices which are legitimate as long as the counterparts do not reject them.[9] If they are turned down, then the weak state has no rights to enforce its will and overcome resistance. Likewise, the weak state has no power to prevent other parties from proposing and eventually adopting different institutional sets. Put differently, a weak ruler is like a standard individual or a consultant, with two differences. First, the weak ruler's institutions could apply by default. Furthermore, if required, the ruler also takes care of enforcing all contracts, no matter what their source is, and claims monopoly power in this domain.[10]

When in force, low-cost-opting-out institutions are necessarily efficient, for nothing would prevent actors from introducing better arrangements, so as to reduce the uncertainty about the interacting agents' behaviour and thus increase the value of what is being exchanged. This is in fact the essence of the institutional dynamics typical of a weak, well functioning state. In contrast with the strong version of the state, however, this dynamic is hardly driven by politicians. After all, in the weak context, power plays little or no role and the political prestige one can acquire by introducing institutional innovations is relatively modest. In fact, institutional entrepreneurship is more likely to take place in law firms than in political life. Sometimes the outcome is radical innovation. More frequently, lawyers go for incremental progress. Surely, appropriating the full benefit of these improvements is far from easy. Yet, in the case of law firms, the main source of revenue is less their ability to produce something new, than their proven skills in problem solving. A record in contract innovation provides the appropriate signal to their potential clients, who need specialists in order to cut down the cost of exchanging.

The dynamics of optional rules is likely to be affected by two sets of phenomena. First, given the external setting framed by the coercive rules, optional institutions evolve relatively slowly, following technological change and economic progress; new products and production techniques that require innovative contractual agreements. Change can accelerate, however, as a consequence of alterations to the coercive straitjacket. For instance, as rent-seeking coalitions strive to reduce the competitive pressure, optional rules necessarily adapt, either to conform to the new environment, or to circumvent it.

The second group of issues relates to credibility. As mentioned earlier, the relevance of any institutional system ultimately depends on its ability to make behaviour predictable, which relates to the effectiveness of its enforcement mechanisms. Sometimes these mechanisms rely on non-violent means: the potential offender might be restrained by the prospective loss of reputation, which implies contempt in a limited community and the inability to carry out transactions on a wider scale. In many other cases, loss of reputation is not a satisfactory deterrent and violence or the threat of violence is required. Hence, the evolution of optional institutions inevitably depends upon the features and dynamics of enforcement. Given the weak nature of the state which characterizes the institutional context described in this section, the relevant rule enforcer should of course be the judiciary (including the police force). Therefore, optional institutions can survive and develop successfully only when (*a*) the judiciary adapts to and accepts the consequences of technological progress, for instance with regard to the principle of individual responsibility; and (*b*) the judiciary resists pressure from other sources such as public opinion, politicians, special interests, which might favour an extensive interpretation of the coercive framework and ultimately choke the optional set.

Unfortunately, in modern societies the second situation described above has rarely prevailed, not so much because of judicial weakness, but because the weak-state solution has hardly ever been agreed to and suitably protected. In past centuries, the ruler did not accept a weak status and had the means and possibly the legitimacy – mercenary troops, blue blood or divine blessing – to claim and enforce his strength. More recently, industrialization has generated new categories of powerful rent-seeking groups that have transformed a potentially weak state into a guarantee for their privileges. As will be discussed in the next chapter, during the twentieth century a new vision of society emerged, a society in which coercive regulation has been gradually crowding out most optional institutions and in which institutional entrepreneurship has been increasingly stimulated either to find ways of turning the potential for coercion to the advantage of selected interest groups, or to pursue protective purposes against state encroachment. To the origins and legitimacy of this coercive setting we now turn our attention.

4.3 The foundations of coercive institutions

During the Palaeolithic era the state was absent and, therefore, coercive rules were out of the question. Geography, demography and the genetic evolutionary drive ensured that the natural and only relevant social unit at the time was the family. Cooperation among families was by and large restricted to what was needed to hunt down big mammals and clearly generated optional institutions: those who did not like the rules of a given hunting party could just leave and join another party or hunt on their own: neither land, nor game were in short supply (Baechler 2002: chapter 1). Formal rules were not absent, for the roles of each individual within the family or the group were well known and infringement was punished. But leaving was indeed feasible. This alternative could have been less than attractive, but the cost of exiting was low.

Coercive rules came to the surface with political organizations.[11] These gradually emerged within agricultural societies, in which goods and services were characterized by variety as well as scarcity. Variety created opportunities for specialization and exchange, while scarcity generated occasions for plundering and thus the need for effective defence on the part of the potential victims, as well as for effective aggression (Benson 1999). Put differently, agricultural societies made it easier to accumulate wealth: power structures and hierarchical political organizations thus came to the surface as complex social arrangements,[12] designed to create, protect and even loot wealth (Baechler 2002). Agricultural societies also began to face the problem of economic uncertainty, which was virtually unknown in earlier historical periods (nomadic civilizations), when survival was based on hunting and when mobility and bad harvesting were not significant problems. With increased uncertainty, a new role arose for religion and for those in charge of religious practices, who sometimes acted as healers and intermediaries between the divinity and the individual, and in other occasions used their alleged gifts to predict the future or to influence it by interacting with the gods. The importance of the religious element could hardly be overestimated: once it was recognized that the future could be anticipated and possibly controlled, the presence of a superior design and of an elite of intermediaries was also accepted, thereby paving the ground for the traditional notions of legitimate rule, both direct and indirect.[13]

Not surprisingly, the connection between the religious and the political spheres was close. And as the need for complex social arrangements intensified, political organizations with coercive powers developed. From this, arose the need for legitimacy. Legitimacy is either direct (intrinsic), in that the rule complies with widely recognized principles such as religious doctrines, efficiency and nature; or it is indirect, in that it stems from a legitimate authority in charge of interpreting those principles and possibly enforcing them. Legitimacy through religion pertains to the text and the interpretation of the Holy Scriptures. The notion of legitimacy through efficiency has emerged only during the twentieth century and will be the object of later chapters. As for nature, justifying coercion because it is natural is not an easy task. In our context, "natural" refers to a trait which stems directly from the individual or – better yet – a trait which is an essential element of each human being.[14] As mentioned earlier, it is generally accepted that man exhibits a very limited number of natural elements: the instinct to survive and preserve the species (procreation) and the ambition to improve one's well-being. To these we would also add vanity, or self-love, as Mandeville in the early eighteenth century defined man's pleasure in being accepted and admired by other people, a notion to which even Adam Smith subscribed. A second order of natural elements is frequently related to man's alleged "social nature", not unlike animal species that exhibit some kind of instinctive social structure – the pack, for instance.[15] This approach has a long and authoritative tradition, as documented in Buckle (1991): for instance, Grotius claimed that since history proves that all individuals want to be part of a social body, sociability is necessarily a divine gift and therefore can well be qualified as natural. About half a century later, Pufendorf made a distinction between sociability and natural social rules (institutions). The former were meant to reflect our alleged intrinsic propensity to be useful to the others (and therefore natural, according to our terminology), while the latter referred to the historical origin of coercive rules, revealed by – and acquired through – experience as the best answer to the problems raised by social situations.[16] Put differently, the main point is that "natural" can be what exists originally, but it can also be what evolves out of those original givens. Thus, it can refer either to the individual or to a social arrangement, or to both. The Aristotelian tradition inclines towards emphasizing social arrangements,[17] while in modern political thought, for example, Grotius, Locke and even Hobbes[18] consider the individual and the social spheres jointly.

To which extent are these views helpful in framing a free-market assessment of coercive institutions? The answer depends on how far away one is willing to depart from the Aristotelian positions, although Grotius's benchmark is probably not enough to meet the free-market set of requirements. As a matter of fact, we are inclined to believe that consistency with subjectivism and methodological individualism (see Chapter 1) suggests an answer closer to Mandeville than to Grotius and Pufendorf. History teaches that man is not naturally social, unless we call one's family or circle of friends a society, or the need to cooperate in order to enhance defence against outside aggression a manifestation of sociability.[19] Evolution has indeed selected those human beings that formed solid family units; it has rewarded collective groups which developed formal rules designed to protect property rights, strengthen cohesion and reduce conflict; and it has also favoured the ability to develop cooperative behaviours with total strangers (impersonal trade). Yet, sociability is far from spontaneous. It is the result of a conscious choice to cooperate in assuring exchange and defence, ultimately inspired by the desire to enhance one's own well-being.[20] In other words, we claim that sociability does not follow an instinctive, unconscious urge, but is the result of human purposeful action which is not other-regarding. Men are not driven by instinct to confer their property to the common pool and create a communist society. More generally, they do not cooperate in order to please other people, but to please themselves and promote their own interests (including "flourishing"), to give expression to their emotional impulses or to live up to their sense of justice, which of course does not exclude that benefiting the others can also be a source of satisfaction.

The upshot of these considerations on the philosophical foundations of social behaviour is that methodological individualism and subjectivism combined ensure that all forms of coercion are illegitimate, except when coercive rules are implemented by divine command and the legitimacy of such command is recognized by the individual as superior to his own. Surely, most readers would note that coercive rules may serve the individual in that they meet some categories of alleged market failures, with emphasis on opportunism. Under such circumstances, formal institutions would enforce transactions that all the members of a community would be willing to engage in *ex ante*, but that would be unlikely to take place spontaneously because people are likely to cheat *ex post*. By doing so – the traditional story goes – coercive rules would actually fulfil the cooperative agreement originated by sociability, be it from a Mandevillian perspective or from Grotius' natural interpretation of the term. Still, one should also observe that coercive rules are not necessarily the only solution to a problem of desirable (and desired) cooperation. Market failures could also be corrected within an institutional context featuring optional rules, in which the individuals interested in cooperating agree to behave following the proposals put forward by an institutional entrepreneur, possibly the ruler himself, and acknowledge that the ruler (or somebody else, if the weak state allows) is also the enforcer of the agreement. Put differently, an optional institutional arrangement might indeed include coercive elements which come into force after the contract has been signed. From this perspective, therefore, the solution to opportunism would not require coercive rules, but only credible enforcers.

Can one then conclude that the argument against coercion ultimately relies on the reader's agreement with the Mandevillian perspective? We are inclined to answer in the negative. As a matter of fact, even if one accepts that man is naturally sociable, the legitimacy of coercive institutions eventually depends on the existence and definition of natural social contracts, a subset of the class of collective agreements known as implicit social contracts.[21] The presence of a natural social contract would imply that when the individual is not "social enough", he positions himself out of the polis and goes against his very nature. Thus, he loses his privileges as a human being, i.e. his natural right to freedom from coercion and deserves to be taxed against his will. Not unexpectedly, therefore, the definition of sociability might weaken the linchpin of the free-market approach considerably. Put differently, one cannot be a free-market supporter and at the same time believe that natural-sociability is an essential component of the human being. If this term merely describes the human instinct to live with a limited number of relatives and friends, then optional, Tocquevillian institutions formed by individuals who choose to get together, exchange ideas and cooperate would do. But as soon as one departs from the concept of sociability as the result of purposeful individual action, in favour of sociability as social health, then a criterion to identify this social health and socially legitimate actions is in order. For instance, taxation may be necessary in order to provide adequate defence against invaders who might threaten our lives or deny us the possibility of improving our condition through oppression and possibly enslavement. However, some might prefer running away or compromising with the newcomers to fighting, others might prefer low-cost defence arrangements to more expensive reactions; or perhaps might choose to die (with honour or with as little pain as possible) and maximize consumption before the day of conflict arrives. Under different circumstances, we could also observe that A's low propensity to solidarity might conflict with B's high propensity to solidarity. Certainly, one may conclude from the above that the appropriate answers require that someone legitimately rank natural social preferences, which of course implies that some members of the group turn out to be less than natural or less than human; or that natural social preferences eventually coincide with those defining the lowest common denominator of the group.[22] This marks the difference with respect to the free-market position, according to which no such ranking is possible. Therefore, the concept of natural sociability would have no operational meaning and coercive rules (including policy-making) would necessarily be arbitrary.

To sum up, coercive economic institutions are seldom the product of a bottom-up process, according to which agents design and agree upon rules of the game that are subsequently transformed into coercive formal rules, either to enhance publicity and transparency, or to justify the nature and boundaries of a political covenant, especially to control those responsible for operating the social contract, the bureaucracy. Instead, coercive economic institutions tend to be the instrument through which rulers or ruling coalitions justify their right to exercise power. Therefore, their nature and depth ultimately depend on the role they are supposed to fulfil at a given historical and political moment, as well as on the threshold beyond which tolerance of coercion is no longer guaranteed and revolt goes off.

4.4 On the dynamics of coercive rules

The previous sections have tried to make two points. Coercive institutions are not essential for the existence and orderly working of a society. In addition, their legitimacy is questionable. Reference to efficiency and natural sociability (civic duty) also provides a weak defence. Most mainstream economists would agree that many rules actually harm growth since they inhibit contracts, discourage entrepreneurship and reduce competition. Furthermore, there is also evidence about the negative effects of coercive rules on virtue, since the introduction of formal coercive rules might well encourage individuals to take advantage of their counterparts' good faith by following purely rational optimizing criteria.[23]

To summarize, coercive institutions, thus, hold their ground only within a functional environment. They are not created and enforced because they are part of a spontaneous social context that would justify them insofar as they are natural or efficient, as in the case of optional rules; but because they serve purposes defined by selected individuals or selected groups of individuals. It then follows that a theory of institutional dynamics must necessarily be based on the dynamics of politics and power, i.e. on the way individuals or groups become rulers and on their chances and strategies to stay in power. This explains the link between coercive rules, the ruler's legitimacy and thus the notion/origin of the state. It also explains why the dynamics of coercive rules ultimately depends on how individuals perceive the presence of the enforcer.

As in most cases, generalizations are dangerous also when examining institutional dynamics: each civilization has its own distinctive features, which sometimes evolve and change significantly over time.[24] This is also – and particularly – true when analysing the role of the state. Yet, if one considers the history of the West, a notion which probably acquired a more clear-cut meaning as of the time the universalistic project failed,[25] three epochs can be singled out for our purposes. One can be characterized as the Gregorian Centuries, the second as the Secular Period, the third as the Age of Social Responsibility, which can in turn be subdivided into an elitist and a popular phase.[26]

During the first period, which de facto lasted until the mid-seventeenth century, coercive institutions were not viewed in terms of social organization and cooperation, for either formal rules were optional rules (contracts and customs), or they were simply perceived as an instrument of oppression applied by the incumbent rulers. With a few partial exceptions (e.g. England), there was little effort to hide the fact that the purpose of coercive institutions was for the ruling elites to get richer, preserve their privileges and prevent palace coups. Not surprisingly, the prince would then use his power to prevent any kind of competing group from coming to the surface, or to buy the loyalty of the people's elites, so as to evict the aristocrats.[27] As a result, in those centuries the dynamics of coercive institutions boiled down to a story of short-sighted exploitation: establishing the threshold of tolerable and revenue-maximizing taxation in a world characterized by long periods of stagnation and generalized poverty, with large areas threatened by potential uprisings and devastated by banditry and petty warfare.

The context changed when rulers ceased to be opposed by powerful aristocrats, no longer needed compromising with the religious authorities, and when they exercised their power by relying heavily on a comprehensive and hopefully loyal bureaucratic machine to reach their aims. Coercive institutions were thus a critical instrument, both to operate the bureaucracy and to obtain the chosen goals. Mercantilism, modern fiscal systems and regulation were the name of the game. Tampering with money was also attempted, but less successfully.[28] Once again, however, looking for the key to a theory of institutional change during the secular centuries by analysing some kind of rational-efficiency pattern is illusory. Instead, one should simply accept that during that period, historical and technological changes forced the rulers to mobilize large quantities of resources for military and administrative purposes: they could no longer afford to hire mercenaries in sufficient numbers and they could no longer rely on a small number of local aristocrats. Hence, two essential institutional traits remained constant during the whole period: coercive institutions (*a*) were to serve the state as the symbol and substance of a centralized authority; and (*b*) were shaped by the need to enhance the wealth of the nation and meet its military requirements. Period. No such phenomena as path dependence or evolutionary selection were at play, unless these terms are understood very loosely.

With regard to legitimacy, it is clear that when God's blessing as granted by right of birth was no longer considered valid (or not valid enough), new sources had to be conceived of and put forward in order to justify large state bureaucracies and heavy taxation. Not surprisingly, political theorists replaced theologians. Besides, there was no shortage of forerunners: as of the thirteenth century, St Thomas Aquinas and the Scholastics had already been encouraging systematic speculation and the use of reason in order to apprehend the divine order.

Likewise, Roger Bacon had devoted his entire life to experimenting in order to discover God's design in nature.[29] Experimenting with political constructivism began in earnest with the Westphalia Treaties, according to which kingdoms and political arrangements were man-made and governed by mutually guaranteed international agreements, with little role for acknowledgement – let alone approval – by the religious authorities. It would not take long before the notion of natural order would turn into that of rational order and become the benchmark for evaluating the adequacy and acceptability of coercive institutions. In particular, by the twentieth century, industrialization and urbanization ensured that greater numbers of people were being included politically and power sharing on a large scale could no longer be avoided. The notion of the ruler's legitimacy therefore evolved into a matter of his consistency with the current notion of rational state action. In a word, public opinion and consensus became critical, and coercive institutions were the instruments through which public opinion could be shaped and consensus obtained.

This history explains why we believe that the traditional view on institutional dynamics needs to be reconsidered. When summarizing the essence of the institutional approach, Douglass North defined institutions as "the external (to the mind) mechanisms individuals create to structure and order the environment" (1994: 363) and argued that "organizations that come into existence will reflect the opportunities provided by the institutional matrix" (ibid.: 361).[30] By contrast, our view posits that within the rational state, institutions are neither a fixed system of constraints, nor the intermediaries by means of which given interpretations of the outside world (representations) generate "societal and economic structures". Instead, our story differentiates between two possible environments – elitist and populist.

When the elitist environment prevails, the ruler applies coercive institutions in order to promote the interests of those very elites. Put differently, policies are not proposed and enforced for the sake of free-market principles, nor because it is believed that free-market contexts create better opportunities for growth. Instead, the dynamics reproduces what is required to keep the boat on course while exploiting the available rent-seeking opportunities. Thus, free-market policies are an option and they often generate only partially deregulated frameworks. For instance, free trade applies to some industries, but not to others. Adjustments in the institutional structure may still be required in order to adapt to gradual changes (technological progress or new market openings), or to face military confrontation. Be that as it may, however, there is no path dependence, but simply corrections in the face of unavoidable pressure, either from outside – technological change or foreign aggression, as mentioned above – or from inside – for instance when the elites perceive that they can legitimize their power only through international tensions (aggressive foreign policy, ultimately leading to war).

The second scenario applies to situations in which the political game can no longer be carried out without extensive popular consent, i.e. when the state (and the armoury of coercive institutions it employs) is not solely required to preserve or adapt rents, but when it is also expected to redistribute wealth on a vast scale subject to three constraints: that no alternative system can do better; that its rule-making procedure offers credible prospects for higher living standards; and that the cost of changing the political context is too high. Under such circumstances, coercive rules tend to be cumulative and ultimately turn out to be the instrument through which discretionary policy-making is developed. They are cumulative because when the ruler owes his political fortune to consensus, and pressure for special-interest legislation is frequent and pulls in opposite directions, the rational response is to give in each time pressure builds up, co-opting the leading interest-group representatives and making enforcement the object of case-by-case evaluation. Hence discretion is bound to prevail over rules, as we know since the time of Aristotle: "when, as in our modern overgrown cities, pay is given, the state is governed by the multitude who have nothing else to do, and not by the laws" (*Politics*, book IV). The outcome is twofold. On the one hand, the state machine expands, in order to accommodate the newcomers and to manage an increasingly complex system of coercive formal rules. On the other hand, policy-makers rapidly lose control, for after a while they hardly know what they are deliberating about. Enforcement then depends upon the bureaucracy and the judiciary.[31] As a result, the role of the politician ends up shifting from conceiving of appropriate institutions, to ensuring that the three requirements to their maintaining power are met and possibly taking action, by means of legislation, of demagoguery, or both. To repeat, self-preservation and expediency are frequently the names of the game and coercive rules are the tools of these trades.

4.5 Veblen's legacy and challenge to today's institutionalism

Langlois (1989) has persuasively argued that the institutional contribution to economics began with Carl Menger's insights: economics is about interaction under scarcity constraints, and institutions are the tools by means of which individuals try to create, expand and consolidate the opportunities for cooperation. Today's institutionalists have indeed accepted that cooperation needs rules, and they deserve credit for having relentlessly underscored the shortcomings of the so-called mainstream, fundamentally Walrasian approach, according to which transactions may be conveniently studied within an environment characterized by complete contracts, perfectly informed individuals and no incentives to cheat. In particular, thanks to the institutional approach, during the past three decades the repeated failures to implement textbook blueprints for efficiency, full employment and growth have rekindled interest in the nature and effectiveness of incentive systems. In truth, though, Menger's lesson did not go beyond urging future generations to study and understand the dynamics of institutions in order to apprehend the essence of the evolution of economic activity. This study, however, could have no normative ambition, since in Menger's view the institutional dynamics is driven by the acquisition of knowledge, by men's effort to break through the curtain of uncertainty. Of course, you can't have normative goals if you don't have a goal.

Yet, and despite important exceptions (Oliver Williamson, for instance), institutional research in these days has often taken a different path and has engaged in forecasting, with forays into regulatory recommendations. Rather than considering the evolution of institutions as an instrument for acquiring knowledge and exploiting opportunities, it has become common practice to regard technological change as the engine of institutional change. In particular, the current prevailing approach is indeed inclined to accept Veblen's attempts to describe how institutions affect individuals' preferences and choices – their very perception of the world and ultimately moral standards and judgement. But the prevailing approach also supplements the Veblenian descriptions by considering technological change the major determinant of the new rules. The challenge for most institutional research has thus been to predict how technological progress and growth influence preferences and behaviours, with the institutional context acting as go-between. Not surprisingly, the temptation to treat institutions as the instrument through which behaviour can be modelled and virtue protected from the deviations induced by technological effects has been all but irresistible.

Put differently, Veblen's failure to articulate a consistent and clear theoretical structure[32] did not deter the post-Veblen institutional authors from echoing the determinist convictions of the historical school and from pointing out the need for active institutional intervention in order to rein in vicious institutional inertia/spontaneity.[33] More importantly for our purposes, the Veblenian legacy continues to make itself felt in repeated resistance to the individualistic foundations of the economic way of thinking and in arguments that since institutions can affect human preferences and perceptions, human behaviour is no longer the expression of human nature. Three conclusions follow from this (Veblenian) line of thinking. First, standard economic reasoning would then suffer from an endogeneity bias, in that institutions are indeed the origin and the consequence of individual actions, but also of individual preferences. Second, it then seems that the only way of breaking the circle is by opening up to methodological holism and considering economics in sociological terms, with more emphasis on macro-analysis, of course. Finally, the prospects for active, centrally-directed policy-making would be enhanced by the fact that since individuals may be influenced by bad institutions, their behaviour and choices could become questionable from the standpoint of "naturalness", thus paving the way for ever-increasing intervention in those choices and behaviours. The upshot is that for those who resist the neoclassical fascination for general equilibrium as the leading criterion for economic policy, the Veblenian perspective offers alluring alternatives – fairness, growth, social efficiency – that are going be confronted in other chapters of this book. In such a context, however, the distinction between optional and coercive rules would no longer be a matter of moral superiority, but of consequentialist selection: is freedom better served by spontaneous evolutionary mechanisms (optional rules) or by a satisfactory definition of the general will (coercive rules)? And what about growth? Or fairness? Clearly, the questions may vary, but the methodological tack would be the same.

To be fair, the institutional view actually stops short of making normative suggestions. Yet, the proposals are nonetheless on the table, visible and problematic. Once the institutional scholar admits that the rules of the game should make the most of human rationality, and that individual preferences can be shaped by the institutional context, one is necessarily caught by the double whammy of being forced to overcome individual sovereignty in the name of social virtue or efficiency (the common good) and of being obliged to turn down democratic procedures to define the common good whenever the individual might be socially irrational and might be voting by pursuing his own welfare, rather than according to social-rationality criteria (Veblen's point). After all, why should one bother with voting if the decision-makers know in advance what should be done? In the end, one has the impression that prudence suggests avoiding the question, but at a price: the institutional perspective turns descriptive, rather than explanatory, and determinist rather than normative.

By contrast, we maintain that the free-market standpoint remains immune even to the Veblenian trap. As pointed out in this chapter, subjectivism and methodological individualism are interwoven with the principle of human dignity: absent an explicit and voluntary contract to that effect, nobody has the right to choose instead of somebody else or to enforce his own preferences by means of violence. That ensures that coercive institutions, therefore, have little or no legitimacy, and the weak state de facto is not an issue: it is accepted by default when wanted, and it is sidestepped when it is inefficient, either because it fails to put forward satisfactory institutional proposals, or because it fails to enforce optional institutions.

Surely, all rules can affect people's preferences, as Veblen would have argued. So what? Contrary to what some neoclassical and even Austrian authors would suggest, nothing in the free-market position asserts the existence of constant or genetic-only preferences. Indeed, the very presence of uncertainty, the continuous acquisition of knowledge, the trial and error process through which we adapt our behaviour and improve the result of cooperation ensure that preferences undergo changes all the time. Centuries ago some authors would have ranked those changes by referring to man's innate social nature. Today some would probably mention the influence of the media and education; or perhaps the weight of new social arrangements, defined by new and sometimes indeterminate natural units. Be that as it may, freedom to acquire and process knowledge is always desirable. Mistakes can be made and evaluations can differ across a population. Yet, acceptance of these possibilities represents the very essence of the principle of individual responsibility, which of course also implies that no human being has the right to pass the buck to other (wiser or simply luckier) parties and to encroach upon their property rights – or any other rights – without explicit consent.

This explains why, in a free-market perspective, the relevant institutional question is indeed the legitimacy of coercion and ultimately of the state (and what kind of state). Far from being just a normative issue, the divide between optional and coercive rules offers an alternative key to the well-known debates about the interaction between formal and informal rules, which has played such a prominent role in the recent institutional literature and beyond.[34] The explanatory power of the formal/informal juxtaposition is well known, but it has yielded very little other than descriptions of the obvious: formal institutions succeed when they do not collide with the informal structure, which is usually defined as "culture". Thus, either successful formal institutions merely reproduce cultural habits and traditions, or their very effectiveness brings about some kind of cultural shock. When these phenomena fail to take place, the system will be characterized by simmering or overt conflicts between the rulers/reformers and the rest of the population.

To conclude, satisfactory as it may look, the institutional juxtaposition sketched above falls short on two accounts. First, it has nothing to say about situations in which there is no apparent conflict between sets of rules and yet the economy does not perform according to expectations. Second, it takes for granted that formal rules are designed and introduced to enhance efficiency, possibly neglecting strings of unintended consequences that might rapidly go out of control. The optional/coercive divide proposed in this chapter offers the answers. In fact, the core institutional question does not consist in assessing where the rules come from and whether they fit the existing cultural environment. Instead, the core question consists in establishing the extent to which rules allow the individual to create and modify cooperating agreements; or the extent to which rules are instrumental in pursuing privileges. This does not eliminate the possibility that social contracts might be framed so as to include both cooperation and rent-seeking. As will be further detailed in the next chapter, however, when social contracts apply, the free-market approach requires that they are either explicit or integrated by low-cost opting out clauses.

5   Social contracts and historical rules

5.1 On the making, credibility and stability of norms

This is an imperfect world. Democracies frequently suffer from bad norms promulgated by short-sighted politicians, most of whom ignore what they are legislating about, but who are often prepared to give in to interest groups and please representative or noisy enough layers of the voting population. As the public choice tradition has explained by applying the rational-choice postulate to the rule-makers, this is hardly surprising. Politicians are human beings like all others and the procedures by which they are chosen do not put a premium on honesty, let alone altruism. If anything, the selection process operates in the opposite direction. Independent thinking is not a plus and occasionally even being reasonable might develop into a liability. In short, rule-makers are rationally inclined to act and legislate in order to enhance their own welfare, and to do whatever is necessary to secure the consensus, popularity and reputation required for election, re-election or appointment. In many occasions party loyalty prevails upon moral integrity and the quality of the laws is affected as a consequence.

To be fair, the outcome of the legislative process is not always counterproductive or ruinous. It does happen that norms are consistent with common sense and the interests of the community broadly understood. Still, even when one abstains from evaluating the quality of the rules, and even when funding is not a problem, nothing guarantees that the rules are applied properly. For instance, the bureaucrats frequently strive to adapt them to their own requirements and preferences. They may also find it advantageous to increase the cost the citizen must incur to qualify for protection under a given piece of legislation. It need not be a matter of blatant crime and corruption. Sometimes it is shirking; sometimes civil servants deliberately delay, or multiply the decision-making layers in order to avoid responsibility; sometimes it is just an effort to enhance the bureaucrat's own discretion in accordance with man's natural longing for prestige and power, or to create additional demand for the bureaucrat's services, which justifies his job and possibly breeds chances for career advancement.[1]

Likewise, the judiciary can also be a source of uncertainty, whenever the actors adhere to their own reading of what legal rules actually mean, or to their own convictions on how to adapt them to specific circumstances. Given that most cases can be branded as "specific", the application of the same rule can easily generate different outcomes and thereby undermine its credibility, that is its ability to provide clear and consistent indication about what is legal (or illegal), and precise enough predictions about people's behaviour.[2] This phenomenon is compounded by the fact that more and more legislation results from political log-rolling and compromise, thereby leading to hazy texts, possibly characterized by loopholes and inconsistencies. Not surprisingly, they create ample scope (and need) for interpretation, and might also be the terrain where the judiciary and the legislative collude or come to blows.[3]

This phenomenon is even more evident when the activities of international and supra-national agencies are taken into account, requiring adjustment by the national legislation, a task which is far from easy, quick or flawless. The judiciary usually tries to solve these inconsistencies by interpreting the original intent of the legislator, or by referring to some higher notion (e.g. constitutional super-laws), or by making use of general principles, more or less vaguely defined. Social justice, fairness and equality are well known examples of such principles. The bureaucrats also play a role in cutting through the hundreds of thousands of pages of new legislation that an advanced country with a reasonably "productive" rule-making apparatus creates every year. In such cases informal rules of conduct might emerge and ultimately prevail, as each office/agency tends to develop its own routines and codes of conduct.

Whatever the outcome, the bottom line is that contradictions and all but insurmountable complexities are inevitable. They create room for discretionary clarification and ironically demand for further legislation. In the end, credibility suffers and potentially counterproductive effects result. Sadly enough, while technological progress makes exchange with private counterparts in the marketplace more and more impersonal, the opposite holds true when dealing with the world of rule-making and rule enforcement.

This increased complexity inevitably affects regulatory and legislative stability. As old rules prove ineffective or obsolete, and pressure for "reform" rises, expectations about policy-making encourage rulers to take action in a wide range of areas of allegedly common interest, that is whenever an occurrence – no matter whether determined endogenously or exogenously – affects a large enough or sensitive enough portion of the electorate. Hence, uncertainty about what the rule might be prescribing in the future creeps in, opportunistic behaviour increases and the agents' time horizon shortens. Not only does uncertainty reduce the discounted value of future income streams and therefore, *ceteris paribus*, negatively affect growth[4] and individuals' welfare, but many agents would actually spot opportunities to engage in contracts while hoping in forthcoming reforms with retroactive enforcement (or retroactive enforcement criteria). They would bet on the conflicts that might eventually arise, and thereby contribute to sapping the coordination and perhaps the reliability of property-right structures as well.

5.2 Looking for constitutional solutions

All the above shows that even when the legislator means well, the traditional notion of rule of law – i.e. a system of credible, consistent and stable coercive rules that people acknowledge as fair and effective[5] – rests on fairly shaky ground. Nonetheless, a large part of the economic profession believes to have found a solution.

Following the Ordoliberal tradition,[6] most economists tend to take it for granted that the recipes for economic prosperity and happiness are known: a mix of economic freedom (more or less rigorous enforcement of private property rights), redistribution for the sake of social fairness and tranquillity, plus variable amounts of regulation, in accordance with the proponents' convictions about the extent and relevance of the so-called market failures. In particular, two possibilities have opened up. One is characterized by a neoclassical orientation. It focuses on the design and enforcement of the appropriate institutional context required to follow the optimal policy-making blueprints and to provide the necessary fine tuning. A second perspective is indebted to the classical-liberal tradition. Its supporters stop short of advocating extensive constructivist engagements. Instead, they tend to concentrate on the rule of law as the only relevant operational device and identify spontaneous evolution[7] as the engine leading to efficiency, fairness, and overall wealth. In this light, constitutional engineering is assumed to provide the meta-structure within which virtuous evolution unfolds and the rigor of the rule of law does not turn into abuse.

Common to these two approaches – detailed agency modelling and broad institutional design – are economists' efforts to transform the evolutionary and the rule-of-law questions into procedural issues, whereby deviations should be kept in check by better planning, more effective bureaus or voting mechanisms, suitable (economic-) constitutional means. In particular, economic constitutions tend to adopt a consequentialist view, whereby meta-rules are engineered and evaluated according to their economic consequences, rather than according to their philosophical foundations or their moral principles. As will be pointed out later, this approach serves two purposes: it offers the possibility of suggesting an objective measurement of the quality of a legal system (e.g. by observing GDP per capita or GDP growth) and it encourages efforts to conceive a process of gradual change, from the current situation to a better one, with each discrete step being appreciated one at a time. That allows doing without inter-temporal modelling and simply settling for easy-to-perform, what-if exercises (groping). In other words, when coercive institutions fail to achieve the desirable objectives of economic prosperity and social cohesion, it is assumed that the rule-making process has gone awry, and that a new corset of rules and meta-rules is called for. These new rules might not succeed in forcing the rule-makers to behave in the most desirable way, but at least they are believed capable of restraining potential abuses. This is the essence of both constitutional economics and of its extended, neoclassical-oriented counterpart – the new political economy.[8]

The sections that follow will ignore the solution based on agency design. Such analysis would necessitate a case-by-case study of the policy objectives to be attained, which either requires the (hopeless) identification of a suitable social welfare function, or falls within the realm of L&E, which is explored in the next two chapters. As for the constitutional alternative, we obviously discard situations where meta-rules are based on individual explicit or quasi explicit[9] consensus, for these are actually exchange agreements, or at most extended versions of default contract law with opting-out clauses; certainly not constitutions. However, when explicit or quasi-explicit consensus is ruled out, we are able to raise two objections. First, we shall maintain that all meaningful constitutions do in fact rest largely on a set of arbitrary, non-accountable decisions. In particular, when based on a general social principle which subordinates the individual to the polis, then constitutions are in fact decrees defining the general will. In addition, we observe that constitutions are made by human beings, most of whom are also responsible for ordinary law making. And those meta-rules, no matter how solemn and grandiose they sound, are enforced by other individuals, closely connected with the rule-makers. Either the latter appoint the former, or the former contemplate the possibility of becoming rule-makers themselves or of occupying positions that require approval by the rule-makers. This mixture is not without consequences.

As a matter of fact, we posit that the only substantial differences between constitutional laws and ordinary laws are the historical events that justify the former and, once constitutions are introduced, what it takes to change them – simple majorities vs. more stringent numerical requirements.[10] Still, there is no a priori reason to believe that laws approved by larger coalitions are better than others, or that they necessarily provide effective restraint. In order to assess whether constitutions are good or bad, one has to clarify what kind of ordinary law-making they are supposed to prevent or generate. To do so, one needs reference to everlasting principles. Relativism provides flexibility, but porousness at the same time. When a large number of robbers are involved in a crime, possibly on a massive scale, the crime is not necessarily transformed into a noble deed or into a tolerable evil just because it involves many aggressors and many victims. Redistribution and bailing out at the taxpayers' expense a bankrupted large company are fitting contemporary examples, respectively. More realistically, it is easy to imagine that the larger the number of people required for approval, the greater the probability that the outcome turns out to be a set of vague platitudes, rather than effective barriers against abuse. In a sentence, unless they establish objective principles, virtuous meta-rules are wishful thinking for the scholar, a valuable façade for the rule maker.

The practical consequence is that the more stringent the majority requirements needed for change, the more likely it is that modifications are carried out by judicial interpretation, rather than through legislative processes. This can have advantages, if one believes that rule-making should be shielded from demagogic pressures. But the same argument can also be used in the opposite direction, if one believes that in a democracy rules should reflect popular will, or that it is easier to appoint and influence a small number of constitutional judges than large numbers in Parliament.

The second part of this chapter suggests a different, mainly explanatory approach to the features and dynamics of policy-making based on what we call "deep institutional changes".[11] The fundamental idea is that the grand principles characterizing a civilization and driving the institutional environment – rule-making and the reactions to rule-making – undergo fairly sporadic changes through time. In particular, the alterations in the ways social interaction is recognized and accepted by the members of a community vary through time as a consequence of ideological evolution. Of course, ideological developments are not sudden and their origins can be traced throughout decades and even centuries. However, it is here upheld that the translation of ideas into shared perceptions and norms takes place rather quickly and is often the result of accidents, or of a combination of accidents: obvious examples are famine, the presence of outstanding or extremely poor leaders, war. Nothing, however, happens to the institutional context if there is a famine and only a famine. Similarly, nothing happens if a revolutionary set of ideas is brought to the surface by brilliant intellectuals and effective popularisers, but the spark to ignite change is absent. By contrast, grand history may be born anew once the rise and spreading of new ideas coincide with a major accident – such as a war or a natural disaster – that forces people to look in new directions and seek new solutions. In such moments the perception of politics is also altered, with repercussion upon people's beliefs about the nature of political action and ultimately expectations about policy-making.

The periods of time defined by the deep institutional changes are named "historical periods". Common to all historical periods is the fact that policy-making remains driven by a single engine, the quest for authority and power; and that it is subject to two constraints: the ideological environment and the available technology. It is therefore maintained that all the rest, including evolutionary selection processes or other path-dependence mechanisms, play a secondary role or perhaps no role at all.

With this ultimate goal in mind, Section 5.3 critically reviews the constitutional approach, while Section 5.4 discusses the notion of deep institutional change as a way of exploring the nature and working of meta-principles. Section 5.5 compares the deep-institutional-change thesis with the institutional and the evolutionary views and Section 5.6 concludes by developing a cautious agenda to test the implications and predictions of the various propositions.

5.3 Social contracts for policy-making

As aired in the previous section, today's political economy investigates the mechanics of politics by relying on the modelling tools typical of modern neoclassical economics, thereby making deliberate use of extremely simplified assumptions and ultimately leaving economic reasoning in the background.[12] Its ultimate aim is to design the rules of the game required to reduce the impact of rents and rent-seeking structures on efficiency and growth. No serious effort is undertaken to investigate the ideological or moral foundation of the rule-making systems. Hence, the nature of the bond which keeps together rulers and citizens is taken for granted (and thus ignored), while research focuses on analysing how rule-makers interact to share and maintain power, on assessing what kind of economic consequences the various idealized patterns of interaction are likely to generate in an allegedly value-free environment,[13] on testing the effectiveness of distinct governance options to create incentives for allegedly virtuous rule making and rule enforcement.

A different and possibly more interesting approach from the speculative standpoint is offered by the "new contractarians", a group we consider to be synonymous with "constitutionalists". Their view suggests that although the principle of atheistic democracy[14] is an adequate foundation for a political system consistent with the classical-liberal standpoint, economic policy-making also requires meta-rules, which define the boundaries of state action and avoid or restrain abuse by the rulers. The foundations of such meta-rules are thus spelled out in a new version of the social contract, the analysis of which forms the object of the present section.

The reason for concentrating on the constitutional contract is that it currently represents one of the two credible attempts to develop a system of principles in favour of policy-making – the other one being the L&E vision (or part of it). In a word, the twentieth-century constitutionalists[15] contend that under certain circumstances, the state can legitimately encroach upon individual rights, even without explicit consent. Legitimacy to do so is based on the implicit/tacit social contract, through which the individual has passively accepted the authority of the state. The tacit option is made acceptable by the fact that the content of the contract is such that the individual would never abstain from accepting it, if given a chance to express his opinion. That is why an explicit contract is redundant and the cost of obtaining it can thus be ignored. If this presumption is agreed to, then coercive action would not conflict with a free-market context and it would also avoid the post-Millian tradition's slide into utilitarianism. That explains why the contractarian claim has appealed both to those who believe that government intervention is excessive and to those who cherish the idea of extensive (good) government, but do not like to be accused of disguised socialism.

Of course, the "new contract" is articulated along arguments far away from those typical of earlier times (prior to the second half of the seventeenth century). Despite their unquestionable success – its two major advocates, Friedrich von Hayek and James Buchanan were both awarded the Nobel Prize – we believe that these new versions require assumptions that are bound to conflict with the notion of individual liberty and are therefore intrinsically contradictory. One can perhaps still call such attempts "contracts", since they are based on the assumption that the individual strikes a deal with the authority. Nonetheless, we maintain that they can claim neither moral legitimacy, nor consistency with the real world to which they are supposed to apply, i.e. with the typical traits of the Age of Social Responsibility to be described later in this chapter. The opposite view, which is upheld in these pages, is that the actual social agreement rests on other, possibly less noble bastions: the ongoing engagement in large-scale rent-seeking and the repudiation of individual responsibility. In short, we claim that the social agreement typical of the collective-responsibility period to be discussed in Section 5.4 has little or nothing to do with the (new) social contract.

Since the whole argument deals with the meaning one should attribute to the implicit contract, we find it useful to shape the discussion in terms of tacit agreement. This comes in two versions, depending upon the content of the silent pact between the individual and the authority. One version can be defined as constitutional *stricto sensu* and will be examined below. The other is the quasi-minimal thesis and will be discussed in the subsequent sub-section.

5.3.1 Questioning the constitutional contract

According to the constitutional version, current institutions have been designed or inherited by actors who have rents to preserve and who therefore try their best to prevent a virtuous evolutionary path from running its course. This explains why we live in a bad world and not much is being done to move toward a better state of affairs. Thus, according to the constitutional view, in order for people to agree on a social structure, the ground must initially be cleared from pre-existing power structures that de facto make it impossible to agree on a social covenant among equals (non-equal meaning conditioned by the past). Of course, implicit in this statement is the belief that absent consolidated rent-seeking, the individuals would spontaneously choose the "best" system of meta-rules, which would in turn eliminate or drastically limit the possibility of having bad norms. This rent-free environment where the ideal (tacit) covenant takes place is created and characterized by a "veil of (Knightian) uncertainty",[16] behind which people agree on the meta-rules that define a society. This spontaneous optimal choice taking place in a world without a past is the constitutional, tacit, social contract.

In particular, the veil of uncertainty does not deny that rents might be created, but it ensures that the meta-rules are agreed-upon and enforced before any individual has had a chance to create or enjoy privileges. In order to identify these meta-rules, the following thought-experiment is suggested. Suppose that a group of individuals came to earth with no past (i.e. no rents), had to decide whether to form a community and debated about the rules that should characterize such a community. Most likely, their fundamental choice would regard the amount of rent-seeking that the social rules of the game to be would allow. In order to make his choice, each potential member of the community would then rationally evaluate his/her chances of successful rent-seeking in a future society. Every individual knows what the world out there looks like and has some notion about his likely positioning in such a world (Knightian uncertainty does not mean ignorance). Nonetheless, he is assumed to be unable to assess his chances for rent-seeking and, more generally, his ability to exploit the opportunities that life may offer, or the probability of suffering from failure. This inability is greater, the longer the time horizon. As a result, if the constitutional features are to extend over a long-distance future in order to enhance stability, and if the constitutional meta-rules are abstract enough (i.e. they consist of very general principles about what rulers can and cannot do), uncertainty ensures that risk-neutral or even mildly risk-loving individuals opt for a system of constitutional norms that severely restricts the ruler's decision-making power.[17] In other words, behind such a veil, individuals believe that their expected rent-seeking gains are significantly negative, so that even the risk-loving members of the society are inclined to subscribe to a constitutional rule that prevents rent-seeking and sets substantial limits to the regulatory and spending/taxing power of the state.[18]

Two sets of comments are in order. First, this line of reasoning rests on critical assumptions about – for instance – the probability of winning the rent-seeking game, which declines as rent-seeking becomes increasingly concentrated in the hands of the elites, which affects the bearing of the risk-aversion element; the profitability of rent-seeking; the sustainability of rent-seeking (if the rent-seeking opportunities are periodically randomly redistributed, the incentive to strive to create privileges and appropriate them is weaker).[19]

Second, it is equally clear that within the constitutional framework the role of the state has little or nothing to do with the protection of fundamental rights (e.g. natural rights), since the existence of fundamental, objective rights is explicitly denied:[20] according to the contractarian view the social agreement is sovereign and ruled by moral relativism. One can indeed define the First Principles or cornerstones of a social order, but these are by no means eternal and do not necessarily apply to all mankind. Even the notion of justice takes an unusual meaning, for "just" no longer reflects compliance with principles, but is made equivalent to submission to the agreed-upon meta-rules.[21] Therefore, consensus prevails upon ethics in three different ways: (*a*) when the tacit agreement behind the veil of uncertainty defines the meta-rules, so that justice is ultimately the content of such meta-rules; (*b*) when justice acquires a normative dimension, in that "just" is what eliminates contradictions among possibly conflicting rules;[22] (*c*) when the object of politics is established and the role of the state is ultimately understood to be the production and financing of merit goods, even when this may imply encroachment upon individual liberties.

These remarks help understand what we consider to be two weaknesses of the constitutional perspective. One is logical, the other operational. From a logical standpoint, the main problem is the role of the veil of uncertainty as mainstay of an agreement on the meta-rules. Even if one accepts the veil as realistic, the existence of such an agreement can only be imagined, for individuals are not identical and therefore – contrary to the constitutional view – they do not necessarily share the same wishes with regard to the way a society should be run and state intervention restricted. For instance, some might want the state to protect the individual from coercion; others might claim that coercive taxation is tolerable to relieve poverty or to compensate people from natural or "systemic" catastrophes; still other groups might favour equalitarian redistribution no matter what. Hence the tacit contract would not be too far away from an exercise in figuring out how a typical individual imagined by the social scientist would behave and what he would choose. To be fair, the constitutional response would be that the tacit contract is in fact a residual contract, in that it identifies the body of meta-rules from which nobody has opted out.[23] This is hardly convincing, though. On the one hand, one could therefore conclude that the constitutional state is not a real state, but only an agency that provides services on demand to those who want to buy protection, redistribution, fairness, etc. On the other hand, if the state that emerges from the social contract maintains its standard monopolistic prerogatives, it is hard to see how one can opt out of a set of rules that does not allow competing systems to come to the surface. For instance, can one opt out of a state educational system if all private education is outlawed or severely restricted in a given territory? Or can one build his own house on his own piece of land after having rejected a law that prescribes that building permits are compulsory for all activities in the construction industry? Surely, one could object that these two examples refer to ordinary laws, rather than to meta-rules. It should be observed, however, that if meta-rules are not about absolute moral principles, then they are necessarily about objectives to be attained through ordinary legislation. Changing the required majority for approval does not transform an ordinary norm into a meta-rule. At most, it changes the decision-maker, as pointed out earlier.

In short, it seems that the purpose of the constitutional state is to legislate more or less at will, and then allow the members of a society (as defined by the state?) to decide whether they like the various pieces of legislation or whether they would like to opt out. Not only would this be hardly manageable from an operational standpoint, but it would lose all its "constitutional" content. Instead, the state would become either an insurance company among many others, with no monopoly power, let alone on violence; or an advanced stationer's shop where one can buy pre-printed contracts, possibly with a guarantee of enforcement provided by the stationer himself, either by default or on demand. Put differently, either the state no longer exists (for a state without absolute power to enforce its rules is no longer a state), or its meta-rules drop their distinctive meaning and are reduced to a mere façade.

From the operational vantage point, the constitutional proposal does deserve credit for not attempting to design an optimal set of meta-rules *ex novo* or to engage in constructivist experiments, but "merely" to reform the institutional context in democracies, where all individuals are allowed to express their views. However attractive this may appear, the difficulties remain daunting. For in order to unleash a constitutional evolutionary process, individuals must be pushed back behind the veil of uncertainty, be reduced to the typical agent so as to make sure that they all share the same notion of the collective good, and/or their time horizon should be stretched considerably. Otherwise, individuals would be fully aware of their chances to acquire privileges and would raise the cost the losers would face by opting out, or even prevent them from doing so. Put differently, reform presupposes that individuals be denied their current status, but in order to do that one should claim that the present meta-rule framework and the present distribution of income is illegitimate (unjust), or declare the coercive power of the state an act of unfounded violence.

To conclude, the constitutional contract would be not only hard to enforce, but also difficult to rationalize in the very light of the (questionable) constitutional notion of justice, which is defined according to the prevailing rules, rather than to general principles outside man-made legislation. Then, in order for the constitutional project to see the light, the accent would have to be on revolution rather than on reform. Nonetheless, even if the constitutionalists were happy with revolutions (which is not the case), revolutions are by nature teleological, which means that some kind of constructivist engagement is unavoidable; or that First Principles (objectivism, eternal natural rights) must be accepted. Still, both of these propositions run against the very claims of the constitutional vision.

5.3.2 Doubts on the quasi-minimal contract

Jasay's quasi minimal approach[24] was conceived as a response to the classical-liberal view derived from John Stuart Mill, according to whom the state is legitimized to act in order to prevent individuals from being harmed. This classical-liberal, almost Hobbesian statement, however, supports two deceptively convincing concepts of liberty: freedom from damage, as maintained by Mill himself (1859/1879: chapter 1), "the only purpose for which power can be rightfully exercised over any member of a civilized community, against his will, is to prevent harm to others";[25] and freedom to follow the rule of law: "when we obey laws, in the sense of general abstract rules laid down irrespective of their application to us, we are not subject to another man's will and are therefore free" (Hayek 1960: 153). Both are open definitions, in that they offer much room to interpretation and have ultimately become rather porous. Thanks to J.S. Mill himself, for instance, freedom from damage has become the right not to suffer as a result of the actions of other members of the community. The Hayekian definition goes in the same direction in that the rule of law is meant to protect the individual from other people's misbehaviour. In fact, in both cases it all comes to defining and interpreting the border between encroaching upon one's legitimate rights (which requires action) and suffering from indirect effects (which doesn't).

This shift of emphasis, away from the traditional idea of freedom-from-coercion, had been noted long ago by the old institutionalists[26] and has in fact gradually led to the crisis of the classical-liberal framework, which has lost much of its identity by engaging in hopeless fights over interpretation and hair-splitting. Confusion and ambiguities have followed. For instance, liberty as the right not to suffer damage inevitably imposes limitations on the others' freedom of action; whereas liberty as the ability to follow procedurally correct rule-making, not unlike what we have already observed in the constitutional case, leads to a notion of justice (and legitimacy) equivalent to compliance with the rules, a conclusion that not every classical-liberal brought up in the Scottish tradition would subscribe to.[27]

Jasay is very clear about the classical-liberal ambiguity and rightly believes that neither damage avoidance, nor Dewey's pragmatic moral philosophy[28] are sound bases to justify violations of the freedom-from-coercion principle. Instead, he claims that since the state can only be the expression of the will of a community (as opposed to the will of God, let alone of an autocrat), the state can only be founded on a contractarian approach. In particular, in Jasay's view the typical feature of a legitimate contract is its ability to originate Pareto-improvements, whereby none of the agents involved is made worse off in comparison with the situation prevailing before the contract is signed and put in force. All actions or policies enforced by the state are then subject to the same validation criterion. In addition, and contrary to the constitutional perspective, the quasi-minimal approach has moral foundations. They are individual liberty from coercion, as mentioned earlier; and private property based on possession, unless possession is derived from violence or fraud (both circumstances being of course departures from the personal-freedom principle).[29]

The quasi-minimal proposal is attractive, in that it contains neither implicit and possibly questionable assumptions about the individuals' attitude towards risk, nor arbitrary and less than plausible conjectures about the nature and dynamic features of rent-seeking. In addition, the political construction Jasay envisages does not necessarily depend on religion and thus on concepts that require the existence and acceptance of a divine order. The emphasis is on the secular version of the natural-right approach, which rests upon the concept that each individual is born a free man, which in turn implies that nobody can uphold any right on the newly-born creature.[30] This is indeed all one needs to postulate in order to develop an argument based on natural rights. In this particular case, the nature-based claim to freedom rules out the right to exercise physical aggression, and thus the duty for the victim to accept it or to negotiate compromises within the social body.

It then follows that when it comes to formulating sets of formal rules in order to discipline social interaction, the role of the state actually becomes a matter of individual choice. It is up to the individual to decide whether and under which conditions to engage in trading with the rest of the community (one or more individuals), how to act or not to act in certain ways while obtaining goods or valuable behavioural commitments by his counterpart(s), how to choose an enforcing agent. Since no exchange would take place voluntarily without at least one party being better off, and with none of the parties being worse off, Jasay's Paretian social contract is indeed moral (i.e. "just" in the traditional way) and persuasive.

Still, the quasi-minimal contract also presents a number of unresolved issues. On the one hand, it depends on the a priori general recognition of an alleged man-centred natural right (individual freedom), which is indeed readily enough conceived, but not necessarily accepted by everybody. For instance, one can also argue for a natural-right vision based on the social nature of man, as explained in Chapter 4. If moral (and therefore just) is what leads to the realization of human nature, and the human being is supposed to realize himself only in the social context, then freedom is subject to what is needed for the individual to be part in a social context, which of course necessarily requires that the nature and goals of a virtuous society must be defined in advance. Hence, two possibilities open up.

Either the individualistic notion of freedom is rejected, which would however imply the downfall of the Paretian-optimality constraint on the quasi-minimal social contract. Or, one upholds the strict individualistic line, but at the cost of undermining the very notion of a social contract, which would be in fact reduced to a set of individual agreements (voluntary exchange) to do or not to do.

Indeed, and this is a second point, one wonders whether state interference legitimized by Pareto optimality needs any coercion at all. If the answer is negative, then there is no reason to have a state enjoying the monopoly of violence and the power to use it. Furthermore, and from a broader standpoint, one may wonder whether Pareto optimal deals are indeed suitable to legitimize a social contract. In theory, one may welcome an agent that reduces the cost of carrying out business. But of course this is not enough to justify monopoly power, and even less the use of violence. Put differently, Jasay's quasi-minimal contract is really a standard contract. Calling the counterpart "the state" makes no difference, especially if one deprives the states of its main prerogatives (monopoly of violence and impunity when infringing upon individual liberty).

Equally important, one should also solve the practical problem of designating those in charge of assessing whether a given course of action is actually conducive to a Pareto improvement. The standard literature sidesteps the question by referring to the existence of public and collective goods: it does not really matter who is in charge as long as he takes care of producing the necessary public and collective goods and gets punished or removed if he fails to do so, or does it at an exceedingly high cost. But definitions are not enough from a subjectivist standpoint. As we have observed in Chapter 3, the very fact that an individual might consume goods or services without affecting the scarcity constraint others are facing, and that the producer is not able to detect who is actually consuming (and how much), is not a reason to tax the individual and force him to pay the (fixed) costs of production. In other words, free riding is not enough to make a good a public good.[31] Yet, even in a world characterized by a quasi-minimal social contract, discretionary/arbitrary power in the name of fairness is required to guess both the amount of presumed consumption and the subjective value associated with such an activity and subsequently assess the existence of Pareto improvements. By doing so, however, one necessarily violates individual freedom. Claiming or guessing that the victim (the taxpayer in this case) is actually free-riding makes little difference to the essence of the question. Envy or frustration are hardly good enough reasons to generate a presumption of fraud and thereby "legitimize" intrusion.

The case for the so-called collective goods[32] would of course be even weaker, for in this context the very definition of collective good depends on the ruler, who may of course have his own ideas about what is good for society, what should be provided by the state and at what conditions. From that vantage point, and contrary to the primary design of the advocates of the quasi-minimal state, the Pareto criterion might thus turn out to be the key to legitimize discretion, rather than to delegitimize extended government intervention.

Finally, and similar to the constitutional case, one might object that Jasay's quasi-minimal state is actually a proposal for revolution, where change requires starting from scratch, rather than for reform, where the starting point is the current given context. Clearly, if the appropriate size of the state is defined by incremental steps based on the Pareto-optimality criterion, the experiment can only start from a situation in which there is no state. Downsizing a large state would go nowhere, unless nobody was enjoying rents, which is wishful thinking. The only way out would then be a what-if exercise behind some sort of veil, which however would meet objections not unlike those already raised earlier on within the constitutional context.

5.4　Deep change and historical periods in Western civilization

The preliminary conclusion of the argument developed so far is that the foundations of economic policy-making are logically weak, unless one is ready to identify and able to justify the notion of social welfare. This possibility has been here denied. In particular, modern social-contract theory offers little help, for either these theories boil down to academic what-if exercises based on questionable assumptions, or they actually refer to the state as an entity which has little to do with the traditional state, and thus would have no power to enforce policies.

As previously suggested, a different and perhaps more fruitful way to consider the legitimacy of today's policy-making is to take for granted that the large majority of the population does support substantial government intervention in most areas of economic activities, and therefore to put a different type of question. Rather than asking "how can one churn better rules?", or "what is the optimal size of legitimate government?", we suggest raising the question of "what makes government intervention perceived to be legitimate?".

The answer we provide revolves around the notion of the historical period, which spans from one moment of deep institutional change to another. Each historical period is characterized by a distinctive, general perception of the rules of social interaction. A modification in these perceptions may lead to new procedures to designate the agents in charge of enforcing the agreed-upon coordination devices (including contracts), to select those responsible for producing rules, goods and services on behalf and to the benefit of the community, and also to determine how desirable "collective" services are identified and paid for. When so, deep institutional change (i.e. change in the shared perceptions) coincides or brings about political transformation and a new historical period begins.

This does not ignore that constitutions exist, but it emphasizes that the content of a constitutional framework is defined or at least heavily influenced by what a political agent believes to be desirable (to enhance/legitimize his power) and acceptable (to his counterpart) at the time of drafting. It also encourages those interested in exploring the constitutional and institutional environment of a period to pay particular attention to the features of the historical phases under scrutiny, which are here assumed to be far less dynamic than commonly believed. In particular, it is here maintained that within each of the three historical periods defining Western civilization to be presented in some detail in this section, the rules of the game did not adjust following any recognizable evolutionary pattern (contrary to the path-dependence thesis), and that efforts to innovate through constitutional law-making are bound to be vain (contrary to the constitutional-economics literature). Top-down projects are successful only insofar as they reflect the shared ideologies of the given historical moment. Thus, they are a by-product of their time, rather than an innovation per se. This does not exclude that constitutions can bring about or ease change. But when successful, even their innovativeness springs from a certain context, and not "any" context would do. On the other hand, proposals relying on a bottom-up approach tend to share the weaknesses of the contractarian approach examined in the previous section.

Our thesis is that the history of Western civilization can be split into three periods: the Gregorian Centuries, the Secular Period and the Age of Social Responsibility. To each of them specific grand rules of the game can be attached, which help understand why economic policy-making became an issue only towards the end of the second period and why it developed into a major component of societal interaction only in the last.[33]

5.4.1 The Gregorian Centuries

There is a general tendency to locate the birth of the West in the High Middle Ages,[34] more or less when ancient political philosophy – stoicism in particular – met Christianity[35] and a number of simmering questions were put on the table. By and large all such questions converged onto two basic issues: defining the legitimacy of political authority and establishing the purpose and the boundaries of political power. The result of the debate – which for some decades actually meant bitter conflict – was a body of shared values usually referred to as "the Gregorian Revolution" (late eleventh century). Such values were critical to the formation of the West, for they identified the "true" source of power and authority, the relationship between the authority and the rest of the community, the role of each individual within the community. For the purposes of the present discussion, we call these features the first deep institutional change in the West, which marked the beginning of the first historical period of our civilization, lasting for some 600 years.

The Gregorian Revolution takes its name after Pope Gregory VII, who in AD 1075 challenged the primacy of the secular ruler by issuing the "Dictates of the Pope", a declaration that disavowed a long tradition whereby the emperor was recognized as the supreme authority in both religious and secular matters.[36] In order to reach his goal, Gregory VII had to raise the question of legitimate power. As a matter of fact, the outcome was already secured as soon as the very issue of legitimacy became open for debate, since all the parties concerned acknowledged that the answer could only come from the notions of natural order and divine will on the one hand, and from the assessment of the nature and goals of the individual within society on the other. In both areas the authority of the

Church was virtually undisputed. Put differently, from a speculative standpoint, the Pope was a clear winner from the very beginning.[37]

In addition, the emperor had to accept the change in the rules of the game imposed by Gregory VII and his successors for one very practical reason. Until the eleventh century, the secular sovereign was a barbaric ruler: rather than ruling, however, he would act as coordinator of a more or less large number of tribes. They would share the same religious faith (a very soft and accommodating version of Christianity) and be forced to cooperate in order to oppose attacks from outside (Magyars, Normans, Arabs). The only way to show sovereign power was thus leadership in battle and the only tangible sign of civilian rule was the somewhat symbolic right to administer justice (even Charles the Great was travelling from one corner to the other of his domain to this purpose, thereby ensuring he would still be recognized as the current ruler). As we know, the substantial decline of threats from outside Europe, the increase in wealth that followed, and thus urbanization, led to a situation where the emperor became de facto redundant militarily, while the prevailing version of Christendom was not enough to make him necessary as the head of a religious structure: bishops and monasteries were more than enough to meet believers' needs. In a word, the emperor had to emphasize his role as judicial authority to justify his existence and to rely on the Church in order to legitimize his power. Destroying the Church would have been hazardous, almost suicidal.[38]

The most important result of the Gregorian Revolution was the birth of the law (Berman 1983). Both the Church and the empire were forced to recognize the existence of rules, embedded in the divine order, discovered by reason and revealed by God, to which all secular and religious authorities were subject: "rule by law and under the law". Other important outcomes were the notion of equality of all individuals before God, to whom we are individually responsible; and the teleological view whereby the individual has come into this world with a purpose, which is/was living according to God's will (i.e. in compliance with the divine order) while preparing for death. In other words, all individuals are children of God, who loves all men equally. But all God's children have to accept the earthly order as sacred and immutable, for it is the expression of God's will. We are alive because we have been presented with a chance to serve God to the best of our abilities while on earth and – more important – to get ready to die in the best possible way, so as to obtain redemption from sin, avoid perpetual damnation (first defined as the sheer absence of God, then complemented with Hell), and enjoy eternal happiness.[39]

One can of course debate at length on the details of how the belief structure of the Gregorian society came about, but there is little doubt that those mentioned above were actually the foundations of all Western early social structures:

1   Equality with respect to God, but passive recognition of God-designed social hierarchy and inequalities in this world;

2   The existence of "just" rules, either conceived by God or by man, but never-

theless consistent with God's design – in case of conflict, just rules were to prevail over habit and tradition;
3   The partition between a secular and a religious world (against universalism).

In this context the features of human behaviour – the perception of what governs social interaction – can thus be translated into the following terms: The notions of authority[40] and of almost fixed social positioning were not open for discussion. There were limits to the rulers' discretionary powers, but these could only be defined by the religious authority, definitely not by the members of a community. Efforts to improve one's own well-being were not forbidden, but such efforts had to take place within the limits of the individual's (allegedly God-assigned) social status. Not unexpectedly, all that might appear as contempt for the divine order and will on earth was met by widespread suspicion, if not hostility.

As a result, economic activity and technological progress were modest, below the critical threshold required to spark fast and sustainable growth. It was indeed enough to provide for substantial population growth, but not to escape the demographic trap: In normal times individual well-being for some 90 per cent of the European population remained barely above what was necessary to survive, but when population grew too much, catastrophe was inevitable. The social stigma attached to the production of physical goods and manual labour in general did not help, either. Of course, expensive transportation and communication, low and scattered populations (absence of potential large-enough markets to remunerate innovation) also contributed to restrain the motivation for technological advance.[41]

This does not mean that nothing within these social structures changed. Still, institutional change was almost random. For instance, one can certainly say that the Middle Ages witnessed the birth of a number of institutional innovations; guilds, urban political structures (the city-states), mercantile law systems, the use of money on a large scale. In addition, there is no doubt that the rules of the game in the feudal economy were different from those prevailing – say – in fifteenth-century Flanders, in sixteenth-century Spain or in seventeenth-century Holland. Similarly, the nature of the contracts typical of the feudal system surely had little in common with those characterizing an urban economy based on mercantile capitalism. Nonetheless, institutional innovations were the results of the greater wealth produced by a combination of some technological progress, less warfare, extensive colonization of new lands; and/or by the quest for power, which often implied the creation of rents preserved by violence. It was not a question of path dependence or evolution, but rather of expanded opportunity sets that could have presented different features if some battles had ended differently, if famines or diseases had struck harder or not struck at all, if the world had not warmed up significantly at the beginning of the second millennium of the Christian era.

Nor do we disavow the important contributions to the history of economic ideas, or to the history of ideas in general, that occurred from the end of the twelfth to the end of the seventeenth centuries. But we suggest that the new ideas failed to affect the references (1) to (3) mentioned earlier. Therefore, they altered neither the general rules of the game, nor the very nature and dynamics of policy-making, the moral boundaries of which stayed the same. In a sentence, the ruler was designated by God; and the Church guaranteed the calling. Concerns for the common weal were either restricted to the religious sphere (charity) or to small, geographically limited communities where interpersonal relations took place following unwritten customary guidelines.

In this light policy-making was clearly a non-issue. As the concept of legitimate authority became clearer, and the position of the prince more vulnerable, the ruler needed to consolidate his secular power, and engage in the gradual transformation of the notion of political structure: from one dominated by religious elements (universalism being one of the options) to one based on territorial control. For historical reasons the only pre-Gregorian example of this phenomenon was Venice, where the ruling oligarchy did without God's blessing and relied on its ability to secure mercantile success and later territorial expansion on the "Terra Ferma".[42] The first large-scale post-Gregorian example was Philippe Auguste's enterprise, ultimately decided at Bouvines, where Philippe Auguste could have lost, as he almost did, with potentially far-reaching consequences on the history of France and perhaps of Europe as well.

Put differently, the Gregorian Revolution articulated the concept that policy was a race for power, and that all secular authority is fragile. Power could be expanded and authority secured through exploitation. Of course, at the time there could be no room for a social contract, for the contract was not between the ruler and the subjects, but between the ruler and those who were supposed to confirm divine appointment and consent.[43] This also explains why policy-making tended to be directed towards the acquisition of more and more resources, and therefore towards the expansion in territorial claims: to consolidate authority and pre-empt potential rivals and aggressors.

To conclude, since rulers were not chosen by anybody, but appointed by a divine agent, in Gregorian times the development of coercive, pragmatic institutions was functional to the interests of the ruling rent-seekers. In the early Gregorian Centuries, when power could be exercised by relatively small armies of highly trained specialists facing equally small armies, rent-seeking was very basic: the ruler would grab what was available, possibly restrained by the religious authorities, and be held responsible to God only. In later periods, military technology (the introduction of artillery and fire arms) made it easier for competitors to challenge incumbents[44] and more sophisticated (and expensive) arrangements had to be elaborated. Sometimes, this led to the creation of the bureaucratic state, so as to improve control over the territory (Philippe Auguste was the major early innovator in this field);[45] sometimes to alliances with the affluent elites, either when money was needed, or when centralized control was ineffective. In turn, there were situations when the elites were affluent enough to maintain or buy their independence, which meant that anointed rulers abstained from claiming rights on certain portions of territory.[46] In yet different environments, the elites bought or acquired privileges (freedoms) and rent-seeking capacity (the case of the guilds is typical, but not unique). Indeed, one can figure out so many different path-dependent or evolutionary processes that one wonders whether these notions actually carry a useful operational content.

5.4.2 The Secular Period

All along the Gregorian period one can surely trace trends, ideas and events that ultimately led the human thought and man's general perceptions away from the medieval frame of mind described in the preceding paragraphs. In other words, there is no doubt that many ingredients that turned out to be the essence of the Secular Period were elaborated and shaped during Gregorian times, following up on issues that had been raised during the Gregorian Centuries, if not earlier. One of such issues is the drive to secularize sovereign rule and create the essential features of the modern state, a notion that was seldom aired explicitly during the Middle Ages, but that quickly became a political necessity for the elites: The Gregorian Revolution had indeed marked the separation between the secular and the religious world, but the fact that God had remained the sovereign source of authority made it apparent that the monarch could obtain full sovereignty and legitimacy only by escaping the religious hold. The Secular Period reveals the consequences of such efforts.[47]

Not unexpectedly, the key, and therefore the critical divide between the Gregorian and the Secular Periods, revolves around the assessment of the relationship between the ruler and its subjects. As mentioned earlier in this section, this relationship bears on two different levels: authority and power, although it is obvious that once the latter is questioned, the former is inevitably also open to scrutiny. The Westphalia Treaties gave practical content to the notion whereby in order for the divine order to be obtained, religious guidance and interference were not needed (Koselleck 1979). Of course, this declaration applied to the Catholic Church as well, which in fact refused to recognize the treaties.

At that time, the new, entirely secularized perception of international politics clearly made little or no difference to the life of common people. But once the management of international power ceased to be a matter of religious interest, and once the Thirty Years War had demonstrated that God could be on all sides,[48] it was hard to claim that domestic rule was accompanied by God's blessing. There were two solutions available and the last Gregorian rulers pursued them both. The first was to ignore God's blessing or any other justification altogether, while extracting rents and preserving power by the sheer exercise of violence. The other was to formulate a rational (which actually meant secular) theory to justify authority and subsequently let power derive from authority as if this notion per se implied the right to exercise discretion (which often meant a good deal of discretionary violence, once again). Such a rational theory was based on two pillars: a reformulation of the natural-right theory and the introduction of the social contract, the latter being what today is more frequently mentioned as a constitution.

The crucial question was addressed explicitly during the second half of the seventeenth century and its practical consequences unfolded a few decades later (Goldstone 2011). In order to secularize the state, four steps had to be taken. If legitimacy for the state could no longer come from above, it had to come from below (the individual or the head of the household, depending upon what the elementary constitutive part of a society is assumed to be). Here lies the original need for a contract between the individual and the authority. In addition, natural rights had to be re-defined in order to ensure that it would be natural (i.e. morally compelling) for the individual to engage in a social covenant. Third, for the contract to be valid or to make any sense, it had to take place between equals. Finally, in order for the contract to be a "social" contract, it could not concern direct, personal exchange, but rather focus on the development of the state as a way to protect society.

As aired above, the completion and widespread acceptance of these passages marked the transition between the Gregorian and the Secular historical periods. Political or natural accidents would then open the way to new political regimes and possibly new sets of pragmatic institutions.[49] The race for power and rent-seeking would of course continue unabated, but with different rules and different technological constraints. Still, the underlying driving force – the quest for power broadly understood, which includes prestige and material wealth – was the same as the one observed in the Gregorian period and in the one which would follow, the Age of Social Responsibility.

The transition was not easy,[50] but it turned out to be successful. As we know, the Enlightenment brought about the switch from government based on compliance with the divine order, to government as a result of a contract. The contractarian element was deemed inevitable, since a natural social trait/instinct was recognized as typical of the individual, as the Greeks had already claimed over 2,000 years earlier. The vision of the Secular Period differed from the Greeks in two crucial aspects, though. First, all men were now equal (the Gregorian legacy), especially if Christians and with a white skin. They occupied different roles on earth, but human nature was one. Second, whereas for the Greeks an individual acquired his human nature only by becoming an active member of society, in the Secular Period the individual is born a human being: he antedates society and consciously decides to form a community. The relation between man and society – the substance of the (social) contract – can take different forms. For example, the individual's determination to be part of a society can be motivated by his desire to enhance his prosperity or his mere survival (e.g. Grotius and Hobbes);[51] or by the instinctive, God-instilled quest to obtain the ultimate goal of the divine order, rationally discovered to be peace (e.g. Pufendorf); or by an encompassing utilitarian choice (man needs society in order to interact and become a rational being), which leads to a contract, which in turn defines the limits of state action (Thomasius).[52] As mentioned above, common to all these views is the notion that human beings follow their nature only by joining a social context.[53] In other words, the individual is a human being because, and only because, his very living in a social context gives him his human qualities, develops his ability to reason and obtain his natural goals.[54]

Of course, this reverses the Gregorian/medieval perspective, whereby man is born endowed with a bundle of natural rights and society is just a product of interaction, possibly a tool of self-improvement, definitely not an actor in its own right.[55] Surely, the contractarian vision also requires that all individuals (including the ruler) are subject to the law. But this no longer means equality before God and God's law, for there is little room for God in the Secular Period. Rather, it is equality before man's created law, which inevitably implies equality under the ruler's law.

From the standpoint of economic theorizing, the secular vision obviously eased the transition to studying "political economy", i.e. the technical and moral features of economic interaction. This led to speculative and practical consequences. In fact, by introducing legitimacy by rational contracting and by removing much of the religious component out of morality, the Secular Period transformed the economic problem from an individual issue to be solved within the household, possibly interacting with other households; into an issue for society as whole. In a sentence, the welfare enhancement of the whole also became part of the social contract. Hence, proper understanding of economic investigation turned out to be one of the critical elements required of the ruler.

As pointed out in Chapter 2, the early classical economists saw their role cast in this very mould, and recommended limited government intervention in order to obtain social happiness and peace, with arguments partly based on efficiency (wealth creation) and partly on morality (non-interference with natural rights).[56] Practically, however, the secular vision opened the way to policy-making spurred by the rule-makers' judgement and justified by results. Although lip-service continued to be paid to individual rights, these gradually became defined only within the framework of a social moral standard. This is hardly surprising, since individual compliance with such a social moral standard is what certifies that the individual has subscribed to the social contract and is therefore part of society.[57]

5.4.3 The Age of Social Responsibility

All in all, the Secular Period failed to provide a satisfactory solution to the debate about (*a*) the non religious sources of legitimacy of the state and (*b*) the possibility of conflating a secular theory of power (why and to which extent the ruler could use violence) with a religious theory of authority (why the ruler was sovereign and sacred at the same time). The fundamental flaw in the contractarian approach of the Secular Period was its very ambiguity towards the role of religion. Its weakness became particularly clear during the American Revolution, the French Revolution and the Napoleonic interval. Ironically, the American Revolution turned out to be sustainable because it rejected the contractarian solution and went back to a new Gregorian system based on a set of God-given individual rights enforced by a Lockean ruler endowed with minimal power.[58] The French Revolution failed because although the peasants and most of the bourgeoisie were more or less happy about the goal of the contract (equality before the law and private property), almost everybody also thought to have full rights to his fair share of power. This was not what the revolutionary leaders had in mind: the goals of the revolution changed as it unfolded, and while it became clear that the "Will of the Nation" was not the same as the "Will of the People" (Jouvenel 1993 [1945]: 55), disorder (and terror) ensued. As we know, chaotic conditions in France during the last years of the century were the primary cause of the rise to power of Bonaparte (originally Buonaparte), a successful general who promised and delivered peace and order (at home). But it is also no accident that that very general never considered the social contract a serious basis for his power and quickly resorted to building up some kind of divine legitimacy for him and for his offspring – first through Papal crowning, then through marriage to Marie Louise.

In fact, the new historical environment that emerged at the beginning of the twentieth century drew heavily on the lessons taught by the French experience of the late eighteenth and early nineteenth centuries and took advantage of the opportunities offered by the industrial revolution. In particular, the new age featured a holistic agreement that proceeded from the elites down to the people. It was a promise of peace, prosperity, qualified power sharing (through modern democracy), and it eliminated the need to conceive or refer to a suitable, legitimate contract between the individual and the ruler. Put differently, the solution to the threat of revolutionary instability and chaos was not a new definition of justice and legitimacy, but a consequentialist claim by the elites: "We rule for the good of the people and we have the right to rule as long as we fulfil our commitment." In turn, the promise to deliver prosperity involved (and involves) three central ideas: all the members of society are given privileges, thereby transforming the economy into a system of interacting rent-seekers; all citizens are offered a chance to obtain a share of discretionary power, i.e. the race to power is open to everybody; and the notion of personal responsibility is reformulated and de facto reduced within an encompassing social context guaranteed by appointed rulers. Thus results the notion of social responsibility. As can be observed, such three promises are not a contract in order to legitimize a ruler or define the essence of "good government", but rather a general agreement to share the newly created wealth, the only restraint being provided by the need to prevent possible reaction by the victims of this new rent-seeking game.[59]

The First World War and its immediate aftermath marked the beginning of this new era.[60] As a matter of fact, global war could not have been waged without a new covenant that provided credible guarantees against poverty and uncertainty, while calling-up millions and millions of people, many of them persuaded that the new dream was threatened by foreign aggressors. Indeed, no war could have been won or fought through without some sort of national agreement and total, sometimes even jubilant mobilization. And no after-war period could have been managed otherwise, especially in Europe, where the effects of the conflict were more devastating. At the same time, global war was crucial in delegitimizing opposition to the new encompassing deal. The result was and is a new version of the Rousseauian "general will", where managing the will and taking action has become more important than the defining the will; where consensus (populism) has replaced virtue; and where the democratic process has solved the authority problem.

The rent-seeking element of the deal makes all the members of a society feel entitled to take part in an illusory win–win game that distributes privileges – "freedoms", according to the vocabulary of the Gregorian Centuries – following a flexible and pragmatic (i.e. consensus-driven) criterion, subject to political contingencies, as well as to agreement about the desirable outcomes, expectations, available resources. The system of privileges must be complex enough not to make it clear whether one is a net winner or a net loser at the end of the rent-seeking game. But one must always be given hope to acquire further privileges in the future, so as to reduce the incentive to rock the system even if at some moment in time one suspects he is getting the short end of the stick. Put differently, each component of society must believe that looking for alternative political solutions and enforcing them would be useless, exceedingly expensive, or even counterproductive. This is actually the case in relatively affluent contexts, in which the expected losses from social conflict are greater and therefore tolerance of abuse possibly more generous.

Of course, the system is self-reinforcing if growth is satisfactory. When so, even the unhappy members have an incentive to confirm the rent-seeking principles of the social-responsibility system, and to confine their efforts to reforming its operational devices – e.g. ordinary laws – in order to change the identities of the beneficiaries and the size of the benefits. But self-destruction looms if growth is sluggish or negative, so that free lunches become manifestly scarce and promises lose credibility.

Power sharing and consensus are the other pillars of post-First World War Western societies. Power sharing reinforces the rent-seeking mechanisms and enhances consensus. Contrary to past historical experiences, power sharing during the Age of Social Responsibility represents the possibility of climbing the power ladder broadly understood, either within the political structure or within the bureaucracy, possibly jumping from one to the other, not to mention the revolving-door options already referred to. This is now workable thanks to the greater wealth, which allows for unprecedented increases in taxation and thus an expansion in the public sector. Success sometimes depends on loyalty to the rulers' elite (top politicians), most frequently it takes place within autonomous, self-governing structures (the bureaucracy). Crucial in this game is that attempts to climb the ladder seldom fail completely. In most cases, real power sharing remains a dream, but those who give it a try remain with the hope of having a chance to do better next time and always end up with micro-rents in their pockets. Even a petty job in the civil service becomes a (passive) rent if one shirks and de facto transforms it into some sort of anticipated state pension. In this light, destroying the machine becomes pointless. Those with the political entrepreneurial abilities to do so usually find it more rewarding to try their luck and apply their skills within the system, while the less able go for the passive rents.

This forms the foundation of consensus (or lack of conflict) and defines the limits of discretionary policy-making by the authorities, who are required to feed the rent-seeking game and at the same time generate enough wealth to meet expectations. This context also defines the notion of social responsibility, which reflects the position of the individual within society and the way he perceives and reacts to experience. In a word, social responsibility means that individuals believe they live in an environment in which they are presented with opportunities. However, opportunities are not equally distributed, and a society based on consensus is legitimized insofar as it is able to hand out privileges (freedoms/ rents) to compensate those that can claim to have been the victims of unfairness (bad luck, nature, some forms of exploitation).[61] Put differently, whereas the notion of economic fairness (access to minimum wealth) defines what is needed in order to guarantee consensus and stability, the concept of unfairness defines the point at which individual responsibility ends and taking action becomes a social obligation. It therefore happens that large areas of economic activities fall under the umbrella of social responsibility. Noticeable examples are the labour market, but also health, education, savings (pensions) and even some manufacturing. In this light, for instance, a piece of legislation which creates a rent is no longer perceived as a crime, as it would be in a classical-liberal world, where it would be pointed out that A's privilege is actually paid by the simultaneous creation of a duty imposed upon the rest of community. Instead, it is regarded as an act of collective quasi-compulsory fairness towards individuals who are not guilty for their misfortunes, who are not required to react to overcome their problems or to work hard to reach their goals, or who are simply entrusted with a mission for the common weal. Of course, whenever the agent acts in order to achieve a collective objective, individual responsibility for the outcome declines and the potential cost of failure becomes a cost for society as a whole to bear.[62]

5.5 Summing up: the historical rules in perspective

In a way, the historical approach put forward in these pages does accept the contractarian starting point, in that it recognizes that a society can only be created by individuals, who agree to cooperate in order to obtain a set of goals. And we also believe that the intrinsic strength of a community depends on the extent to which a set of interacting agents believe that cooperation serves their own interests. Likewise, it is fully acknowledged that cooperation works better when institutions are consistent with the purpose of the agreement. For instance, if the goal is economic growth, institutions should protect and enforce property rights and should not distort relative prices, which therefore reflect scarcity and provide suitable incentives to those engaging in entrepreneurial activities.

The difference between the mainstream, the contractarian and the historical projects is where you want to go from there. The neoclassical and the socialist approaches (which include all varieties of third ways)[63] emphasize some notion of social efficiency, ranging from counteracting alleged market failures so as to maximize wealth, to enhancing politically defined priorities, including redistribution. On the other hand, the contractarian agenda is less concerned with defining the social goals. Instead, it tends to underscore the need to constrain policy-makers' abuse by introducing meta-rules, which are determined either behind the veil of uncertainty so as to enhance a quasi-holistic, procedurally flawless solution, or by applying First Principles (e.g. freedom from coercion or solidarity, as noted in Section 5.3.1 above). Within both contexts – mainstream and contractarian – the role of the rule-maker boils down to suggesting and promoting an ideal state of the world.

By contrast, the historical view does not pay much attention to how the world should be, where it should be going or how its rulers should be selected or constrained. This does not deny that a social scientist – or any other human being – can have his own ideas on these issues. But it does mean that an opinion is not a theory and has little or no normative power. Opinions do not explain. If anything, they express personal preferences or informed guesses about risky or uncertain events. In fact, the analytical strategy suggested here focuses on identifying the axiomatic principles that keep a community together, the First Principles characterizing a "historical period"; and on explaining the sets of institutions and policy actions consistent with – and imposed by – those principles. It is surely interesting to detect and possibly quantify the consequences of those rules on aggregate or sectorial economic performance, a task that economic statisticians have been confronting for decades with increasingly sophisticated tools and mixed success. From our standpoint, however, such exercises have an informative/documentary value, but little explanatory or predictive content.[64]

Put differently, although it is not denied that we are living in an imperfect environment, the way the world changes and advances does not depend on the various categories of substantial and/or formal piecemeal solutions that social engineers might suggest. Progress hardly means better social goals or top-down improved meta-rules. Instead, the evolution in political structures and in the attitudes towards policy-making depends on historical accidents and deep institutional changes, which in turn occur as a result of a combination of new ideological constructions, accidents (again), technological progress, decay affecting the previous set of First Principles. One might contend that this perspective smacks of relativism, since First Principles may evolve as a civilization moves from one historical period to the other. Or perhaps one can retort that First Principles remain the same, although the way they are acknowledged changes, thereby affecting human behaviour and interaction. A typical example is the modification in the perception of the sacredness of property rights and the extent to which they can be legitimately encroached upon. Another example is the notion of punishment for criminal behaviour, which in the past was often maiming and death, today is generally imprisonment or relatively mild constraints on the criminal's freedom to move.

Still, the role of the relativist debate within the present context should not be over-emphasized. It is of course true that all normative ambitions necessarily depend on the definition of First Principles, and that according to a large group of political philosophers these are not necessarily eternal. The very fact of continued disagreement on this question across time proves the point. Nonetheless, two additional aspects should be kept in mind. Those who raise the relativist question, no matter which answer they offer, are bound to develop their argument by accepting subjectivism as the basic operational principle of a community. This holds true even when the reasoning is turned on its head, and it is claimed that a principled society is one that offers a collective identity to its members. For even in this case the ultimate judge remains the individual. Thus, concentrating on the subjectivist debate is probably more relevant than coming to terms with social relativism.[65] Besides, this book is about explanations, rather than prescriptions. And explanations require a proper understanding of what communities do, of why they do it. That shows the importance of apprehending the belief structure with reference to which the members of a community operate, of clarifying what policy-making is expected to do, rather than focusing on what it ought to do in order to pursue an abstract goal (e.g. virtue, as the classical Greeks asserted, or peace, as Hobbes claimed, or consensus, as Hayek wrote).

To conclude, in the Western case neither relativism, nor natural law provides an *ex ante* explanation of why the overwhelming majority of Westerners are rather happy with the incumbent political structures.[66] The former is almost tautological, whereas the latter is either ad hoc (when in the Rousseauian sense) or simply remote from the current way of thinking (when in the Gregorian sense). As we have already seen, in the Age of Social Responsibility individuals might not be all satisfied with the prevailing distribution of rents, or with the dominant redistribution patterns of income and wealth, but the presence and desirability of the rent-seeking activities is hardly questioned. The (democratic) procedure through which the rent-seeking structure is to be altered is also generally accepted. This does not imply that the present context is morally sound or coherent. Today's democracies are not a benevolent version of the Hobbes–Leibniz concept of the state.[67] The ruler's assurance of extensive rent-seeking weakly backed up by a legitimate threat of violence should the members of the community refuse allegiance is not a substitute for the seventeenth-century promise to pursue happiness (lack of conflict). Similarly, protection from (which actually means spreading) the cost of uncertainty and accidents is not the same as guaranteeing protection from physical violence. Yet, even if those who believe in everlasting natural laws rightly maintain that these are violated, the substantial firmness of post-First World War Western societies proves that the First Principles typical of the Age of Social Responsibility are being complied with; hence, the features and implications of such principles are crucial when trying to understand the dynamics of norms in general and of normative economics in particular. By contrast, the alternatives are not exciting: as will be put forward in the final paragraphs of this chapter, the contractual, the institutional and the evolutionary approach are of little help in explaining today's policy-making contexts.

5.5.1 On the contractarian shortcomings once again

Starting from Veblen, over a century ago the paleo-institutionalists[68] rightly held that both atomism[69] and holistic institutionalism are fragile starting points for economic theorizing. On the contrary, they maintained that the challenge for any economist (and social scientist, one might add) is to understand the nature and consequences of the rules of the game (institutions) on individual behaviour. The individual, however, is not a *tabula rasa* where rules operate by creating incentive systems. Instead, he is a moral agent who reacts to outside stimuli following his perceptions, preferences and ideologies.

Unfortunately, although lip service is often paid to the paleo-institutional insights, their implications are almost systematically ignored. True enough, these classes of interaction are difficult to grasp, let alone to model or quantify. Still, difficulties do not justify oversight or outright blindness.

The contractarian view is no exception: its advocates are also deaf to the paleo-institutional lesson, with consequences. Earlier on in this chapter it has been shown that the contractarian solutions to the many imperfections of today's policy-making are less than adequate because they strive to legitimize the state through arguments that rely on arbitrary consequentialism, including weak forms of utilitarianism. As a matter of fact, constitutional theories *stricto sensu* include both features: They ultimately validate restricted personal freedom and therefore government action, when this is perceived by the legislator as necessary to obtain the best of all possible worlds. The illusion of the human being tacitly signing the constitutional contract behind the veil of uncertainty de facto empowers the policy-maker to resort to ordinary law-making to pursue a goal that the veil makes sure nobody can really identify. In contrast, the quasi-minimal view does distance itself from consequentialism, but is nevertheless unable to overcome the *liberum veto* problem[70] unless the ruler is endowed with the power to sidestep subjectivism. By doing that, however, even in this case some degree of discretion and utilitarianism must necessarily be accepted.

Last, but not least, contractarian theories say very little about the interpretation of the social contract. If interpretation is subjective, then all contracts become a matter of good will and informal- or self-enforcement (as opposed to coercive enforcement). The state vanishes as a consequence.[71] If interpretation is entrusted to a third party, then designation becomes a political question. It doesn't take much to fear that discretionary powers will be exploited to promote personal advancement and vanity (e.g. making the headlines), to pay political debts, or even to pursue one's honest belief about the real meaning of the constitutional covenant. In other words, the very tools that must be put in place to give the social contract operational content are the instruments that sink it. Recent examples along these lines abound in the American constitutional literature, which opposes those who believe that the Founding Fathers should be read as the authors of a document stating eternal and uninfringeable principles, to those persuaded that the Bill of Rights is a living text that acquires new meanings as time evolves and the notion of morality changes.[72] No matter who is right, there is no gainsaying the rules of the game prevailing in today's American politics are far from those the Founding Fathers had imagined over two centuries ago.

5.5.2   On the institutional temptation

The institutional approach is probably more attractive, in that it escapes consequentialism (and thus utilitarianism), while offering a number of statements with which it is easy to agree: institutions matter, what happened in the past has an impact on individuals' present and future decisions, individuals sometimes take action to modify existing organizations or to create new agencies altogether, formal rules interact and sometimes conflict with informal rules. From the institutional perspective, change takes place in two forms: as a consequence of a shock (e.g. a war) or following a "representational description", that is a situation in which the conflict between informal and formal institutions forces the individual to wake up, abandon the ongoing smooth path-dependent process, and shape new beliefs. When this happens, the old rules of governing interaction with the institutional environment are disrupted and if a new system of social, economic, political variables consolidates, a new path-dependent context comes to the surface (Poirot 1993; Fiori 2002).

The major flaw in the institutional story is the fact that unless one crosses the border into determinism, it offers a description rather than an explanation. As a result, the nature of policy-making must necessarily be left out of the picture, since it is not conceived as the origin of institutional legitimacy. If anything, it is presented as the result of activities carried out by some organizations (including the state) that have been created by groups of individuals with the purpose of reducing transaction costs or of generating and exploiting rents, the only restraint being consistency with the prevailing informal rules. This is plausible when informal rules exist, are firmly in place and openly affect individual behaviour, as exemplified in Ellickson (1991). But it is not very useful when informal rules do not exist (or are almost irrelevant, as it frequently happens in a world characterized by impersonal exchange/transactions), nor is it useful when rule-making is about redistributing income or regulating the relationship between the individual and the state (a citizen's duties and privileges), rather than among individuals. The latter case applies of course to policies in general.

By borrowing the institutional terminology, one could therefore refer to the features of our historical periods as to the institutions typical of the old institutional school. Nonetheless, the notion of path-dependence becomes all but useless, as it is now taken to identify the mechanisms through which, for each historical period, technology and ideology direct the main policy-making actors playing the game of power and competing for power. The rest is a matter of accidents, no matter how important they might be. More important, and contrary to the (old) institutional argument, we maintain that institutions do not greatly affect individual perceptions.[73] Ideas/ideologies do. And when the rules of the game (institutions) run against those perceptions, then society cracks, loses its cohesion, perhaps falls apart while individuals revolt.

5.5.3 Is policy-making evolutionary?

How does our approach compare with the evolutionary approach? According to such view, economics should study how individuals adapt through production, consumption and exchange, led by their efforts to improve their conditions in the presence of variable rules of the game and scarcity.[74] In the past, the emphasis was on the role played by physical constraints (Malthus). Towards the end of the nineteenth century, more importance was devoted to men's way of thinking and to the established social relations (Veblen). More recently, the focus has moved towards the role of legislation and institutions widely understood: for instance, the free market system is one of the possible selection mechanisms, which forces agents to adapt and provides sets of incentives that direct people's actions and reactions, thereby creating a competitive process (Alchian).

All in all, even if mainstream economics maintains a different perspective, it is hard to disagree with the fundamental evolutionary argument: agents do not compete to maximize their happiness (or their profits). Instead, they adapt in order to improve their well-being or avoid worse conditions. The way they do so depends on their psychological patterns, on the behavioural routines inherited from the past, as well as on the characteristics of every human being (against the typical-agent assumption).

Of course, these evolutionary statements are not denied here. Rather, the matter of contention regards the role played by culture, which is here synonymous for mental habits and systematic informal rules of social interaction. From the evolutionary vantage point, culture is subject to gradual change according to a path-dependent process, punctuated by accidents that can eventually alter its speed and direction. Thus, economic life would reflect the evolving nature of culture and scarcity (technology, demography). Yet, from this vantage point, unless one has a theory of cultural path-dependence, social interaction and its developments can only be "explained" *ex post*, which is indeed what happens when one describes. As a consequence, and quite understandably, the evolutionary school has little to say in terms of policy-making, other than claiming that there is scope for intervention whenever the cultural legacy leads people to behave inefficiently,[75] and at the same time warning the rule-maker about the potential damages provoked by the introduction of formal rules that run against the prevailing informal environment.

Put differently, we do not object to the evolutionary (and paleo-institutional) notion, according to which ideologies shape social interaction and affect social dynamics. However, we also claim that the ideological framework does not evolve, but is simply subject to a very limited number of deep changes. Within such ideological framework, a selection mechanism operates, driven by the quest for power and constrained by the current technology. The evolutionary school defines a stable regime as a situation resulting from repeated actions that have proved successful through time, but which continue to be subject to gradual and continuous change. In fact, stability as commonly understood is ruled out almost by definition. Instead, according to our historical perspective, within each historical period stability means constant psychological patterns in accordance with the First Principles of the time, which by definition remain fixed within each period. Interactions might change behavioural features, of course, as a result of new technological opportunities, which sometimes expand the range of possible individual choices, sometimes increase the scope and opportunities for additional policy-making. Nonetheless, feedbacks on the ideological structure are moderate or altogether absent, since the structure remains characterized by the last deep institutional change.[76]

Hence, culture does matter, in that it can be claimed that First Principles define the cultural environment, which amounts to saying that culture counts if one defines this concept as the content of the deep institutional change. And there is no doubt that a community can go through cultural changes. For instance, we conjecture that the West went through three such changes. Similarly, one can make the case for different societies or civilization featuring different cultures, since one presumes that not all societies underwent the same deep institutional change.

But it can also be maintained that culture does not count (much) if one regards it as a system of steady, resilient behavioural patterns dictated by tradition, established informal rules and habits. One can surely observe that people do follow informal rules, for there is no doubt that those informal rules are quickly abandoned when they do not work, or when they become an impediment to obtain higher levels of well-being. An example is provided by generations of immigrants or, more recently, by how quickly young people in post-communist countries have adopted "Western values". Likewise, one can definitely observe habits, such as the use of monetary means of exchange or language. But these can hardly be called "culture" in an evolutionary sense: money is not used because our ancestors used it, but because it is useful and its use makes nobody worse off. In fact, as soon as the technology allowed for new means of payment (e.g. plastic cards with a magnetized strip) many individuals rapidly reduced their use of bills and coins. Similarly, we do not speak a language because our ancestors spoke that idiom, but because that is what our parents taught us and because we find it more difficult to express ourselves in other languages. But there is of course no cultural barrier that prevents millions and millions of people from learning another language in order to make sure that others understand what they are saying or read what they are writing (or vice-versa).

To conclude, we posit that evolutionary economics offers rather limited help in understanding the nature or the foundations of policy-making. Surely, it emphasizes the role of the social environment and predicts that policies evolve according to the way accidents affect – and generate routines that are ultimately incorporated into – culture. Yet, we do not believe this to be enough and we therefore make a different point. That is, we maintain that successful policy-making is about gathering consensus on a fixed set of issues defined by the last deep institutional change. One can of course discuss about how deep a deep institutional change is; or how large consensus must be in order to define First Principles. That is indeed today's challenge for the policy-maker, who might have to look for new ways and identify a new agenda to bolster consensus, should the features of the current historical period weaken.

5.6 A programme for (hard) empirical work

To repeat, our perspective considers historical periods as characterized by the fact that given rules of the game are more or less accepted by the members of a community thanks to a system of shared social postulates, if not ideologies. In each period, such members might not like the ensuing political outcome and might want to have a better system, a better ruling elite, or both. But within each period neither the exercise of power nor the boundaries of power are seriously questioned. With very limited exceptions, not even the procedure to select the ruler is an issue.

In particular, during the Age of Social Responsibility, the prevailing ideology (First Principles) has accepted top-down policy-making for the sake of peace, qualified power sharing, extended rent-seeking, and reduced individual responsibilities within the economic domain. Hence, it is apparent that a society can break down when the rulers are manifestly incapable of avoiding turmoil and/or unable to provide satisfactory opportunities for rent-seeking and/or ask its members to be economically responsible. Put differently, as long as individuals share the First Principles typical of the Age of Social Responsibility, rule-makers confronting a crisis will make the "right" decision in coming to the rescue of those who suffer most, in ensuring that major shocks are avoided, in making promises guaranteeing a soft landing should further disturbances occur. The very fact that these policies make little economic sense is of course irrelevant, for in the Age of Social Responsibility there is little room for efficiency and other text-book criteria (e.g. moderate taxation, little redistribution, concerns for long-run effects such as inflation and moral-hazard).

Reactions to an economic emergency from a (new) contractarian standpoint would be different, for in this context a crisis is actually irrelevant. In the constitutional situation, policy-making should respect the veil of uncertainty, behind which people have ruled out rent-seeking and redistribution. As a result, the principle of individual responsibility is protected and collective/merit goods only are produced. Failure to do just that would imply a violation of the social contract and therefore elicit overt hostility towards the rule makers. The quasi-minimal version would lead to a similar conclusion, with two differences: the Paretian constraint would ensure that the production of collective goods is smaller and – more importantly – legitimate policy-making would not be driven by consensus or (democratic) majorities, but by Paretian straitjackets and thus explicit-consensus guidelines. It then follows that while the constitutional contract has both a (strong) normative and a (mild) explanatory goal, the quasi-minimal contract is merely prescriptive, and thus hardly suitable for empirical verification.[77]

On the other hand, testing the evolutionary approach to policy-making is equivalent to testing the role that an evolving culture plays in determining the nature of state intervention. In this context, the analysis should investigate and compare the changing nature and driving forces of policy-making as culture dictates new requirements and constraints. That implies that such changing nature and driving forces be identified, and that long-term policy trends be cleansed of short-term expedience. Certainly, technological opportunities should also be taken into account, since their presence can potentially generate new evolutionary paths, thereby requiring updated rule-making approaches. Of course, the historical view would simply maintain that there is no substantial change within each historical period (other than those provoked by the new technological conditions). Hence, both the evolutionary and the historical approaches would predict somewhat variable and possibly erratic policy-making. The difference, however, is the question of origin. According to the former view, policy-making is just the result of more or less rapidly changing cultural patterns driven by expanding, technologically-driven sets of opportunities. Still, clear trends should be discernible, with differences across countries or geographic areas. According to the latter view, policy-making consists of a set of ad hoc measures that follow accidental events, normally have a short-term horizon and tend to expand the rule-makers' power without alienating consensus. The tools are diffused rent-seeking and universal access to privileges.

Finally, the institutional approach can also form the object of empirical scrutiny, although some caution is in order. In particular, two theses can be verified. One regards the possibility of institutional change taking place as a consequence of a path-dependent process driven by pressure to lower transaction costs. In other words, the institutional argument is that institutions evolve because technological progress creates new situations and these require new organizational arrangements. Although data gathering may present significant empirical and methodological challenges, the economic statistician should investigate whether transaction costs per unit of exchange (or their weight out of values exchanged) actually follow some kind of monotonic process,[78] controlling for (*a*) the increases in productivity provoked by better technologies (rather than by better institutions), (*b*) the fact that as time goes by, more and more transactions (and transaction costs) are observed just because lower transaction costs make exchange affordable and thus feasible, (*c*) the fact that many transaction costs are not observed and thus are hard to quantify.[79]

The second institutional concept open for investigation refers to the occurrence of institutional change or conflict following acute friction between formal and informal rules, as long as formal rules are relevant, i.e. enforced. This kind of exercise, however, also presents significant problems. For instance, one must differentiate between those tensions generated by formal rules at odds with the informal rules and those created by simply bad (inefficient) rules. The former would provoke a cultural crisis and a systemic shock, whatever these terms mean; the latter would simply require a change in the legislator, or in the incentives that drive the legislators' activities. In some cases, drawing the distinction may be easy; in most cases, it might be quite difficult and identification problems might arise.

Possibly more relevant from a theoretical standpoint is the informal/cultural question. In order to have a conflict between formal and informal rules, one must have resilient informal rules. The early institutional view held that informal rules come first, while good formal rules would and should add transparency, publicity and credibility to sets of agreements based on shared, consolidated values (culture). Hence, formal rules contradicting informal rules would simply be bad rules, which would be amended or would lead to turmoil, as mentioned above. More recently, however, it has been observed that informal rules take time to form and pass the filter of habit and tradition, while fast technological progress often makes behavioural patterns obsolete even before they become stable, shared routines and thus real informal rules. Thus, in today's societies, standardized behaviour never succeeds in becoming an informal rule. And formal rules no longer fulfil the role of codifying informal rules; rather, and in the best scenario, they anticipate the informal rules that would eventually develop, if those patterns had time to go through the time-filtering process. Hence, one might have second thoughts about considering the tensions between formal and informal rules a relevant question, since the potential for conflict then arises when the incentive structures and perceptions generated by technological progress are found inconsistent with the sets of formal rules introduced by the legislators. This includes policy-making, of course. Once again, designing reliable experiments that take these issues into proper account and distinguish the historical hypothesis from the institutional argument (First Principles and ideologies are more powerful than incentive structures in shaping individual perceptions) is not impossible, but is hardly amenable to the current statistical techniques of which economists seem to have grown particularly fond.

6 Legitimacy and efficiency

An introduction to transaction costs and L&E

6.1 Ways out of the legitimacy deadlock

The argument developed so far has focused on three main points. First, the delusive quest for man-made equilibrium has transformed most economists into potential policy-makers in search for the perfect society. As a result, the case for economics-as-a-hard-science has become increasingly popular. In particular, the economics profession has attracted many bright minds who have correctly understood that by combining inductive theorizing and social engineering, one can more easily obtain political status and worldly success broadly understood. Second, policy-making[1] efforts have been justified by referring to men's unfortunate lack of information, to their undesirable and regrettable short-sighted greed (if not outright stupidity), as well as to the impossibility of achieving strategic rationality. Hence – our third point of interest – the case for coercive rules aimed at correcting irrational behaviour and offsetting failures in strategic interaction (and market failures in general) has been forcefully put forward and has occupied a prominent position within most research agendas.

The upshot is that once the need for policies is recognized or accepted, the social scholar is called to come to terms with the problem of coercion, i.e. of drawing the line in order to obtain an acceptable compromise between legitimacy and abuse. As observed earlier in this volume, and as will be recalled in this section, different criteria have been used in this endeavour. Whatever the prevailing standard, all reflect a typical trait of Western societies, in that coercion requires justification. Certainly, this does not imply that the justifications given have always been persuasive or that they have served as effective constraints upon rulers' discretion. In fact, attempts to validate coercion have frequently smacked of exploitation and oppression. Yet, the Gregorian deep change ensured that encroachment upon individual freedom would not be taken for granted. This is actually the essence of the legitimacy question, which still holds true to this day: although nobody doubts that humans suffer from occasional or systematic myopia and rational dishonesty (a subset of opportunism), or that intelligence and talent present significant differences among the population, violent intervention still requires a legitimate explanation.

In truth, the manner in which many economists have taken this requirement into account is barely satisfactory, since they have simply circumvented explanations by referring to the existence of a social utility function to be maximized (the social-efficiency criterion). Maximizing something that remains to a large extent undefined has thus become the dominant operational principle. This is regrettable, for by doing so, the economics profession has actually assumed away one of the very problems – if not *the* very problem – to be addressed by any social science, i.e. the nature of society and of the relations that should characterize personal and impersonal exchange within a community and among communities.[2] This is another reason why economists with prescriptive ambitions should make explicit their philosophic premises. Their failure to do so has produced the major weakness of a significant part of today's normative economics, which oscillates between ad hoc regulation on the one side, and recipes for "optimal" taxation and discretionary monetary policies (including debt financing) on the other. The somewhat confused reaction of the profession to the 2007/2009 crisis – especially within "free-market" quarters – has been a powerful illustration of this lack of consistency.

Economists in search of fundamentals do not need to go very far, though. By and large, the history of political thought has offered three ways to articulate viable solutions to the question of legitimacy. One refers to the paternalistic and socialist arguments, whereby legitimacy is provided by the quest for the individual or the common good, as defined by an "elite", whose claim to rule is based upon its enlightenment by God or by the cannon (the Gregorian and the secular options, respectively), or upon its election (the democratic option). A second response has been offered by the (Ordo)liberal approach, according to which legitimacy is generated by a social contract signed by the whole population behind a veil, which however, upon closer inspection, sometimes looks more similar to an iron gate, as suggested in the previous chapter (Section 5.3).[3] Not surprisingly, since one can imagine different kinds of typical individuals and various thought experiments with different veils, one also comes up with diversified notions of the fair, agreed-upon social environment within which the authorities can rightfully exercise coercive powers in the economic sphere. Finally, a third possibility has been articulated in value-free terms by the classical-liberal scholars: this is the view to which the neoclassical school has subscribed by claiming that intervention is legitimate whenever there exist market failures, technocratic solutions are feasible and government malfunctions are relatively modest.

The conclusion reached in the previous chapter is that the argument for socialist legitimacy is either very strong or not an issue at all. As long as one assumes that society comes first and that human beings can only realize themselves within the context of a community, then there is no doubt that legitimacy originates from the political philosopher's definition of the "true" nature of man and from the ruler's capacity to pursue the ideals of social and individual "virtue" with rigour, no matter how much they cost, as Plato argued when describing ideal states ruled by philosophers-kings or as the visionaries of the

French Revolution advocated at the end of the eighteenth century. But if one assumes that individual liberty is the starting point and the essence of human nature,[4] that a society is no more than the product of men's sociability, or the instrument that they consciously create in order to enhance their individual well-being, then it follows that there is no "true" nature of man outside of one's own preferences. Similarly, there is no such thing as "social virtue" or "common good" prevailing upon individual virtue and individual preferences. When so, there is obviously no room for social(ist) legitimacy, let alone paternalism.

As for the Ordoliberal claim to legitimacy, Chapter 5 has tried to show that its foundations are vulnerable, in that the constitutional perspective[5] requires questionable moral assumptions about the notions of justice, individual freedom, and blind or tacit commitment. One might have doubts about its consistency as well. On one hand, if individual liberty (from coercion) cannot be encroached upon, then norms cannot be coercive, but merely voluntary contracts or informal rules.[6] On the other hand, if man's freedom can be violated for the sake of the collective interest (society), then social values clearly take precedence over individual rights and the socialist perspective should follow. The Ordoliberals actually tend to elude this alternative by redefining and narrowing the notion of liberty (e.g. by making freedom equivalent to the absence of rent-seeking), and by transferring responsibility for the ultimate decision to the constitutional authorities or to democratically elected legislators. In these cases, however, the constitutional veil might shrink and its constraining power might become subject to interpretation, especially if the world behind the veil turns out to be defined by an oligarchy (a constitutional court, for instance) or by constituent politics reflected by an elected legislative assembly.[7]

The neoclassical regulatory ambitions have already been mentioned in Chapters 2 and 3, in which it has been repeatedly shown that the normative implications of that research programme are characterized by the search for static efficiency in a world in which Walrasian perfect competition is not the rule, but is nonetheless the benchmark; and in which wealth is supposed to be dissipated whenever prices deviate from marginal cost. Put differently, within the neoclassical context, static efficiency remains the core of economic inquiry, and social efficiency becomes the element legitimizing intervention, even at the expense of individual liberties, including freedom of contract.

That a substantial number of influential scholars maintain that the best way to serve social efficiency is to refrain entirely from violating the freedom-from-coercion principle (or not to violate it excessively) and thus to preserve private property rights is not denied. But even that is a partly deceptive statement. First, such an argument offers only utilitarian or – better – consequentialist support for freedom and private property, for if it should become apparent that encroachment upon private property enhances growth in key industries, then private property and individual freedom would be violated. A recent example is provided by the hugely popular literature on endogenous growth, which would justify taxation as well as government selection of the winning industries (including education). Likewise, caution is in order when appreciating statements like "judges can hardly avoid using some criterion of social welfare in fashioning rules of decision, and efficiency is a more libertarian criterion than any other I know" (Posner 1975: 777). As a matter of fact, both the view on growth and that on judicial decision apply to the study of the means to obtain given goals. Rather than comparing outcomes, the libertarian standpoint consists in a statement about the moral constraints that characterize human action. Second, much also depends on the manner in which social efficiency is defined, for at one extreme, the term can accommodate some notion of Rousseauian "virtue" and thus ultimately turn towards the socialist vision, while at the other extreme, it can be understood as the pursuit of high GDP growth over an extended period of time, which was the goal of Soviet economics, even on the eve of its collapse.

6.2 From neoclassical institutionalism to L&E

The most important attempts to deal with the efficiency criterion without dodging the issue of legitimacy have been generated by the extension of the orthodox context so as to include an institutional perspective. In other words, rather than merely focusing on imagining Walrasian, perfectly-competitive outcomes and recommending policies to reproduce them,[8] over the past three decades neoclassical economists have reformulated their normative agendas by concentrating on the gap between private and social costs within an environment featuring institutions; and by conceiving suitable, "well behaved" policies and regulatory frameworks.[9] The normative upshot has been that the economist should therefore help design laws and directives so as to (*a*) enhance the creation of wealth that otherwise would be dissipated because of rent-seeking, (*b*) enforce rules of the game so that the benefits of potential exchange are not nullified or lessened by the presence of the so-called "transaction costs", (*c*) modify spontaneously determined property-right arrangements in order to reduce social costs (waste). Point (*a*) forms the primary object of the public-choice literature, while the tradition originated by Coase (1960) has focused on points (*b*) and (*c*) and has represented the essence of the new L&E, which draws on the rationality-based efficiency paradigm to develop and justify a consequentialist, softened approach to institutional design.[10]

From a broader perspective, the L&E normative vision surely represents a break with the past, in that it develops an explicit argument in favour of a new notion of morality, one in which the debate about right and wrong (just and unjust) loses weight and the economist's cost–benefit analysis acquires a moral and prescriptive status. Not only does the new L&E approach underscore that "in a world of scarce resources, waste is regarded as immoral" (Posner 1975: 777), but it also makes clear that

> The demand for justice is not independent of its price. My guess is that when the issue of justice is studied generously and when the many pseudo-justice issues are eliminated, it will turn out that society is in fact willing to

pay a certain price in reduced efficiency for policies (e.g. forbidding racial and religious discrimination) that advance notions of justice, but that society does so to preserve intact the social fabric – to forestall rebellion and other forms of upheaval. I am suggesting, in short, that we will eventually develop a utilitarian theory of justice.

(Posner 1975: 778)[11]

Put differently, the L&E argument developed in three blocks. First, the role of transaction costs was emphasized as the key to understanding economic institutions and economic action.[12] Second, the legacy of sociological jurisprudence supported the refusal of the moral element as an essential component of the legal structure, with two consequences. On the one hand, the twin concepts of harm and victim have become ambiguous: the principle of reciprocity presented in Coase (1960) has ensured that liability ultimately depends on man-made legal ruling. On the other hand, and following Bentham's footsteps, it was argued that morality means social happiness, and that therefore social happiness should be the reference point for rule-making, for the politician as well as for the judge. Hence, property-right assignment and policy-making are eventually justified by consensus – explicit or hypothetical.[13] Third, the contributions (primarily) of Duncan Black and Anthony Downs in the 1940s and 1950s delivered serious blows to the ideal of virtuous democratic policy-making and sparked a rapidly expanding public-choice literature which took for granted that state-enforced rules are needed, but which also affirmed that politicians and bureaucrats are not necessarily the best architects or administrators of such rules. In fact, the L&E solution shies away from political interference and – especially in America and as of the early 1970s – it prefers to assign the responsibility for creating and applying the law to judges. These are perceived as quasi-technocrats, less dependent on short-term, electoral horizons and less prone to create or threaten to create rents by tampering with the idea of the common good and eventually expand the size of the state.[14]

In this light, the following pages do acknowledge the role of externalities and the importance of the institutional questions raised by the divergence between private and social cost. Far from offering a comprehensive review of the huge L&E literature, however, we try to shed light on some key methodological issues that have characterized much of these contributions. Our purpose is to show that such issues in fact involve a number of critical and perhaps questionable assumptions. As a result, the L&E approach might lose some of its free-market appeal or some of its normative strength and reveal itself as an elusive compromise between deceptively neutral cost–benefit analysis and ideologically-biased policy-making.

To illustrate these doubts, the remaining pages of this chapter investigate the nature and operational value of transaction costs, as they are generally treated within the L&E framework. This is of course both necessary and crucial, since the institutional design proposed by the L&E literature is centred on the attempt to minimize these costs and approximate the results presumably obtained through frictionless exchange. Consistent with this analytical purpose, Sections

6.3–6.5 define the components of transaction costs and discuss the way they have been treated within the L&E approach. Section 6.6 argues that the transaction cost (TC) concept is in fact a terminological trick, which should be replaced with the clearer notions of institutional and exchange costs. As shown in Section 6.7, failure to solve this ambiguity runs the risk of stoking encroachment upon individual liberty.

6.3 What is a transaction cost?

Transaction costs are acknowledged as the centrepiece of the L&E programme. They "refer to any use of resources required to negotiate and enforce agreements" (Cooter 1987: 457), they are "associated with the transfer, capture, and protection of rights" (Barzel 1989: 4) and "are incurred when property rights are exchanged in market transactions (based on contracts)" (Kasper and Streit 1998: 197).[15] The basic idea is that if there were no transaction costs and individuals behaved "rationally", a system of smooth, voluntary exchanges would make sure that property rights are transferred to those who value them most.[16] Put differently, once TCs are defined as the costs that prevent Walrasian efficiency from coming true, the absence of TCs would tautologically imply the existence of a perfect world, since this is indeed how most economists would define a perfect world. It might not be Nirvana, since scarcity would not disappear and the possible persistence of natural monopolies might make some people uneasy. Still, it would definitely be a world in which minimal or no improvement can be obtained by outside intervention. In particular, rule-making at large (efficiency-driven assignment of property rights and liability) would make no sense and economics would become either the quantitative handmaiden of political philosophy or the branch of the history of technological progress devoted to assessing the impact of scientific advancement on people's well-being.

There is no need to illustrate that the role of transaction costs is crucial in this reasoning about the departures of the real world from Nirvana. In fact, during the past decades the notion of TCs has been extremely popular. Nowadays TCs are frequently resorted to in order to explain all kinds of undesirable phenomena and feature prominently in microeconomics textbooks. Nonetheless, we maintain that TC economics should be taken with a grain of caution, and that its operational significance might be less important than commonly understood.

It seems appropriate to start our reassessment of the TC notion by looking at where transaction costs apply – exchange. Of course, the very fact that voluntary exchange is desirable reveals that the agents involved present different opportunity costs. This applies to barter, when, at the margin, individual A draws more satisfaction from α units of X than from β units of Y (and is therefore willing to give away at least βY to obtain αX), while the opposite is true for individual B, who is therefore willing to give away no less than αX to obtain at least βY. It also applies to a monetary economy, in which individual A perceives the price of X (Y) as the amount of purchasing power he must sacrifice (can gain) when he buys (sells) one unit of X (Y).[17]

In this light, a transaction cost then usually identifies whatever generates a divergence between a situation in which dreams come true as long as they are compatible with somebody else's dreams (frictionless exchange or, better, preferences compared), and a situation where desires and hopes are stifled, so that part of the anticipated net gains vanishes for at least one of the parties exchanging the good. The emphasis is of course on the so-called deadweight losses: It is therefore ruled out that sacrifices made by one agent are transformed into gains for the other agent, e.g. as a result of bargaining. Obvious examples are the presence of shipping costs or of information costs, which often have to be incurred, but do not provide any direct benefit to the parties originally involved.

Put differently, while carrying out his economic activities, a rational individual sustains categories of expenses that do not relate to physical production and are nonetheless instrumental in making exchange successful.[18] These categories will be analysed in the next two sections, devoted to enforcement, assignment and definition.

6.4 Property-right related TCs: enforcement

As one may have already gathered from our previous reference to the Coase–Posner line of thinking, most L&E authors do not consider property rights as the operational counterpart of the (philosophical) principle of justice,[19] but as instruments created in order to ease human interaction and enhance efficiency, subject to political constraints.[20] This surely applies at an individual level: "property rights arise when it becomes economic for those affected by externalities to internalize benefits and costs" (Demsetz 1967: 354). Nonetheless, the same efficiency-driven, consequentialist vein is also maintained within a more general social context: "the main allocative function of property rights is the internalization of harmful effects" (ibid.: 350). It follows that as long as it is claimed that desirable exchange fails to take place because the instruments are not effective, and as long as TCs are defined as those that prevent desirable, Pareto-improving exchange from taking place, property-right enforcement is necessarily part of the TC set.

Nobody would dispute the above statement. In the L&E perspective, however, property-right enforcement is not a mere police problem, whereby an authority ensures that the rules are complied with. Instead, it turns into an economic problem. In particular, the L&E approach considers the desirability of a rule to be positively correlated with the material benefits it is supposed to generate, and negatively correlated with the cost of its enforcement. Hence, the "efficient/optimal" rule is the rule that maximizes the difference between the wealth agents are in a position to produce by complying with it, and the cost it takes to enforce it.[21] The rationale for this ostensibly amoral view is critical to much of the L&E literature, which considers rule-making and rule enforcement as the optimal solutions to the externality problems. But how robust is this (undoubtedly convenient) amoral view, as a result of which the object of the enforcement may change according to the cost the enforcer must suffer? In order to shed light on this question let us go back to the original issues at the very core of the whole L&E vision: the presence externalities and the solution offered by an efficient distribution of (private) property rights.

Of course, there would be no externalities if resources were abundant: unless A and B both enjoy having a fight, there would be no need for A to take any good away from B, who might instinctively react and strike back. Hence, in a world without scarcity there would be no need to develop and enforce a system of property, as Demsetz made clear. However, when scarcity comes to the surface, it affects all the members of the community who appreciate a scarce good. Following up on that, the crucial logical step implicit in the Coase–Posner tradition is that scarcity emerges as a social question or as a problem within a community. If the community does not introduce institutional answers (private property or centralized regulation), it ends in the tragedy of the commons, loosely identified as the result of compounded externalities.[22] That explains why from the L&E vantage point, the solution cannot depend on subjectivist constraints. In a word, the assignment of property rights is a social answer to the externality problem. It must therefore comply with commonly-accepted social criteria; and the minimization of TCs makes the difference among the various assignment possibilities.

Surely, the recognition and enforcement of private property is the key to peaceful exchange and social cooperation.[23] In particular their role becomes crucial in a world of scarcity. Nonetheless, and contrary to what the quotations offered in the previous paragraph seem to imply, we maintain that property rights are not the institutional reaction to scarcity. Indeed, the very fact that a good is scarce implies that it has been already appropriated and taken away from the common pool. Otherwise it would not be scarce; and there would be no externalities, but only undesirable effects, if any. Along the same line of reasoning, the tragedy of the commons is not generated by the lack of property rights on the final-consumption goods, but by the lack of property rights on the production factors, which in the common-pool case continue to be treated as an abundant resource.[24] Of course, the tragedy can be limited by establishing property rights to final goods, but unless property rights to inputs are appropriated and enforced, the property and output of the final goods can only be determined by some sort of central planner, who is the de facto owner of the production factors.

Certainly, one could predict that a previously unappropriated good might become scarce. If so, he might want to claim property rights to anticipate scarcity. Does this identify a situation in which scarcity leads to property rights? The answer is no: for although the object of his claim might be scarce in the future, it is not scarce when the claim is made, otherwise it would have already been appropriated by somebody else.[25]

These are important qualifications, for a superficial reading of the argument advanced by Demsetz (and much of the property-right literature) might induce the reader to believe that property rights come to the surface as solutions to a problem of social inefficiency, i.e. as the result of the gap between private and social cost. That is not only logically weak, as explained above, but also factually inaccurate. Anthropological studies have shown that scarcity prevented neither the so-called Pleistocene overkill, nor – more recently – over-hunting in most parts of the world, e.g. in Polynesia, Europe, the Americas.[26] Similarly, but from another perspective, commercial law was not created in order to define property rights, but to formalize pre-existing rules of the game accepted by most agents, so that such rules could be enforced more easily and effectively.

Instead, the problem of social inefficiency is solved through the enforcement and exchange of property rights, not through their creation. Put differently, creating property rights is not an issue, since property rights are implicit in the very notion of scarcity. As a result, internalization does not depend on the emergence of property rights, but on the rewards obtained from property-right enforcement and on the costs that enforcement involves, as the L&E cost–benefit approach would suggest. Likewise, evolution does not reward societies that have developed property rights, but societies that have found ways of enforcing them at relatively low cost (and thus overcome the prisoner's dilemma). The difference may look as an exercise in hair-splitting. Yet, it has normative implications of some consequence.

If the creation of property rights follows the appearance of an internalization problem, as the mainstream view would maintain, then it would be reasonable to assume that the definition and assignment of property rights can be formulated as social questions, rather than as matters that concern the individual and have to be decided upon by individuals. By contrast, if the rise of private property rights antedates scarcity, then property remains an individual issue (the Lockean first-user-first-owner principle), rather than a social one. The upshot is that scarcity does make a difference, in that it makes enforcement important and thus makes private property relevant to others. In other words, scarcity explains why owners are willing to incur the cost of enforcing their property rights. From this perspective, however, scarcity does not create rights. To summarize: in the scarcity-first case, property rights can be tampered with by society, for they originate from society; in the second case they can't, for such rights originate from the individual.

These remarks also affect TC theorizing. If enforcement is deemed to be the response to the externality problem, as a cursory reading would suggest, then enforcement is the cost of obtaining efficiency, it affects exchange and should be rightly subsumed under the general heading of transaction costs. But if enforcement is regarded from the alternative standpoint – ensuring that property rights are recognized and protected – then enforcement costs are an "institutional cost"[27] and affect the value of the good one owns. In this light property-right enforcement is not merely a way to ease transactions, but a tool to ensure that spontaneously-born rights are recognized and respected.

The difference between a transaction cost and an institutional cost becomes apparent when one considers that limited protection of property has relatively little consequences on the satisfaction generated by goods and services consumed immediately, whereas it definitely affects the expected value of goods and services to be consumed in the future. One may not be concerned about the protection of his property of the cookie he is about to eat in a few seconds. But one might worry if the cookie is left unattended on a desk in a kindergarten for a few hours. If so, it is clear that the quality of enforcement does not concern just the cost of carrying out a transaction, but rather what one can reasonably expect to benefit from owning something which could possibly be snatched away or damaged without full compensation, independent of whether such resource is exchanged in the future. In a word, institutional costs affect the structure of opportunity costs in general and the market for property-right enforcers in particular.[28]

6.5 Further TCs related to property rights: assignment and definition

As mentioned earlier, two other concepts frequently recur in the transaction-cost literature: the assignment and the definition of property rights. As a matter of fact, we deliberately ignore the assignment issue, which in our view is neither a transaction, nor an institutional problem. If anything, it is a meta-institutional question, about the grand rules of the game. In a free society property is not assigned. It is acquired by individuals through their very actions: either as a result of a contract, or by appropriating previously non-scarce resources. In contrast, in a socialist society the collective body is assumed to have priority over the individual. Clearly, in the latter case "society" owns all resources by default, and goods and services can subsequently be partially or totally assigned to its members according to political criteria (including absolute discretion by the ruler/dictator). And of course they can also be taken away from them. Put differently, in a free society, nobody is entitled to assign any property to anybody, whereas in a socialist society the state has property and can temporarily transfer it to individuals, or allow individuals to keep part of what they find or create. There is no third possibility and nothing else should be added. To illustrate this point, we refer to two well-known examples presented in Demsetz (1967: 348–349): slavery and the draft. Contrary to Demsetz's argument, from our perspective slavery was not inefficient because slaves were not allowed to buy their freedom. Rather, it was inefficient because the state rules insisted on assigning property rights that in a free society could have never been created, let alone assigned. In other words, the economic problem of slavery was neither a question of poor/inefficient property-right assignment, nor of exceedingly high transaction costs. Rather, it was the problem of a system which assumed that "society" owned the slaves (as opposed to a situation where each person owns him/herself), distributed them to the slave masters according to a set of default rules and enforced the distribution of its property.[29]

Similarly, it is not entirely accurate to describe the introduction of the military draft as a veto on transactions. The draft actually means that the government owns a man's time during a given period of his life and can thus legally force him to serve in the army. If the draftee pays his way out (e.g. by corrupting a medical officer who certifies his alleged inability to serve), then a transaction takes place. If not, it means that the price is too high and the young man has to comply with the owner's wishes. Once again, property rights are assigned (to the government) and transaction costs are negligible, for they boil down to finding out how much should be paid and to whom. The problem is not a question of non-internalization. Rather, this situation implies that rulers deem that the draft-ee's service is infinitely valuable to the community at large; and that sometimes a bureaucrat breaks the rule – breaches the contract with the state – if rewarded adequately. In other words, what Demsetz defines as a preclusion to internalize externalities because of high transaction costs is in fact his own understandable disagreement with the evaluation of a young man's time by the government.[30]

As for the second concept, the task of improving the definition of property rights was first mentioned by Hardin (1968) and has become the object of renewed attention over the past decade, especially after De Soto (2001) pointed out that in many countries accumulation and development have been hampered by the inability to demonstrate property rights. In particular, De Soto's point is well taken and has the merit of showing that property rights are not relevant just for the rich: Their role is in fact crucial for development as well. But that is only part of the story, since it remains to be assessed whether the assets are absent or "dead" – to use Hardin's and De Soto's vocabularies, respectively – just because they are not defined, or because property is not protected and contracts are not enforced. The view taken here is that the latter situations are more likely to apply: we believe that long-term investment is discouraged (dies) not only because agents do not know who owns the fixed capital or the land; but also because both the capital and its fruits are too vulnerable to expropriation;[31] including – and sometimes primarily – by the government itself, of course.

To conclude, the importance of the costs other than those incurred in sheer production is beyond dispute. As explained in Sections 6.3 and 6.4 above, however, if one wants to understand why differences in preferences and skills do not always generate exchange, Coasean TCs can be put aside without too much harm and two sets of different elements brought forward. One set refers to those variables – the costs of exchange – that produce a divergence between opportunity-costs in a Nirvana world and opportunity-costs in reality. Still, these are no different from any other cost required to produce goods and services and deserve no particular attention. A second set relates to those factors that have been here named institutional costs and that relate to enforcement. No more than that: other alleged TC categories – such as those relating to the assignment and definition of property rights – are in fact a misunderstanding and can be misleading.

One may thus wonder about the motivation to keep Coasean transaction-costs alive. After all, by attaching the TC label to whatever stands in the way of an individual making his dreams come true, one runs the risk of confusing a tautology with an explanation, and possibly creating ambiguities. For instance, a separate treatment devoted to transaction costs necessarily implies a rather narrow notion of production, in that one must imagine that all the accessory acts of exchange have already been dealt with (or will be dealt with separately): inputs have been acquired and are ready to be used, all outputs have already been sold and the buyers are lined up to collect them.[32] We devote the final sections of the chapter to answering this question.

6.6 Transaction costs, true and false

Let us start from the irrelevance of transaction costs mentioned above, and ponder why the costs of exchange should be so distinctive as to deserve being singled out for special investigation. There is no doubt that exchange comes into the picture whenever an individual wants to alter his own condition by peacefully interacting with others over the creation and use of resources. This is actually what scarcity implies for economic action. If resources (including time) were not scarce, there would be no need to exchange.

Now, when the individual acquires goods and services that he is unable or unwilling to produce and that do not fall on his lap from the sky, he obviously considers how much it costs to consume what he is about to buy, for the ultimate goal is consumption, not purchase.[33] That includes the expenses incurred in order to obtain information, to negotiate, to have the goods delivered. Put differently, information, contracting, manufacturing, shipping, rewarding innovation are all part and parcel of the same game – satisfying needs/desires at the lowest possible cost. Hence, when economics is understood as a set of exchanges, manufacturing and production lose much of their relevance as specific categories of expenditures: for even the "producer" is actually exchanging goods and services that are themselves the result of an exchange mechanism, as Coase (1937) himself acknowledged.

Thus, TCs would perhaps make a difference if the ultimate goal was ownership per se, not consumption. Otherwise, TCs are just the same as "the traditional treatment of transportation costs in the already existing literature … transaction costs are productive in precisely the same way that resources used up in the physical transformation of inputs into outputs are productive" (Dahlman 1979: 144–145). In other words, in any world the opportunity costs of X correspond to the value of everything that individual A must actually give away in order to obtain one marginal unit of X. And it is apparent that "everything" should also include the value of the time and resources devoted to acquire information, to searching and to contracting. Hence, the opportunity cost of X for individual A is not the inverse of his opportunity cost of Y. Once all the exchange costs have been taken into account, it may well be that A, who is willing to get X, actually finds out that his opportunity cost of X referred to Y only (Ya/Xa) is in fact lower than his potential counterparts' opportunity cost of X (Yb/Xb); or higher, when interested in acquiring extra units of Y. When that happens, no exchange takes place.[34] No more is required.

Why then should one articulate an opportunity-cost based theory of exchange if some of the relevant costs are left out, and then fill the gap by a terminological trick? Of course, we do not deny that each potentially desirable transaction actually involves costs that are suffered in different time periods by various actors.

Some of these are sunk costs and could turn out to be deadweight losses, should the last step of the transaction – contract enforcement – fail to be completed satisfactorily. Still: Is there really a need to rename fixed and potential sunk costs as "transaction costs"?

Of course, things are different when it comes to contract enforcement: the expenses related to which are indeed special, since they fall outside the domain of mutually voluntary exchange and apply only after the will of the contracting agents has been expressed, accepted, and all the sunk cost of exchange have been incurred. In fact, contract enforcement is the cost of protecting individual liberty, rather than of carrying out an economic activity.[35] Once again, that explains why enforcement costs are here ascribed to the class of institutional costs,[36] together with those incurred to protect property rights in general. As a matter of fact, neither group – enforcement nor protection of rights – forms the object of the transaction, but both make the transaction more or less attractive by affecting expectations about the possibility of being cheated and about the value of what is being exchanged.

6.7 Exchange costs, institutional costs and policy-making

To repeat and summarize the argument put forward in the previous paragraphs, by identifying transaction-cost economics as a branch on its own, the distinction between the political and the economic domains has been strengthened. In particular, this logical construction has offered theoretical support to the argument according to which economic growth does not depend on the nature of the political regime, but on the ability of the political regime to enhance low transaction costs: "The success stories of economic history describe the institutional innovations that have lowered the costs of transacting and permitted capturing more of the gains from trade and hence permitted the expansion of markets" (North 1990: 108). A typical example is the present interest in the costs of the bureaucracy, which has led to repeated efforts aimed at reforming the administrative machine, making it better and corruption-free; with little regard to whether these reforming attempts are at all compatible with the First Principles characterizing the Age of Social Responsibility. Not surprisingly, the results have been modest and little thought has been devoted to considering the origin of failure.

Furthermore, since Coase (1960) cast new light on the economics of transaction costs, the economic profession has striven to give theoretical support to efforts aiming at finding optimal institutional arrangements to internalize externalities and, more generally, to fix alleged market failures. Although this might not have been Coase's original aim, his contribution in fact ended up supporting the view according to which under some circumstances government property is wealth-enhancing (and thus legitimate, in a utilitarian perspective).[37]

Finally, over the past few decades constitutional economics has almost become a branch of macroeconomics and ultimately an issue of optimal institutional design (the object of modern political economy) developed upon all but collectivist utilitarian foundations. However, by merging the exchange and the institutional costs into one category (TCs), constitutions turn out to be less the tool to protect the individual from external aggression by other individuals as well as by government, than the instrument to protect rational (optimal) policy-making from populist interferences. By doing so, the gap between the classical and neoclassical branches of Ordoliberalism is all but bridged. Still, even if the design of the bridge may appear elegant, one wonders whether its foundations are very firm.

We have put forward a much simpler alternative by positing that economic action – defined as man's behaviour with the purpose of increasing his welfare under scarcity constraints – entails two categories of expenses: exchange and institutional costs. The former refer to what it takes to satisfy our needs, once we decide to explore the possibility of exchanging. The latter consist of monitoring and enforcement: they are the cost of defending our liberty.[38] Of course, liberty is not necessary for exchange to take place. But the effectiveness with which liberty is preserved affects opportunity costs.[39] The replacement of TCs with exchange and institutional costs not only clarifies an important methodological point. But it also calls attention to the fact that from a free-market perspective, governmental intervention should aim at fixing institutional failures, rather than market failures; and that exchange costs are more likely to be reduced by voluntary cooperation, rather than by coercive centralized action.

7 The normative agendas of the L&E approach

7.1 From transaction-cost economics to Coasean L&E

Transaction-cost economics is certainly at the very core of modern institutional economics and Coase is surely recognized as one of its fathers. Nonetheless, as we have underscored in the previous chapter, the methodological foundations of this approach are not entirely satisfactory, especially from a free-market vantage point. In this chapter, however, we shall argue that other theoretical features of Coasean economics – reciprocity, the departure from uncompromising subjectivism, the potential welfare-enhancing mission of the authority – are fragile and do little to provide clear normative prescriptions. As a consequence of these underlying ambiguities, the flexibility of the Coasean perspective has generated different institutional visions, most of which share an effort to set guidelines for the policy-making authorities and possibly put a limit on arbitrariness. This chapter considers two broad sets of agendas developed in that vein. One plays down the social components of transaction costs and casts severe doubts on the scope for rule-making (Section 7.2). The other analyses Posner's and Epstein's more "pragmatic" solutions (Section 7.3). The hidden methodological assumptions and implications of the different visions will then be summarized and reassessed in Section 7.4, while Section 7.5 draws some conclusions with regard to the role of the judiciary and the transition from the rule of law to the law of rules typical of the Age of Social Responsibility, a transition to which the L&E perspective has surely contributed.

To begin with, let us examine the thrust of the Coasean argument, as it emerged from Coase (1960). Four points are relevant for our discussion:[1]

- Economic actions often produce undesirable effects. In particular, production may involve costs that are imposed on third, "external" parties, without their consent.[2] Under such circumstances, two different situations may emerge. When actor A is liable, then the third party C has a right to ask for compensation, or to require that A discontinues his activity. If A is not liable, then C can either suffer the damage or buy the discontinuance of A's activity. Thus, harm can be provoked both by acting (production of goods and services) and by preventing an agent from acting; and there is no victim until the assignment of property rights (and thus liability) is clarified. This is the essence of the Coasean so-called reciprocity principle: "the harm recognized as a negative externality should be interpreted as reciprocal" (Fox 2007: 388).

- If all men act rationally (that is, they are not subject to emotions, passions, whims) and if all goods and services can be exchanged at given prices, which are constant and the same for all the members of the community (perfect competition with zero transaction costs),[3] then exchange will take place and property rights on the scarce resources will be transferred to those who can use them in the most profitable way. As a result, under these conditions, exchange guarantees that resources are allocated efficiently and that efficient allocation "maximise[s] the value of production", i.e. social wealth (Coase 1960: 6). In particular, the initial allocation structure of ownership/ wealth does not prevent exchange from obtaining the allocation of resources that maximizes social wealth.

  This defines the economic perspective on the role of the judge in a zero-transaction-cost environment, which consists in defining and assigning property rights: "the immediate question faced by the courts is *not* what shall be done by whom *but* who has the legal right to do what" (Coase 1960: 15).[4]

- On the other hand, when impediments to trade exist, but the outcome of a theoretical transaction is nonetheless deemed desirable, then the judge should intervene, examine various possible property-rights structures and assign rights so as to reproduce the desirable outcome: "the proper procedure is to compare the total social product yielded by these different arrangements" (Coase 1960: 34).[5]

  In other words, the authority should carry out cost–benefit analysis the proper way (whatever that means)[6] and assign property rights and liabilities *also* by considering the outcome of such analysis. That applies whenever transaction costs are positive, even if they are not high enough to prevent the transaction from taking place: "even when it is possible to change the legal delimitation of rights through market transactions, it is obviously desirable to reduce the need for such transactions and thus reduce the employment of resources in carrying them out" (ibid.: 19).[7]

- Government regulation may be desirable when exchange is difficult and cooperation among the various actors cumbersome. In these cases government intervention is justified in that it enhances social production. This applies even when it may entail "legalized nuisance", although "it is all a question of weighing up the gains that would accrue from eliminating these harmful effects against the gains that accrue from allowing them to continue" (ibid.: 26).[8]

In the end, once all ambiguities are netted out, the essence of the Coasean L&E programme remains the reciprocity argument: the victims are not necessarily those who suffer from the voluntary but not evil-meaning effects provoked by those who carry out some kind of economic activity. In this light, and quite simply, the role of the judge is to decide who owns what, so that interaction and exchange may take off. In fact, following Coase, in a world with perfect information and knowledge the mainstream economist would even tolerate judiciary oversights and mistakes, since in a "perfect" world featuring symmetric exchange, which therefore excludes endowment effects and in which the opportunity cost of X is the inverse of the opportunity cost of Y, resources will end up maximizing the value of social production no matter how the judge assigns property rights.[9]

The other components of Coasean economics apply to the real (imperfect) world, but their functioning is far less precise and the consequences they generate unsatisfying. In this imperfect context, reciprocity no longer guarantees that the judge has mere redistributive functions, since when exchange is less than seamless, the distribution of property rights affects the final allocation of resources. Under such circumstances, decision-making by the judicial and the political authorities should be inspired by the criteria of wealth-creation, social and institutional efficiency and stability (Coase 1960: 19). Justice and morality play little or no role at all.[10]

From a broader perspective, one could remark that this approach is still compatible with some sort of consequentialist free-market view. For instance, one could rely on public-choice reasoning and argue that by allowing the judge or the legislator to depart from wealth maximization, one might end up with unpleasant surprises. Nonetheless, Coase's caution and qualifications cannot hide that much of his normative lesson also implies a substantial departure from subjectivism:[11] Coasean actors always consider that the value of the good to them is no greater than the market value of its marginal use.[12] Thus, the consumer's surplus has all but disappeared, which is somewhat paradoxical, since the very notion of efficiency is not about maximizing production, but rather about maximizing the surplus enjoyed by the individuals (Rizzo 1979/1980).

The departure from subjectivism is not without consequences. When one takes into account the possibility that the value of the good is greater than the market value of its marginal use, which is in fact what happens in everyday life with final-consumption goods, then anything can happen: for instance, A might not be able to buy a million-dollar house from B, even if A likes that house more than B (i.e. that house is more valuable for A than for B). When so, the allocation of property rights matters even if "transaction costs are zero", as Block rightly emphasized. But it also matters if A is able to buy the house from B. To illustrate this point, suppose that individuals A, B and C initially own Y, X and $100, respectively. Y and X have each a market price of $100. Now, suppose that A wants to buy X, which gives him a surplus of 10, while Y offers him a surplus of 5 only. Assume also that Y generates a surplus of 3 to C, who is indifferent between $100 and X. Finally, B is indifferent between having X, Y or $100. Then, individual A decides to sell good Y to C, so as to obtain $100 necessary to buy X from B. Now, this round of transactions has led to a situation where A's welfare has risen to 10 (+$100 worth of X) and C's welfare has increased to 3 (+$100 worth of Y). On the other hand, if A had owned X and Y from the start, A would have had a surplus of 15 (+$200 worth of X and Y); B would have had nothing and C would have had $100 in his pockets. No trade would have taken place, but the distribution of the surplus across the community would have been different: in the previous example it was 13 (+$200 worth of goods), whereas now it is 15 (+$200 worth of goods). The upshot is that even when one accepts the utilitarian standpoint (according to which personal feelings can be compared following an objective standard and added up), once subjective values are taken into account, the absence of "transaction costs" is not enough to bring about social-wealth maximization.[13]

To sum up, although much of the literature has actually focused on the implications of the zero-transaction cost hypothesis, Coase's assumed equivalence between subjective value and market value is at least equally important and "heroic", since it often happens that for at least one party the value of the good is actually prohibitively greater than the market value of his marginal productivity.[14] However, these two acts of heroism lead in different directions. When one drops the zero-TC assumption, one is forced to face the utilitarian dilemma that indeed characterizes much of the L&E context.[15] Whereas if one drops subjectivism, one must necessarily give in to (hopefully benign) forms of central planning.

Hence, one does not need to accept Becker's or Posner's extreme positions to see why the original L&E message has appealed more to the "scientific" researcher engaged in cost–benefit investigations related to market transactions among identical individuals (the typical agent once again), rather than to the post-marginalist economist aware of the difference between value and price. In particular, the mainstream economist was well aware that

> if you can persuade a judge or jury that it is in the general public's economic self-interest to allow your client to steal income from another person's property, then scientific economics teaches that you are helping to restore economic efficiency.
>
> (North 2002: 76)

By contrast, "less progressive" lawyers and old-style institutionalists have remained perplexed.[16] On the one hand, technocratic functionalism is not necessarily a good substitute for rights, especially when legal systems are deemed to be based on – or at least constrained by – some overarching moral code. On the other hand, the more arbitrary and the more frequent the assignment or reassignment of property rights, the more likely are the tensions between formal and informal rules and the less reliable are the formal rules themselves, by definition. From an institutional perspective, both phenomena are hardly conducive to social wealth (whatever it means) and economic growth.[17]

All in all, the ambiguities of the original Coasean approach make it difficult to assess how far the normative ambitions of social cost–benefit analysis can go within the L&E context. After all, although Coase (1960) opens the door to technocratic accounting to deal with externalities, Knight's lesson and teaching are not altogether forgotten (Coase 1960: 43). As a result, the L&E literature has unfolded in at least three different directions: one has emphasized the need to intervene in order to reduce transaction costs, another one has underscored the ability of the market to do better than the regulator, a third one has suggested a more pragmatic approach, *pace* for principles and fine tuning. The next two sections try to shed some light on the consequences that have ensued.

7.2 The first L&E agenda and the institutional legacy

As a matter of fact, the normative consequences of Coase's solution to the TC problem were not so evident at its inception. Part of the explanation is perhaps due to the fact that the institutional facet was perceived as dominant. Put differently, the less-than-sweeping normative content of Coase (1960) and Calabresi (1961) ensured that the L&E message was more institutional than Posnerian (as we would say today). It emphasized that the distribution of property rights has economic consequences.[18] It showed that the distribution of property rights affects the production of goods and services for material consumption; and also illustrated that economic performance ultimately depends on making exchange possible, i.e. on extending the range of goods that can become the object of voluntary exchange. But it went no further than that, consistent with the very environment in which modern L&E was born: pre-Coasean Chicago and Virginia.[19]

Indeed, although the Posnerian view ultimately prevailed on both sides of the ocean,[20] the original mistrust with regard to government encroachment has remained clearly discernible in at least two different L&E approaches, which have subsequently evolved into disciplines in their own right. One strand, led by Henry Manne's pioneering work, has analysed sets of contracts that did not present particular issues in terms of "transaction costs", but that have nevertheless been subject to increasingly popular regulatory intervention, generally for the sake of efficiency. Corporate governance and financial-markets regulation are typical examples.[21]

A different research programme has been developed by Oliver Williamson, who also ignored most of the Coasean view on transaction costs and clarified instead that "transaction costs" are in fact the cost of cooperating, i.e. the cost of avoiding opportunistic behaviour: "opportunism is a central concept in the study of transaction costs", while the economics of transaction costs explains "the main governance structures of transactions, and indicates how and why transactions can be matched with institutions in a discriminating way" (Williamson 1979: 234). From this standpoint, therefore, L&E can indeed be approached as a branch of new institutionalism: a research effort on the origin and features of complex contractual agreements designed to reduce opportunism under different monitoring conditions.

These perspectives help us understand that the L&E and the new institutional school differ on a crucial point: causality. The main subject matter of L&E is how the rules affect economic performance. Under such circumstances, technological progress and possibly political ideologies define the optimal property right structure, thereby reversing the earlier direction of causality maintained by the old institutionalists. The new institutional school, on the other hand, pays attention to both mechanisms: how institutions affect human behaviour, and how economic events affect the evolution of rules and of organizations, including property rights. More generally, the (new) institutionalists investigate the interaction mechanisms between the two areas, thereby including also the role of politics typical of the public-choice approach.

Yet, with the passing of time the new institutionalists have de facto frequently neglected Manne's and Williamson's contributions and warnings.[22] Instead, they have become open to the possibility that the rule-makers (judges or legislators) intervene in order to reduce the costs involved in new sets of transactions made possible by technological progress. With its emphasis on technological efficiency as the engine of growth, and by admitting that the rules of the game must adjust to the new technologies, the Coasean L&E contribution to institutional economics has eventually come to the surface as an ongoing encouragement to monitor and/or fine-tune the property-right structure, even at the expense of the freedom-of-contract principle.

In contrast with these views, and consistent with Manne's and Williamson's agendas, we suggest that the "institutional problems" of a dynamic society are simply a matter of institutional costs, as defined in Chapter 6. The engine of growth is not technological progress, but entrepreneurship, while the way entrepreneurial efforts are translated into economic growth depends on the ease and cost of cooperating. As a result, the rule-maker should abstain from tampering with entrepreneurship,[23] acknowledge that the costs of cooperation can only be assessed by the contracting parties, and understand that cooperation ultimately depends on the ability to secure and enforce property rights and contracts, which include both the transfer of rights and commitments to act or not act. In particular, the role of the judge is to find out what is to be enforced (as argued in Leoni (1961) and Hayek (1960)), reduce the cost of enforcement and apply general principles in order to provide "just" solutions when property rights are in doubt.

A fitting example of the difference in these two institutional readings is provided by the treatment of idiosyncratic exchanges that involve significant sunk costs at the beginning of a project[24] and generate streams of benefits over an uncertain future. According to the Coase theorem, idiosyncratic exchanges per se are not relevant since they do not relate to divergences between private and social costs, i.e. they do not involve externalities associated with property rights. Nonetheless, a Coasean institutional view would lead one to focus on the existence of high transaction costs as the origin of opportunism, which might prevent the market from doing its job – i.e. ensuring that a mutually beneficial contract is completed – with subsequent losses of wealth. This would justify government intervention: Bureaucrats or government-controlled managers would be called upon to act as fair, non-opportunist producers of the goods that fail to be supplied because of their underlying idiosyncratic-exchange requirements. Alternatively, the judiciary might be relied upon to establish and enforce strict liability rules in order to reduce the cost of uncertainty for one of the contracting parties.

In short, contracts would be created and enforced when deemed socially desirable.

Our perspective differs, in that any contract must follow an explicit voluntary agreement. Once the parties involved consider a transaction desirable, the transaction takes place if the enforcement of property rights identified by the parties involved (which includes Williamson's concern for how idiosyncratic transactions are described and monitored) is credible; and if the counterpart's behaviour is reliable (especially when all contingencies cannot be predicted – incomplete contracts). The latter case is of course what cooperation is about: a matter of trust, reputation, default routines defined by statutes or by precedent, but which can also be bypassed by the cooperating parties if they decide otherwise. From this vantage point, the institutional challenge is thus restricted to two issues: the enforcement of existing rights and of the agreed-upon transfer of rights on the one hand, and the introduction or application of default criteria of adjudication on the other. Clearly, since the object of the contract is not always the same, it often happens that different contractual features emerge from negotiation. In our view, however, this is where the analysis should call it a day. In particular, it should stop short of drawing the distinction between market and non-market (hierarchical) arrangements, which is not persuasive and perhaps even misleading, as it gives the impression that some agency should step in whenever the market is unable to fill the spaces.[25] When cooperation fails to materialize, the key to proper understanding is bad enforcement (high institutional costs), not transaction costs.[26] Transaction costs as traditionally understood merely describe technical impossibilities and are therefore a synonym for wishful thinking, with little or no operational value.

To conclude, Manne's and Williamson's perspectives are complementary, in that they both underscore the role of the institutional costs in enhancing cooperation. And of course, they oppose Holmes's, Becker's and Posner's wealth-maximizing drive, to which both the legislator and the judge should to a large extent acquiesce. As a result, the former view considers the L&E approach as a method to understand how different property-right regimes affect economic action. Not surprisingly, the normative implications are cautious and tend to focus on the credibility of the commitment and the predictability of human behaviour. The latter view, on the other hand, understands the purpose of social-science scholarship to be the design of social arrangements that pursue some pre-defined objective. This is sometimes conceived in terms of general equilibrium, as in the neoclassical tradition; sometimes in terms of partial equilibrium, closer to Coase's, Calabresi's or Demsetz's perspective; sometimes by referring to more politically-tainted objectives such as consensus (Holmes and Posner).[27]

It is apparent, however, that as soon as one leaves the Posnerian guidelines, the policy-making implications of the L&E approach become ambiguous. There is no doubt that most of its founders are generally considered staunch advocates of the free-market principles. Still, this is not entirely correct. If in order to qualify as a free-market supporter one must believe that the price mechanism is generally the best welfare-enhancing mechanism to allocate scarce resources, and that the burden of proof that legitimizes some kind of coercive intervention by a third party – either the state or the judiciary – necessarily falls on the proponent of the alternative, then it is true that most L&E supporters would qualify as free-market advocates. However, this is a rather porous filter, for the litmus test is the definition of welfare. If it is accepted that free-market economics requires a subjectivist approach to welfare, then the rules should aim at protecting individual liberty, including property rights and freedom of contract, no matter what.[28] In this light, however, most L&E authors would not qualify under the free-market banners. On the other hand, if the notion of social welfare is introduced as a concept in its own right, worthy to be pursued independent – or in spite – of some individuals' happiness, then suitable combinations of justice and efficiency may actually play a critical part in the definition of satisfactory solutions. From this standpoint, the L&E contribution is useful and promising. The consequence, of course, is that morality is replaced by some form of pragmatism: "just" actually means "fair"; and "efficient" means "to the best of the decision maker's knowledge".[29]

7.3 The second legacy: pragmatic L&E

If one must articulate operationally normative guidelines rooted in the Coasean L&E lesson, it is impossible to do without pragmatism: rule-making must show some degree of consistency and comply with common sense (consensus). If anything, the role of the social scientist is to point out when discretion becomes arbitrariness and possibly to suggest procedural solutions on how to provide adequate protection to that effect. The discussion of the role of coercive norms has already been presented in Chapter 4, while the constitutional possibilities of defining appropriate boundaries have been the object of Chapter 5. In this section we set out to evaluate the nature and consistency of the pragmatic choices, without venturing into the area of moral judgement. In particular, Section 7.3.1 below puts forward a critical overview of Posner's approach, which rejects traditional, centralized constructivism, but considers the law as an incentive system, supports moral relativism and sometimes draws near to populism. This is compared to the alternative pragmatic view in Section 7.3.2, according to which Epstein tries to conflate the principle of individual liberty with the need for cost-minimizing default rules, *pace* for optimality and fine tuning. This will enable the reader to draw some "grand lessons" from the L&E vision (Section 7.4) and evaluate their role within the historical perspective outlined in Chapter 5 (Section 7.5).

7.3.1 Posner's pragmatism

The traditional constructivist strand in economics would claim that some sort of command system delivers better results by comparison to what can be obtained by groups of voluntarily-interacting individuals. This may happen because of irrational behaviour and opportunism made possible by market failures (the neoclassical view), or because people do not perceive that there is a common interest worth to be pursued for its own sake, such as income equality or the eradication of greed and envy (the socialist view).[30] The most popular L&E pragmatic approach differs from both. This Holmes–Posner tradition assumes that we live in an imperfect world in which the quest for perfect solutions is vain, if anything because the very notion of perfection implies the definitions of a standard, which is also necessarily subjective and therefore unsuitable to be applied uniformly to a community. Hence, when courts are to rule, the Holmes–Posner view is that judges must apply a notion of justice which coincides either with what in a given historical moment people consider to be acceptable (moral relativism), or with what serves the purpose of obtaining widely approved-of results (populism).

The borderline between the two is thin. In essence, it depends on whether one wants to attach a moral connotation to the rule-making process. But one can confidently claim that the Posnerian L&E view is squarely consequentialist, consistent with the Beckerian (and positivist) amoral approach to economics. According to this perspective, the purpose of a legal system is not the protection of a principle, such as an a priori notion of justice (e.g. the protection of the individual from others' unjust conduct), for "truth" does not exist, and thus the very notion of meta-principle does not exist. Rather, the law should be framed in order to allow human beings to pursue their goals (material well-being). Therefore, the law and the legal systems are effectively one, an incentive system that allows a social body to obtain an agreed-upon (or agreeable-upon) purpose: efficiency, fairness or wealth.

Nonetheless, the essential feature is not the choice of the goal. Although Posner himself has indeed been repeatedly criticised for his emphasis on social wealth, this is not the real issue. Instead, the core question is whether the legal system should be seen as a satisfactory set of incentives, or whether it should be conceived as a moral system, to protect society and what could be defined as social virtue, or to protect the individual and his liberty from coercion. Once again, Posner's answer is clear: his system goes for the first option. Hence, positivist economics necessarily dominates in this framework and the legal scholar is encouraged to engage in what-if exercises leading to sets of predictable and falsifiable potential outcomes. In this light, justice means that there is an a priori known and stable super-criterion according to which the "just" outcome is selected. In other words, justice ultimately relates to the features of the selection process, rather than to those characterizing the goal. Justice is procedural rather than substantive. With regard to substance, the Posnerians choose wealth, which is convenient because it is somewhat measurable, it is amenable to the Kaldor–Hicks compensation criterion[31] and it is easily agreed upon: Who would not agree on rules that enhance personal wealth? Not surprisingly, unless one is willing to accept the Austrian extreme outlined below, the Posnerian default super-rule seems to be all but irresistible (Harnay and Marciano 2003).

The Austrian alternative as represented by Bruno Leoni and (to a lesser extent) Hayek, asserts that the judge's task is to "discover" the law.[32] In particular, the

Austrian notion of the law relates to a system of formal and informal rules that define just behaviour, where "just" is a negative concept that ultimately means refraining from violating man's freedom from coercion. This is the criterion according to which the line between just and unjust is drawn, as well as the principles according to which, when it comes to torts and crimes, the legal system must provide for compensation and reasonable punishment to discourage injurious behaviour. Whatever one may think of the Austrian desiderata, however, this is not the way most judges see their role. In civil-law contexts, the judge is clearly supposed to apply legislation, not the "law". When legislation is not precise enough, he is supposed to fill the gaps and find out what the legislator actually meant, i.e. the spirit of the legislator (not of the law). Even when the judge ends up giving in to his own opinions, he nonetheless pretends to be following the spirit of the legislator. In present common-law contexts, the potential for exercising discretionary power is probably larger, but it offers the judge the possibility of ruling in accordance with the "present day concepts of right and justice", with precedent being some sort of weakly-binding default rule;[33] and of bypassing the application of any overarching principle. Once again, philosophy is supposed to give way to the judge's notion of fairness, collective interest and common sense.

Thus, it seems that today the Posnerian approach offers an attractive solution to all those unhappy with the arbitrary rulings: the efficiency standard turns out to provide a valuable guiding standard and ultimately makes the Posnerian judge's action credible and stable. Of course, one may question the very meaning of efficiency. Hence, the accent on material wealth, the market value of which is measurable and therefore supposedly able to reduce the scope for discretion.

7.3.2 An introduction to Epstein's third way

Once it is acknowledged that the L&E vision is necessarily consequentialist, the next query is whether the choice is limited to the Chicago and Yale alternatives – that is, whether rules can only be drawn either to pursue neoclassical efficiency or broader collective aims such as fairness through redistribution. As a matter of fact, Epstein (1995) offers a third option, by arguing that rules should be framed in order to solve the problems of interaction at minimum costs. This would make economic sense (who can be against cost minimization?), it does not run against morality (cost minimization hardly runs against individual liberties and everybody is presumably happy to reduce the cost of litigation, with the possible exception of lawyers), and it does not prevent policy-making.

In order to achieve his target, Epstein puts forward two sets of apparently simple rules that in his view the courts should follow and with which the legislature should not tamper. The first block defines the right to individual liberty (self-ownership), the right to appropriate what has not been appropriated previously by others (first possession), the right to engage in voluntary exchange (freedom of contract), the right of exclusion (each individual has the right to use what he owns in the way he likes best). The second block relates to default rules affecting the interaction between the individual and the rest of the world. In other words, compulsory exchange applies when the counterpart's very life is at stake (the rule of necessity) or when coordination is too expensive and the state must step in (the rule of just compensation).

Epstein falls indeed within the L&E orthodoxy, in that he does not believe that a legal system's evolutionary process is necessarily virtuous, i.e. leading towards desirable results. In particular, he does not believe that in the absence of shock, appropriate starting points (history) are sufficient guarantees of a well-behaved path dependence process (the power of tradition).[34] Thus – Chicago again – he maintains that external intervention and guidelines are necessary and that efficiency is the benchmark. The consequentialist vision is indeed spelled out clearly. This is particularly apparent when Epstein explains the legitimacy of private property, which is not articulated in Lockean terms, but is justified by the fact that it works better: "its functional roots are so powerful that it should be treated as a moral imperative, even though the most powerful justification of the rule [of ownership over labour] is empirical, not deductive" (Epstein 1995: 59). However, and contrary to the technocratic vision put forward by the Posnerian approach, in the case of Epstein efficiency is shaped in Bastiat's clothes: as mentioned above, rules should minimize the cost of the invisible effects they might generate, whatever the law-makers' original intentions. The primary targets are of course litigation and administrative costs. In this light, Epstein argues that simplicity, credibility and stability are best guaranteed by a "legal regime that embraces private property and freedom of contract" (Epstein 1995: xii). The consequentialist connotation, however, remains crucial, for it turns out that these requirements are default criteria rather than rigid standards,[35] as the Austrian or the natural law visions would maintain. This is evident in Epstein's arguments in favour of private property (see above), of first possession (it should be enforced because it allows exchange), of freedom from coercion (coercion would prevent welfare-enhancing exchange), of vicarious liability (justified by a mix of deep-pocket and easy-business-with-strangers expediency), as well as his arguments against anti-trust legislation (too cumbersome to apply).

Two consequences follow. From an operational standpoint, it is apparent that much of the neoclassical efficiency that characterizes most modern L&E remains on the sidelines of Epstein's framework, in which there is no room for optimality and little faith in fine tuning. From his vantage point, efficiency means reducing enforcement costs by reducing statutory regulation, enhancing predictability by using simple rules and transparent vocabulary, limiting dependence on expert advice other than in relation to fact finding. Second, and from a broader standpoint, Epstein's approach emphasizes the nature and virtues of a law system that should not be conceived as a means of designing or enforcing the legislators' law, but rather as a practical way of solving disputes. Therefore, adherence to private property and freedom of contract is neither a deontic priority, nor is it directly instrumental in achieving wealth. Instead, it is the guiding criterion for obtaining a low-cost, stable and credible judicial system.[36] In turn, such a judicial system is likely to enhance growth and prosperity. But growth and prosperity would remain a consequence, not the primary objective.

To conclude, the third way outlined in these paragraphs is surely a compromise between advocating a legal system in which target-driven efficiency is the default rule, as suggested by the Chicago tradition, and conceiving of a judicial context driven by moral criteria, a softer version of what the neo-Austrian tradition would put forward.[37] In fact, such third way is characterized by its underscoring the role of means-driven efficiency as the base reference. Ideally, this third way would retain the flexibility of an amoral system, while also limiting discretionary power by imposing a measurable, behavioural straitjacket upon the judges: whenever the decision-maker moves away from simplicity, private property and freedom of contract, it is up to the decision-maker to prove that such deviation benefits the parties involved and does not harm those that are not involved.

7.4 Preliminary conclusions: the L&E story in perspective

The argument developed in this and the previous chapter has made a number of general points. First, we have tried to look at the intellectual origins and success of the L&E approach from a partially new perspective. In particular, we have maintained that its major contribution has been its ability to successfully combine on the one hand the legal profession's efforts to depart from formalism without falling back on arbitrariness, and on the other, much of the economic profession's labours to transform the institutional (exogenous) variable into an endogenous element amenable to some kind of prescriptive modelling. In order to articulate and open up what quickly turned out to be an almost boundless research agenda, the L&E community made use of a number of a priori claims: (*a*) the judge is a better rule-maker than the politician or the bureaucrat,[38] (*b*) the notion of harmful economic activity is relative, for the reciprocity postulate ensures that identification of the victim ultimately depends on the assignment of property rights, (*c*) the law is not about morality, but about maximizing social efficiency in the presence of transaction costs,[39] (*d*) the selection of the social-efficiency criterion is agreed upon behind what could be defined as the "veil of efficient precedent", according to which it can be presumed that when in disagreement, two parties or the members of a society would opt for the solution that maximizes wealth or growth, with precedent being the default rule.[40]

Second, we have pointed out that the emphasis on transaction costs is at least partially inappropriate, if not outright confusing. If one agrees that economics is the study of exchange, then the study of economic behaviour and of its consequences is necessarily defined by two sets of variables: what it takes to explore the opportunities to satisfy one's needs and what it takes to define one's position – rights and obligations – in an interacting system: that is, individual freedom and the rights freedom involves. The former have been identified as exchange costs, the latter as institutional costs. From this standpoint, it then becomes apparent that the existence of possible market failures should be studied within the realm of exchange costs, whereas rule-making failures fall under the heading of institutional costs. To put it bluntly, there is no room for transaction costs.

Third, we have examined the role of the Coase theorem in new light. Despite Coase's own qualifications in applying his efficiency-driven line of attack, his main contribution remains the reciprocal nature of harm and therefore the endogenous nature of the victim. In the absence of transaction costs, harm boils down to the issue of (re)distribution, whereas when transaction costs are significant, two possibilities open up. It is the judge's task to step in and single out the victim when the conflict is between individuals unable to reach an agreement. It is government's job when opportunism prevents otherwise desirable coordination.[41]

Fourth, we have emphasized that L&E is both explanatory and normative, and that there is a lot to gain by keeping the two sides separate. The explanatory side sheds light on the market-generated, "spontaneous" arrangements that individuals conceive in order to overcome coordination problems in contracting (Williamson's TC economics) or in obtaining efficiency after wasteful situations have been spotted and transformed into potentially profitable opportunities (Manne's contributions to the market for corporate control). As for the normative side, one conclusion is of course that when it comes to spontaneous arrangements, regulators should think twice before they interfere, or perhaps they should simply abstain from interfering: although one can always think of better solutions, interacting individuals can do a pretty good job, whereas regulators often seem to fall victim to obsolete economics or non-economic prejudice (e.g. envy cloaked in fairness). A second facet of the normative side focuses on using the common-law system to bring about judge-made "virtue", with this notion especially defined in terms of technocratic, static efficiency and/or income equality. Other issues include the role of government in overcoming coordination problems or situations in which indirect effects have substantial negative consequences for the community as a whole. For instance, Epstein refers to the indirect effects provoked by appropriation of natural resources: although no property right is infringed upon by the first owner, it is argued that the damage generated by his monopoly power on the scarce natural resource can be so large, that some form of regulation is required in the name of social efficiency.

Modern L&E is now the prevailing theoretical framework that social scientists have at their disposal in support of free-market economics. It is clearly based on utilitarian foundations across its spectrum. In this context, the content of the (social) utility function marks the differences among the various L&E branches. As pointed out earlier, however, the utilitarian-consequentialist approach provides only partial and temporary protection to free-market principles, which can be on safe ground only if buttressed by the freedom-from-coercion postulate. Put differently, since this postulate is generally rejected by modern L&E, the broad free-market recommendations put forward by L&E quarters end up being porous and ready to accommodate regulatory deviations in specific but far from negligible cases and areas of economic activities. The L&E

view on a number of real-world situations – anti-trust, natural-resource management, systemic banking – provides plenty of examples.

Surely, unless one takes pleasure in intellectual speculation, it makes little sense to engage in finding out whether the utilitarian approach is right, or whether it should give in to a natural-right based system. It is a fact that utilitarianism prevails both in academia and in the world of real policy-making. True enough, the argument of the utility function is not necessarily the same throughout the profession and similar remarks would also apply to the meaning attributed to its various elements/components: "fairness", "social justice" and "social welfare" are obvious examples. But once the utilitarian context is accepted, its content is often a matter of political expediency or common sense, ultimately depending upon the decision-maker's opinion about what is reasonable. Further illustrations are the notions of "adequate compensation", "risk spreading", "wealth-enhancing cooperation" and "collective interest".

On the other hand, it is perhaps more fruitful to pause for a moment and ponder the operational promises disclosed by the L&E vantage point. As Henry Manne already perceived some 40 years ago, the first grand lesson is that the bridge between economics and the law is primarily a matter of learning and education. From a historical perspective, it is true that common-law judges have frequently acted in compliance with economic-efficiency criteria – a statement that upon close inspection is almost a tautology.[42] Nonetheless, it is also undeniable that today's common-law regimes have been heavily contaminated by statutory law and regulations, and it is equally apparent that rapid technological change has gutted the *ceteris paribus* condition, a crucial requirement for precedent to apply meaningfully.

Two results follow. In general, routine has become a less than reliable source of wisdom. Thus, when discretionary rulings are requested, a proper understanding of the economic consequences of judicial rule-making helps avoid painful, protracted and sometimes hard-to-reverse mistakes. Put differently, L&E has little to add to the institutional idea that institutions "matter" and that institutions affect people's behaviour, informal norms, economic performance and sometimes even the individual's way of thinking ("psychological patterns").[43] Nor has L&E discovered efficiency, or the easy way to a mechanical notion of justice. Still, it has provided an important standard of reference for appreciating and evaluating the behaviour of the courts and has made it harder for those blinded by an ideal vision of the world to neglect the actual consequences of uneducated or uninformed judgement. A second result concerns rule-making. If the backbone of the Age of Social Responsibility holds true, one may predict that the judge is bound to lose his role of law-maker and act as a regulator, possibly competing with the bureaucrats to fill the holes left open by the legislators. But there is an important difference. Politicians are subject to consensus, while high-ranking bureaucrats are subject to a double constraint: they must be co-opted by their peers and must be agile enough to please all political colours. In both cases, but especially when it comes to the high bureaucracy, the key is the ability to develop clienteles and do favours, which in turn generates some blackmailing leverage. By contrast, according to the L&E perspective, the judiciary is definitely more independent of vote- and favour-trading mechanisms. Thus, it is better placed to make use of more technical criteria to enhance its prestige and de facto create a system of rules that are applied more or less systematically. These rules are not laws, for they are derived neither from a tradition of voluntary contracting, nor from political or semi-political bodies formally endowed with a power to legislate (legislators or bureaucrats). Nonetheless, they do act as effective guidelines for human behaviour. Not surprisingly, in reality the quality of these rules is closely related to the quality and features of the judiciary, which often vary systematically across countries: sometimes judges are expected to solve problems, while other times they are expected to establish fair compensation for inflicted harm.[44] In any event, the judge has to grapple with expediency and in order to avoid controversies, he is necessarily inclined to decide according to objective (i.e. little objectionable) criteria. In this light, microeconomic reasoning is perhaps the only instrument available, and L&E explains how to bring it into play.

The second grand lesson originates from the comparison of the different L&E approaches. Somewhat paradoxically, the Coase theorem offers little help to rule-makers in search of a solution to social problems, for it says very little about exchange costs and even less about institutional costs. If anything, it reminds the reader that both categories exist and that they affect economic behaviour as well as economic performance. Moreover, the theorem clearly shows that the power of the Chicago tradition depends heavily on the willingness to articulate and accept a consequentialist, wealth-maximizing theory of property rights based on the reciprocity-of-harm postulate. This route is not without snares, though, and one might have some doubts about what would happen once the decision-maker felt free to pursue neoclassical representations of an ideal competitive equilibrium with all the complexities that Calabresi (1961) illustrated some 50 years ago. But one can be pretty sure that in the end Manne's and Williamson's admonitions would be put aside and that the temptation to give in to more populist, deep-pocket solutions would be almost irresistible.

In this perspective, Epstein (1995) has probably offered a sensible and yet relatively flexible answer to the double whammy – wealth maximization against broader notions of the social good – that seems to have characterized much of the normative ambitions of the L&E tradition. Once the consequentialist choice has been made – and most of the L&E literature has little doubt about this option being the only one sensible or at least the only one realistic – the problem is not to find out the perfect goal or the optimal instrument to obtain it, but rather to minimize or reduce the chances that consequentialism goes astray and turns into arbitrariness, even if for the sake of the noblest of causes.

Epstein's primary goal is the reduction of institutional costs (enforcement and administration). Freedom of contract and therefore entrepreneurial spirits are the instrument through which exchange costs can be effectively reduced. By this argument, Epstein achieves two goals. On the one hand, he can develop a theory of private property (self-ownership, first-possession and right of exclusion) without relying on the freedom-from-coercion postulate. On the other hand, and precisely for this very motive, he can open up to (moderate) government intervention (*a*) to fill the gaps of coordination, (*b*) to care for common resources (prevent abuse by the first possessor), (*c*) to ensure that each case brought to court does not become a question of scholarly debate, research and eventually prey for the lawyers, (*d*) to pursue purely political goals or accommodate political expediency (e.g. by means of moderate redistribution). All this (and more) can be accomplished without worrying too much about individual freedom, since this concept never actually enters his construction by the ontological door.

This approach might sound like a watered-down adaptation of the L&E normative ambitions and perhaps a simplistic account of the L&E explanatory potential, which is frequently characterized by sophisticated reasoning and does not refrain from using high-powered technicalities. Nonetheless, Epstein's underlying scepticism towards normative fine tuning injects a healthy dose of realism into a discipline which seems to have been taken over by bureaucrats and agencies (that is, regulators), rather than judges. This "invasion" is hardly surprising. There is no doubt that today's judges should know much more about how the economy works if they have to exercise their discretionary power in assessing negligence, setting compensation, evaluating punishment so that rational criminal behaviour is effectively discouraged. In this light, Henry Manne was right in insisting on making the legal profession aware of the economic elements that must necessarily enter the legal decision-making process. Nonetheless, as the drive towards Walrasian efficiency becomes dominant, acceptance of the technocratic suggestion makes the task of the judge exceedingly complex, often entailing less credible and less stable rules: judicial ruling according to L&E guidelines would take more time, involve much higher costs and ultimately require skills that judges or jury members cannot be required to command.[45] Furthermore, it would also create tensions, as some judges do not necessarily consider themselves as technocrats, but rather the positive face of politics, an elite in charge of enforcing the daily rule-of-law system, and translating political whims and populist intemperance into commonsensical, fair guidelines for decent social behaviour, as much as possible in accordance with people's expectations and sentiments.

The upshot is that the L&E legacy seems to generate two different approaches that stand a good chance of gaining mileage in different environments, even if in those environments are not quite in accordance with the expectations of some of the L&E founding fathers. One is Epstein's simple-rule view, which appeals both to the judiciary and to public opinion. Surely, this might not represent a substantial departure from today's practice in the courts (especially in common-law countries) or from the generalized perceptions of the public at large. Nonetheless, it provides an easy-to-understand, substantially amoral argument to pursue and enforce a legal system based on promptness and clarity, possibly with some chance of counterbalancing a long-term trend in policy-making, which is in fact moving in the direction opposite that suggested by Epstein's fairly neo-liberal canons which conflate transparency with low administration costs for most situations.

The second approach regards rule-making bureaucrats, who seem to have been the greatest indirect beneficiaries of the Posnerian L&E vision. Of course, regulators could (and do) rely on standard neo-classical microeconomics when introducing rules to compensate for market failures, or for people's irrationality, or for the consequences of people's irrationality. But they need more than that in order to encroach upon somebody else's turf – such as the judiciary. Why does one need an anti-trust authority if the law says that price collusion deserves punishment, or that exceedingly high profits are the consequence of a crime (abuse of dominant position), or that being the only guy in town is an act of aggression to consumers' welfare? Why does one need an agency to monitor the packaging of food or the positioning of the brake-light in vehicles, if the law says that poisoning or fraud are crimes and that the seller of a faulty car is liable for the damages provoked by its malfunctioning? Wouldn't it be enough to take the criminals or alleged criminals to court, possibly in front of judges with some knowledge and experience in the relevant areas? Of course, the answer is that once the gap between the private and social good acquires a reciprocal dimension, efficiency requires that general rules be abandoned and that each situation be the object of an ad hoc technical investigation. When this is the case, justice understandably becomes the outcome of a wealth-enhancing decision and the legal rule is legitimized by that very same principle. Seen in this light, then, one can indeed consider removing these cases from the range of action of the judicial and political authorities, and entrusting specialized agencies with the task of doing their economic research and coming out with the efficient solution. Clearly, the more the notion of justice is subordinate to that of social wealth and the less marked its moral connotation is, the greater the role for specialized, technocratic agencies and the quicker the gutting of the traditional state branches, to the dismay of those who care about the balance of powers as an effective way to restrict abuse.

7.5 The historical perspective and the law of rules

The various arguments articulated in the sections above show that the whole vision characterizing the currently prevailing L&E approach has very little evolutionary content. In fact, L&E is not about finding the law, as Bruno Leoni and the idealized common-law system would recommend, nor is it about easing the slow, but spontaneous and altogether virtuous unfolding of the institutional process towards better rules, following Friedrich Hayek or some contributions by Douglass North.

Stated differently, the L&E approach acknowledges that changes in the structure of property rights might fail to materialize, despite their manifest advantages in terms of efficiency (Libecap 1989b). That explains why both Chicago and Yale definitely advocate active law-making by the judge, so as to obtain fairly well-indentified objectives that neither tradition nor evolutionary selection are likely to bring about.[46]

Surely, this fits well within the general framework characterizing the Age of Social Responsibility. From the economic standpoint, most L&E scholarship is consistent with the constructivist orthodoxy (man-made equilibrium): it assumes that efficiency is primarily a static issue and that if any dynamics come into the picture, they are merely a sequence of static situations, which therefore require gradual adjustments in property rights. By assigning the task to the judiciary, one reduces the chances that the necessary corrections are corrupted by populism and log-rolling, while also ensuring that compensation mechanisms remain transparent and that change is brought about relatively quickly. In addition, the more the system is made independent of fundamental moral standards, which are by definition not subject to debate, the more its assessment becomes subject to cost–benefit evaluation. As a result, the selection and enforcement of institutional architectures (including suitable property-right structures) become fallible, and therefore "scientific", according to the current meaning associated with this term.

To some extent, the L&E stance also matches the current ideology in at least two other major respects. First, it complies with the view according to which political failure does not necessarily imply a loss of legitimacy by the regulatory bodies as a whole, but rather a shift in authority away from the legislators. This is clearly discernible in public opinion, which seems to have little trust in politicians, but has faith in the possibility of getting the rules right. Consequently, public opinion maintains that the task of improving the rules cannot be left to the vagaries of voluntary individual interaction, and it believes that some sort of state authority has the duty to intervene. If anything, the problem is perceived as one of selecting the suitable rule-maker, while much less emphasis is laid upon the rule-making process itself. Hence, the arguments in favour of judicial activism and judicial review.

The second point regards the notion of "rule of law". We know that the current, widely-accepted, efficient-institution blueprint includes a requirement – the rule of law, whatever it means – which seems to sum up whatever a society needs for prosperity. After all, who can be against the rule of law? L&E does not fail expectations in this domain, either. The topic is duly addressed and solved by conflating a loose version of the free-market property-right structure justified by wealth-enhancement with the need to confront the problem of rational opportunism (hence government intervention) with an ill-concealed propensity to lean upon deep-pocket solutions in order to reduce transaction costs and/or enhance competition. The outcome looks appealing and exhibits all the desirable traits of an ideal rule-of-law system: stability, credibility, efficiency and flexibility. In particular, the first two features are guaranteed by the judges' acceptance of the common-law reliance on precedence and by their control on political activity (judicial review); the other two are guaranteed by the allegedly superior knowledge of the judges (judicial activism) and by the incentives in place, which drive their action (as opposed to the incentives typical of the bureaucrat or of the politician).

Yet, reliance on the judiciary and on the rule of law also raises some questions, since hope and ideal design usually differ from reality. This justifies the broader analysis suggested in the last paragraphs of this chapter, which are devoted to a reconsideration of these two issues from the historical perspective put forward in the previous chapter.

7.5.1 On the role of the judge

The medieval emphasis on the quasi-sacred nature of private property did not prevent plenty of abuse, but together with the sacred nature of authority it contributed to making judicial review and judicial activism irrelevant. The former would have been a task for the Church, while the latter would have been perceived as undue interference with the freedom of contract and the ruler's prerogatives.[47] During the Secular Period, the role of the judge was equally restricted: because the social contract was between the ruler and his subjects, the judge was little more than a bureaucrat on the one hand, an intermediary in personal disputes on the other. His role under Napoleon's rule was exemplary. Common to both periods was the absence of the modern state: hence, in those centuries law was not the result of the activity of a recognized (i.e. legitimized) legislative entity, such as Parliament. Rather, the legitimacy of the law was based on religion, on tradition (as long as tradition implied some sort sacredness), on customs (default behavioural patterns enforced by social pressure) or, as it gradually emerged during the first part of the Secular Period, on speculative reasoning. Definitely, law did not rely on consensus about a set of goals in competition with other goals proposed by candidates to power. Indeed, one could argue that in a social environment in which the judge had replaced the philosopher, speculative reasoning might have supported judicial activism and perhaps even judicial review. As we have already seen, however, this did not happen for two reasons. First, during the Enlightenment, economics was not about man-made equilibrium and optimal social choices. Second, since the social contract was not about the assignment or the enforcement of property rights (including regulation), the judge was not regarded as a key player. The same could be said of the legislative assemblies in their early stages, when they were supposed to be little more than ornamental. Even in the newly-formed United States, the Founding Fathers thought that Congress would have had little to do, although they were clearly worried about the tendency to legislative tyranny. Hence their attempts to avert the problem by means of federalism and the separation of powers, with checks and balances. The only prominent exception was Great Britain, where the House of Commons had an effective power to keep the sovereign in check.

The outlook and the prospects for judicial review and activity changed dramatically during the Age of Social Responsibility. Chapter 2 has already explained in some detail the economic meaning and consequences of the reliance on constructivism as a means of obtaining both static efficiency and fairness, which accommodates redistribution and a substantial amount of collective responsibility, as opposed to a view of the world that relies on the agent's consciousness. The partial but significant and altogether accepted replacement of the family by the state as the fundamental social point of reference for individual action and accountability is a powerful proof of how deep the shift in the underlying psychological patterns has been. Indeed, it is now widely accepted that private property can be violated for good enough reasons of social interest, and that a ruling elite is generally expected to enhance growth in people's purchasing power. That is in fact what the principles of reciprocal harm and wealth enhancements are about. The L&E context simply posits that the world has become too complicated to be dealt with by legislators alone and that judges should take over the pursuit of the common good, while legislators should be entrusted with consensus-gathering (populism).

Can we then conclude that the match between L&E and the First Principles of social responsibility was (and is) all but seamless? Not necessarily, for the Age of Social Responsibility also posits a third set of requirements. As we have seen in Chapter 5, within this ideological system the community acknowledges the existence of the democratic state as a guarantee of power sharing, it expects and tolerates reduced accountability for the mistakes committed in the quest for the common good, and it insists on the possibility of entering the political competition at low cost. In a word, the Age of Social Responsibility identifies a system of interactive rent-seeking, accompanied by the multiplication of the layers of power, which in turn waters down individual responsibilities.

It seems to us that these "promises" can hardly be met by delegating the rule-making power to the judge, whatever one may think of his technical skills and intellectual honesty.[48] As experience shows, recent attempts by the judiciary to acquire some sort of political status (judicial activism) have faced resistance. In the American case the role and even the legitimacy of the Supreme Court have been the subject of debate,[49] while in many European environments the inefficiencies of the ordinary courts are celebrated almost every day.

Rather than supporting judicial supremacy, it appears that the First Principles typical of the Age of Social Responsibility shore up the case for a technocratic bureaucracy characterized by strong personal and institutional ties (including numerous revolving doors) with the world of politics. In short, if one takes the Posnerian approach, we conjecture that the appropriate model would be the French *énarchie*.[50] Put differently, the judge who enhances wealth and commands compensation schemes in order to combine efficient property-right assignments and fairness is no longer there. His place has been taken by the educated bureaucrat who is expected to create a quasi-perfect system by means of optimal regulation. In this context, rent-seeking would still be allowed in the lower layers of the bureaucratic apparatus as well as in the political sphere, and the democratic principle of open access to the state machine would not be contradicted. Not surprisingly, therefore, the *énarchie* represents the system towards which several developed countries are moving and provides a matching answer to the request for greater government intervention formulated by qualified and highly trained regulators able to design better rules, monitor the system and take over troubled situations declared of national consequence.[51]

In partial contrast with the Posnerian vantage point and our own, the emphasis of the Yale perspective on the equalitarian notion of the collective good suggests a reduced role for the bureaucrat and seems to welcome closer interaction between the judiciary and the legislative, with the latter having however the last word. In particular, the judge is considered some kind of advisor on legal matters, whose task is to shed light on the economic consequences of the application of different general rules. He is then expected to apply such rules once the political rule-maker has reached a decision. In theory, the bureaucrat plays a minor role. Nonetheless, it might be observed that in this environment the judge is in fact an expert working in a specific branch (the legal sector), and that his job is not unlike what a qualified civil servant is supposed to do in other areas of the state apparatus: they both apply the written rules as defined by the legislators and, when necessary, they are both supposed to fill in the gaps according to criteria defined by politics or public opinion (common sense, current moral judgement).

Within this framework, therefore, the standpoint suggested by Yale appears as the best match between L&E on one side of the scale and the constraints set by the Age of Social Responsibility on the other. The fundamental reason is that the Yale L&E version ensures that the technical recommendations end up subject to the political decision-making process, and therefore filtered by the mechanisms typical of a "consociational" social structure, rather than of a competitive one.[52] By rejecting the notion of reciprocity, but accepting the fact that rules have economic consequences, Yale L&E offers guidelines for informed evaluation, with rather mild normative content. Put differently, it creates opportunities for negotiation, rather than issues for potential conflict. It is of course hard to say whether this is going to be the prevailing pattern in the future. Yale promises some sort of political oligarchy supported by legal experts, rather than run by *énarques*. In such a society, politicians are better equipped to meet their promise of adequate growth without allowing the rise of a new class of barely-legitimized rule-makers which society might find difficult to accept.[53] As the reader might have guessed, we doubt that this promise can be kept.

In this light, Epstein's proposals seem to be off the mark, in that neither liberty of contract, nor (qualified) private property, nor transparency are at the core of the First Principles typical of our age. In particular, Epstein's attack on bureaucratic rule-making power (regulation) appears to be running very much against the so-far successful attempts to share responsibility by fragmenting accountability. Somewhat paradoxically, the cost-lowering implications of Epstein's recipe turn out to be the very burden that prevents it from being accepted as sensible, relatively easy to enforce, and even wealth enhancing.[54] This is of course regrettable. Although its inherent consequentialism does not qualify it as a free-market approach, its basic tenets provide a satisfactory compromise between a Lockean rule-of-law environment (against state encroachment of all sorts) and the softer Hayekian view focusing on stability and predictability (but quite flexible on the content of the rules). As we have tried to illustrate in these pages, however, its failure is not due to intrinsic weaknesses, but to the prevailing notions of the rule of law, which oscillate between the enforcement of optimal regulation and the credible enforcement of socially desirable rules (the law of rules).[55] To these ambiguities we now turn our attention.

7.5.2 From the rule of law to the law of rules

The record of the L&E vision with regard to the rule-of-law question is mixed. Today the rule of law has become a synonym for good government (who can be in favour of bad government and say so in public?) and thus tends to be defined both in the positive, as a system of credible and stable rules, and in the negative, as the absence of arbitrary decision-making. As we have pointed out elsewhere (2007), the result is that today the rule of law has not much to do with economic freedom, but rather with the quality of the rules that are enforced, as well as with the consistency of the legislator and the effectiveness of the enforcers. Not surprisingly, a broad spectrum of social scholars can therefore claim with reason to be advocates of the rule of law.

The Age of Social Responsibility has provided a fitting framework to this soft approach to the rule of law. Although it has become a recurrent synonym for good government, it is undeniable that during this period the rule of law has been transformed into a system of procedural guidelines, the main purpose of which is to provide legitimacy to the political authority and to its activity. In a word, today the rule of law requires that the rule-maker be selected through democratic procedures, that he legislate according to agreed-upon guidelines (majority or super-majority) and he refrain from creating privileges unless for the common good. In this scheme a privilege is no longer a privilege, but a moral obligation dictated by fairness. The result is that the rule of law has ceased to become a principle that regulates social interaction, and has turned into a way of identifying well-behaved policy-making in the common interest. The critical notion becomes the common interest, which therefore gives substance to the rule of law.

From our vantage point, the L&E contribution has definitely ensured that the rule of law identifies more than just a set of desirable meta-procedures and a gross test for political activity (credibility, stability, lack of corruption). In other words, the wealth-enhancing principle has provided a much-welcomed (consequentialist) benchmark to assess whether "good rules" are in place, thereby encouraging rule-makers to focus on the institutional context: rule-making criteria as opposed to single pieces of legislation. Furthermore, it has provided a much-needed boundary between the political side of social responsibility and the rent-seeking, consensus-capturing drift. Indeed, when it comes to property rights, L&E and the rule of law are actually one, in that the decision-maker should endeavour not to generate deadweight losses. As we have observed earlier, within the Age of Social Responsibility the L&E approach suggests that this goal is obtained more easily if the judge supersedes the politician; or if the judge acts as the supervisor and ultimately enforcer of the (rule of) law.

Unfortunately, the flipside is that in the Coasean L&E perspective the reciprocity principle can be easily used to conceal arbitrariness; whereas resort to compensation might lead to populist redistribution. Put differently, the L&E approach could turn into an instrument to redefine and ultimately weaken the rule of law in societies in which First Principles of social responsibility prevail. Of course, this idea can get additional traction by the very concept of property typical of much of L&E scholarship, according to which property rights emerge as a response to a social problem (see Section 6.4 in the previous chapter), an idea which has been all too easily accommodated within the ideology of social responsibility.

7.5.3 What about the future?

The Age of Social Responsibility is not going to vanish soon. Some of its main-stays are indeed being questioned, as the growth rates of people's purchasing powers in several Western countries have declined and even fallen into negative territory. Nonetheless, the reaction seems to boil down to assorted requests for reform and possibly additional guarantees (same blueprints with better managers and enforcers, with little attention to costs). Deep historical change seems to be far away. The notion of the regulatory state with momentous nationalistic con-notations is very much alive and kicking, and in extreme situations – e.g. the 2009 financial crisis – it has been unreservedly supported even by numbers of self-proclaimed free-market scholars. When conflict arises, it seems that the demand for extended guarantees prevails over demands for positive growth. In the end, more than a serious financial crisis is required in order to bring about a deep change.[56]

To conclude, we believe that despite the undeniable contribution that the L&E literature has offered on the economics of liability, the economics profes-sion could have done a better job. First, it has revived from Pigouvian times an old subject which seemed to have been settled – negative externalities – and framed it in a misleading context by using a rather deceptive terminology. As we have argued in the previous chapter, the presence of externalities is a con-sequence of exceedingly high institutional costs, not of transaction costs. This is why the normative analysis should consider whether ad hoc institutional arrange-ments stand a chance of working better than those that develop spontaneously and avoid tampering with property rights. If the politician, the bureaucrat or the judge can do better than the individual, then let the individual take advantage of the options these actors can offer, but if and only if he wishes to do so. This is in fact the legacy of – say – Manne, Williamson and Epstein. Instead, by taking transaction costs seriously, both Chicago and Yale have somehow transformed an institutional question into a technological (or, better, technocratic) one, thereby encouraging creeping constructivism and providing "moral" legitimacy to discretionary power and enforcement in the name of the social weal.

Moreover, the economics profession should be blamed for having blurred the difference between negative externalities (which imply a violation of property rights) and undesirable effects. It has given the impression that negative exter-nalities can be reduced by reassigning property rights (which is self-contradictory or self-explanatory)[57] and that undesirable effects and behaviour do not exist (reciprocity) or can be corrected (mandatory acceptance of statutory coordination). Finally, economists should also be blamed for having concealed the fact that in a dynamic economy the gap between private and social benefits/ costs is inevitable and for having led social scholarship to focus on the quest for Walrasian equilibria. Once again, the reference to transaction costs has been treacherous. Either the gap is a matter of exchange costs, in which case the solution is technological progress driven by entrepreneurial efforts, or the gap is a matter of institutional costs, in which case the solution comes from the closer examination of the inner failures of the institutional mechanisms and the lack of institutional competition, rather than from the analysis of what the institutions do or should be doing.

Sadly, one fears that much of – but not all, to be fair – the L&E scholarship has been instrumental in justifying and possibly accelerating the century-long transition from the principle of the rule of law (no matter how poorly applied) to the principle of the law of rule mentioned earlier. To an extent, this has been inevitable, for the law of rule is part and parcel of the Age of Social Responsibility. In particular, this transfer reflects and illustrates the difference between the free-market recommendations based on the freedom-from-coercion postulate and those based on consequentialism. It also therefore explains why one can advocate free-market visions while keeping the door open to the possibility of enhancing the holistic notion of the common interest. It is hard to anticipate what it might take to change this attitude, not to mention that many would deny that such change is at all desirable. Several well-known, free-market authors have made this explicit by rejecting their earlier free-market ideas and switching to the popular version of Keynesianism (Wolf 2008). But if the approach proposed in these pages is correct, it will take more than a crisis or a new burst of intellectual entrepreneurship. It will take both at the same time, or perhaps in sequence, but in reverse order. If not, the crisis that might spark the next historical period might well come too early to generate real change.

8 Growth and crises reconsidered

8.1 On the economics of growth and happiness

Economic analysis has generally been conceived of as an attempt to understand and evaluate the outcomes generated by individuals who interact in order to improve their well-being in a world characterized by scarcity. Few would doubt that these activities could equally well be described as man's "pursuit of happiness", and that whenever positive economics gives way to normative attempts to fulfil the common interest, the analytical focus tends to move from the pursuit of individual happiness to the ruler's quest for "social happiness".[1]

Of course, the emphasis on social happiness played an important role some three centuries ago, when the early classical economists called attention to the fact that happiness is not a zero-sum game and that individuals could obtain progress in material terms without looting their neighbours. In particular, understood as a comprehensive increase in the standard of living, the quest for happiness has contributed to explaining the birth of policy-making, which gradually shifted its focus from how to restock the prince's coffers or annihilate opposition, to the study of (*a*) how to design and enforce the most suitable institutional framework to promote aggregate growth, (*b*) how the ruler's command should replace individual choices, so as to overcome the lack of coordination or rationality (short-sightedness), for the sake of the individual himself or of the common good, possibly at the expense of growth. For instance, as long as people enjoy safety more than income, and envy reduces happiness; privileges, regulation and redistribution are welcome for the sake of social happiness, even if entrepreneurship and working efforts might suffer as a result.

These two research agendas – desirable rules of the game and optimal decision-making – have characterized to various degrees the Smithean legacy, which emphasizes specialization, free trade and firmly established property rights. They have been typical of the Ricardian tradition, which insisted on the role of accumulation (investment). And they have influenced myriad post-marginalist contributions, which articulated their conceptual guidelines and efforts in terms of dynamic equilibrium and entrepreneurship.[2] To these explanatory structures we shall devote our attention in the next sections. Before we do that, however, the remaining paragraphs in this section draw attention to two methodological issues that justify some caution. One concerns the origins of the shift, from the analysis of trial-and-error processes in an uncertain environment to the engineering of wealth creation or, put differently, from the pursuit of individual happiness to the economics of aggregate growth. A second one regards the very notion of growth, the measurement of which raises a number of questions and sheds light on the choices policy-makers are required to make when working at their own personal goals. We conclude this introductory section by articulating some reasoning on what we can expect from the economics of happiness.

8.1.1 From individual happiness to collective growth

As we have observed in Chapter 2, the early economists did not advocate policies for growth. To begin with, the notions of happiness and satisfaction were frequently approached within the framework provided by cautious versions of subjectivism and methodological individualism: although the "philosopher" could give advice and shed light on the true meaning of happiness (not necessarily a synonym for high income), it was acknowledged that the perception of happiness necessarily comes from the individual, and that only the individual is in a position to know or judge what makes him happy and possibly revise his evaluations.[3] As a result, the term "happy society" identified a set of happy individuals or families, the family being often recognized as the smallest social unit. Moreover, and in accordance with our earlier remarks, for a long time before the Age of Social Responsibility that expression usually alluded more to the prevailing recognition of "social virtue", to the absence of political turmoil, to the quiet acceptance of one's position in society, and less to the achievement of high living standards in the aggregate. In fact, the notion of happiness was by and large absent during the Gregorian Centuries and started to surface only during the Secular Period.

Thus, the normative implication of this (classical-liberal) agenda is straightforward: Policy-making should be about the rules of the game within which the individual operates in the search for his own happiness. And as long as strict subjectivism prevails, rule-making should of course be restricted to formalizing and enforcing the moral boundaries within which humans can act: for instance, the minimal Lockean state.

By contrast, and consistent with what we argued in Chapters 4 and 5, the introduction of the economics of growth (and development) as a specific branch of economics in its own right originates from a different conception, according to which improving individual well-being is a social concern and thus a legitimate object of active policy-making.[4] In other words, when the dynamics of living standards became an element of the social contract characterizing the Age of Social Responsibility, the issue of individual happiness turned into one of collective growth and social happiness.

8.1.2 *Measuring growth in the Age of Social Responsibility*

That helps understand why measurement has all but become an obsession. Clearly, if solving or easing the scarcity constraint remains an individual endeavour, there is no need to quantify happiness or to measure changes in happiness (growth). Why use the scales when everybody is expected to be the judge of his own choices? When failure strikes, shouldn't one's frustration, anger and complaints be directed against the coercive power of the authorities, guilty of preventing the agent from making the most of his chances? Or against nature and misfortune, guilty of having given the poor peasant or the indigent beggar the "wrong" position in society, born to a destitute family or with little chances of migrating away from a country devastated by vicious warlords or raiders?

Nonetheless, we have already observed in Chapter 5 that typical of these last decades has been the idea that the authority should guarantee a constant minimum improvement in collective material well-being. This "minimum" is broadly defined as a constant rise in aggregate consumption: it ensures that nobody is permanently worse off, and that a substantial portion of the population enjoys higher living standards with the passing of time.

Yet, assuring the electorate non-decreasing incomes and wealth comes at a price, for guarantees regarding income, wealth and employment also imply lower social mobility, the preservation or creation of rents, biased risk evaluations and the misallocation of resources (bad investment). This clearly slows down the overall growth rate in material consumption, which weakens political consensus. More generally, in the Age of Social Responsibility decision-makers face the difficult choice between rising equality and falling living standards; moreover, they become vulnerable to cycles, which are often ignited or escalated by accidents and might easily get out of hand. For instance, high social mobility and low rent-seeking promote higher growth, which in turn exercises a downward pressure on the demand for rent-seeking and social safeguards (European-style welfare state). This keeps up momentum. But if a shock (e.g. globalization, a financial crisis or a bitter electoral campaign full of promises) creates a higher demand for rents, and if this demand is satisfied, then growth slows down, which in turn creates further demand for social guarantees and – *ceteris paribus* – further downward pressure on growth.[5]

Be that as it may, the role of figures when politicians interact with – and possibly influence – public opinion is undeniable. Specifically, measuring the dynamics of material well-being has become both tempting and in the end inevitable. In the past, temptation came from the belief that policy-makers could actually plan and obtain growth, as long as they had enough information.[6] In more recent times, faith in the wonders of planning has subsided, but the possibility of deluding the members of a collective body with limited access to transparent, easy-to-read information, has remained appealing. For example, by posting positive aggregate growth figures, rule-makers do not claim that everybody has become better off. That would be too obvious a lie. Nonetheless, those figures witness that new wealth has been created, with two implicit messages: more opportunities for redistribution are available, and all individuals stand a chance to improve their well-being in the future. Furthermore, those who have ended up worse off in the recent past are led to believe that their personal situations could have been just a matter of bad luck, and that they might be more fortunate in months or years to come. Even when growth is weak or negative, spreading the information could be the right thing to do from a political rent-seeking stand-point: in particular, it justifies policy-action, which typically means guarantees and privileges to selected interest groups and, more generally, populist redistribution.

All in all, even those who might fear they could become vulnerable to criti-cism for poor performance must recognize that the citizen wants hard data in order to assess whether his complaints and expectations are reasonable, while the politician needs figures to justify his action, acquire consensus, and fend off opponents. After all, access to the data has become relatively easy to researchers, to the media trying to attract attention, as well as to interest groups looking for convincing evidence to support their claims. Controlling and possibly manipulat-ing the production of the numbers is more productive than hiding or ignoring them.[7]

8.1.3 So, what's wrong with measurement?

Assessing the value of the data on income and growth is a different matter. As Frey and Stutzer (2002) pointed out in their rich survey of the empirical literat-ure, people's happiness surely depends on material consumption, but also on how they perceive their role in society (an issue that had already been raised by Mandeville and Smith in the eighteenth century) and on how they compare their current status with their expectations, their perceived prospects to meet them and their recent experiences. Taken together, these elements explain why, under certain conditions, individual happiness turns out to show little change over time even when GDP per capita increases (aspirations rise at the same time),[8] and also why happiness usually varies across individuals within a community, controlling for income (since envy is negatively correlated with relative income, while the opposite holds true for vanity and self-esteem). Time also matters: a pay rise might be a source of happiness, but happiness diminishes as time goes by and new expectations or ambitions build up. Put differently, an individual might not always be happier when his income rises, but he is generally worse off as his income declines, especially when the decline is not common to the other members of his community of reference.

In short, although economic statisticians might know what affects individual happiness, their assessment hardly helps rule-makers to get it right. Unless one has a moral recipe for utilitarian comparison and aggregation that justifies coer-cion and redistribution, the only sensible goal is to boost productivity growth, so that constant inputs generate more valuable output, in quantity and/or quality. Long ago, Alchian (1950) pointed out that the key is adaptation to new environ-ments – new preferences and new technological opportunities. This implies the capacity to react quickly, to gather and elaborate information, to imitate and to innovate through groping (trial and error); as well as the ability to pursue systematic research strategies (scientific investigation). In this light, therefore, the purpose of policy-making is multiplying the free lunches we enjoy every day with no extra charge on breakfast and dinner. In practice, this means that structural adjustment should be facilitated, so that greater factor productivity translates into higher purchasing power for the factors in higher demand and more and more members of the community acquire or develop with relative ease the bodies of knowledge essential to operate complex machineries, create and absorb new skills and carry out exchange in far away markets. Furthermore, although it is obvious that not all individuals are in a position to reap quick gains from technological progress (candle producers, for example, are going to suffer when electricity is introduced), the idealized policy-maker living in the Age of Social Responsibility should also ensure that even those who do not immediately benefit from growth ultimately revise their expectations and perceive that they can be winners in the not too distant future. In short, they should not retard growth; rather, they should promote it.

Certainly, Alchian's key is realistic and growth enhancing policy responses feasible if individuals are self-confident and self-reliant, so as to acquire the ability to look at change as the norm and as a source of opportunities, rather than as a threat to acquired rents. Unfortunately, this very prerequisite has been gradually and significantly eroded in the past decades, through a period of "deep crisis" during which generations

> have witnessed a turn towards collectivism in the law, toward emphasis on state and social property, regulation of contractual freedom in the interest of society, expansion of liability for harm caused by entrepreneurial activity, a utilitarian rather than a moral attitude toward crime.
>
> (Berman 1983: 36–37)

This erosion has also been typical of the economic literature on growth. Thus, not surprisingly, growth-theorizing has generally failed to deliver, while policy-making for growth has turned into policy-making for sustainable rent-seeking.

Before we analyse the gap between the economics of growth and the reality of policy-making, it is nonetheless necessary to assess what the growth process consists in. This will be the object of the next three sections, which offer a critical appraisal of the traditional growth theories (8.2), of the interaction between technology, science and growth (8.3), of the engines of growth from a historical perspective (8.4).

8.2 What do growth theories tell us?

Theorizing about economic growth can be framed by two simple observations. The first observation is that communities do not exploit all the opportunities to increase their living standards and frequently live well inside the so-called consumption-possibility frontier. The second consists in the awareness that the frontier changes continuously, thereby expanding the set of opportunities open for exploitation by the individual or by groups of cooperating individuals. Hence, the main challenge for the economics profession has been finding out (*a*) why individuals fail to take advantage of their opportunities, (*b*) why this failure varies across countries, (*c*) why the frontier moves at different speeds, both through time and across countries. The classical-liberal, the extensive and the entrepreneurial agendas have offered some answers.

8.2.1 The agendas

The classical-liberal research programme was launched by Mandeville and Hume and subsequently expanded and popularized by Adam Smith. These authors identified exchange as the main engine of growth. In particular, the size of a geographic market would extend the possibility of trading and therefore enhance specialization according to talents, natural-resource endowments and chance. Specialization would create the resources required to maintain an adequate stock of scientists, who would then promote technological progress. In short, exchange facilitates approaching the frontier; at the same time, however, the further a society moves away from the origin, the greater sustainable number of scientists and the greater available opportunities expand that frontier.[9] In modern terminology, exchange sparks an endogenous-growth process, which is simple, logically consistent and persuasive.

The second agenda has emphasized extensive growth, promoted by the use of larger and larger quantities of inputs, either with constant technology, or by considering technology itself a higher-order input generated by making use of other resources such as capital and labour. The former version is the now obsolete classical approach to growth, which for decades has validated central planners' action all over the world, although under different headings: indicative planning in the West, central planning in the Soviet bloc and Mao's China, forced industrialization and manpower planning in most undeveloped countries. According to the latter version, still popular in the 1980s and 1990s, planning growth turns out to be an exercise in calculating the optimal amount of resources that should be devoted to the "appropriate" production of new technology.[10]

The last research agenda has focused on the notion of entrepreneurship. Motivated by profit and/or vanity, individuals defy uncertainty, looking for opportunities, obtaining major or minor breakthroughs and creating new products, new production processes, new organizational and contractual structures to meet demand and enhance the buyers' purchasing power. These new advances can be summarized as "growth", which therefore depends on the ability of the institutional framework to encourage entrepreneurship. In particular, according to a large part of this literature, the appropriate institutional framework should protect economic freedom (private property rights, freedom of contract, contract enforcement) and therefore set substantial limits to government intervention.

All the above insights are confirmed by robust empirical evidence. The richest countries are indeed those that have promoted trade, both within their own borders and with the rest of the world. By contrast, it is undisputed that the introduction or the strengthening of trade barriers hampers growth in poor areas and leads to crisis in more affluent regions. Indeed, this should not surprise those familiar with the notion of opportunity cost: voluntary exchange is always beneficial to the parties involved, and the greater the opportunities for exchange, the greater the possibility of exploiting differences in opportunity costs.

At the same time, there is little doubt that fixed capital enhances labour productivity, and that the state-of-the-art vintages of technology embodied in the new machinery ensure that decreasing marginal returns are no longer a binding constraint. Put differently, this empirical literature emphasizes that higher productivity is the key to higher living standards, that technology is crucial to enhancing productivity, and that fixed assets are the main vehicle of technology, which is thus transferred from the laboratories and the innovators' desks to everyday economic life.

The theoretical arguments in favour of entrepreneurship also find convincing support. The comparison of the performance of the centrally-planned economies of the Soviet bloc with the Western economies during the second half of the twentieth century has struck public opinion. Similar comments hold true for the Chinese miracle following the partial liberalization of the Chinese economy. More detailed and systematic investigations on the connection between "appropriate institutions" and economic performance also point in the same direction: a sound institutional framework – economic freedom – enhances productive and entrepreneurial energies, which in turn generate economic progress and growth.[11]

8.2.2 Convergence

Yet, the discrepancies among these three visions are less sharp than meets the eye. Although the approaches outlined above are indeed different, they tend to complement each other. For instance, the eighteenth-century picture can be easily enriched with Hayek's view on the acquisition of knowledge through the market process, conceived as a mechanism that provides information on scarcity as well as on the opportunities for investment and entrepreneurial challenges. Hence, the role for new vintages of machinery and for suitable institutions.

As for extensive growth, the emphasis on investment in fixed and human capital (education) as autonomous goals worthy of pursuit in their own right has probably lost traction during the past decades. The traditional neoclassical approach to growth underscoring total factor productivity (TFP) has also been put aside.[12] However, technological path-dependent processes driven by scientific curiosity and entrepreneurial abilities have rightly become critical in understanding the nature of technology as an input in its own right.[13] Furthermore, and not surprisingly, it has also been acknowledged that the effectiveness of investment and the benefits of technological progress depend heavily on the size of the markets available to producers and on the incentive structures (institutions) with which they are confronted. As a result, such elements have been duly incorporated in all kinds of technological, extensive-growth models and theories. Conditional-convergence, exogenous-growth theses are the primary set of examples.

The same applies to the entrepreneurial approach favoured by the Austrians, who understandably refer to Mises and, more frequently, to Schumpeter's creative destruction and Kirzner's alertness.[14] Entrepreneurial theories tend to refer to the carriers of technological change, to the actors who transform progress into growth. These are crucial agents, of course; but they are by no means the only ones. Scientists and technological innovators matter, too. Put differently, scientific advances, technological progress and productivity growth are hard to capture by the rather simplistic notion of creative destruction, which is actually more apt to describe competition. Similarly, although nobody denies the role of being alert, waking up and having a sharp eye are not enough to grow. To summarize, entrepreneurship works well in explaining the movements towards the technological frontier, but is somewhat inadequate unless it incorporates other theoretical elements to entwine the "movements towards" with the "movements of" the frontier.

8.3 Science, technology and the limits of growth theorizing

Although generalizations always require prudence, the main lessons from the past 50 years are that there are no limits to scientific advance and technological progress,[15] and that these are critical in ensuring sustained economic growth. A community can reach the consumption-possibility frontier by working harder, easing communication and exchange, designing better organizational architectures. Advancing the frontier, however, is virtually impossible without technological progress, which in turn depends on, and is fed by, scientific developments.

Scientific advance operates by opening up radically new perspectives, which engineers subsequently exploit by creating new general-purpose know-how, such as the steam-engine, electricity, the field of information technology; or by developing new insights, thanks to the innovations that have already occurred and the new directions of research that they have suggested by stimulating new categories of demand (e.g. miniaturized data storage).

Technological progress translates scientific knowledge into technical uses of economic relevance or, put differently, makes the most of scientific knowledge in order to lessen the scarcity constraint. Sometimes technological progress results from innovation. Sometimes it is imported (adopted) through imitation and possibly adaptation, which allows a society to bridge the gap between its current and its potential situation. Be that as it may, the bidirectional interaction at work is manifest: scientific advance supports technological progress, which in turn offers new stimuli to the researchers. Sustained economic growth is thus stronger, the stronger the interaction mechanism and the more effectively the institutional context allows entrepreneurs to transform technological opportunities into the production of desirable goods and services.

This helps us understand why the notion of path dependence has become so prominent (and perhaps a little frustrating) in much of the growth literature. It also explains why it is so difficult to make significant progress in the theorizing about growth processes: the feedback system that characterizes the relation between innovation, science, entrepreneurial and managerial skills is extremely dense, complex and very difficult to articulate. And of course, it is heavily dependent on the institutional context, the rules of the game. More radically, however, once growth is associated with the notion of newly-acquired knowledge, growth theorizing necessarily becomes a wild-goose chase. If growth is made possible by the discovery and exploitation of previously unknown scientific and production possibilities, then the very notion of uncertainty ensures that we can't predict when new forms of knowledge are going to be acquired, of what they consist, or what their economic effects are going to be. Indeed, the best one can do is to engage in more or less sophisticated extrapolations (predictions) with regard to different classes of situations, and to put forward rather extensive and sometimes boring taxonomies describing potential and necessarily incomplete feedback systems, each of them leading sets of opportunity boxes to open up,[16] with little or no knowledge about their content.

To be fair, by emphasizing that breakthroughs and alertness promise advance, the entrepreneurial vantage point seems to be simpler, and more consistent and realistic than all other approaches. Its particular strength lies in its ability to explain why scientific advance and technological progress are necessary, but not sufficient, for growth. Moreover, the typically-Austrian accent on individualism is logically and methodologically sensible: scientific knowledge and innovation do not drop upon communities out of the blue. Instead, they are the result of individual talent, alertness, efforts and breakthroughs. Hence, the entrepreneurial context is possibly the only one where institutions are a set of value-free stimuli to which individuals react while trying to acquire knowledge, rather than sets of coercive rules aiming at optimality within a hypothetical dynamic-equilibrium setting. Nonetheless, although the relation between entrepreneurs and institutions is certainly critical and leads to important results with regard to the role of economic and political liberties, big questions remain on the table: why do some societies achieve better results than others and why do they show different reactions to historical accidents? Why do catastrophic events have different consequences across time and space? And how do we explain that the same community experiences different growth rates over time, and that slowdowns occur even in periods of high technological progress? Can history offer some clues?

8.4 Growth theory in historical perspective

From a historical standpoint, three general statements go undisputed. First, for many centuries the world was capable of producing increasingly large quantities of food. By and large, that translated almost completely into demographic expansion.[17] As a consequence, until the eighteenth/nineteenth century, the food surplus was frequently not enough to meet the needs dictated by demography, and even less was it possible to make substantial amounts of resources available to industries other than agriculture. Second, sustained growth began sometime in the nineteenth century and was characteristic of the West. The United Kingdom began the First Industrial Revolution, followed by other Western countries a few decades later. It took the rest of the world at least a century to catch up, in most cases with limited success. Finally, growth has never been a regular, smooth phenomenon, especially if one takes into account the dramatic and violent events that severely disrupted the incumbent economic structures – bad harvests, wars, epidemics, protracted political turmoil. This obviously applied to the period prior to the First Industrial Revolution, when agricultural output was heavily influenced by the weather; but it also applies to more recent times, when farming has played a smaller role in aggregate production, and the damages of localized bad luck (bad weather) could be offset through trade and/or smoothed through international financial transactions, including insurance. In a word, it seems that from a historical standpoint, slow aggregate growth accompanied by rising population, and therefore quasi-stagnant GDP per capita has been the norm, whereas the dynamic of the past two centuries – higher, sustained aggregate growth with declining birth rates – has been the novelty.

These facts cast some doubts on the explanatory powers of the classical-liberal and neoclassical agendas. We know that "exchange for mutual benefit has been part of the human condition for at least as long as *Homo sapiens* has been a species. It is not a modern invention" (Ridley 1996: 200).[18] We also know that since man started to produce spears, the contribution of capital to human welfare was manifest. Yet, it took at least a million years before growth meant something to the typical individual. Lipsey *et al.* (2005) have gone a long way in explaining what happened. Their work clarified that the secret of Western success was the rise of the scientific approach to economic bottlenecks: The rational, scientific mind can help understand natural phenomena and this knowledge can be applied to soften the scarcity constraint and make people better off. F. Bacon (1561–1626) and G. Galilei (1564–1642) were the foremost precursors of this new way of thinking; R. Descartes (1596–1650) and especially I. Newton (1643–1727) were the spiritual fathers of a new era. They and myriad other scientists who followed their footsteps marked a break with the past in several respects. In some cases their investigations stemmed out of sheer intellectual curiosity, with no immediate concerns for issues of economic relevance. In other cases they were moved by the need to solve practical problems, e.g. the demand for man-made fertilizers or for precision instruments to measure time to ease high-seas navigation. Common to all these scientists, however, was the belief that all natural phenomena have rational explanations with little to do with religion, myth or magic; that such explanations are part of very general laws, which can be exploited to apprehend extended sets of events; that within the realm of natural philosophy (the hard sciences, as they are known today), the inductive approach is far superior to deduction;[19] and that such laws can be made use of in order to produce outcomes that are not directly observed in nature, or even to correct or offset undesirable natural events.[20] Perhaps more importantly, their inquiries no longer took place in semi-isolation, but unfolded within a fairly thick network of physical and epistolary contacts that made it possible to conceive of research programmes on a continental scale. This ensured that the so-called "eureka-moments"[21] did not go unnoticed or lost; and that they could more frequently hit the bright and even the not-so-bright minds as a consequence of constant interaction among peers and perhaps also as a result of incursions by amateurs. Thus, beginning in the eighteenth century, scientific progress sparked research programmes that allowed other research agendas to take off; while also creating opportunities for entrepreneurial endeavours. The result was progress and feedback effects that stimulated further research.

Is this then all we need to know about growth? Not quite, since the elements of the Western miracle shed light on new questions. Was the causal nature of Newtonian inductivism inevitable? Was it an accident? Were the earlier scholastic enquiries and Descartes' deductivism a mistake or a necessary step to obtain success? Is another leap forward just around the corner? Or has it already taken place?

Economists are generally ill equipped to provide reasonable answers to these questions. We are no exception. Nonetheless, some general conclusions seem to come to the surface. First, genius is always an accident, but bright minds are relatively frequent, although such minds might often be wasted, their potential goes unnoticed and progress ultimately suffers as a consequence. In fact, the existence of a proper setting makes the difference between waste and success: in the late seventeenth century two countries – England and the Netherlands – provided the appropriate environments, characterized by openness, appreciation for scientific inquiry, tolerance for intellectual freedom (which included a relatively free press).[22] Of course, "appropriate" is not the same as "ideal". But both in the Netherlands and in England central government was weak and the burden of religious intransigence relatively light.[23] Tolerance ensured that these were the countries in which scientific insights had the best chances of being developed and of fertilizing sustained growth.[24]

Second, the translation of scientific knowledge into entrepreneurial endeavours is surely easier when scientists and entrepreneurs are close to each other. Still, the role of developing local scientific communities should not be overemphasized: today the transfer of scientific knowledge is generally smooth and inexpensive. Even when that is not the case, it yields a lag in knowledge transmission, rather than loss of knowledge and stagnation. Hence, we posit that modest interaction signals a lack of entrepreneurial abilities, rather than of insufficient research inputs. Engineers have poor incentives to transform scientific insights into technological findings and/or potential entrepreneurs are unwilling to transform those findings into opportunities to meet previously unsatisfied needs. If this is true, advocating policies for research and science would be vain, to say the least. Instead, the observer should wonder why technicians/innovators and entrepreneurs are induced to concentrate their energies on other, apparently more profitable targets, or not to concentrate at all and to take refuge into what could be defined as "technical and entrepreneurial numbness".[25]

Third, comparative economic history – once again China and the West are the best candidates for this kind of exercise[26] – suggests that until the eighteenth century institutional competition and "culture" did not make much of a difference as far as living standards and economic progress were concerned. Surely, those institutional and cultural differences were critical when individual speculation turned from inquiring into natural philosophy towards conceiving and pursuing scientific agendas. Once past the scientific threshold, however, it became clear that the ability to make progress depended to a larger and larger extent on the ability to fertilize those agendas by exposing them to entrepreneurial stimuli. China and the non-Western world failed on this account as well. But it also appeared that when progress turned out to be led by supply (entrepreneurial abilities), rather than by demand (the need to solve specific problems related to the exploitation of natural resources), the forerunners of the First Industrial Revolution – the United Kingdom, France, Belgium – were left behind. In their stead, new actors came to the surface: the United States, Germany and later Japan, the main characters of the Second Industrial Revolution.

To repeat and conclude, today it would be a mistake to worry too much about scientific progress. Luckily, there is no way to undo the Newtonian revolution. And once the Newtonian threshold has been crossed, progress takes place anyway, even if its speed is inevitably also affected by luck, genius and institutions. Instead, and consistent with the Austrian perspective, the key ingredient becomes entrepreneurship, which plays a role both when acquired scientific knowledge is going to be transformed into opportunities for growth (new products and production processes), and when catching-up (imitation) seems more promising.

8.5 A theory of endogenous entrepreneurship

As mentioned earlier, there is no disagreement about the fact that trade, technological progress and entrepreneurship are the key to sustained economic performance. In a growing economy scientists and innovators successfully strive to acquire new knowledge, while productive entrepreneurs[27] take risks by exploiting and applying knowledge in order to meet demand. Rather, the main differences among today's various growth theories consist in how they interpret and emphasize these statements. The neoclassical agenda ultimately ignores the role of uncertainty and focuses on an "extensive" research programme – how welfare can be enhanced by employing larger quantities of resources combined according to a set pattern.[28] The productivity of such inputs is thus determined by a production function that generates technology. By contrast, the Austrian school underscores the role of uncertainty, which characterizes both scientific insights and entrepreneurial attitudes. Three consequences follow from their vantage point. First, since growth is about changes in the production function brought about by innovators and entrepreneurs (this is what "intensive growth" means), attempts at formalization are futile, for one cannot formalize an unknown production technology. Thus, there can't be a positive theory of intensive growth, but just a rather porous set of statements. Second, extensive-growth theories also miss the point, as the Ricardian tradition has witnessed. At most, one can advance a theory about the institutions that enhance virtuous productive interactions and helpful feedbacks, so as to correct mistakes and avoid wastages – this is the subject matter of normative institutional economics. Third, since the rules of the game are crucial in assessing when and how an individual decides to break through the veil of uncertainty, scholarly research should focus on the appropriate rules of the game, which most Austrians believe to be spontaneous order within the rule of law.

8.5.1 What's wrong with Austrian entrepreneurship?

We have already mentioned that the economics profession is not quite happy with the orthodox, neoclassical approach. Economists have realized that individuals are not maximizing agents operating in a certain environment and that model-making per se does not create ideas, but often times leads to scientistic illusions. Growth modelling is no exception. Moreover, it is not factually true that an economy can only experience extensive growth.

To be fair, the profession is also less than ecstatic at the Austrian approach. The Austrian perspective is indeed helpful, for it does not deny the existence of increasing returns to knowledge and high cooperation and/or enforcement costs. Moreover, Austrians accept that in a perfect world some sort of intervention could reduce the cost of cooperating, overcome the cost of contract enforcement and internalize externalities. Yet, they justify resistance to governmental interference by acknowledging that this is not a perfect world, and that the potential benefits from R&D subsidization would be necessarily offset by a host of counterproductive effects. Austrians argue, for example, that R&D subsidies weaken the feedback mechanism between entrepreneurship and science, as the scientists would now respond less to entrepreneurial incentives and more to bureaucratic preferences, the two sets often times leading in different directions. Furthermore, productive entrepreneurial skills would be transformed into rent-seeking efforts aimed at influencing the allocation of public funds, at the expense of economic performance.

Although these objections are certainly well-founded, it is hard to deny that in the end they strike a consequentialist note: there is a scope to pursue (the acquisition of knowledge) and limited governmental intervention is the best way to promote that goal. Hence, the debate comes close to an argument about figures, estimates, social outcomes. In a word, there is no solution in sight. For instance, the Austrians could comment on the German success stories in the late nineteenth century and early twentieth century, or on the Japanese and South Korean miracles in the 1970s and 1980s – all situations in which the role of government intervention and direction was undeniable – by claiming that a restrained government would have led to superior performances. Yet, the strength of this argument is questionable and its counterfactual content is far from convincing.

We hope to bypass the consequentialist hurdle that lurks even behind the Austrian claims by offering a partly different approach, which emphasizes the creation and enhancement of the scientific and entrepreneurial spirits, rather than the way such spirits are applied. With this in mind, the following subsections turn to the role of ideology as an explanation. The reason for this attention to ideology is that despite its many virtues, the weak spot of the entrepreneurial-institutional literature consists in its assumption that entrepreneurial propensities and abilities are more or less equally distributed across regions and historical periods, and that it only takes the right set of institutions to ensure that those talents come to the surface and are employed in productive ventures.[29] Persuasive as it might sound, however, we challenge this statement, and borrowing from biology, we argue that individuals have a genetic disposition to become entrepreneurial. Having that disposition is a necessary condition for entrepreneurialism, but it is not a sufficient one: entrepreneurship is neither an exogenous variable, nor is it a natural, constant and permanent feature of any human being. As shown in the subsection below, we also suggest that once entrepreneurship is no longer exogenous, the returns on skilful institutional design and tampering pale in comparison with the role of First Principles.

Human nature might well be the same: we are genetically inclined to improve our material and emotional state, we take chances to enhance our purchasing power and/or to satisfy our vanity. However, this does not necessarily imply that the way people think, and the goals they conceive of, are always constant. In particular, individuals' behaviour can be modified by deep institutional changes, which also influence the very meaning they attribute to "being better off" or, put simply, to "success". Sometimes success is mere survival. Other times it is the ambition to expand the range of opportunities (social mobility, with the risks it implies). Under different ideological contexts, it becomes the right to secure a fraction of the median income and to benefit from wealth transfers accordingly. Non-material components also play a role. For instance, as argued by Rousseau, both scientists and entrepreneurs can be vain, and can act in order to enhance their prestige in society. And of course, the stronger the social status of science and business skills, the greater the willingness to take chances and engage in growth-related activities.

Of course, all human beings feel a desire to improve their condition, but they apply their rational qualities in different ways. Likewise, all communities of a certain size include individuals who possess natural talents that enable them to look at natural phenomena with a scientific eye, who are alert enough to catch sight of opportunities for profit and entrepreneurial enough to organize resources, evaluate risks and take chances. Yet, it frequently happens that the rules of the game and the incumbent ideological context encourage individuals to ignore or repress their talents and instincts. This not only implies a move from productive to unproductive entrepreneurship, as Olson and Baumol had it; but also from creative alertness to outright submission and acceptance of the current state of the world, or to what we defined as "entrepreneurial, scientific and technological numbness". When this attitude lasts long enough and the individual perceives it as successful, it can turn into an established, hard-to-eradicate behavioural routine, possibly a psychological pattern.

Put differently, we posit that it does not take a historical shock for entrepreneurial spirits to appear or to disappear. Understanding and absorbing the setting that defines the reward system to entrepreneurship relies more on imitation than on shocks or trial and error. For instance, it is probably fairly easy and quick to acquire entrepreneurial attitudes when an individual migrates into countries in which such mindsets are common. Conversely, it is somewhat slower when the individual finds himself in an environment which tends to thwart risk taking and social mobility. In the opposite case, the entrepreneurial mindset can be lost when the environment is built upon exploitation, and when access to the ruling elite is a matter of birth or proven compliance with the rulers' will. Be that as it may, according to our line of argument there exists a dynamic of entrepreneurship, which is shaped both by institutions and by ideas, with an emphasis on the latter. The next step is then to analyse the causality mechanisms.

8.5.2 What happens when institutions are no longer exogenous?

As mentioned above, the literature on entrepreneurship assumes that institutions are exogenous and that entrepreneurship reacts to the rules of the game. This is certainly true. Still, this is not the whole story, since causal mechanisms work in the opposite direction, too: from entrepreneurial attitudes to institutions. On the one hand, the lack of shared, free-market principles makes it easier for the policy-makers to expand their rent-seeking activities. By contrast, in relatively prosperous, fast growing communities, productive entrepreneurs are more likely to create powerful enough coalitions to oppose the restrictions introduced by the policy-makers – either by influencing public opinion or by persuading the policy-makers themselves (lobbying).

Which of these effects prevails? Rent-seeking pressure or productive entrepreneurship? The public-choice school and the political-economy approach claim that it all depends on the political and governance structures. These are obviously important elements, but other factors might tilt the balance and lead to conjecture that in the Age of Social Responsibility productive entrepreneurship is eventually bound to come under pressure and succumb, even when growth is satisfactory. Progress, structural adjustment and competition create disgruntled entrepreneurs who are likely to be tempted to invest in unproductive ventures (possibly tapping somebody else's money). To illustrate this point, one may observe that fast growth is usually accompanied by changes in relative prices: new products and processes make their appearance, the structure of demand evolves as the range of choices widens, and companies must adapt, sometimes rapidly. Likewise, growth is also characterized by ongoing structural change on the supply side: technologies and innovations do not develop at the same speed across industries, nor does competition present the same challenges. In addition, the very notion of competition implies that some agents do better than others, and that those who do poorly meet trouble and eventually go out of business. In the end, for some companies manipulating the institutional environment can be less expensive and demanding than adjusting to competition. When their efforts are successful, the institutional context is affected, and the rewards to unproductive entrepreneurship increase further.

The timing might differ following historical circumstances and the balance between the extensive and the intensive growth components. If extensive growth prevails, there are few losers, and therefore little incentive to pursue unproductive actions.[30] The opposite holds true when growth is intensive and involves substantial structural adjustment and/or intense competition. This has been the case in much of the West during the past couple of decades, as the so-called "globalization" unfolded. China and India exemplify intermediate situations, in which structural phenomena have been accompanied by robust extensive components. Thus, in the end it appears that pressures for rent-seeking and against productive-entrepreneurial attitudes slow down only when extensive growth is significant. On the other hand, when the opportunities for extensive growth are exhausted (as in much of the West today), entrepreneurship is in trouble and growth is bound to stall. Within such a context, intensive-growth spurts are not altogether absent. But intensive growth brings in itself the seeds of unproductive temptations, and the more successful the unproductive undertaking turn out to be, the lower the ongoing capacity to transform scientific advances into opportunities for economic growth.

These phenomena are also a warning to the observers of changes in real GDP or in other similar variables, for those data actually incorporate three different, difficult to disentangle components. One is a short-run story: data are affected by sudden changes in relative prices or in the producers' perception about future demand, so that new inputs are brought into operation or expelled. This is the extensive component. A second story regards the medium run, and reflects the unfolding of overlapping technological trajectories.[31] A third element is the long-term dynamics of entrepreneurship, which usually encourages the rise of unproductive factors when intensive growth is substantial and extensive growth is weak. This last phenomenon may well be self-reinforcing: as rent-seeking intensifies and the policy-makers give in to the demand for redistribution, the economic system loses flexibility and new demands for safeguards (privileges) emerge. In particular, the chances to engage in extensive growth patterns after a crisis are reduced.

8.6 Can entrepreneurship be rescued?

The previous paragraphs have presented a rather dim picture, dominated by some sort of ratchet effect, according to which there are always good reasons to slow-down, but acceleration is harder to bring about, even in the presence of satisfactory technological progress. Should one then conclude that the long-term drift from productive to unproductive entrepreneurship or to entrepreneurial numbness is all but inevitable? After all, economic history after the First Industrial Revolution has shown that periods of sluggish growth have indeed been followed by rebounds (Maddison 2005), and that it did not always take a new "industrial revolution" to jump ahead.

To address this question we recall our previous claim: sustained growth requires some minimum amount of productive entrepreneurship, in order to transform Newtonian technological progress into innovation, and innovation into growth by means of new fixed capital (embodied technological progress). In this light, the periods of sluggish growth after the industrial revolutions can be traced back to two sources. One relates to the steady decline of productive entrepreneurship following the rise of rent-seeking. In this case, reversal may be triggered by government intervention, as the Keynesian view would argue (see also Section 2.6 in Chapter 2). Another possibility relates to the very features of the historical period during which the slowdown takes place. When so, long-term rebounds might require deep institutional changes. These two scenarios are examined in the next two subsections.

8.6.1 The Keynesian gloom

The Keynesian position is that stagnation or slow growth tends to take place when entrepreneurship features unproductive traits: entrepreneurial skills are devoted to acquiring rents and even productive activities are carried out under the shield of the rents created by policy-making. By borrowing from macroeconomics terminology, one may thus conceive of the existence of some kind of a vicious circle. Regulation, rent-seeking and the general provisions and guarantees characterizing the Age of Social Responsibility, ensure that relatively large quantities of productive inputs stay idle: unemployment figures move upwards, while the meagre prospects for the future depress net investment, no matter how low interest rates might be. Sluggish investment fails to transform technological progress into higher productivity on a large enough scale to bring about a new phase of growth. In this context, therefore, productivity gains translate into modest growth and can even be partially offset by renewed, wealth-destroying, rent-seeking efforts, both in the private and public sectors. The obvious examples are the acquisition or strengthening of privileges; and the expansion of the civil service, respectively.

The Keynesian recipe to escape the trap advocates intervention by the policy-maker, who is supposed to offset the lower propensity to consume private goods by the larger consumption of government services. Of course, the trick is performed by issuing public debt, possibly financed by foreign creditors. Although today's debt might be perceived as a promise of future taxation, present consumption patterns are unlikely to reflect the full amount of the debt. Put differently, the trick might work even in the presence of the Ricardian equivalence.[32] As long as those who buy government bonds do not expect default, the Ricardian equivalence is at least partially neutralized if it is believed that the Treasury bills will be reimbursed by issuing new debt. When so, at least a fraction of the Treasury bills in circulation are considered financial wealth, and therefore hardly generate a reduction in consumption.

In the end, according to this view the trap can be avoided and the policy-maker go scot-free if: (*a*) despite the higher propensity to save, the policy-maker brings about higher consumption, thereby leading to temporary extensive growth; (*b*) the "trick" soothes pessimism about the future and restores confidence;[33] and (*c*) the opportunities for unproductive entrepreneurship are barred and investment resumes. In other words, extensive growth must be feasible and debt financing must provoke a change in individual preferences: under the conditions listed above unproductive propensities are hopefully turned around by the period of extensive growth triggered by debt-financed spending.[34] Whether the conditions are within reach is of course another matter.

8.6.2 Entrepreneurial numbness and the role of education

The first scenario of sluggish growth has focused on the observation of entrepreneurs choosing between productive and unproductive options in accordance with the prevailing institutional context. Instead, the second scenario considers that the ideological foundations of the rules of the game also affect the very features of entrepreneurship. Today's fiscal requirements of social solidarity have become a heavy burden on successful entrepreneurial endeavours, while the widespread diffusion of rent-seeking has gradually eroded the legitimacy of risk taking. A number of consequences have followed. For instance, although both productive and unproductive entrepreneurial ventures involve risk and possibly failure, in the Age of Social Responsibility success tends to have a legal foundation in the latter case only: rents are often guaranteed by formal norms passed by government or governmental agencies and almost become moral. Even when such privileges meet opposition, disapproval is at least in part directed towards the authority that issues the privilege, rather than towards the beneficiary; and censure is ultimately watered down by the privilege being perceived as one of the many elements that compose the political debate at large.

From a broader vantage point, the gradual weakening of our (genetic) propensity to engage in productive entrepreneurship and the silent acceptance of unproductive behavioural routines originate from an attitude of psychological numbness that starts very early in the life of most individuals. From its inception, a typical ingredient of the Age of Social Responsibility has been state-controlled education. Private schooling has not been formally outlawed, of course. But in many countries, the state schooling system has enjoyed all sorts of privileges. In addition, the central authorities have almost total control over what is being taught and often times influence the recruiting of the teachers even outside state schools. The result is that state education has now become a rent-seeking system for many teachers – hence the opposition to the voucher-system – whose power and willingness to fail or expel students is frequently limited and whose teaching abilities are hardly monitored. In turn, lack of competitive pressure and slack accountability for the results have not only caused a deterioration in the quality of education, but they have also often created an environment in which the notions of social good, forced solidarity, and lack of individual responsibility have prevailed, either through direct action (what is being taught) or indirectly (by observing how the system works and ultimately feeling part of it). Now, since most youth in the developed countries of the West spend some 10–20 years of their life at school, it is not surprising that the way they are trained to confront difficulties and to respond to challenges reflects the environment they perceive during those crucial years, especially when those behavioural examples or schemes are consistent with the moral standards adopted through their parents.

Put differently, one can imagine two different environments, both in harmony with the traits typical of the Age of Social Responsibility. One consists in the development of an incentive system that encourages rent-seeking at all levels.[35] In such an environment, risk-taking may be directed in unproductive directions (the creation and exploitation of privileges), but if it is not quenched through education at large, entrepreneurial spirits remain alive. Examples along this direction are provided by regimes in which bright individuals often move up the social ladder by making use of their alertness and intellectual skills, as well as of their understanding of the dynamics of the system.[36] Not surprisingly, a different and more competitive system under these same circumstances might redirect such entrepreneurial energies towards productive purposes. On the other hand, an environment might feature an educational system conceived in order to make the individual feel part of a community of consumers supplied by a static production structure guided by regulated prices, in which long-run growth is fed by adopted constant technological progress, rather than by innovation. Under such circumstances, the ideal environment for most model-makers, individuals are trained to be happy with what is being given to them by a fair society ruled by a benevolent planner.

At first sight the outcomes might appear similar, for in both cases, one would observe unproductive, rent-seeking entrepreneurial activities. The substance, however, is rather different. In the former case, success is the result of risk-taking, of a vision, of the awareness that you need a strategy in order to get to the top. In the latter case, success comes from the ability to fill the gaps or from luck. In other words, in the former case you need to act in order to exploit the opportunities and be the author of your future, while in the latter case you must be lucky, either to be co-opted by the elite, or to be chosen to solve the technical needs of the elite.

Of course, these phenomena are not peculiar to the Age of Social Responsibility. Still, we claim that the second scenario has characterized much of the West during the past decades and that the weakening of the entrepreneurial idea – both productive and unproductive – has been triggered by the deterioration of the educational system together with a weakened family fabric, sometimes unable to oppose the mind frame inherited from schooling, and frequently unwilling to do so.[37]

Numbness does not imply that innovation is altogether lost. But when numbness prevails, progress and growth clearly become a matter of imitation, whereas the task of transforming technological progress into economic performance takes place in other parts of the world. The process is not irreversible, either. The traditional literature, however, claims that one would solve the problem by enforcing the proper institutions: better regulation and lower taxation. We, by contrast, maintain that once the very notion of entrepreneurship is disgraced, long-term rebounds can only come from the educational sector.

8.7 Policy-making for the long run: technology and entrepreneurship

From a policy-making standpoint, the challenge presented by the growth question can thus be articulated in fairly simple terms. To begin with, the methodological foundations inherited from the Newtonian revolution are unlikely to be much affected by state intervention. Unless science is systematically obstructed over the whole planet, technological progress is going to advance anyway. It simply takes place in the areas that present more favourable institutional settings.[38]

Hence, there is no significant technology challenge. If at all, one might observe a free-riding phenomenon, as sooner or later entrepreneurs in one region might profit from research carried out somewhere else, possibly by imitation. But the importance of this occurrence should not be overestimated, for when free riding occurs in the high-tech industries, for example, the quasi-rents (profits) enjoyed by the innovative producers are already modest and the benefits created by the imitating innovators are almost entirely appropriated by the buyers. Under such circumstances, the policy-maker plays a merely redistributive role, in that he must decide whether the surplus generated by innovation/imitation accrues to protected/privileged producers or to consumers. While this is not without consequences – and the recent EU record with regard to R&D and anti-trust is eloquent – it is hardly a strategy for technological growth.

Policy-makers have also devoted some attention to the entrepreneurial challenge, which has justified action (subsidies) in favour of young, new entrepreneurs and efforts to keep alive ailing companies. We let the statisticians compute the questionable effectiveness of such programmes. Nonetheless, there are reasons to believe that a normative response to this alleged challenge might be missing the point. One wonders, for example, how the marginal projects could be identified and whether it would not be easier to eliminate the "marginal-project" question by means of first-best intervention.[39] For instance, if the gap between the private and social value of innovation is created by excessive taxation on profits, the solution is a reduction in tax pressure, rather than handing out subsidies. If the gap is provoked by regulation for the benefit of a specific counterpart (the consumer, the worker), then the first-best solution is the abolition of those privileges.

Yet, ambiguities abound. The attempt to enhance the creation of new companies while also making it harder for inefficient suppliers to go bust is puzzling, to say the least. It implies that consumers are willing to sustain all kinds of producers, even those who have shown poor performances. That contradicts the evidence, of course; for if consumers had appreciated them enough, the bad performers would not need help to stay afloat. Moreover, those very same policy architects consider the market as a constant pie to be fairly distributed among consumers, rather than producers. Thus, by penalizing risk-taking, planners end up generating fierce battles to acquire or protect bundles of privileges. Put differently, the economy is squeezed by the double whammy of rules of the game that protect inefficient producers, but prevent the pie from growing; and of strategies aiming at redistributing meagre portions of that pie among an increasingly large number of hungry guests. As Gordon Tullock pointed out over 40 years ago, fairness thus degenerates into a fight for privileges.

Rather than looking for ad hoc policies, and consistent with the argument articulated above, we suggest that the core problem with long-term declines in growth rates is historical. By ignoring the historical, quasi-ideological nature of a long-term crisis, policy-makers end up enforcing a piecemeal mix of measures that ultimately boil down to the redistribution of a shrinking – or slowly growing – pie. The system can still thrive as long as the rent-seeking temptations are kept in check and productive entrepreneurs continue to carry the ball by creating wealth and by providing the necessary feedbacks and stimuli to the world of science. But surely, the system enters a period of crisis as soon as the rent-seeking disease is no longer kept in check and the perceived political costs of backpedalling outweigh the gains from reviving the productive-entrepreneurial component.

When long-run decline is also accompanied by the decay of the entrepreneurial culture within the educational system, the balance among the various forms of entrepreneurship is clearly no longer an issue. Targeted policies become irrelevant. To repeat, this does not mean that entrepreneurship has disappeared altogether, but it does mean that the surviving productive entrepreneurial ideas will be developed and exploited somewhere else, outside the entrepreneurs' native communities.

To conclude, there is not much the incumbent policy-making authorities in advanced countries can do to forestall or exit long-run crises. The very fact of being "advanced" – that is, that the majority of the population is relatively affluent – means that violent unrest is going to be unlikely: individuals would have too much to lose by overt turmoil, especially if the institutional alternative is far from evident. Nevertheless, peaceful, traditional recipes such as fiscal or monetary tricks are unlikely to provide satisfactory solutions. These policies do not address the real problems – a regulatory environment leading to unproductive rent-seeking and/or an educational system devoted to entrepreneurial numbness. In fact, they sometimes aggravate it: higher taxation and tampering with interest rates do nothing to unravel the root of the long-run question, let alone fix it.

Instead, hope for growth in the Age of Social Responsibility can only come from technological advance and structural flexibility. These can keep productive entrepreneurship alive despite the influence of the dominant First Principles of the age. Technological advance does create opportunities that would-be entrepreneurs might want to exploit, but it is obvious that the myriad technological agendas do not always have the same economic value. As they unfold their potential, some sectors will grow faster, while others will lag behind. If these "better" industries are characterized by relatively lax regulation, opportunities might indeed be developed and successfully transmitted to the rest of the economy. When this happens, bouts of productivity create growth and second chances for the political class in trouble. Otherwise, stagnation is almost unavoidable and falling purchasing power for vast layers of the population becomes a realistic threat. Political disquiet or – more likely – disaffection is a frequent by-product.

8.8 Policy-making for the medium-run: countercyclical intervention

From the medium-run perspective, the purpose of policy-action is taming the business cycle. Not surprisingly, countercyclical action is both appealing and frightening to all policy-makers. It is appealing because dealing with the business cycle[40] justifies intervention in front of public opinion. Especially, when it affects several countries at the same time, the business cycle provides an excuse to pay little heed to long-run issues, to rally the electoral body around the flag, and to silence opposition. By contrast, countercyclical action can backfire, for when ineffective or counterproductive, it can weaken the incumbent policy-maker, who therefore becomes vulnerable to his competitors. This explains why a general cyclical crisis is usually handled with mixed feelings and why, in the end, political expediency tends to obscure all other considerations.

Groping is further enhanced by the fact that during a crisis – or a situation perceived as critical – individuals might modify their preferences, and thus transform a transitory adjustment into a behavioural question. For instance, it is plausible to imagine that when dealing with a deep crisis, individuals reduce consumption and try to save more in order to face future adverse contingencies. If demand for consumption goods falls and if expectations about future consumption darken, investment also slows down and part of those savings are bound to be wiped out. In particular, some of the resources that are not going to be consumed will end up in "malinvestment": fixed capital that is not going to be employed in the production process. The upshot is that the excess supply of production inputs (including labour) will generate deflation, while aggregate production will drop until the demand for investment goods matches savings. The decline in production will of course be greater in a regulated economy, in which the legal context does not allow nominal wage rates to fall enough.[41]

This explains why, when the behavioural threat becomes real or the timing of the crisis differs from what the political situation requires, the policy-maker has a good reason to draw attention to its general (worldwide) dimensions, describe its dynamics so that one has the impression of reaching the trough relatively early and step in with expansionary, countercyclical policies: by printing money, or by transforming domestic or foreign savings into domestic consumption (public debt). These actions are politically sensible, in that they are consistent with the contract characterizing the Age of Social Responsibility. In addition they are understandable in that they aim at offsetting behavioural changes that might cause the political class serious damage. Yet, from an economic stand-point, these actions miss the point and can be counterproductive. The following subsections explain why.

8.8.1 Countercyclical actions, strategies, results

If one considers the two major crises that occurred in the past 100 years, three elements stand out, all consistent with the governmental strategies articulated in the previous paragraph. Throughout the 1930s all governments emphasized the universal nature of the crisis, which affected the whole industrialized world and was even considered unavoidable, since capitalism was supposed to be the carrier of prosperity, but ultimately self-destructive. Keynes himself owed a large part of his popularity to his ability to "predict" the crisis of capitalism well before 1929–1932.[42] Second, all governments engaged in massive intervention, which ultimately led to partial nationalization and heavy political interference on economic activity. Not surprisingly, private investment stalled, while the central authorities tried hard to transform private savings into public expenditure. Third, public opinion was erroneously led to believe that the crisis actually struck in 1929/1930, while the years that followed could be interpreted as a long period of quasi-stagnation along government-supervised, corporatist guidelines.[43]

A similar approach has also characterized the 2008/2009 crash, even if it was more a financial (sectorial) phenomenon than a generalized collapse of the eco-nomic fabric. Policy-makers again hesitated before acknowledging what was happening, then declared that the world financial system was on the verge of implosion, and finally responded by underlining the systemic nature of the crisis, which was proclaimed to be the consequence of the alleged "neoliberal" atti-tudes (i.e. lack of stringent regulation) adopted in previous decades. Not surpris-ingly, regulation and a new form of corporatism have been introduced as "new" measures to avoid similar catastrophes in the future and to make sure that uncer-tainty would no longer be a carrier of unpleasant surprises. At the same time, the authorities have engaged in massive injections of liquidity in order to rescue troubled financial institutions and even some large manufacturing companies.

As reactions to these crises reveal, in the Age of Social Responsibility there is only one pattern of reaction to a crisis. But not all crises have the same origin. Some are provoked by accidental negative shocks in the relative price structure; some are provoked by systematic mistakes. The 1973 oil crisis is an example of the first category; the 1929/1933 crisis exemplifies the second. These two cat-egories are examined below.

8.8.2 Sometimes crises come from accidents,...

Of course, there is not much to do in order to offset deteriorations in the terms of trade, other than to remove whatever can obstruct structural adjustment: producers modify their techniques, expand the production of the goods and services that have experienced price rises and move away from the industries hit by price drops. From a free-market standpoint all measures aiming at softening the transition make little or no sense. If the price change is unexpected,[44] bad luck hardly justifies violation of property rights. The indiscriminate endorsement of subsidies, trade policy and regulation to protect incumbents belongs to the realm of privileges, rather than of voluntary solidarity. It is acknowledged that adjustment has a cost, as the social, consequentialist approach would argue. Nonetheless, even if one neglects to consider where to draw the line when it comes to bad luck,[45] the free-market supporter would doubt that there is a criterion to determine the optimal speed of adjustment, allegedly determined by the trade-off between the benefits obtained when the economy moves to an efficient production structure, and the opportunity cost of the resources staying idle while unfettered adjustment is underway.

The nature of the problem is radically different, however, if a change in the terms of trade degenerates into a behavioural crisis, in which risk aversion dominates and uncertainty leads to a drop in the demand for both consumption and investment goods. Under such circumstances, the community fails to see or is unable to seize the opportunity for investment driven by the potential beneficiaries of the new context[46] and heads towards stagnation or decline. In other words, the difference between a price adjustment and a crisis is the difference between a structural and a behavioural adjustment. When analysing a crisis, one should therefore focus on whether a price shock produces a behavioural adjustment, and how this is accommodated by the entrepreneurial system. For instance, if individuals are hit by a shock and wish to save more, a fall in aggregate demand occurs. But it may also happen that the new propensity to save is matched by an increase in investment opportunities. New investments bring about a new composition in stocks and output may increase even above the levels prior to the adjustment, if individuals permanently believe that uncertainty about the future requires the creation of greater productive capacity. Once the (new) desired composition is obtained, flows return to where they were.[47] In short, in this case the adjustment would remain transitory and the outcome would not qualify as "critical".

8.8.3 ...sometimes from genetics, fraud, bad reading,...

Clearly, not all crises are merely accidental. There are also crises unleashed by systematic mistakes, either because agents misread market signals, or because the market sends out deceitful information (i.e. distorted prices). According to the former hypothesis, agents can misread information because individuals are affected by genetic biases; or because they are trained, and possibly persuaded, to make mistakes.

The role of genetic biases in economic decision-making is well known. For example, the argument in favour of protectionism in "strategic industries" remains popular despite its weak economic foundations. The reason is that the human mind is still affected by calculations about what was needed to guarantee survival to a community in a hostile environment centuries or millennia ago. Agriculture is a prime example when it comes to industrial policies. From a different standpoint, genetic legacies also help explain differences in the perception of ownership: even if the market price is the same and if no specific psychic element is attached, in many communities land is considered more valuable than financial assets.

Despite their weight, genetic legacies can hardly be held responsible for a crisis, though. They do not provoke *ex post* reactions – individuals do not wake up and regret their earlier decisions. If they did, these biases would have been eliminated long ago, as more and more agents become conscious of their blunders and rationally adjust their behaviour. Put differently, this kind of biological biases can help understand systematic errors, but not occasional misjudgement, let alone cyclical mistakes.

Rather than blaming genetics, it is probably more fruitful to concentrate on those situations in which market signals are misread because individuals have been encouraged to make mistakes, e.g. by relying on false information. This may occur because of purposely fraudulent behaviour by private advisors or public authorities. When private agencies cheat, they provide false or incomplete data in the wake of sloppy investigation and superficial analyses. In other words, they break a contractual agreement that usually prescribes that they should perform professionally and to the best of their abilities. When monitoring is carried out by government-related agencies, the public knows that it is their duty to certify – for example – the financial status of companies quoted on the stock exchange or of banks operating in a given territory. It also knows that a state authority has the means to perform its duties, which the citizen rationally expects to be applied. Systematic failure to do so is in fact a form of fraudulent behaviour: in the Age of Social Responsibility individuals trust the state to which they feel bound by an implicit social contract. In contrast with the private context, however, most of the time public agents remain immune to judicial investigation and sanctions, which obviously contributes to increasing carelessness and malpractice.[48]

Finally, misreading can also happen because individuals have been taught/ trained not to read. This is not a genetic trait, of course; it is a behavioural question and is related to the educational problem mentioned earlier on. For instance, today the essence of the (free-)market system remains poorly understood. The market is still perceived as a set of more or less desirable outcomes, rather than a process that gathers and transfers dispersed information generated by voluntary transactions (Hayek 1945). Similarly, the connection between entrepreneurship and growth is hardly grasped, let alone explained in the classrooms. The very notion of profit is often grossly misrepresented, sometimes being confused with the price of capital, sometimes being depicted as a rent, sometimes being described as the result of exploitation. Surely, the widespread insistence on teaching model-making techniques and neglecting ideas has added a great deal to this distorted way of thinking. Likewise, the sheer success of technical analysis when dealing with the dynamics of the stock exchange points to the fact that extrapolating statistical trend is more rewarding than fundamental analysis. Put differently, making money in the Age of Social Responsibility is considered a matter of luck, of beating the statistician. Good luck does not need social sharing, but bad luck does, for nobody must be held accountable for misfortune. The conclusion is that when market signals are ignored or misinterpreted, human action necessarily leads to repeated critical episodes driven by extrapolation and sparked by alleged mishaps.[49]

8.8.4 ... but not from greed or blindness

What about the recurrent effort to blame short-sighted greed and "speculators" for allegedly unjustified booms and the overly painful delusions? As mentioned in Section 8.3, growth implies structural movements, since research agendas generate innovation trajectories that do not necessarily affect all industries to the same extent and at the same time. It may well be that when an industry experiences a boom, individuals get carried away by optimistic extrapolation, especially when they have little information about the technology, its potential economic value, the companies and the competitive pressures the industry may be subject to. Clearly, when the weak fundamentals of the companies and industries involved become manifest, those who do not wake up early enough are bound to suffer. An example has been the high-tech-communication boom and crisis in the last decades of the twentieth century.

Yet, there is not much to do against the yearning for wealth. To begin with, the desire to be better off is not necessarily an evil feature, as long as it does not involve violence. Blindness, on the other hand, can be offset by better information and education. In a world populated by short-sighted people, you will soon witness an increased supply of spectacles. It does not matter whether these new spectacles come from private entrepreneurs or state bureaucrats, as long as nobody cheats and the consumer is free to choose. Surely, some will claim that the bureaucrat might be less knowledgeable, but that he is to be preferred since he is in a position to take into account and prevent the so-called "systemic effects", whereby a greedy minority can imperil the prosperity of the blind majority by triggering snowball effects and "shaking the system". Once again, this is bound to be a moot normative claim, unless one establishes under what circumstances individual preferences can be overruled through regulation, and under what circumstances individual property can be violated for the sake of selected groups (redistribution in favour of those who made the wrong, "greedy" choices). The social view would trust the utilitarian criterion adopted by the rule-maker, whereas the free-market position would of course flatly deny such a compulsory delegation of powers. Searching for a third way would be a vain exercise, for as long as the possibility of encroaching upon individual freedom is admitted, one implicitly assigns the rule-maker the power to set his own boundaries, which therefore are likely to reflect his utilitarian standard and his legal power to modify and enforce them.

8.9 Lessons for impending crises

To sum up our argument thus far, we have suggested that the essence of a crisis is the inability to comprehend, which in turn is the result of fraud or bad education. Although it remains hard to estimate to what extent systematic fraudulent behaviour, bad economic training and lack of understanding lead to crises – a task that we gladly let the statistical economist grapple with – there is a clear difference between situations in which contracts have been breached (fraud) and those in which involuntary mistakes have been made (misreading).

In the case of fraud, the problem and the solution clearly lie with the judiciary, not with the policy-maker. In practice, however, the solution may be elusive. The judges are themselves the product of the Age of Social Responsibility. Their reading of the facts is often a mix of contract enforcement and "common sense", i.e. genetic behavioural biases, conventional wisdom, public opinion, sometimes populism. In addition, the judiciary is not independent of political power. Although the context varies across countries, politicians often influence the appointment of the judges. In turn, the judges frequently do not pass up on the opportunity to become future rule-makers, which requires approval by the incumbent rule makers. All in all, it is hard to imagine situations in which the judges are neutral, and in which policy-makers are taken to court for having fallen short of their obligations and for having led the citizen to make bad choices. It would also be hard to find policy-makers wealthy enough to pay damages or the premium required by an insurance company. Their wages or fees would probably go through the roof, and become an additional burden for the taxpayer. The outcome is what is being currently observed. Taxpayers (reluctantly) accept that these rule-makers be paid substantial salaries so as to run the redistributive, rent-seeking game, that they largely ignore their monitoring role, and hope that their regulatory activity is nonetheless for the sake of the common good.

When market signals have been misread, the educational question seems to be most relevant. Education is a matter of people, parents, friends, teachers, and media. They are all subject to innate or acquired behavioural distortions. Still, the case for compulsory education by a monopolist (the state) is weak. There is ample evidence about the limits of the rulers to define – let alone enforce – good training in economics. The alternative is of course the promotion of open access to education. Competition among educational curricula and teachers does not guarantee that each individual gets unbiased information and judgement, but it does provide more opportunities for debate, careful thinking by the parties involved (students and their parents), comparison, and ultimately the promotion of a less superficial approach to the (self-)responsible development of human beings.

What are then the consequences for countercyclical policy-making? We believe that if one accepts that the dynamics of productivity is the outcome of a combination between technological progress and entrepreneurial innovation, sooner or later regulation will stifle entrepreneurial spirits and reduce the chances of bouncing back. In a closed economy, the result is stagnation. In an open economy, it might be prolonged recession, as competition puts pressure on the quasi-rents enjoyed by the owners of the production factors. Their purchasing power will thus drop, perhaps even dramatically, and such a drop will unleash a behavioural crisis. The effects are of course aggravated if input prices are prevented from falling enough and companies are driven out of business. True, the result is not quite a business cycle, for under such circumstances the economy fails to rebound. But crisis (or stagnation) it is, nonetheless.

This logic applies to the coercive aspects of regulatory intervention, the essence of real policy-making. But the government can also alter agents' behaviour through promises. As noted in Section 8.8.3, promises fall under two categories: commitments to monitor and commitments to refund (guarantees). Monitoring is currently supposed to be enforced by the judiciary or by specialized government agencies, which act in accordance with the principles of social responsibility: unless the government official signals irregularities or missing information, and unless the judiciary intervenes, the public takes it for granted that the information available is correct and proceeds accordingly. Furthermore, when the government offers guarantees of refunds in case of losses, the reduced perception of risk encourages over-investment and reduces the incentives to control firms' behaviour and performance. As a by-product, managers increase their rents and get away with shoddy investment decisions.

Is monetary intervention any different from real policy-making, false promises, munificent guarantees? Surely, the impact of regulatory or fiscal intervention on the incentive structure tends to be permanent. Even if intervention is only temporary, it sets a precedent and therefore affects expectations about the future. It may vary through time as individuals adjust, but some kind of lasting behavioural change does occur. For instance, by increasing tax pressure on capital income, the government leads to a reduction in investment, which might be partly – but only partly – offset by accounting tricks such as tax avoidance or outright tax evasion. Likewise, promise and guarantees do change the way of perceiving risk.

Monetary intervention, by contrast, is never sustainable in the long run, unless it is accompanied by some kind of regulation. For instance, you can carry out an expansionary monetary policy, but unless you regulate the real interest rate by law and make dealing with foreign residents illegal, agents can make such measures redundant by using rival monetary units, or by formulating contracts in a different way. Put differently, monetary intervention is unique in that it can be neutralized as long as capital markets remain relatively free. Still, two questions are to be answered: Does this mean that monetary policy is neutral? And does it imply that the process of neutralization is smooth and relatively harmless?

The answer to the first question is well known and focuses on two points. In paper-money regimes, a change in the money supply always affects different categories of agents to different extents. If extra money is handed out to banks or to governments, the bank shareholders or the recipients of government spending are going to benefit, and the rest of the community is going to lose. For example, if the money supply is reduced and the agents can't get the liquidity they need elsewhere, demand for goods and services weakens and some investments turn out to be unprofitable: owners of capital and possibly the financial sector suffer, while owners of liquid assets gain. Thus, monetary policy is never neutral: as Richard Cantillon pointed out some three centuries ago, it implies redistributive effects and alters the perceived profitability of investment.[50]

Sooner or later the system adjusts, as the relative price structure gradually absorbs the consequences of the monetary shock and investors correct their actions in the wake of their new perceptions of consumers' demand. But the adjustment is neither smooth, nor harmless. On the one hand, the wealth effects that accompany the adjustment process are often permanent. In addition, it has been observed that some investment projects are undertaken because of – say – easy money and booming demand. These will turn out to be the result of a bad decision, once credit becomes more expensive and/or demand drops. And whenever investment plans are disrupted, production capacity is wasted.

There is a silver lining, though. Surely, when investment plans are scrapped and the investment mood worsens, investment stagnates and the existing fixed capital is run down. But once agents at large believe that mistakes have been discounted and that the cleaning is over, consumption can resume and investment will also pick up at relatively high speed, to build up the depleted capital. This new wave of investment will probably incorporate the newest technology and therefore enhance productivity growth above the long-run trend. In a word, monetary policy is most likely to contribute to blurring the overall picture and to enhancing the redistribution of wealth in a rather opaque way. But it does not necessarily create entrepreneurial numbness or ruinous behavioural phenomena. Rather than solving the problems of a structural crisis, monetary mismanagement might well aggravate them – but perhaps not irreparably.

8.10 Summary and conclusions

In this chapter we have shown that as of the beginning of the Secular Period, research and analyses in the areas of political science justified the role of the policy-maker by pointing out his ability – if not his duty – to enhance the prosperity of the community under his jurisdiction. In particular, during the Age of Social Responsibility, growth has become part of the implicit contract between the electorate and its representatives, who have been promising rising living standards for everybody. That promise has not always been kept.

The history of economic thought has underscored different mechanisms that explain aggregate performance. In the end, however, it all depends on the ability to exploit talents and opportunities at three different levels: when acquiring new scientific knowledge, when transforming knowledge into technological breakthroughs and when translating breakthroughs into entrepreneurial initiatives. The emergence of chances follows path-dependent processes and feed-back mechanisms, which are in turn affected by the prevailing institutional and ideological contexts. In recent times, more attention has indeed been devoted to the rules of the game, but the literature has still paid little attention to the role of ideology and First Principles. As a result, even if a reputed literature keeps arguing that it was all a matter of property rights, we know that growth took place as a consequence of the Newtonian Revolution. Yet, we still fail to grasp what happened later. Surely, free-market institutions help understand why the Netherlands and Great Britain took the lead, but this explanation is less satisfactory when it comes to the German or Japanese miracles from the late nineteenth century to the late twentieth.

Our basic argument is that in the Age of Social Responsibility the threat to the advancement of science and technology is minor, when compared to what endangers the future of entrepreneurship. Growth will not taper off because of rent-seeking, which might be reversed by institutional overhaul; but because of numbness, which could be reversed only by a new deep institutional change and which can hardly be stemmed by targeted, pro-entrepreneurship measures possibly driven by expediency. Rather, expediency can transform an accident into a behavioural crisis and therefore a temporary setback into a long-lasting problem, and it can contribute to people's inability and possibly unwillingness to read market signals and take action accordingly.

More generally, we have observed that government intervention runs the risk of generating unintended but nonetheless acute fluctuations through two mechanisms: regulatory illusions and monetary shocks. Regulatory illusions induce agents to believe that companies are not what they really are. When they wake up and run away, fluctuations ensue. Monetary shock, on the other hand, lead agents to believe that the returns on at least some investments are different from what a rational analyst would estimate and from what they turn out to be in reality. Bad investment decisions follow and people eventually adjust, once again after waking up, or after the events force them to wake up. Both frameworks justify booms, depressions and periods of stagnation, that is business cycles. When major crises occur, both mechanisms are often at work at the same time or in sequence. This is no accident, especially during the Age of Social Responsibility, in which governments have an incentive to regulate, and may thus be tempted to neglect the low-growth trap by encouraging relatively generous monetary policies.

In the end, one must realize that economic crises happen because of shocks and mistakes, and unless one denies uncertainty as a crucial element in economic reasoning and reality, crises are unavoidable. From this perspective, therefore, the challenge for the ruling elite does not consist in finding ways of creating the perfect individual or eliminating uncertainty. Instead, it consists in ensuring that agents have the possibility of realizing their mistakes, that they are rewarded for being prudent, and that they are encouraged to engage in risk-taking according to the incentives provided by profits and losses. The notion of self-responsibility and the instinct to be better off[51] will encourage people to react to critical episodes and bet on a more prosperous future. At the other extreme, entrepreneurial numbness and expectations of guaranteed compensation for losses are the recipes for stagnation or low growth at best. Unfortunately, one has the impression that with the passing of time, the nature of policy-action has taken the West closer to the latter edge and that opportunities to grow have been wasted.

9 Poverty and transition

9.1 What it is all about

After the Second World War and until the 1960s, the distinction between developed and undeveloped countries was rather straightforward, although wishful thinking, political manners and a sense of guilt in the aftermath of colonialism had replaced the term "undeveloped" with "developing": Western Europe and its offshoots on the one side, the rest of the world on the other (Maddison 2005). The Soviet bloc was an embarrassing exception, however, and was therefore hypocritically shelved in a third category named "centrally planned economies", as if many developing countries were also not centrally planned. In the past couple of decades, political correctness has led to more articulated and "objective" rankings. For example, the *World Bank Development Report 2010* classifies economies into four categories according to their GDP per capita: High income countries (>\$11,905), upper middle income countries (>\$3,855), lower middle income countries (>\$975), low income countries (<\$976). In 2008, average GDP per capita in these four groups of countries (adjusted for PPP in brackets) were \$39,345 (\$37,141), \$7,878 (\$12,297), \$2,078 (\$4,592), and \$524 (\$1,407).

We simply characterize developed economies by two elements. First, they operate near the consumption and production possibility frontiers defined by the fastest runners.[1] Second, their wealth does not come primarily from the exploitation of raw materials, but from the employment of fixed and human capital. Put simply, developed countries feature a highly valuable (productive) labour force, are well equipped with modern machinery, and make the most of the opportunities created by technology and trade.

It is therefore obvious that a developed economy can be stagnant, but not for too long: otherwise it might be overtaken and eventually outpaced by better players, and fall back to "developing" status. In addition, the standard notion of "developed" is necessarily relative and arbitrary. It is relative, because it is calculated with reference to a moving benchmark – say, potential GDP per capita – defined by the top performers. It is arbitrary, both because GDP per capita measures the amount of production – which many consider an inadequate proxy for wealth and happiness, as argued in Chapter 8 – and because there is no objective criterion to determine how "close" to the front runner one economy needs to be in order to qualify as a member of the elite.

By definition, the economies that do not belong to the set briefly described above are undeveloped. Some of them are stuck in poverty or relative poverty, in that they do not seem able to bridge the gap that separates them from the front runners. They are not necessarily zero-growth areas. In fact, they may well take advantage of shreds of technology that come their way more or less randomly through imports, the effects of which might be magnified by some primitive form of imitation and adaptation.[2] Absorption through imports and basic imitation may also gather momentum as a consequence of aid or of temporary improvements in the international terms of trade. Yet, these advances do not ignite a growth process of much consequence: the rules of the game stay more or less the same, investment continues to be sluggish and the agents hardly modify their behaviours, skills or entrepreneurial attitudes. In brief, undeveloped countries may experience spurts of growth, but no sustained increase in well-being. Indeed, when rent-seeking is particularly intense, the benefits of such short-run bursts of improvements are likely to be appropriated by a restricted number of interest groups. This also applies to aid programmes, which do very little for growth, and can easily be counterproductive (Bauer 1974, 1991).[3]

In contrast, other countries might be in the process of catching up with the front runners, although this catching-up frequently runs out of steam or simply aborts before the standards set by the elite are obtained.[4] These are generally identified as "transition countries", i.e. economies that have been characterized by low income and limited growth for more or less extended periods of time, but that have recently embarked on market-oriented institutional change and are showing evidence of fast growth,[5] with significant and lasting effects on the living standards of the resident population. In particular, the experience of the Soviet bloc after 1989 has helped clarify the existence of a two-stage process, according to which an economy first undergoes an institutional/political transition process, during which catching-up might take off. Catching-up represents the second stage, which is generally supposed to start no later than five years from the beginning of transition (Allsopp and Kierzkowski 1997; Ellman 1997).

Given this broad terminological picture, the next section examines a number of concepts that had been already mentioned in previous chapters and that will be used again in order to frame a new way of considering poverty and transition. In Section 9.3 we explore why a rather large group of individuals living in poverty[6] fails to imitate more successful economies and to take the (institutional) steps required to ignite catching-up. Section 9.4 analyses the phenomenon of transition, with emphasis on the variables that affect the chances of success. Section 9.5 concludes by analysing the meaning of development economics and the role – if any – of development policies.

9.2 Culture, behaviour and social contracts reappraised

In previous chapters, we observed that human action in a social context is characterized by culture, behavioural routines, and people's understanding of the social contract. Of course, these three concepts interact with – and affect – one another. Moreover, they are all influenced by ideological components, sometimes following a deep institutional change, on other occasions as a result of an inertial process (path dependence driven by evolutionary mechanisms). We shall now briefly review and expand these notions, which will be subsequently used to analyse the economics of poverty and transition.

9.2.1 Culture

In Chapter 3 we noted that culture defines the role of what we called the external observer, who generally ensures that the agent feels uncomfortable and encouraged to amend his behaviour if his actions deviate from the expectations of his community of reference. In other words, the external observer informs the individual about the prevailing customs and ethics, the constraints imposed by the group upon his behaviour and possibly the positive and negative incentives that the group provides with regard to (spurious) altruism.[7]

Cultural patterns include personal emotions, as long as their expressions are recognized (codified) by the external observer. In fact, such expressions are frequently desirable, since they generate significant information about the expectations and the behavioural routines of the individual – and thus about his reliability and the terms of possible cooperation. This clearly plays a very valuable role when there are opportunities to interact, but enforcement is weak and expensive, and contracts are incomplete. Culture also reflects deontic principles, which shape how the individual thinks and perceives what happens around him. Deontic principles can be shared with the rest of the community, in which case they define the common notion of moral legitimacy of institutions (the rules of the game) or social action (policies); but it may also happen that the individual develops his own moral standards. These could originate from the outside world, possibly from another culture; they can be the product of new ideologies proposed by persuasive intellectual innovators; or they can be shaped by the inner circle of people with whom the individual interacts more frequently – family members, friends, teachers, colleagues.[8]

Hence, (collective) culture and (individual) psychological patterns coincide for the pure conformist, who believes that public opinion and common wisdom are always right, fair, and just; and that the proper course of action is to imitate and follow the crowd, whatever that means. In vital communities, conformism is of course the exception rather than the rule. In these societies, psychological patterns include curiosity, risk taking, drives for self-betterment, and the skill and willingness to adapt to new environments. These are typically individual features, which vary across individuals and are the engines of entrepreneurial advance as well as of cultural change.

When conformism prevails, culture is static and social relations end in sets of more or less regulated repetitive practices. More frequently, however, the inter-action between the inherited cultural traits, new exogenous ideas and the indi-viduals' own psychological patterns determines the evolutionary path of a culture and eventually the features of social relations. When these cultural traits are intense, widely shared and open to accommodating the dynamics of viva-cious individual action, the environment features an "open" culture and forms an "open society". In this context, the key concepts are tolerance, and deeply-rooted and fairly stable moral principles. Tolerance allows the unfolding of the indi-vidual discovery process, while moral principles ensure long-term cooperation.

By contrast, a goal-driven culture applies to situations in which groups of individuals are kept together by a set of common wishes, rather than by moral standards. This may happen because each subset of a social entity has its own moral standards or, more likely, because moral standards are superficial, fragile, or moulded according to expediency. Hence the notion of "goal-driven society", in which policy tools are accepted as long as they appear instrumental in attain-ing shared targets, and tolerance is necessarily limited by the nature of the goals. Many developed countries fall within this "goal-driven" category.[9]

In a similar vein, an "individualistic society" refers to geographic areas where agents feel more or less the same about the meaning of acceptable ("fair") indi-vidual behaviour, but are much less in agreement with the collective goals defined by a majority (or a strong minority), or with the policy-making tools to be applied in order to obtain such goals. Thus, agents feel entitled to opt out of any "implicit" social contract and legitimized to resist state coercion. Of course, this represents a critical issue for the political scientist and the policy-maker, since it raises the question of whether a group must respect the individual who interacts with the group, but does not share its preferences; or whether it can apply the social rules also to the (cultural) outsider. As discussed at length in previous chapters of this book, the free-market and the socialist vantage points offer sharply different answers. The former would argue that the individual always has a right to opt out from the group, and interact with its members according to rules defined on a case-by-case basis or on a general, agreed-upon default rule (e.g. the civil code, or tradi-tion, or third-party rulings). By contrast, the socialist answer would insist on geographical proximity; residence being enough to justify the imposition of cul-tural conformity and policy-making on the dissident individual. Opting out is not excluded altogether, but it requires – and is equivalent to – physical migration.

The extreme case emerges when there is no prevailing culture: then, a society boils down to a system of formal cooperating agreements to enhance exchange within a purely "rational" context, in which the depth of the rule of law deter-mines the time horizon of the agents.[10]

9.2.2 Behavioural routines

In an ideal world, formal rules and policies merely reproduce the informal canons and meet the recognized needs of the group. Thus, formal rules are introduced to enhance communication and credibility, with limited or no conflict between culture and policies and no intention to create new rules and interfere with spontaneous interaction. In such a world, there is also no need for coercion, except to prevent violence and to enforce contracts previously agreed upon, since policies solve coordination problems in order to attain shared goals according to procedures that have been unanimously accepted. As a result, behavioural routines would originate from the spontaneous interaction between psychological patterns (the way we are, including principles) and culture, with no regulatory interference from the authorities. People would follow their own preferences, their own ways of acquiring and elaborating knowledge and information, their own moral standards. Surely, agents would also be willing to adapt to – and even compromise with – the outside world in order to enhance cooperation. But that adaptation would remain their own choice, out of altruism or greed, need and cowardice; definitely not under the threat of aggression by other parties.

However, things are different in reality. The action of the state is by no means neutral. Regulators and legislators do matter: They have their own goals that originate from a mix of culture, ideological commitment and political expediency, heavily influenced by interest groups. Put differently, governmental action is coercive and creates behavioural rules that might well conflict with the psychological blueprint of at least some groups of people, when not with those of substantial layers of the population, especially in goal-driven or individualistic societies. As the public-choice school has emphasized, the rule-making elite itself tends to evolve into a rent-seeking group that frequently pursues no specific welfare-enhancing mission, except to garner consensus and preserve power. If these rent-seeking activities are kept within the limits defined by the First Principles underlying the implicit social contract, the rule-maker has little to fear and the new behavioural routines will be eventually agreed to. The context becomes much more intricate, however, if First Principles are not in place. Under such conditions, the difference between government action and abusive short-term rent-seeking is faint and turmoil can only be avoided by the threat of violence.

The conflicts created by the various incentive structures and rent-seeking phenomena may explain why given stimuli fail to elicit the same responses across societies (economies). When the First Principles are weak and the formal institutions not shared, state action may be resisted or made ineffective; and large social groups break down into smaller subgroups, held together by culture and common behavioural routines. As will be pointed out in the next two sections, both sets of elements – differentiated response to conflicts and group fragmentation – are critical in explaining poverty traps, the dynamic and depth of transition, and the failure to engage in the deceptively easy path to prosperity.

9.2.3 Social contracts

Chapters 3–5 have analysed at some length the nature and content of the social contract, which is founded on what we have defined as First Principles. To repeat our earlier line of reasoning, the importance of the social contract originates from the fact that it is the bedrock of shared policy-making: it characterizes its nature and the extent to which its authors may deviate without meeting major punishment (loss of power).

In this chapter, the object of the social contract enters the picture in various ways and contributes to our understanding of poverty and (market-oriented) transition. For instance, the contract may be framed in order to meet priorities that exclude economic growth, a possibly puzzling phenomenon for the mainstream observer of poor countries, but not unusual in richer environments, in which the advocates of zero-growth perspectives abound. Or, it might not be framed at all, leading to fragmented societies and possibly to rent-seeking coalitions with diverging interests, a frequent source of conflicts. In a similar vein, the social-contract perspective can also help to explain situations in which individuals have had enough, realize the extent of the oppression to which they have fallen victim, believe that they deserve and can obtain better, but ultimately fail to galvanize into collective action. Put differently, lack of a clear social contract does not prevent the poor from agreeing on the need to modify the current institutional context, but cooperation might easily break down when First Principles must be "revealed", let alone enforced.

To conclude, there is no doubt that some meta-rules are more conducive to GDP growth than others. Nonetheless, it makes little sense to draft blueprints designed to maximize growth or consumption while ignoring the driving ideology that has a bearing on cooperation within relatively large communities. Rather, and in contrast with a 60-year long tradition in development economics, we shall try to emphasize that the presence or absence of a well-defined social contract plays an important role in the development story. In particular, this applies when a community does not come from scratch, nor emerges from a smooth evolutionary process; but originates from artificial political arrangements, imposed from the outside, when the conqueror and the conquered have not merged into a single community; or imposed from the inside, when an autocrat has succeeded in replacing the old behavioural routines with new routines.

9.2.4 The features of interaction

To conclude, the main idea put forward in these pages consists of three elements. First, we disregard the traditional literature that focuses on development as the result of exogenous institutional change, and we also ignore the view according to which (political) transition is sparked by exogenous growth.[11] Although we understand that exogeneity may be convenient – for instance, it spares the econometrician a number of methodological headaches – it does not really explain much. Furthermore, we are persuaded that in order to understand the positioning of a community in terms of economic development, the social scientist should consider the features of cooperation, which must be assessed with reference to its cultural foundations, the reliability of the partners in exchange and the protection granted to property rights (liberty).

Culture defines admissible and non-admissible social goals and extends to First Principles, which ultimately define to what extent violence can be legitimately exercised. Reliability refers to behavioural routines, which are credible only if consistent with the presence of deontic principles or the exercise of violence. Property rights are the essence of a system based on entrepreneurial advance. Finally, we claim that the interaction between culture and behavioural routines is critical to comprehending what happens when the existing behavioural routines are swept away by new guidelines introduced by new external observers and/or new inner judges, that is when the social contract breaks down or when the absence of the social contract is no longer accepted.

9.3 Poverty

The history of development economics has consisted in the quest for recipes to fix various kinds of malfunctioning. Traditionally, economists have identified three different categories of inadequacies, which in turn have been singled out as the ultimate reason for misery in large areas of the world: lack of fixed capital, lack of schooling, lack of appropriate institutions.

For decades, distinguished scholars have developed remedies and policies to make up for these deficiencies.[12] First came the theories advocating central planning in order to enhance fast growth in heavy manufacturing, possibly supported by foreign loans to compensate for low savings at home and problematic credibility abroad. The result was rampant corruption, a host of military regimes, a hodgepodge of "cathedrals in the desert": large, Soviet-style plants that hardly produced anything, soon to be abandoned for lack of maintenance, managerial skills, and buyers. Later came the development programmes aimed at creating human capital (with an emphasis on technical training). The outcome was equally disappointing. Considerable resources were wasted in phony projects, which were frequently controlled by local elites with limited interest in educating their countrymen. As a result, they ended up rewarding only the trainers (both locals and foreigners) or being a paid holiday for limited numbers of hand-picked trainees, or creating a captive market for builders, providers of equipment, consultants. Sometimes the curricula had little to do with what was needed or feasible. On other occasions they concentrated on higher education (prestige projects for future political leaders) and neglected that education is all but useless if there are no incentives to engage in entrepreneurial activities and invest. When the projects were indeed designed properly, some of the best trainees migrated (or remained) abroad in order to make the most of their newly-acquired skills. The others soon found out that their human capital was not necessarily welcome by the local producers and administrators, and that their talents could be employed more profitably in rent-seeking ventures. And even when aid concentrated on primary education, the outcome has been perplexing.[13]

Beginning in the late 1980s, the scholarly response started to focus on the presence of distorted or inefficient incentive systems: bad rules of the game enforced by undependable judiciary, corrupt agencies and organizations backed by coercive powers and arbitrary decision-making by the rulers. Not surprisingly, the next wave of recommendations proposed by the so-called experts consisted in transferring Western institutions, legal systems and – of course – experts to the undeveloped world. As we know, the results have been mixed. In some cases, the local rulers just pocketed the reform sweeteners and ensured that reforms remained no more than an exercise in window dressing. By contrast, in other areas the rules of the game were indeed amended for the better: productive entrepreneurship was encouraged by deregulation, withdrawal of government-guaranteed soft-budget constraints and a more credible protection of private property.

As pointed out in Lin (2005), there is no doubt that granting governmental privileges to bad incumbents enhances poverty: it allows inefficient producers to waste resources and it prevents more efficient competitors from entering the market. Therefore, it is not surprising that institutional change leading to the removal of these distortions generates better performances. Most, however, would question the claim that the adoption of "good government" is the result of Western transplants and advice. Rather, they would argue that good government follows political change, and that political change is definitely not the result of expert advice or improved human capital. For instance Opper (2004: 577) offers evidence suggesting that "International Financial Institutions are not actually able to import liberal ideology with their financial involvement". In a similar vein, Berkowitz *et al.* (2003) show that the way a particular legal code is adapted to the specific conditions of – and consciously accepted by – the recipient country is far more important than legal origin and sophistication:

> First, for the law to be effective, it must be meaningful in the context in which it is applied so citizens have an incentive to use the law and to demand institutions that work to enforce and develop the law. Second, the judges, lawyers, and other legal intermediaries that are responsible for developing the law must be able to increase the quality of law in a way that is responsive to demand for legality.
>
> (Berkowitz *et al.* 2003: 166–167)

We do not deny that good laws are better than bad laws. Yet, we believe that this does not justify today's propensity to consider development economics almost a playing ground for empirical work in institutional design, as if suitable institutional design was a sufficient condition to implement the appropriate micro- and macro-policies geared to alleviate poverty. This tendency is certainly understandable: after decades of research and generous amounts of money disbursed, the substance of the mainstream recipes remains uncertain (Marangos 2009), their quality debatable and the results disappointing. To some extent, it might even be argued that the most prominent success stories refer to countries that have ignored neoclassical advice (Stiglitz 2002). Nonetheless, we underscore that the way laws are perceived and applied is at least as important.

Be that as it may, nowadays three basic results are firmly acquired. Aid helps when it aims at meeting catastrophic situations such as famine, droughts, epidemics and earthquakes; although a heavy toll is levied when assistance is channelled through public or semi-public organizations.[14] Second, the institutional perspective has underscored that poverty is not just about bad economics. Economic performance depends on the rules of the game, and the evolution (or stability) of these rules is also the result of the politicians' ability to select the tools that best enhance their interests. Finally, the institutional emphasis has shown that politicians do not operate in a vacuum: the effectiveness of their action depends on the cultural environment and the cost of enforcement depends on their legitimacy, which helps understand why a number of quick-fix solutions have been ignored by their alleged beneficiaries even when they have proven their worth in the developed world. We add that both elements can only be appreciated within an interdisciplinary context, which can provide general guidance for research strategies, but which should stay away from generalizing across communities.

In perspective, the institutional story ultimately boils down to a matter of economic freedom, which has brought to the front stage a group of advanced countries to catch up with and which has enhanced the production of enough resources to feed and educate larger and larger amounts of human capital (Weede 2006). In turn, economic freedom requires legal structures that produce stable and credible private property rights. Thus, not unexpectedly, the economics profession has increasingly been attracted to studying the features and the origins of the various legal systems. For instance, La Porta *et al.* (1997, 1998) opted for a consequentialist approach (the legal system is chosen or interpreted in order to pursue a given goal); while Mahoney (2001) underscored the role of history (legal families come from the past). Yet, one cannot overlook that the foundations and the conclusions reached by this literature have come under heavy criticism;[15] and that although economists have acknowledged the importance of politics, they have tended to neglect the history and foundations of political regimes. In particular, political conditions are assumed to be exogenous, or are studied in a short-run perspective (vulnerability to coups and rebellions).

The upshot is that we believe that this line of research offers only partial results and that the explanations it suggests are sometimes weak or not deep enough. Furthermore, we maintain that the concepts mentioned in the previous section of this chapter – culture, behaviour, social contracts – provide more promising insights into the different contexts that characterize poor communities and into the reasons why such poor economies fail to make sustained progress.

9.3.1 *Starting from the bottom*

Let us begin with the obvious: a poor country is not poor because its inhabitants prefer misery to wealth, but because the cost of becoming better off is unbearably high. One can surely imagine different definitions of wealth. For some, it means consuming material goods and selected categories of services (e.g. health, tourism, education) in large amounts; for others, wealth has weaker material connotations and more importance is attributed to quiet, slow-pace living, even if there is less opulence. In whatever way one defines wealth, however, one can easily accept that in all poor economies, (*a*) a large number of people would like to improve their material condition and many have at least some ideas about how to acquire information, knowledge, and about how to act in order to obtain their (material) goals; (*b*) the expected net benefit from the actions they should undertake to improve their tangible well-being is very often negative. In other words, poor areas are not populated by masses of dim-witted people or ascetics who believe that there is no way one could be better off, irrespective of the circumstances. Yet in these countries many perceive that the institutional circumstances would nullify or oppose their endeavours.

As we have observed, the institutional and property-right literatures recommend "economic freedom", which is frequently employed as a synonym for "capitalism" and is sometimes supplemented by references to "good regulatory institutions".[16] Still, this "solution" misses the point: capitalism describes a desirable state of affairs, but says little or nothing on how to obtain it. Additionally, capitalism is generally put forward from a consequentialist standpoint, according to which economic freedom is not intrinsically good, but it is good because it works:

> Much more important to me are freedom, compassion for the poor, respect for the social contract, and equal opportunity. But for the moment, to achieve those goals, capitalism is the only game in town. It is the only system we know that provides us with the tools required to create massive surplus value.
>
> (De Soto 2001: 242)[17]

We do not deny the correlation between economic freedom and economic performance. Yet, we posit that this correlation offers little help in explaining what prevents a large number of societies from attaining better rules of the game, including economic freedom, and from solving the problem of poverty by unleashing productive entrepreneurship (freedom per se saves nobody from starvation). Put bluntly, the economic-liberty story is actually a tautology. Poor countries are far away from free-market principles by definition. Thus, it makes little sense to suggest recipes that make them richer "by definition". By contrast, the relevant question should address what makes it so difficult for poor people to follow free-market guidelines and what explains their partial failure, i.e. the fact that attempts to change the rules of the game break down before significant success is obtained.

The essence of our answer is fairly simple and can be summarized in two sentences. On the one hand, historical, political and geographical accidents in poor countries have led to the establishment of exclusive rent-seeking elites.[18] These have become part and parcel of the cultural and institutional context and have continued to operate to maintain their hold on power. Poverty cannot be eliminated unless this context breaks down (or is broken down). On the other hand, these societies find it difficult to coalesce around shared First Principles that would justify substantial institutional changes and eventually originate new, "righteous" behavioural routines. Hence, the fight against poverty depends crucially on the ability to establish new cooperating agreements buttressed by a renewed cultural fabric.

9.3.2 The rent-seeking story

As a matter of fact, the puzzle of poor societies is not the presence of exclusive rent-seeking groups, but the nature and resilience of such groups. If it is true, as we believe, that interest groups in undeveloped countries are the main culprits for involuntary material poverty, then one should investigate in what ways these coalitions differ from those we observe in developed economies, why they have been so deviously successful and why, when overturned, they often tend to be replaced by coalitions with similar goals and ruling strategies.

To be fair, rent-seeking coalitions do not always lead to poverty. Surely, one can refer to the extensive literature on the (mainly static) deadweight losses associated with monopoly power. Still, these losses are serious only when supported by legal buttresses denying freedom of entry, a point which was clarified by Tullock (1967) long ago, but which has been virtually ignored by policy-makers throughout the world until today. For our purposes, the key element of Tullock's analysis is the separation between rule-makers and rent-seekers. To simplify Tullock's argument, rule-makers create sets of acceptable rents that they believe public opinion is likely to accept; and then put them up for sale. The rent-seekers are the buyers, who compete for the privileges available.[19]

The separation of these roles reproduces rather accurately the Western context. It is indeed possible that interest groups influence the political system prior to the elections. Nonetheless, it is important to point out that their control on the political system is weakened in different ways. A developed economy usually generates many coalitions, with contrasting interests. As a result, the presence of many masters ensures that the servant enjoys considerable degrees of freedom. While looking for compromises, the politician becomes a broker, possibly a dealer, and may acquire independence in the process. Second, interest groups may put pressure on politicians when the elections approach, but they tend to lose their grip soon afterwards. One might certainly argue that frequent electoral rounds increase the dependence of the political class on the business community or on other, equally powerful coalitions, such as trade unions or consumers' associations. After all, repeated games (and requests for funds and votes) tend to strengthen loyalties, cooperation and collusion. Still, one should also consider that the political players involved in "big" rent-seeking games are not all those who hold political office, but just the top brass; and that once they become leaders, their careers may be more or less successful, but seldom crash. Even when they fall (for instance, when "hit" by the judiciary), they are usually provided with golden parachutes, which further insulate them from pressure. Moreover, and especially where strong party systems prevail, politicians go through revolving doors, which makes revenge by the interest groups a potentially bad move. Finally, the power to create or destroy rents impacts on the balance of power. Thus, if the political class is in the hands of charismatic leaders, the balance tilts in their favour.

In brief, we agree with Tullock's description of the rent-seeking game. But we also emphasize that Tullock portrays an environment typical of developed societies: a relatively open game about competing coalitions, all of them trying to create and profit from privileges without rocking the boat. Yet, poor economies offer a different picture, consisting of different representations of the exclusive rent-seeking game. The first representation suggests a situation in which rent-seeking is carried out by a small elite which brings together in the same hands political authority and economic power. Like in the developed world, under concentrated rent-seeking the ruling interest groups try to get rich; but unlike what happens in the Western context, in which the elites strive to keep power through consensus, in this poor-world context the elites stay in power by ensuring that competitors do not stand a chance to oust them. This goal is pursued by violence, by the threat or violence, or by enacting rules that prevent the opposition from collecting the financial means required in order to build effective resistance to abuse and to develop a credible challenge. Hence, not only catching-up is irrelevant, but it could even be harmful to the incumbent elites. The production of wealth mirrors the fact that the owners of the production factors are rewarded. If such increased wealth affects large layers of the population, it means that a "middle class" is born. As a result, once income levels rise, tolerance with regards to authoritarian leaderships might weaken and the legitimacy of the exclusive elites is questioned. Once repression is no longer viable, institutional transition begins to take off.

We can thus imagine the existence of a tipping point: as long as the ruling rent-seekers keep the country poor, wealth and power can be concentrated. In these situations, poverty is in fact the goal, not the problem. Beyond a threshold, possibly defined in terms of median income, transition is virtually inevitable and can only be avoided through massive foreign intervention, military or financial. Clearly, the threshold varies according to the opportunity cost of ousting the incumbent rulers. For instance, communication makes it easier for dissidents to get organized, acquire funds from third parties and also obtain information about what one misses out by being poor. The "openness" of the society also plays a role, for the more culture is goal-driven, the more difficult it is to define political alternatives, and the higher the chances that the hoped-for transition is merely a palace coup followed by chaos and/or tribal warfare.

The second representation refers to a situation characterized by diffused rent-seeking: as one can observe in countries with significant endowments of natural resources (Robinson *et al.* 2006), the ruling elite still appropriates much of the wealth produced in the country and garners consensus by guaranteeing a relatively low purchasing power, acceptable to the rest of the population and more or less independent of the individual's working effort. The creation of vastly overgrown state bureaucracies often serves this purpose. In contrast with the previous situation, poverty is now relative, since it depends on the notion of "acceptable". Of course, in this case rent-seeking takes place at two levels. There are active rent-seekers, who create, manage and distribute the rents. They have no interest in enhancing wealth for society as a whole, but unlike the conditions prevailing under "concentrated" rent-seeking, they pursue a target framed in terms of relative poverty. There are also passive rent-seekers, who are the beneficiaries of the redistribution process. In truth, this is often the case in the developed world, too. And similarly with the previous situation, this case also presents a tipping point, defined by the ability of the economy to meet people's income expectations. When the rent-seeking structure no longer allows satisfactory performances, the system meets crisis: political unease, turmoil, possibly transition. Once again, however, in the poor country context this is not an open game. Access to the active rent-seekers remains discretionary, since it is a matter of co-opting, rather than of electing.

To conclude, when it originates from exclusive rent-seeking situations, poverty is indeed about privileges, frequently enforced by violent means. Once given tipping points are reached, however, trouble breaks out. The outcome can be civil war, tribal conflict, a palace coup, or transition. Put differently, confrontation may lead to chaos, to the establishment of significant new interest groups, or to significant changes in the rules of the game. We believe that culture and First Principles shape the conditions that make the difference between the various classes of outcomes.

9.3.3 Tipping points in open cultures and goal-driven societies

The road to the tipping points mentioned in the previous paragraphs is paved with unrest, resentment for missed opportunities, frustrated ambitions. Certainly, these perceptions are sharper when comparisons among living standards are easier. For instance, satellite TV and the diffusion of the Internet during the past two decades have probably done more to fight poverty than most previous development plans combined.[20] In this vein, easier travel and communication surely played a major role in the downfall of the Soviet empire in different ways. People became aware that Western morality was no worse than Eastern corruption and alienation, that Westerners had no intention of aggressing and looting the East. And of course, they also realized that Western living standards were much higher than theirs and that the gap was growing. As a result, by 1989

> The moral base of communism had vanished. The elites had lost confidence in their legitimacy. ... Those who had had hope, during the 1940s and 1950s, were replaced by those who had never had hope and who had grown up knowing that everything was a lie.
>
> (Chirot 1991: 18–19)

As Rostow (1991: 64) put it, "There is an aura of defeat in the USSR, as well as shame and cynicism at having been cowed or taken in by the communists for so long".

On the other hand, nationalism and religion can be – and have been – resorted to in order to nullify the effects of comparison and create or strengthen alternative open cultures in opposition to potential substitutes. For instance, the luring image associated with the economic performances of the developed countries can be offset by referring to the alleged decay of Western morality, to its drive towards aggression, exploitation and imperialism. Furthermore, the typical individual in poor countries may be persuaded to make introspection and spiritual enrichment his lifetime goal, to be preferred over material advance or hedonic greed. Clearly, as communication becomes easier, the role attributed to these ideological elements rises and extremism becomes tempting. One can thus conceive of some sort of polarization: either the consequences of communication eventually ignite transition, or they elicit extreme reactions, by and large based on anti-Western propaganda.

Still, communication might not be enough. It makes people aware of the opportunities and lowers the threshold of tolerance, but the conditions to be fulfilled in order to take advantage of those opportunities are much more difficult to apprehend. Stated differently, those who go past the tipping points often believe that poverty can be eliminated by a "simple" change in the political regime, with little awareness of – and consensus on – the behavioural routines required to create wealth. As a result, the economy remains inherently frail and political change turns into a revolving-door exercise: "Negative consensus" may be enough to create political instability, but can be of little or no use when it comes to wealth creation. In particular, in contexts characterized by goal-driven cultures, intolerance or geographical specificities,[21] the poverty trap applies and one palace coup follows the other. Open cultures are also vulnerable, for not all open cultures are conducive to growth: hence, frustrated ambitions for immediate results could lead to political conflict for power and scraps of wealth, however open the cultural bonds are. For example, tribal societies might have problems in accepting the notion of an independent but accountable judiciary that enforces property rights with clarity, speed and little heed to political pressure, while side-stepping personal propensities towards social benevolence enhancing fairness and redistribution. Time and patience are also relevant. For no matter how open the underlying culture might be, countries in which dictatorial systems have been overturned are usually unable or unwilling to wipe out bloated bureaucratic apparatuses in just a few months. Yet, employees and civil servants are unlikely to become efficient managers, motivated workers or creative entrepreneurs overnight. Given the fundamental role of property rights, this also applies to the features of the judiciary, which is in charge of their enforcement (Dam 2006). As in the case of the bureaucracy, the judiciary cannot be replaced overnight and, if it has a tradition of servile cooperation with the political elites, it will continue to look for guidance and support from the (new) elites. Catching-up is thus delayed and ultimately stalls.

To conclude, poverty is the result of deliberate attempts to thwart growth in order to preserve an exclusive rent-seeking game. When strengthened by ideological pressure, behavioural routines resulting from concentrated rent-seeking may be supine adaptation, especially in the presence of goal-driven cultures. Unrest is likely to be pervasive, but the efforts to oust the ruling coalition are a mere power game, of little or no economic consequence. Culture plays a minor role or – better said – it plays a major role by being unable to create a new pattern of social cooperation. Diffused rent-seeking, on the other hand, offers more interesting outcomes, and the behavioural routines it engenders could well be transformed into a cultural phenomenon. In this context, when culture is open, the chances of starting transition depend on the underlying psychological patterns. When culture is goal-driven, turmoil breaks out.[22] When culture is individualistic enough, relative poverty becomes tolerable and transition/development is not on the agenda.

In fact, the way out of poverty ultimately depends on people's attitudes with regard to entrepreneurship, property rights and unfettered competition. Thus, when trying to move out of poverty, cultural openness is necessary, but not sufficient. It is necessary, because you need First Principles in order to delegitimize the incumbent rulers, restrain factional conflict, cut rent-seeking and introduce new patterns of reliable, peaceful cooperation. But it is not sufficient, for not all cultures lead to material wealth and not all societies are ready to wait. As history shows, it takes years, possibly generations, for a new (or renewed) culture to emerge.

9.4 Transition

The previous paragraphs have discussed what it takes to fight and shake off rent-seeking in poor countries, concluding that when the record of poverty rests upon consolidated behavioural routines moulded by prolonged and possibly diffused rent-seeking, cultural transition must necessarily precede institutional and economic change. Such cultural transition might be rapid, if society is swept by a sudden, deep ideological change – say, as a consequence of globalization, charismatic political or intellectual leadership, or dramatic crises of some kind. Otherwise it can only take place slowly and sometimes unpredictably, as history and the external environment stimulate actors to adapt and subsequently transform new behavioural routines into psychological and cultural patterns.

However simple and persuasive the above assertions might sound, the traditional approaches to transition have been different. On the one hand, transition became an issue worth of investigation only in 1989, as the Soviet bloc imploded and policy-makers started to wonder how to transform a centrally-planned system into a free-market economy. The implicit (and wrong) assumption was that transition relates to former communist regimes only, and that its purpose is the transformation of a hyper-regulated, centrally planned economy into a capitalist system. This is of course an unwarranted simplification, since transition can also consist in the dismissal of a relatively free-market context by rent-seeking elites. For instance, this is what happened when the protectionist wave swept the whole world as of the late 1920s. The history of industrial organization is also a source of telling examples. In those very years cartels played a major and very explicit role in designing the National Recovery Plan (antici-pated by the Swope Plan) in the United States. Likewise, cartels aiming at regu-lating steel, chemicals and other industries were formed all over Western Europe, not to mention Fascist Italy and Nazi Germany, where cartels became compulsory.

On the other hand, and partly as a consequence of the previous oversight, it has usually been taken for granted that transition should be designed from the top, by means of a strong government with the ability to enforce appropriate rules leading to success and legitimized by the very fact that it is guiding the country through transition, as if transition were actually the ultimate goal of policy-making. In some cases the top-down approach was qualified, as in Jowitt (1992: 223): "[successful transition in Eastern Europe] will take the type of liberal authoritarianism that existed in nineteenth-century western Europe". Other times it was more radical, as in Brabant (1993: 98–99): "only an authorit-arian intervention in economic affairs ... may successfully move the process along the coveted new development path". In general, the failure to grapple with the problems of constructivism characterized the well-known and largely inef-fectual debate typical of the 1990s, when much of the economics profession was pitching gradual transformation against shock therapy. The advocates of the former view emphasized the need for strong and virtuous governments, which would be competent and steady enough to bring about "stabilization", preserve price controls and various forms of central planning for an extended period of time; and guarantee that structural reform would not be opposed by – or fall victim to – old or new interest groups. By contrast, the partisans of fast change were focusing on the need to prevent the outgoing coalitions from freezing the reform process, and on the desirability of creating new coalitions with an interest in supporting private property and entrepreneurship: in a word, in establishing and preserving a business-friendly environment.

In theory, they both made sense and were appropriate responses to specific problems: avoid invalidating transition by stoking uncertainty and discontent on the one hand and, on the other, ensure that the old guard does not take control in the new context, and that it does not reproduce the old privileges under a decep-tively new constitutional shell. As surveyed by Marangos (2005), the main-stream literature of the 1990s dealing with the former communist bloc was facing the same dilemma when arguing about sequencing. What comes first, then – institutional development or market-oriented reforms (price liberalization, pri-vatization, sound monetary policy, balanced budget)? In the end, the suggested solution – which in fact amounted to less than a solution – was "both": you need strong institutions before you unleash free-market forces; and you need free-market forces to drive institutional changes.

In practice, however, both were/are bound to fail and to be replaced by expe-diency. First, because macro-stabilization (keeping inflation and public expendi-ture under control) and structural adjustment (privatization and institution building) are goals rather than instruments. Transition strategies are not chosen by academics or technocrats in a vacuum, but by political leaders dirtying their hands: old leaders who choose a new strategy to preserve their power; or new leaders who choose or promise a novel institutional context to legitimize their ambitions. As a consequence, we maintain that the key to understanding the dynamics and the potential of transition is political. Second, because the features of mainstream transition also reflect the evolution of the political coalition in charge. As the new rules of the game are introduced, and greater exposure to the outside world follows, it might well happen that the initial plans go awry, that the ruling interest groups change their nature and composition. Put differently, transplanting capitalism won't do, because the meta-dynamics that characterize the poor and the developed countries are different. Of course, that also includes transplanting capitalist legal principles and institutions, especially when transition is underway (Teitel 2000; Milhaupt and Pistor 2008). As we have pointed out, and contrary to what occurs in the developed world, the introduction of new rules in poor countries is a matter of credibility, flexibility, recent (bad) memories. These components affect behavioural routines and shape new inner judges and external observers to a much larger extent than economic or legislative technicalities.

We have observed that growth in the developed countries is spurred by the hopes for non-decreasing living standards, which the incumbent rulers are expected to satisfy; and is moderated by the parallel need to create and distribute rents in accord with the implicit social contract. In democracies, both the governing parties and opposition pursue the same goal, more or less in the same way: to create and distribute rents, to preserve and exploit power without violating First Principles. Success goes to the most credible coalition led by the most convincing leaders.

Transition differs, in that the linchpin of the whole exercise is the definition of the rules of the game – once again, to preserve and distribute power – in an unstable and uncertain environment, in which legitimacy is fragile and expectations are necessarily disappointed. Thus, during transition the social contract is to be defined, discovered, possibly rediscovered. The search for compromises and solutions may be easier if the process is led by charismatic and effective leaders who have acquired indisputable prestige through their opposition to the previous regime, and perhaps also accreditation in the eyes of the outside world. But the outcome is by no means guaranteed. For instance, if transition is led by a democratic regime, the race to redistribution is inevitable. Failure to redistribute would imply the loss of power to the benefit of those who promise to do so. Effective and charismatic leadership is just an extra that allows those in charge to restrain the rent-seeking game without running the danger of losing out to (more) populist opponents. While the idea of a strong government/leader that can do without rents is frequently shared by gradualist and shock-therapists alike, the real world offers few or no examples of this. If transition is guided by autocrats, then institutional change actually refers to the creation of new rules of the game suitable to the new ruling elite. Surely, this type of transition has little to do with "mainstream transition". In particular, if the new rules of the game are just formal window dressing, then so-called transition is merely a palace coup.

On the other hand, if the cultural environment has changed, and the new autocrats are skilful enough to understand the new priorities, then transition can take
off, even if the goal has little or nothing to do with catching-up.

9.4.1 Three different transition stories

In the end, there is no single blueprint for transition. Yet, although what really
happens depends on a mix of cultural and historical variables, a limited number
of rather general patterns can be emphasized.

A first set of transition stories refers to situations in which transition starts
from within, is motivated by discontent, but is not supported by much cultural
change. In these stories, the behavioural routines typical of the pre-transition
period are indeed part of the existing cultural heritage, which remains more or
less the same: people are not against the "old" system as such, but they believe
it can perform better once its shortcomings are fixed and those responsible for
mismanagement are removed. For those aspiring to grab power, advocating
change may thus be a strategy good enough to topple political opponents, but
inappropriate to win lasting support. As a result, uncertainty prevails, economic
activity slows down and transition stalls early. Free-market institutions (protection of property rights and freedom of exchange) might indeed be launched and
enforced on paper, especially if this helps to attract international donors and
approval. But the reality is that transition is aborted. Behaviours will hardly
change, and it will be business as usual, with some variations in the redistribution mechanisms, and little turnover concerning the structure of the final beneficiaries. For instance, top-down transition from a centrally-planned to a partially
decentralized economy will hit the central authorities and benefit decentralized
"mafias" and oligarchs, with whom the policy-maker at the centre – strong
enough not to be booted out, but not strong enough to enforce his authority at
the periphery – will have to strike some kind of a deal. As we have seen, once
power has been redistributed, the new behavioural routines originated by a
mafia system – for dealing with a mafia boss is not the same thing as dealing
with a party secretary – might eventually weaken the original cultural fabrics,
especially when demography, communication and geography contribute to
transforming a goal-driven society into an individualistic one, possibly more
open to alternatives and tolerant with regard to the principle of individual
responsibility.

Clearly, the outcome depends on the nature of such new psychological patterns, if any. Education, therefore, plays a critical role, although not all educational models lead to the same result. For instance, if the moral standards
transmitted through education reproduce those typical of the developed West,
including the Western social contract, transition will be attained from a political
standpoint, as representative democracies are established and possibly strengthened by international recognition. Nonetheless, growth will soon slow down and
the opportunity for catching up disappear, as the Western rent-seeking mechanisms also take root and absorb a large share of the productive energies.

A different situation materializes in the opposite case, when transition is sparked from within as a result of a cultural shock[23] or, more likely, following the breakdown of the constraints that had driven behavioural routines in previous periods, but that failed to transform those routines into a culture. This is what happened, for instance, in some European countries, in which central planning failed to destroy the pre-existing psychological patterns. Absent the political constraint – which in the European case was ultimately identified in Soviet occupation – it did not take much for the incumbent leaders to remove the symbols of the old regime and ignite transition to the past. In these countries, however, catching up with the group of the developed countries was/is not the name of the game. It was a political catchword or – frequently – the means by which a symbolic goal could be achieved. Catching-up may happen, but as result of reform linkages,[24] rather than by policy design. For when one society reverts to its past, the social scientist never really knows what kind of interacting mechanisms are going to prevail, or how the old psychological patterns, filtered by the recent routines and confronted by new technological environments, are going to evolve. Understandably, the new political elite will endeavour to avoid liquidating the old nomenclature and will hope for the best. The "best" actually depends on the nature of the underlying cultural system, which sometimes is conducive to productive entrepreneurship, but other times is characterized by emphasis on some notion of collective cohesion (e.g. nationalism), which is far less favourable to economic performance. And it also consists in the ability to attract foreign investment, which is the only chance to create new wealth in a short time. Foreign investment, in turn, depends on a number of elements. The ideal combination is offered by small countries that are characterized by a high level of literacy and proximity to large markets. In these cases, even a small amount of foreign direct investment could make the difference and create enough opportunities that will induce the population not to regret the liquidation of many old companies, raise living standards and keep uncertainty within tolerable levels. On the other hand, if foreign investment does not flow in sufficient quantity, and behavioural routines do not adapt quickly enough, transition won't go very far.

A third possibility is provided by situations in which transition starts from the top and is engineered by enlightened rulers who realize the need to take the steps necessary to increase living standards, to prevent potentially violent uprising and thus to preserve power. This has been the strategy pursued by the Chinese authorities, a choice which is in sharp contrast – say – with what is happening in Iran. Clearly, if the institutional changes required to destroy the old rent-seeking mechanisms run against the existing cultural fabric, then the experiment is likely to end in failure and ultimately weaken the authorities that promoted change in the first place. However, if such change is consistent with the incumbent psychological patterns, and gradual and subtle enough not to alarm the rent-seeking layers of the privileged, then economic success may ensue. A typical solution is to undercut potential opposition by ensuring that the old rent-seekers will be occupying key positions in the "new" system: for instance, by acquiring managerial or supervisory responsibilities in newly-formed companies in which the government exercises formal or informal influence. Two further requirements must be met, though. First, the political environment must not deteriorate too much. A major political crisis would create uncertainty and ultimately discourage investment and productive entrepreneurship. Second, the speed of growth also plays a crucial role, especially in large countries. If transition regards the passage from a centrally-planned economy to a relatively free-market system, major imbalances such as sectorial unemployment come to the surface. These can be kept under control only if the winning industries grow fast enough to absorb the unemployment generated by the rest of the economy and to reduce the cost of uncertainty, relocation and training. Moreover, transition must be quick enough to reach a critical threshold, beyond which the individual perceives that fighting for political change may be too expensive. Beyond that threshold, the choice would no longer be between different regimes, but rather between leaders within the incumbent system.

9.4.2 On transition and rent-seeking

To conclude, transition consists in replacing one rent-seeking system with another; and in ensuring that the agents involved do not react to uncertainty by shortening their time horizon, but instead by cultivating cooperation in a long-term perspective.[25] As a result, it would be a mistake to evaluate the success of a transition process by referring to the gap between developed countries and the economy under scrutiny. It would be equally wrong to relate successful transition to the achievement of some kind of free-market goal. This may happen, of course, when cooperation is accompanied by the development of both productive entrepreneurship and risk-taking attitudes. More importantly, however, we believe that one should try to classify and "read" the significance of transition according to a framework defined in cultural terms. This explains why understanding transition is inevitably a difficult task. For no matter where transition comes from – clash between formal and informal rules, dissatisfaction with living standards, anticipation of future turmoil – it seldom turns out the way it was meant to be. Although one can list myriad variables that can affect the political and economic environment, the upshot is that the transition process itself shapes new psychological patterns and new behavioural routines, thereby modifying culture and generating new societal visions. The only safe conclusion is that in most cases, transition tends to make societies goal driven, following our definition in Section 9.2.1. There are of course notable exceptions – for instance, when the ruling elites succeed in creating new bonds (or re-establishing bonds inherited from the past) based on nationalism. These efforts are nonetheless going to be less and less successful as the media portray – and the new generations absorb – the features of globalized cultures based on different First Principles. In these cases nationalism takes the form of nation-centred welfare states, rather than of ethnic, historical or political identities. A manifest example is the eagerness with which all transition countries long to acquire international standing and recognition, even at the expense of what decades earlier would have been considered national pride.

Understanding and grappling with the ongoing change generated by transition is in fact the challenge that prospective policy-makers are almost invariably unable to do. The challenge is simply put. Transition leaders necessarily come to stage equipped with their views on the shared (or enforceable) behavioural routines accepted by the population. And they build their rent-seeking structures on those bases. As the transition process is under way, however, psychological patterns evolve, and so do expectations, and behavioural routines. This almost inevitably leads to cultural fragmentation,[26] or to a cultural move towards a goal-driven structure, which in turn is less tolerant with respect to rent-seeking and perhaps more open towards some forms of benevolent paternalism, as in Pelikán (2010). Yet, paternalism needs leadership and when leadership is poor, crisis breaks out.

This underscores a final element, partially referred to earlier on: transition is a process of incremental steps, and requires the attainment of given thresholds in terms of credibility. Unfortunately there is no way to model the "optimal" path to a credible institutional setting, since the definition of threshold varies across societies. In some cases it is a matter of affluence (say, income per capita), while in other situations it is a question of demography. More generally, it is simply a matter of time, as the new behavioural patterns evolve and possibly consolidate into partially new, predominantly goal-driven, cultural structures.

9.5 What remains of policy-making for transition and growth?

Just as in developed countries, policy-making in undeveloped and transition environments is ultimately an exercise in rent-seeking, although the absence of clearly-defined and widely-shared First Principles makes the picture less stable and policy-making less credible. As a matter of fact, breaking away from poverty and catching-up with the wealthy elite has little to do with policy-making, although misdirected intervention can obviously distort incentives and make things worse. In contrast to many theories of development, we have argued that poverty can be understood as the consequence of a historical holdup created by a violent environment: an autocrat that imposes his will and rent-seeking practices against the people's preferences, or endemic turmoil that makes property insecure and shortens the individuals' time horizon dramatically. Be that as it may, violence denies individuals prospects for peaceful, voluntary interaction. It therefore prevents preferences and behavioural routines from evolving under the impulse of new ideas and from making the most of the opportunities provided by the available technologies.

The historical holdup is closely connected with the existence of cultural traps: the constraints responsible for poverty create an environment in which the role of deontic principles is thwarted by the behavioural routines induced by exclusive rent-seeking, both concentrated and diffused. As a result, behaviour becomes less predictable, cooperation more risky, and entrepreneurial numbness prevails. Such cultural traps may evolve into cultural crises; that is situations characterized by a significant gap between the shared values of a community (say, the informal rules broadly understood) and the rules of the game necessary for growth, growth being a sought-after goal. Put briefly, poverty is obviously an undesirable state. Yet, the presence of exclusive rent-seeking weakens the purpose for cooperation and is likely to bring about a gradual attenuation of the cultural ties. When society is to an increasing extent goal-driven, populism affects the political legitimacy of the incumbent leaders or of their competitors. If crisis breaks out and its unfolding leads to an individualistic culture or to the lack of culture, as defined in Section 9.2.1, the probability of turmoil is lower and the burden of political oppression is lighter. Nonetheless, the chances of escaping poverty in less than open cultural environments remain dim, since it is virtually impossible to garner and preserve enough consensus in the absence of a clearly-identified common goal, particularly in the presence of diffused rent-seeking.

In fact, escaping poverty requires that the new, shared notions of right and wrong be defined and that the violent restraints upon productive economic action be removed. These are no easy tasks and they represent necessary, but not sufficient, conditions to obtain material prosperity. In particular, these conditions emphasize the limits of most aid programmes (even when they do not end up in extended corruption scams), of expert advice (even when it is not a demonstration of arrogant paternalism), and of deceptively cheap loans (even when the public borrowers do not transform them into overblown expenditure programmes). Thus, focusing on the virtues of the rule of law, the miracles of appropriate legal systems and the wonders of optimal sequencing and institution building may turn out to be all but pointless. Of course, we do not deny the importance of an effective legal system. Yet, we argue that all legal systems are transformed into more or less reliable and desirable rules by the way people think and see their roles in society: by culture and political structures. "People" also include the judges, of course. As a result, we suggest that the juxtaposition of common-law to civil-law families does not shed much light on the depth of the so-called "rule of law" in poor or transition countries. Rather, we believe that one should focus on how the notions of the state and of the common interest are perceived (or imposed) in areas that were previously characterized by tribal social structures, in which rule-systems were based on custom and tradition, and in which enforcement relied on the threat of ostracism, rather than on the monopoly of violence by the authority.

By contrast, those interested in changing the rules of economic interaction should consider the chances for development in two key areas – the educational system and the judiciary – and forget about captivating expressions such as "intensive growth".[27] When efforts in these areas are opposed and nullified, development policies remain a matter of wishful thinking and window dressing, frequently an opportunity to create rents and stoke corruption. Under such conditions, the only way to avoid poverty is migration.

9.5.1 Education

Our emphasis on the role of perceptions, legitimacy, deontic principles makes education a key issue, especially in goal-driven societies. On the one hand, education is the instrument by means of which an elite tries to strengthen a goal-driven culture and thus create legitimacy for policy-making. On the other, it is the means by which the moral skeleton for productive entrepreneurship, tolerance, trust and long-term cooperation can be built up. These elements make the difference between a culture associated with a performing social fabric based on cooperation and entrepreneurial spirits, and a culture that degenerates into factional rent-seeking conflicts. Indeed, this is probably the only area in which foreign aid can make an impact, as long as it is accepted by the incumbent ruling elites. This implies that the beneficiary is not the local ministry for education, but the poor family with children.[28]

Clearly, the free-market meta-vision rules out educational policies imposed by the state, which deprive parents from the liberty to choose what they deem best for their children and react to their mistakes by moving students from one school to another, from one curriculum to another. Nonetheless, free-market principles are not necessarily in contrast with the existence of centralized educational programmes, as long as they do not enjoy monopoly power or involve privileges: parents and students must preserve the right of opting out at no cost and of joining other programmes. The open question remains of course taxation, which runs against the free-market moral code, but could nevertheless be acceptable within a social contract that makes subsidized education for the poor, and therefore targeted redistribution, a moral duty for society.

Yet, in reality, the free–market view on education is not on the agenda. In most countries the state quasi-monopoly of education is considered a matter of course. Even neo/Ordoliberals such as L. Einaudi and F.A. Hayek favoured state education, according to which the curriculum is by and large defined by the central authorities. Although private education is not generally outlawed, private schools must comply with requirements set by the government; and subsidies are disbursed only to those attending governmental schools (with no or limited tax exemptions for those who decide otherwise). Part of the reason is that state teachers are usually a powerful interest group, especially in diffused-rent-seeking contexts. Not only are they large in terms of sheer numbers, but they also influence public opinion by means of daily contacts and privileged access to the children's families. The very high regard with which the idea of education is generally held also gives it a unique place; thus, the opinions of educators tend to have disproportionate weight. No reformer can afford opposing them, unless such a coalition acquires a particularly bad stigma during the years (e.g. overt collaboration with the secret police). Moreover, dismantling the state educational system would create substantial uncertainty in the population at large. Of course, the demand for teachers would remain the same and would possibly increase were public education eliminated. But that does little to change the general perception, both because rent-seekers are rationally blind to the potential benefits of competition, and because (rent-seeking) teachers who prefer to work for large bureaucracies do not usually stand out for their entrepreneurial qualities.

However, one does not need to be overly pessimistic. Catching-up and transition might take off even in the presence of a biased educational structure. In particular, one may predict that success stories will more often unfold in countries with educational structures in theory dependent on the central authority, but de facto autonomous and free to adjust to the new, emerging cultural patterns;[29] and in which the central rule-makers do not rely on education in order to create consensus and legitimize their power. Once again, however, teaching is made of teachers, and their skills and mental frames can hardly be changed overnight. Thus, even when they rest on sound bases – shared First Principles in accord with the requirements of long-term cooperation – sustainable catching-up and successful transition take time: the slower the generational turnover, the slower the process.

9.5.2 The judiciary

With very few exceptions, and rather surprisingly, calls for sound institutional development have nothing to say with regard to those who would be operating the institutional context and implement the rule of law. Yet, there is little hope for growth unless contracts and property rights are enforced and that is clearly the job of the judicial system, which is perhaps the most important element characterizing social interaction. In brief, the crucial element to obtaining successful transition is ensuring that the government is strong enough to keep rent-seekers in check and enforce contracts, but does not abuse its powers. This is nothing new, of course.[30] But it is often forgotten that both requirements can be met only if the judiciary performs adequately (proper training and professional pride) and if it is made somehow accountable to sets of virtuous moral standards deeply rooted in public opinion. Accountability vis-à-vis a political ruler won't do and can be easily made irrelevant or transformed into dependence. In poor countries, judges tend to be highly dependent on the incumbent ruler, who makes the law and changes it more or less arbitrarily. As a result, two sets of behavioural routines follow. Agents adapt by shortening their time horizons and by relying on local, informal enforcement mechanisms (including mafias). Furthermore, the judiciary tends to perceive the law as a vehicle for political expediency. Regrettably, these routines are not likely to vanish overnight.

As a matter of fact, the new (reformed) judicial systems must be consistent with deeply rooted informal structures that have to be reckoned with for extended periods of time. Yet, these systems must also be strong and credible enough to outperform mafia-style competitors. These are daunting tasks. But even more taxing are the efforts required to change the judges' behavioural routines. Lacking strict political guidelines and controls, and in the absence of an open culture that restrains and delegitimizes arbitrary action, "reformed" judges in poor countries are likely to replace the politicians and make the law themselves, hopefully in the pursuit of efficiency or cultural consistency, but certainly at the expense of the rule of law. For instance, in many countries the distinction between private and public property remains ambiguous. If resources are to be shared and profits are thus equivalent to looting the common pool, even an honest and competent judge would not enforce property rights. This might explain why – say – after the fall of the "Soviet Empire", the Czech Republic performed differently than the Ukraine: the notion of private property in the Austro-Hungarian Empire was not the same as that in Tsarist Russia.

To summarize and conclude, poverty can be fought only if the poor find their situation avoidable and consensus coalesces around strong cultural points (revolution) or at least an implicit contract (First Principles) strong enough to support at least a watered-down version of Leoni's rule of law. Hence, there are no policies for development or for transition, but there are visions regarding the content of education and the role of the judiciary. Contrary to what happens in developed economies, however, in poor countries these visions are blurred by historical hold-ups, distorted behavioural routines that have been transformed into psychological and cultural patterns, and weak deontic guidelines. In most cases, the escape from poverty is in fact a trial and error process, with no clear-cut First Principles to rely upon. Shortcuts (e.g. nationalism) are tempting, but counterproductive. Peaceful fragmentation might be more promising, although virtually impossible to obtain when geography matters (the presence of valuable and concentrated natural resources would easily ignite civil war). There are no safe recipes with regard to political structure, either. Democracy works if it protects against abuse and violence, but it fails when it becomes factionalism and a way of legalizing diffused rent-seeking. Early attempts to jump-start a growth process by enlightened authoritarian governments are more likely to succeed, since in these cases patience can be imposed, rather than hoped for. But we also know that populist and rent-seeking autocracies are more frequent than autocracies strong enough to resist rent-seeking pressure and legitimized enough to resist populist attacks. That is why, in the end, we are convinced that the ability to reshape the judiciary and the cultural foundations of its strength remains the ultimate test and the best guarantee of development.

10 Final remarks on the economic way of thinking

10.1 Describing, explaining, advising

Economics deals with the ways individuals behave in order to enhance their well-being in an environment characterized by scarcity, formal and informal rules of the game, and uncertainty. Thus, economics is clearly about human action, particularly about preferences and choices, since scarcity implies that when we strive to obtain our preferred sets of goods and services, we necessarily decide to surrender other goods and services (including leisure).[1] Furthermore, economics is about the acquisition of knowledge and – sometimes – about engagement in entrepreneurial activities, which are sparked by disequilibrium and are the major instruments through which individuals endeavour to satisfy their aspirations. Finally, since individuals often try to meet their goals and to achieve more ambitious aims by cooperating and exchanging, economics also necessarily concerns the interaction among human beings (exchange and cooperation).

Unfortunately, this is how far agreement within the economics profession goes. From here, however, questions begin to arise, particularly concerning what economists should do and what the relationship between economics and the other social sciences should be. We have tried to show that the work of the economist is usually expected to fall into three categories: describing, explaining and advising. Consistent with the Austrian tradition, this book has suggested that economics should focus mainly upon "explaining". In contrast with the Austrians' claims, however, we emphasize that explanations rest upon embedded value judgements, and, thus, we have argued that "explaining" requires that value judgements be made explicit. In particular, we have opposed the drive towards scholarly colonization that has characterized much of the mainstream economics literature over the past 50 years, and have argued that the rationality assumption has been instrumental in shaping amoral individuals and – paradoxically – in shoring up social rationality. We have concluded that for economics to better fulfil its explanatory function, the discipline itself must open up and take advantage of the rich insights offered by other fields, such as history, sociology, political philosophy and psychology. In the following pages, we shall further illustrate these points and summarize the main lessons to be drawn from the previous chapters. Specifically, in the remaining part of this section we recon-sider the implications of the different approaches to the role of the economist. Section 10.2 calls attention to the tensions between the subjectivist, the social and the theological perspectives on economic interaction, as well as on the illu-sory attempts to solve the good-government issue by referring to the rule of law and by selecting the allegedly optimal legal family. Section 10.3 underscores the fragility of the free-market claims of those who do not realize – let alone ques-tion – the challenge presented by today's prevailing First Principles. The last section concludes with some remarks on how economists could make more effective contributions in the aftermath of the most recent crisis and possibly prepare for the next one.

10.1.1 Describing

The importance of descriptive economics is patent. Facts and numbers define the phenomena we want to explain and provide elements that help verify the explan-atory power of theories. Yet, the task of data mining and describing pertains to the field of statistics, and possibly history. Accomplished economists must of course be familiar with these disciplines, for these other fields tell economists what their studies should address and assist them in discerning broader views: a historical perspective on factual evidence is a powerful eye-opener and ensures that the social scientist avoids getting entangled in a corner and being misled by accidents or partial-equilibrium delusions. Still, factual evidence should be con-sidered with caution. Bad history and poor statistics can cause considerable harm, as crucial details might be overlooked, bad data might generate confusion and mistakes, and even good theories might be falsified. Likewise, correlation is not the same as causality, and extrapolating from good descriptions of the past is not equivalent to predicting. In a world subject to ongoing change, rear-mirror gazing is tempting, but dangerous. In a word, facts are not and cannot create the-ories, and the mirage of a-theoretical economics is in fact all but an oxymoron.

In a different vein, we have also taken issue with an alternative descriptive agenda, which has focused on portraying allegedly ideal equilibrium features, rather than data. In Chapters 2 and 3 we have argued that the Walrasian vantage point raises serious reservations, in that it implies a vision in which human beings are expected to act like robots, no new knowledge is acquired, prefer-ences are constant, uncertainty is absent and non-rational behaviour is an evil to be ignored or – better – effectively counteracted. In this context, normative eco-nomics draws its legitimacy from what has been called social irrationality, which originates from market failures and cognitive distortions, and ultimately leads to new forms of technocratic paternalism (Rizzo and Whitman 2009). Exercises in theoretical equilibrium structures have value for teaching purposes, in that they help students to learn the tools of their trade and double check the consistency of their reasoning. Yet, static equilibrium has little to do with reality and even less with the market system, a discovery process characterized by imitation, chance, and trial and error. Put differently, the market is a process driven by disequilibria

– unsatisfied needs and unexploited opportunities – and by the acquisition of new knowledge, rather than by the search for stationary conditions. By taking the economics of equilibrium out of the classroom and into the field, the intellectual energies of scholars are wasted, and the most critical elements of human behaviour are overlooked.

10.1.2 Explaining

We are persuaded that the core of economic theorizing consists in explaining. Regrettably, however, the history of the economic way of thinking has failed to produce widespread agreement on the methodological guidelines that should drive explanations. The key issue is the role attributed to inductivist theorizing. According to its supporters, economists should observe selected phenomena and detect correlations that are subsequently interpreted as relations of causality between variables. Hence, a-theoretical efforts at systematization, possibly smacking of a revival of the historicist tradition, should lead to articulating more or less sophisticated theories, the quality of which would ultimately lie with their predictive power. Put differently, descriptions are transformed into explanations; and policy-making boils down to choosing among the different hypothetical states of the world, the feasibility and optimality of which are scrutinized by the economist, who looks at Walrasian equilibrium as his prime benchmark. Against this claim, which today dominates the economics profession, this book has sided with those who believe that theorizing in the social sciences must rely on deductive reasoning. To repeat, even a sceptic would accept that checking for consistency and common sense by looking at the world of facts is essential.[2] But since the nature and features of human interactions experience continuous change in a world characterized by uncertainty, prediction necessarily remains an illusion, unless one can guess what kind of knowledge individuals are likely to acquire in the future, how they are going to transform it into entrepreneurial endeavours and how successful such endeavours are going to be. Thus, understanding the mechanisms that govern such ongoing change can only be an exercise in logics: a theory remains a way of reasoning, a set of mental structures that help the observer put into context and understand what he sees and anticipate how individuals are likely to react to incentives. In particular, there is no room for equilibrium economics in a world of uncertainty, for within this framework, equilibrium can never be known and, even if known, it would become obsolete as new knowledge is acquired and new preferences are developed. Progress is powered by disequilibrium, by curious and never–satisfied consumers interacting with productive entrepreneurs. Surely, it is not led by some mysterious force pulling individuals towards a goal, and definitely not by Walrasian equilibrium, an abstract and imaginary notion marshalled only by self-referential technocrats.

As noted in Chapter 3, in orthodox economics the concept of equilibrium is germane to that of rationality. From this perspective, droves of scholars have claimed that as long as economic modelling based on rational behaviour offers good predictions, the rationality assumption is acceptable and even necessary, since it represents the key to backward induction and logical positivism: from factual analysis, to theorizing and ultimately to forecasting. Furthermore, the mainstream view recommends its adoption by all social sciences as their main working tool. In truth, others schools of thought have been more cautious. They have steered away from economic imperialism, making it clear that their interest is deliberately confined to the rational area of individual behaviour, and they have justified their position by arguing that irrational behaviour lies outside the realm of economic investigation. Thus, they have transformed economics into the analysis of human action "as if" people were rational.

No matter what shape it takes, however, the rationality approach is fundamentally flawed, since it makes economics equivalent to a mechanized process bordering with determinism – wealth maximization by means of cost–benefit analysis. The rationality approach, however, has carried the day, with important consequences. When related to human behaviour, the cost–benefit methodology has often been applied to areas of human action outside economics (another example of economic imperialism), and has suggested that the social sciences could perhaps be reduced to a unified algorithm. Furthermore, the "rational", cost–benefit method has actually strengthened the case for social planning, as long as one believes that the purpose of a society and of the implicit social contract that keeps it together consists in maximizing social happiness. In the end, the need for an objective, measurable standard has made "welfare" a synonym with wealth or, more precisely, with "material wealth". Yet, "it is hard to understand how anyone could seriously believe that GNP could be converted into a significant indicator of social well-being" (Okun 1971: 5), and it is even more difficult to imagine that social planning could be derived from the same foundations as the free-market perspective.

Clearly, wealth accounting is conceptually easy to perform and one avoids many difficulties by keeping morality and other values out of the picture. Nevertheless, the assumption of rational action is not a satisfactory representation of human drives and impulses. Individuals' behaviour, motivations and preferences also depend on their emotions, as well as on their notion of justice: on what they perceive to be right or wrong, on their sense of duty and commitment. Certainly, economists are not required to formulate value judgements when "explaining". Nonetheless, we believe that they cannot neglect individuals' value judgement, since these value judgements may go a long way in clarifying social behaviours, even – or perhaps especially – when social behaviours seem to violate the principle of self-interest simply understood.

In Chapter 2 we have observed that this more robust economic way of thinking – explanations which avoided general-equilibrium benchmarking and rational scientism – has had illustrious forefathers. In fact, it formed the bedrock of the view held by the early classical economists, from David Hume to Adam Smith, including all those authors who considered economics a branch of moral philosophy. Unfortunately, that legacy started to weaken early in the nineteenth century, and eventually gave way to Walrasian marginalism and its followers. That decline has several reasons, two of which we underscore. On the technical side, the classical theory of value paid little or no attention to the role of demand. The labour theory of value became a major burden and before long its inadequacy to explain the real world became apparent. On the political side, about a century after the publication of the *Wealth of Nations*, the economic profession had generally embraced majoritarian democracy as the fitting decision-making procedure and the market process as the efficiency-enhancing result of human design. Thus, the moral foundations of free market economics were gradually eroded by consequentialism and its content – i.e. the set of goals that would give it a meaning – was to be defined by majority voting. Unfortunately, this double line of thinking eventually opened the gate to the advocates of moral relativism, undermining the very foundations of subjectivism and diluting the notion of the market system understood as a system characterized by voluntary interaction among free individuals. Not surprisingly, therefore, during the twentieth century democratic decision-making took care of defining what the market should do and how it should operate. In the past decades, logical positivism, which is a softer and less naïve version of scientism, has supplanted both the moral approach and the explanatory a-priorism of the earlier generations as the guiding principle of economic investigation. As a side effect, the intellectual principles supporting the free-market vision of societies rapidly yielded, and having conceded its own intellectual foundations, the fate of classical liberalism has been compromised.

10.1.3 Advising

Economists' possible third role explicitly calls into question the moral content of policy-making. According to the dominant view, the policy-makers set the goal a society should pursue, while the experts suggest the most efficient – i.e. wealth enhancing – way of obtaining the selected targets. Put differently, according to this approach economists should turn into engineers and instruct politicians about the best way of getting from A to B in a given period of time; or into statisticians and provide the required figures, simulations and predictions. Yet, the requests coming from the world of politics are far from detailed. There are many ways of financing and running a state educational system, of redistributing income to the poor, of awarding privileges to those who allegedly deserve them, and even of dealing with the threat of a worldwide financial crisis. Each way has its own hidden costs and unintended consequences. In the end, it is undeniable that many politicians are ill-equipped to understand the experts' reports and that economic advisors eventually do more than just adding up the figures. Either they present solutions "on demand", so that intellectual honesty and efficiency are sacrificed for the sake of political expediency, or their framing of the various proposals affects how the contents are perceived and which decisions are ultimately taken by the technocrats themselves. In fact, the pretence of technocratic impartiality does not hold water and it is all but meaningless to define good policy-making absent a definition of good government.

10.2   Good government and free markets

In the history of mankind, the notion of good government has been articulated in three different ways, depending also on the legitimacy of the decision-maker. On one hand, "the classical thinkers, from Aristotle to Thomas Aquinas, Jean-Jacques Rousseau, and Edmund Burke recognized the cultivation of civic virtue not only as the test of good governance, but also as its essential foundation" (Bowles 2006). One may of course have different ideas about the content of "civic virtue", but it is apparent that according to this view, government action should not aim at influencing the outcome of human action, but rather at assessing the reasons that power it (virtue). In this case, therefore, the ruler's legitimacy originates from his presumed ability to identify and enforce virtue. At the other extreme, one should consider governments that operate in order to enhance the power of the ruler and his chances to stay in office without losing consensus. Particularly in democratic countries, electoral blessing legitimizes almost boundless and arbitrary rule-making. Within the economic context, such activity takes place in the name of the (majority of the) people and obviously purports to pursue the common good. It may therefore include the guarantee of a minimum income for each member of the community, the production of selected goods and services to be made available in satisfactory amounts at regulated prices, and also the creation of privileges such as trade barriers or inescapable bureaucratic hassles which claim to ward off abuse, but which in fact benefit the bureaucrats. Differing from this consequentialist version of the state, but also far from playing the role of the moral supervisor mentioned earlier, the Lockean and the neo-Aristotelian alternatives consider that the state should be the warden against illiberal behaviour, a guardian shielding the individual and his property from attacks: physical violence and fraud. No more than that. Hence, this (mini-)state draws its legitimacy from a tacit cooperative agreement, by means of which the members of a community minimize the cost of ensuring their safety and their property and create the conditions for enjoying their natural rights and for individual "flourishings". The contract is implicit, but it should be credible and opting out should always be possible.

10.2.1   Free market and personal beliefs

By now, the reader will be well aware of the fact that we do not believe that one can make a watertight case in favour or against any of one these visions. Unless one can identify one and only one source of legitimacy, the verdict remains pending. Surely, from the biological and historical standpoints, the individual – possibly the family – precedes society. This does not mean that the individual is asocial, or that the individual does not need society to fulfil his goals. Indeed, man does pursue many of his aspirations in a social context, by exchanging, communicating, cooperating and developing a wide system of personal and impersonal relations. Nonetheless, the decision on whether to interact, and to which extent, remains a matter of individual assessment. Hence, all social agreements need to be subject to individual control. They need to be explicit, or require that opting out of the implicit contract entails negligible costs. In particular, nationality and residence are not acceptable justifications for banning opting out or for enforcing monopoly powers. This has been our main argument against social consequentialism. However, it should also be recognized that the juxtaposition of the subjectivist and the social standpoints could lose much of its weight if one conceives of another agent – God – ranking higher than the individual. To illustrate this point, suppose that somebody believes that man belongs to God, because God has created all living creatures and all other elements in the universe, and that there exists a Godly design, to which all creatures must therefore conform. Furthermore, suppose that this person is sincerely persuaded he/she knows what God's design is. Wouldn't this "somebody" be thus entitled to claim that legitimacy is equivalent to compliance with his understanding of God's design, and that deviations from such a design might entail the very loss of human dignity and prerogatives?

The upshot is that the case for or against free-market economics is necessarily rooted in one's own philosophical beliefs. Contrary to common opinion, however, we hold that the critical divide is not only between methodological individualism and collectivism, i.e. on whether a person has rights *in qua*, or has rights and duties granted by the political organization (society) the person belongs to according to birth. Rather, the difference is also – and perhaps foremost – between the secular and theological notions of mankind. In the former case, the outcome is the system of fundamental rights defined by Jasay, Hoppe and possibly the neo-Aristotelians. In the latter context, the outcome depends on what the various religions and religious authorities prescribe. In these contexts, free-market recipes are not ruled out altogether, but they necessarily drift towards a consequentialist note, as exemplified in the Christian tradition by Aquinas, Locke, Hayek or Becker, according to whom the main and possibly only justifications for private property and freedom from coercion are peace and/or wealth creation.

10.2.2 What role for the rule of law?

With the benefit of hindsight, free-market consequentialism has paid off. For a variety of reasons – including historical accidents – Western elites have generally and wisely chosen to implement growth enhancing policies during the past two centuries. These in turn have strengthened the case for private property and, more generally, economic freedom. This does not mean that the West always held private property as sacred, for the foundations of private property have always been rather ambiguous.[3] But it is true that the consequentialist approach requires that violations of private property be justified and that when justifications turn out to be weak, the rule-maker loses legitimacy. By and large, in the West this threat has been credible enough to restrain abuse. The Christian legacy mattered, of course, but only indirectly. It did not define the content of the rules. Rather, it specified the guidelines for those who suggested the rules of the game and who strived to obtain or preserve legitimacy; moreover, it successfully introduced political competition, thereby ensuring that the ruler knew that he could not claim self-referential legitimacy.

With regard to content, we have argued that laws are frequently a matter of rent-seeking by the incumbent ruler, subject to the constraints provided by historical accidents and by the prevailing First Principles. We do admit that this book has paid relatively little attention to the "rule of law". As a matter of fact, we do not dispute the appeal of the rule of law, which nowadays has become a captivating catchword identifying a situation in which legitimacy by conquest is denied; violence without justification is not admitted (rule under the law); and rules are credible (i.e. they are enforced). But we do doubt the operational value of this paradigm, which in our opinion says very little about the actual content of the rules, and which looks more like the description of a desirable institutional environment, while being rather weak when detailing how to avoid the abuses of majority decision-making.

In truth, since the early 1960s the constitutional-economics literature – an offshoot of the Ordo/neo-liberal tradition – has tried to give substance to the rule of law. Yet, we have a feeling that all efforts to move away from merely rejecting trade restrictions and overt rent-seeking have been rather ambiguous. Likewise, most attempts at formulating ideal procedures to select suitable policy-makers outside Hobbesian monarchical rule have been less than convincing and they all pale in comparison with the procedural refinements of – say – the Venetian Republic. Possibly as a consequence of this disillusion, several scholars have thus moved from tinkering about constitutional design to investigating which kind of legal system would be more likely to bring about the desired institutional features.

Following Hayek (1960, 1973), the mainstream literature has concluded that an idealized common-law context offers the suitable answer: courts are relatively independent of petty politics, of vote trading and thus of the pressure exercised by interest groups; stability is better enhanced by precedents than by statutory law-making; bad rules are more easily amended by an educated judge than by hundreds of poorly informed legislators. Moreover, common-law systems are usually held to be more deferential to the trading parties' original intentions and preferences, and thus closer to the principle of voluntary exchange. In a word, the common-law vision seems to succeed in bridging the free-market divide and bringing together morality and efficiency. The common law's morality lies in its respect for private property and voluntary exchange, while its efficiency relates to the system's wealth-enhancing consequences of these operational criteria. In other words, a virtuous feedback mechanism seems to emerge, whereby morality legitimizes efficiency, and efficiency ensures that moral standards remain a reliable constraint on both judicial and legislative arbitrariness. The key components in this virtuous mix between ethics and wealth are the *stare decisis* principle based on precedent and, more recently, the judicial review guarantee, whereby a supreme judiciary body ensures that both inferior courts and legislators do not violate agreed-upon meta-rules or super-laws. But does that really settle the issue? Is the common-law approach the handmaiden of the rule of law and thus the magic wand by means of which the free-market vision escapes all methodological and philosophical provisos?

To be sure, the common-law legal structure originated in a world in which private property was of the utmost importance, and indeed, one may argue that it was primarily meant to address situations from a practical vantage point. Just as in the earlier Roman tradition, common-law judges were supposed to provide relatively quick, easily enforceable, understandable and reasonable solutions to conflicts between individuals.[4] Yet the original common-law judges certainly cared very little about neoclassical efficiency, and the role of morality in their decision-making processes was only indirect. In fact, the common-law system consisted of a procedural arsenal designed to ensure that liberties would not be easily encroached upon (precedent); and that common-law judges were operating within an environment in which undesirable features could be filtered out or restrained through an evolutionary mechanism (institutional competition). Put differently, the moral foundations of freedom, private property and institutional competition came before the legal system and were not their consequence. Whatever its actual features, the incumbent legal system worked effectively because it complied with the underlying First Principles of the time.

One could thus conclude by remarking that the world in which the idealized version of the common-law seemed to thrive (with some qualifications) bears very little resemblance to today's common-law regimes. In truth, it is unlikely that today's rule-of-law advocates refer to the common-law experience of the Middle Ages, an epoch when markets were far from free, growth far from buoyant and the autocrats' judicial power hardly disputed. Yet, one should also bear in mind that nowadays rulers in common-law countries are not really opposing rent-seeking and arbitrary decision-making with too much enthusiasm: legislators do not refrain from introducing all sorts of statutory law-making, while judges feel relatively free to deviate from precedent. Judicial review also seems to be porous, as Supreme/Constitutional courts often believe it is their duty to adapt constitutional principles to the current political situations and *Weltanschauungen*, rather than to enforce the original *dictatum* of the Founding Fathers.[5] Perhaps even more significantly, the principles of individual freedom tend to be considered subject to the notion of public interest, which ought to prevail either because the public interest is beneficial to all in the long run; or because talents and luck are a social good to be shared; or because property rights originate from society, which is therefore legitimized to assign and rearrange them to pursue selected collective goals. If this is the proposed notion of the rule of law, it does seem that its common-law foundations are not quite the strongest bulwark against violations of economic freedom.

10.2.3 Back to First Principles

All told, we are still persuaded that First Principles remain a more satisfactory operational tool than the rule-of-law mantra. As noted in Chapter 5, First Principles identify the origin of legitimacy within a society. They can be derived from the sacred scriptures, from sets of values shared within a community, or simply – but also more problematically – from the primacy of the individual and therefore his right to reject decision-making by majority. This latter option identifies the free-market alternative, in which the emphasis should fall on the concept of "freedom", since in this case the term "market" merely indicates that the whole question concerns the application of the freedom-from-coercion principle to economic activities. It follows that free-market supporters are consistent if they embrace freedom from coercion as the only source of legitimacy for restraining human actions, including policy-making. All other justifications belong to consequentialism and expediency and therefore need theological foundations. In other words, once the primacy of the individual is denied, one requires theological foundations in order to make clear value judgements on the outcome of market exchanges and therefore interfere legitimately with the market process.

The ambiguities of a considerable portion of the L&E literature discussed in Chapters 6 and 7 offers plenty of examples in this context. By emphasizing the need to design rules of the game that reduce the cost of transacting or, perhaps more appropriately, the cost of monitoring and enforcing property rights, one ends up with tautologies or with statements of the obvious: one can always suggest hypothetical situations that improve upon Pareto suboptimal states of affairs. But when one argues for government intervention to enhance efficiency, the merit of such policies necessarily becomes a matter of cost–benefit analysis, rather than an enquiry into the voluntary cooperative arrangements that could be proposed and enforced in order to expand the range of opportunities available. One can certainly conceive of interesting solutions applicable to static, possibly partial-equilibrium contexts, as in the Posnerian tradition; or solutions derived from healthy doses of realism and scepticism about technocratic omniscience and bureaucratic wisdom, as in Epstein's proposals. But it is undeniable that sooner or later expediency conflicts with one's perception of fairness, or with one's understanding of his or her rights, the bedrock of which is either nature or a perceived (social) contract. And these can be overruled only by appealing to theological arguments, to a general design superior to individual interest, and therefore not conceived of by individuals.

Not surprisingly, related remarks also apply to the economics of growth, poverty and transition (Chapters 8 and 9), which usually includes detailed studies on how to obtain the desirable institutional context, and which seem oblivious to the relation between legitimacy and individual freedom. Although good institutions are by definition preferable to bad institutions, neglect of First Principles necessarily involves blindness to the mechanisms by means of which effective transition processes are started and kept going, as well as to why paternalistic or neo-paternalistic autocratic regimes are tolerated and sometimes even welcome.

10.3 From socialism to free market and back

As we know, in the last decades of the twentieth century, the advocates of constructivist economics were struck by four major events: the unanticipated worsening of economic conditions and the eventual collapse of the Soviet bloc; the acknowledged inability to solve the problem of poverty in the undeveloped world by means of aid and selective industrialization (picking hypothetical winners and showering them with privileges); the creeping crisis of the welfare state in most developed countries; and the gradual decline in growth rates – once again in most developed countries – despite ongoing technological progress. Not surprisingly, confronted with the evident failure of textbook recipes for regulated, demand-driven growth, since the mid-1980s both the academic community and most policy-makers started to show a more favourable attitude towards the free-market approach. Numerous observers heralded this change as a milestone in the way public opinion perceived economic matters: "Socialism is now defended rather than accepted as a moral imperative. Liberalism is now attacked rather than ignored, and a debate about liberalism permeates the world of ideas".[6] To an extent, optimism in classical-liberal and Austrian surroundings was justified. Although the drive towards free-market principles contained momentous qualifications,[7] free-market ideas seemed to be meeting with much friendlier audiences for the first time since the beginning of the century. Even if the works by Hume, Say and Menger continued to be ignored, the names of Smith, Hayek, Friedman and Buchanan were no longer associated with greed, asocial attitudes and Spencerian selection of the fittest. In some quarters they even became trendy.

Yet, although Marx and Keynes were hurriedly put back on the shelves, hardly anybody paid much attention to the fact that the buzzword had become "static efficiency", not entrepreneurship or individual responsibility. This book has tried to explain why this happened, why many allegedly free-market approaches were intrinsically fragile, and why as soon as free-market principles seemed to be at odd with the hoped-for outcomes, liberalism was more or less dumped and gross interventionism revived. It happened in the recent past and unless proponents of free markets renew a focus on First Principles, and emphasize that the alternative to the illusion of social rationality is individual responsibility, it will happen again in the future.

10.3.1 The consequentialist and moral perspectives once again

We have observed that by focusing on consequentialism, free-market policy-making recipes are generally designed to enhance cooperation and replicate what would happen in a world characterized by low transaction costs. However, the origins of inadequate cooperation might be subject to very flexible interpretation. As a matter of fact, this explains the widespread reliance on the Ordoliberal tradition, according to which a consequentialist version of the free market has been used as an argument against rent-seeking and populist, myopic redistribution. From such a perspective, therefore, it appears that the strength of the free-market approach ends up depending critically on the goal to be obtained (growth) and on the experts' ability to regulate without throwing too much sand in the wheels. However, when growth is no longer a priority or the only priority, and/or the promise of optimal regulation fails to deliver, the case for free-market economics becomes vulnerable.

We believe that such an approach will not take its proponents very far, even when they mean well. Rather, the chances for a lasting change of attitude away from socialism ultimately depend on the nature of the proposed free-market vision. This is true both for the man in the street and for the accomplished scholar. As experience demonstrates, and as Olson (1982) explained years ago, under consequentialism, the technocratic illusion may win the day, but only temporarily. If the market fails to produce the expected results and/or circumstances might alter shared priorities, disenchantment will prevail and the search for social(ist), rent-seeking solutions resumes. In a word, a consequentialist view stands only a poor chance to restrain selected categories of government intrusion, especially when their benefits (on aggregate demand) are immediate and their costs (on ill-structured supply) are all but invisible. In fact, effective restraints can only come if the moral attitude prevails, or if a radical and widely shared transformation in the current way of thinking takes place – that is if major events provoke a deep enough crisis in the very way the rules of social interaction are understood and give substance and power to new, "revolutionary" ideologies.

Not surprisingly, the divide between the consequentialist and the moral visions also affects the essence of positive and normative economics, and as a result the role of the social scientist. Consequentialism focuses on the desirability of the outcomes, which explains why positive economics frequently turns out to consist in the design of what-if exercises driven by the pursuit of previously-defined goals (e.g. growth). As a result, the choice of the appropriate rules and the evaluation of their potential impact in light of those predetermined ends become the purpose of normative economics. Not surprisingly, the development of accurate measurement and forecasting techniques becomes critical, while subjectivism must be abandoned. By contrast, the moral approach analyses individual behaviour by downplaying the role of rationality and by concentrating on the various elements that contribute to shaping preferences (psychological patterns) and to stimulating responses to incentives (behavioural routines). Unlike consequentialism, the moral view does not make use of positive economics in order to assess the desirability of human action. Rather, the moral view offers a consistency check that forces the observer to make his philosophical touchstones explicit from the outset: hence our notion of a-priorism.[8] Value judgements take place within the realm of philosophy or political philosophy, and it is there that standards are defined; not in the realm of positive or normative economics. Thus, selecting the free-market standard is no longer an economic decision. It is a philosophical choice that subsequently affects our understanding of individual behaviour (potential deviations from the rationality guidelines) and puts constraints on the legitimacy of man-made coercive rules, the acceptability of which eventually depends on their compliance with the notion of individual freedom.

10.3.2 The late twentieth century flirtation with free-market gibbering

In perspective, it is apparent that the four major events of the twentieth century (see above) did not really cast doubts on the foundations of the Age of Social Responsibility; and that, therefore, even during those years the trend in favour of free-market ideas remained powered by consequentialism, not morals. The late twentieth-century pull towards economic freedom originated from disappointing growth performances, either because the "optimal" rules of the game were neglected, or because of bad management by the policy-makers. The first context applied to several communist and poor countries, where people had vague notions about the working of a market system; while the second mainly applied to more affluent countries, where very few had reservations about the prevailing rules of the game. In general, the problems were perceived to be the excesses of central planning and the inefficiencies of corrupt and slack bureaucracies, rather than the violation of the individual freedom to choose.[9] Seen in this light, the Western free-market rhetoric of the late twentieth century had little to do with a plea for a new vision, and the principles typical of the Age of Social Responsibility remained in place. Thus, when some 20 years later a powerful mix of overconfident regulation, benign neglect towards grossly fraudulent behaviour and amazingly generous monetary policy almost brought the industrialized world to its knees, the flirtation with free-market ideas came to an abrupt end and the essence of the social contract forcefully came to the surface. Social consequentalism was vindicated: as people confronted the choice between short-term safety and shared responsibility on the one hand and, on the other, long-term growth and individual responsibilities, massive state intervention took the floor to ensure the first goal was met.

Are we then back to square one? Can one conclude that the free-market paradigm is incompatible with the principles governing the Age of Social Responsibility? By and large, this book has answered in the affirmative. The prospects for the economy are not encouraging and the current implicit social contract fails to be honoured in many countries. For instance, in 2011 the state of public finances featured by several Western countries has become dramatic and the future does not bode well, on either side of the Atlantic. People want to be safe, which means that they want to enjoy a high rate of employment (in the United States), and generous provisions for the unemployed and the retired (in continental Europe). The political elites are clearly falling down on the job across the whole line. Yet, we live in a context in which society comes before the individual: individual action is constrained by his implicit duties towards society (compulsory solidarity or fairness) and his position is guaranteed by his right to "human capability".[10] Economic stagnation and political disenchantment are the likely outcomes, at least in the short and medium run.

Although it is commonly accepted that socialism has failed to deliver satisfactory outcomes, and the very term "socialism" has acquired an all but derogatory connotation, the 2007/2009 crisis has made clear that the foundations of the socialist vision and ideology remain intact: It is widely held that it is desirable and indeed possible to design and realize ideal societal models in terms of wealth, opportunities, equality or other valuable goals. Of course, these shared goals are going to be consistent with "human capabilities" and supposedly obtained by adopting "extended neoclassical" blueprints.[11] In this climate of opinion, subjectivism, methodological individualism and personal responsibility continue to be sidestepped. Regrettably, public opinion thus continues to be unaware that the very rejection of these values has costs and that such costs cannot be avoided or reduced unless new First Principles are considered.

10.4 What about the future of policy-making?

Social scientists have no crystal ball. But if one accepts that the role and nature of policy-making boil down to some a priori moral choice, and if one believes that today's First Principles are not really different from what they were almost a century ago, the result is that over the next few years policy-making will be "business as usual". Surely, recent events have altered the emphasis on some of the components of the social contract, and raised new challenges for the regulatory experts. Will that make a difference? And can economists make a difference?

In recent times most economists have taken two different routes. Most of them have strived to create relatively complex mathematical constructions that would fit the macro-evidence; demonstrate that economics is indeed a hard science characterized by more or less exact laws subject to rigorous empirical scrutiny; and suggest that the economic method can be exported to all social sciences and beyond. These economists might not have contributed much to the history of economic ideas, but they have definitely strengthened the perception of economics as a rather eccentric discipline. As a matter of fact, while aspiring to rigour and exactness, this branch of the economics profession has also shown that most models are vulnerable to attack, that changes in the data sets often lead to significantly different results and that each situation deserves its own explanation. Moreover, abstracting from their intrinsic merit, these contributions have ensured that sound economics has virtually disappeared from the current debate. Even a cursory look at the top reputed journals in the profession suffices to understand why: most articles are impervious to those without a PhD degree and the conclusions often contain common-sense platitudes or counterintuitive results by and large explained by rather unrealistic initial assumptions. Furthermore, frustration with modelling has eventually led to econometric testing, so that economic theorizing has been effectively replaced by sophisticated statistics reproducing the past or offering (poor) predictions for the future.

A second group of economists has concentrated on the normative side. By drawing on public choice and new institutionalism, they have mixed the classical-school teaching on the virtues of free trade, qualified laissez-faire and the rule of law with the Austrian rediscovery of entrepreneurship. The result has been a rather strong case in favour of capitalism under the protection of a small, but credible state.[12] Recent history has proved this position right. Economic freedom is probably the best institutional environment to exploit growth opportunities and transform an isolated episode in a long-lasting success story. As we know, some 200 years ago easy access to cheap energy offered those opportunities and economic history since then has been a stunning accomplishment worldwide. No matter how reasonable these recipes have been, today's growth is no longer a priority in many economies and the normative views of the liberal tradition have thus lost their teeth. They are more or less acknowledged, but their targets are no longer at the top of the policy-makers' lists and – perhaps even more importantly – the rules of the political game required to meet those recipes are not consistent with what current First Principles dictate.

From a broader standpoint, it is fair to say that economics went the wrong way at the beginning of the nineteenth century, when it ignored technological progress and entrepreneurship, and focused on how to rationalize eternal poverty. It failed again to meet new challenges after the marginalist revolution, when the focus moved towards mathematical modelling to match the hard disciplines and to statistics to neutralize uncertainty. To be fair, the cost of those mistakes has not been very high. In a way, the economics profession itself has not done much to ensure that economists be taken seriously and influence policy-making choices. As observed in McCloskey (1998: chapter 9), modernism is impractical and its spirit has died long ago, the mainstream economist notwithstanding. As a matter of fact, the proliferation of figures and models and the willingness to please politicians or rent-seeking coalitions has often induced the greater public to believe that economics is a matter of opinions and that you can get almost any answer as long as you ask the right expert. Besides, and more generally, if technological progress saves social democracies from the Olsonian collapse, why should Western policy-makers pay attention to the long-run consequences of their choices, let alone their philosophical foundations? As was aptly pointed out some ten years ago by Kay (2003: 339),

> The economic role of a social democratic government is to determine through the democratic process how society wishes scarce resources to be allocated between competing ends, and to direct the activities of businesses and households in order to bring that allocation about.

In a way, Kay was right, for this is what First Principles prescribe today. And this also explains the status of what Kay calls the (embedded) market, i.e. an exchange system that institutions steer in accord with the guidelines defined by the "social, political and cultural context". In this framework, pluralism and regulatory discipline become the keywords. So much for economics. Yet, one has the impression that the embedded market has been a disappointment and that social-democratic economics is about to collapse. By running after desires and ignoring the nature of preferences (which always imply choice and therefore costs), modern policy-makers have slowed down growth, thrust their hands deeper and deeper into taxpayers' pockets and brought public finance on the verge of systemic catastrophe. In this light, and regrettably, the real tragedy of the economics profession at large has been its failure to go back to fundamentals and offer a consistent alternative. Simply telling policy-makers to beware government failures and to abstain from giving in to special interests and creating consensus isn't enough. While we might (and do) endorse such policies and while they might advance the free market in the short- or even the medium-term, they fail to provide a long-term validation, since they advise on utilitarian rather than principled grounds. The most important task of today's social scientist is to help people – policy-makers as well as those who elect them – understand the lasting case for free markets, the case rooted in those First Principles that have contributed so greatly to the success of the Western world.

Notes

1 Introduction

1 This possibility had already been predicted in Higgs (1987). See also Smith *et al.* (2010), who illustrate Higgs's insight with reference to the recent Troubled Assets Relief Program and the New Deal's National Recovery Act.
2 See, for instance, Taylor (2009).
3 See, for instance, James (2009).
4 Fraud appeared in different ways. For instance, in the private sector, managers and auditors frequently forged the accounts or simply lied about the quality of the company assets. In the public sector, public administrators deliberately accepted involvement in the securitization game so as to please alleged market makers who then returned the favour by making it easier for troubled borrowers to improve their ratings, reschedule their debt and loosen their short-term financial constraints.
5 For instance, according to Akerlof and Shiller (2009: 72), "the sub-prime crisis may be directly traced to a shortcoming of modern deposit insurance". In their view, the solution is a monetary-fiscal stimulus large enough to achieve full employment, plus the proclamation of state-guaranteed solvency of the financial system to restore confidence (ibid.: 96).

From a different perspective, in Europe many public figures ended up blaming the Americans for having ignited the crisis, and unrestrained globalization for having spread it. A similar exercise in logical twisting and bad economics had occurred a few years earlier, when the Chinese had been blamed for exceedingly good economic performance, and globalization had been identified as the culprit for having allowed competitive Asian companies to slow down growth and for having created unemployment in Western Europe.

6 Eichengreen (2007) offers an excellent example of this approach, applied to a multinational environment.
7 A quick look at the role attributed to methodological issues in most undergraduate and graduate curricula in economics throughout the world easily proves this point.
8 This vision owes a great deal to A. Marshall's *Principles of Economics* (book 1, chapter 1): "Economics is a study of mankind in the ordinary business of life; it examines that part of individual and social action which is most closely connected with the attainment and with the use of the material requisites of wellbeing." The path leading to that vision, as well as both the implicit assumptions it implied and its legacy, form the cores of Chapters 2 and 3 of this volume.
9 See Langlois (1989) for a thorough analysis of the methodological shortcomings of the institutionalists research agendas. Chapters 4 and 5 discuss the foundations and legitimacy of the institutional contexts, while Chapters 6 and 7 are devoted to the economics of transaction costs. In all these chapters the mainstream, prevailing consequentialist approach will be juxtaposed to the free-market vision.

10 In a similar vein, see also Infantino (2010), who believes that whenever an action involves the procurement of means, such action necessarily acquires an economic dimension. Several free-market scholars, and especially the "Austrians" would then conclude that the focus on interaction turns the shaping of individual preferences into a matter of secondary importance. As we shall clarify in Chapter 3, this book offers a different perspective.

11 The most authoritative efforts were carried out by Friedrich Hayek, who however also failed to provide the answers to the questions that Veblen had raised and to which Carl Menger had offered tentative solutions.

12 Menger defines pragmatic institutions as the result of man-made, intended design, such as ordinary law making. Organic institutions are spontaneously-born habits and customs that have been developing over time and have been retained and possibly refined (language, money, habits).

13 By contrast, organic institutions generally evolve gradually and, given their nature, they usually have a rather limited impact on the way people perceive reality. Limited, but not absent: for instance, the grammar of the language we speak affects the structure of our thoughts (see Lera Boroditsky's "Lost in translation", published in the *Wall Street Journal*, 23 July 2010).

14 Morality has been assumed to mean different things. An inquiry into the terms of the debate is well beyond our scope. Nonetheless, although we are aware that other categorizations are possible, we make a distinction between ethics, morality and natural rights.

   By "ethics" we mean the rules that the individual believes should govern his way of life in his pursuit of virtue, which of course also presupposes that the individual has an opinion about what "*la bonne vie*" consists of. When we refer to "morality" (the *mores*), we mean the behavioural rules accepted and praised within the community to which the individual belongs (but see also notes 12 and 26 in Chapter 3 of this book). Finally, we identify "natural rights" as the basic constraints that an individual believes to be typical of all human beings and unchallengeable, neither by him nor by others.

   As consequence, ethics determines how the individual behaves within a society; while morality defines the foundations of any social covenant. Thus, both ethics and morality necessarily evolve through time and across societies. On the other hand, natural rights may differ across individuals following their religions or philosophical inclinations, but within those religious or philosophical constraints they are eternal, for eternal is the essence of the individual.

15 Certainly, the effects of such changes and shocks can be different across societies, and can therefore easily generate differentiated outcomes. This happens even if one controls for the variance in the accident, since its impact and perception are always diverse, both across societies and across individuals. *A contrario*, one can observe that different historical institutions may generate similar economic performances. For instance, Pomeranz (2000) has documented at great length that despite vastly different historical institutions, living standards in Europe and China were approximately the same for at least 500 years (until the end of the eighteenth century).

16 "Psychological patterns" describe individual behaviour in a world in which pragmatic institutions are neutral, i.e. in which they are equivalent to procedural or enforcement devices without substantive normative power.

2   On the nature and scope of economic reasoning

1 Lange (1945–1946: 19) defined economics as "the science of administration of scarce resources in human society" and added that "it deals with a subject which depends on the standards and forms of life in human society". But rather than pursuing the matter further, he articulated a list of the sub-disciplines created by such a definition: economics *stricto sensu*, economic sociology, theoretical economics, applied economics, econometrics, welfare economics.

2 More on this will be said in Chapter 3, in which the notion of rationality is discussed at greater length.

3 About a century after Xenophon, Plato would also take an interest in economic issues. Plato's economics thinking, however, seemed to be motivated by his willingness to enforce state control upon most human activities, rather than by a desire to understand their mechanisms. For instance, in the *Republic* he did consider exchange advantageous from a production standpoint, but overlooked the consumption benefits derived from individuals' different preferences. Not surprisingly, Plato actually regarded the division of labour as an area for state supervision: individuals were indeed supposed to engage in (or be assigned to) the activities that best suited their talents, but could not move from one occupation to the other.

4 Socrates emphasized that individual happiness was a matter of the soul, while material prosperity could encourage greed, envy and ultimately corrupt morals. Hence the state had a duty to interfere with allegedly immoral choices and be suspicious of trade and entrepreneurship. See also Huerta de Soto (2008) on the lack of interest of most classical Greek philosophers towards economics as a social science, and on their outspoken hostility towards free-market principles and their institutional foundations. As mentioned above, this was particularly true of Plato.

5 Aristotle recognized the value of money as a measure of wealth and also tried to develop a theory of moral exchange and just distribution. See for instance his *Nicomachean Ethics* (book V, chapter 5) and his *Politics* (book I, chapters VIII–X). Still, it would have probably been better if he hadn't. By arguing that money cannot reproduce itself, he contributed to inhibiting a proper understanding of the "interest rate" for centuries. Furthermore, by theorizing that individuals exchange goods of equal value, he misled generations of economists until the late nineteenth century and encouraged public opinion to despise merchants and trade in general: "Tradesmen in All Ages and Nations have been reputed ignoble" (Edward Chamberleyne 1669, quoted in Stone 1965: 40).

6 A relevant exception is the birth of independent municipalities in the High Middle Ages, especially in Italy and later in Flanders. The composition and action of municipal governments were often influenced by the most important guilds and moneyed interest groups, such as bankers and merchants.

7 The Greeks themselves made a difference between the polis, where virtue should be pursued; and alliances/covenants, through which common material needs should be satisfied.

8 There was a difference, though. From the Catholic and Lutheran perspectives, economic activity was perceived as an instrument: a way of surviving and not being a burden to the rest of the community. From the Calvinist standpoint, labour was a goal: the purpose of man on earth, in order to honour God and his design in this world.

9 According to Delumeau (1983) pessimism dominated the daily life of most people and this vision of fear and guilt started to be questioned only in the eighteenth century. Delumeau's perspective has not gone unchallenged. It is true, however, that with the partial exceptions of the Netherlands and England, until very late for most people the source of optimism was related to the chances of self-fulfilment and salvation, rather than to the prospects for improvements in material well-being.

10 Robert Crowley in *The Voyce of the Last Trumpet* (1550), quoted in Cowper (1975). See also Tawney (1926) and Knights (1937), who offer a wealth of evidence with regard to the general attitude of the time, according to which "every member of the same should live content in his vocation and execute his charge according to his profession", as Gerard De Malynes wrote in his *Saint George for England, Allegorically Described* (1601). More generally, in his monumental work on the social and economic history of England across the sixteenth and seventeenth centuries, Stone (1965: 21) claimed that:

> The notion that ever since the seventeenth century England has been a nation of shopkeepers inspired by the ethics of the market-place and led by a capitalist bourgeoisie is one that dies very hard. In fact as late as 1870 England was basically aristocratic in tone, taking its moral standards, its hierarchy in social values, and its political system from the landed class.

The supreme virtues of which were "obedience and the avoidance of change". This vision did break down in England during the first half of the seventeenth century, but was then prevalent again for the next two centuries. See on this the various references to the work by Habakkuk, quoted in Stone (1965).

11 Nonetheless, it must be conceded that economic matters were regarded as worthy of investigation by experts. For instance, Edward Misselden (1623: 16–17) claimed that only trained people can understand the difference between "Intrinsique" and "Extrinsique" value (i.e. utility/satisfaction and price, in today's terminology), and he also suggested that when merchants seek their "Privatum Commodum", they enhance the common interest: "What else makes a Common-wealth, but the private-wealth, if I may so say, of the members thereof in the exercise of *Commerce* amongst themselves, and with forraine Nations?". Misselden also explained in clear terms the notion of relative prices: "it is the plenty or scarcitie of Commodities, their use or *Non*-use, that maketh them rise and fall in price" (ibid.: 22).

12 Of course, Hugo Grotius and John Locke were the typical champions of this widely accepted natural-order approach. See also Chapter 5 on the connection between the natural order and the implicit contract of secular societies.

13 "Economy" because it dealt with the production of goods and services, not unlike Xenophon's lines of reasoning on estate management; "Political" because it affected the wealth and stability of a community (see also Section 1.3 in Chapter 1).

14 The theistic view of long-run perfection/equilibrium had already been questioned by Hume's *Dialogues* (published in 1779). Definitely a sceptic, possibly an atheist, Hume's argument was twofold. First, our notion of equilibrium is often the measure of our ignorance, in that we define as godly design or will what we do not rationally understand. Second, it is an act of arrogance (and stupidity) to aim at defining metadesigns conceived by God. Indeed, the very notion of "conception" presupposes an anthropomorphic approach which cannot be accepted.

   Yet, the economic implications of Hume's contribution were largely ignored. Perhaps because they weakened the importance of equilibrium within the social sciences, and failed to suggest a different research programme. Or perhaps because they failed to make a strong argument in favour of the individual as maker of his own condition.

15 According to the *Journal of Economic Literature*, in May 2010 economics considered some 19 domains, including some 116 categories. Although some domains and subareas in fact identify subject matters that lie outside the realm of economic theorizing *stricto sensu*, (e.g. economic history, urban planning, econometrics), the fragmentation of economics properly understood remains substantial.

16 See Schabas (2005: 49) and, more generally, Keynes (1926). De Gournay (1712–1759) contributed to economics in many ways: as witnessed by Turgot's *Elegy to Gournay*, he anticipated the Hayekian notion of dispersed knowledge, Smith's much publicized man's virtuous instinct to trade, as well as the phenomenon of rent-seeking by organized interest groups.

17 Contrary to the literature prevailing in seventeenth-century England, Adam Smith preferred to mention "instinct", rather than profit, as the engine of man's economic activities. This choice could perhaps be explained by his efforts to show that the free market is virtuous because it is the result of the individuals' virtuous (and natural) impulses. Greed would have been more difficult to justify and would have called for a discussion of the role of merchants, still a touchy subject in the second part of the

eighteenth century. As a result, whereas in seventeenth-century economic thought profit-seeking was actually enforcing the natural order, according to Adam Smith the source was man's innate virtue. See also Section 2.4 below.

18 See Schabas (2005) for a more articulated picture, in which pre-Ricardian economics is characterized by a natural order regulated by Providence, whereas the post-Ricardian period features a natural order following the laws dictated by natural scarcity.

19 These are the words used by Smith (1982 [1759]) in order to explain cooperation. See Holler (2006) for an in-depth analysis of the notion of sympathy and of some implications for social interactions.

20 J.S. Mill quoted in Jaffé (1976: 516). Contrary to common belief, Adam Smith's contradictory references to the invisible hand have also little to do with man's efforts to enhance his consumption and welfare, or with the importance of individual choices (Grampp 2000). Rothbard (1995) underscored the ambiguities of this Smithean expression, which nonetheless does not stop him from suggesting that most human beings eventually behave like machines (today's terminology would refer to "alienation") and that only public education can restore their dignity (Smith 1981 [1776]: 781–784).

21 For instance, the first edition of Malthus's *Essay on the Principle of Population* (1798) explained poverty as the results of men's drive to generate children, rather than as the consequence of a bad social organization, which was Condorcet's and William Godwin's thesis. In his second edition (1803), however, Malthus presented a much revised version of his original argument.

22 Mandeville's notion of human nature and sociability as expressed in the Fable of the Bees was one of the few remarkable (and at the time definitely scandalous) exceptions. By claiming that men can be evil, he questioned the moral foundations of individual behaviour and created a grey area: could vice be admitted in the name of the common good? Can be a social covenant be acceptable when its actors do not mean well? Should well-meaning intervention be banned because by correcting individual misbehaviour, interference with the public good would ensue? To be fair, the notion of private vice leading to the public good was not entirely new, as witnessed by the works of John Houghton in the early 1680s and Dudley North a few years later. These works also proposed a dynamic vision characterized by competition and entrepreneurship that unfortunately went lost in Mandeville's and (Smith's) visions of society.

23 England was an important exception, though. During the late sixteenth and the seventeenth centuries envy for the Dutch spurred many studies on how to get rich despite the absence of natural resources to exploit. By and large, the answer widely aired was "free trade, specialization and better institutions", an answer that was nonetheless overshadowed since the late sixteenth century by decades of wars and fervent nationalism and that was discovered again only some 300 years later.

24 The benefits of exchange depend on two elements. The first relates to the gain in consumption: even if individual A does not develop his talents (specialize) and keeps his production structure constant, trade would generally allow him to improve his welfare as long as his opportunity cost of consuming good X differs from the relative market price of X (the terms of trade). This benefit accrues to at least one trading partner whenever agents have different preferences, and thus different opportunity costs. The second benefit of exchange concerns relative productivities, which depend on the development of talent: exchange allows specialization and therefore reduces the amount of time/effort it takes to produce one unit of X (or Y), either for self-consumption or to exchange with given amounts of Y (X). As result, exchange allows the aggregate production possibility frontier to expand. Adam Smith grasped this last source of benefits, but not the part pertaining to the consumption gains. See also Rosenberg (1994: chapter 2), who underscores Charles Babbage's critical contribution to the economics of specialization.

25 Perhaps Adam Smith also found it convenient to accept the medieval theory of remuneration, according to which compensation is just as long as it rewards labour, effort. It is worth pointing out, however, that in medieval times, the "labour theory" met needs specific of that period: to justify payments to the sellers of science (for otherwise science was supposed to belong to God) and to accept merchants' profits. A similar comment applies to the early references to instincts in order to explain free trade and trade in general: since instincts are synonymous with human nature, trade is moral because it originates from human nature:

> There is nothing in the world so ordinarie, and naturall unto men, as to contract, truck, merchandise, and trafficque one with another, so that it is almost unpossible for three persons to converse together two hours, but they wil fall into talke of one bargaine or another, chopping, changing, or some other kinde of contract.
>
> (Wheeler 1601: 2–3)

But Smith was not subject to the same constraint, and probably really believed in instinct-driven trade, as his mistaken theory of value proves.

26 Before Adam Smith, the idea of a spontaneous economic order free from religious connotations was already clear in Joseph Lee's *Vindication of the Considerations Concerning Common-Fields and Inclosures* published in 1656 and was later revived by Mandeville's insights into the spontaneous features of the market and into the role of the price system as an efficient allocation mechanism. Yet, Adam Smith introduced a new perspective by rejecting the idea that such order was brought about by greed and self-interest, and referring instead to "mutual sympathy" and "benevolence". More recently, see also Buchanan (1979: 31).

27 Defining Western civilization and dating its birth are daunting tasks that lie well beyond the scope of these pages. Nonetheless, for our purposes it might be worth pointing out that its major traits include the denial of Universalism, which dates to the failure of Justinian's effort to revive the Roman Empire (sixth century), to the Gregorian blows to the Carolingian alternative (late eleventh century) and, later on, to the defeat of the Church by Philip the Fair (see for instance Azzara 2004). The West also emphasizes the role of the individual as opposed to asceticism, which began to lose ground since the fourth century AD and became all but marginalized in the twelfth century, to be replaced by an increasingly strong propensity to accept and encourage the use of rationality and, within limits, the exercise of entrepreneurship (Stark 2006). As summarized by Koch and Smith (2006: 22),

> The essence of the West is an indefinable blend of rationalism, activism, confidence, knowledge-seeking, personal responsibility, self-improvement, world-improvement and compassion. At the root of it all is a sense of ethical individualism that is shared by Europeans and their descendants, and represented today by the peoples of America, Europe and Australasia.

28 This attitude was still present in the eighteenth century, when it was commonly accepted that a different distribution of income would have encouraged the lower classes to squander their additional resources in "weekly debauches" Tawney (1926: 270).

29 The objectivist view aims at defining imaginary long-run, possibly eternal, relative-price structures. By contrast, the subjectivist approach focuses on values, rather than prices. As a result, subjectivism gives origin to an altogether different vision of the world, a vision which denies static equilibrium and long-run foresight, which sets severe limitations on the use of mathematical modelling. Nevertheless, as the subjective theory of value took hold, these last points were appreciated only by the Austrian marginalists.

30 In his *Cours d'Économie Politique* published in 1839, Pellegrino Rossi, the successor to Say's chair in Paris, actually expressed his doubts about the notion of equilibrium

with extreme clarity, but almost accidentally. In the end, and rather unfortunately for the history of economic thought, he was better known as a politician murdered in the 1848 tumults than as an insightful scholar.

31 See also Campagnolo (2009 and 2010).
32 Marchionatti (2007: 303) clearly explains that "Walras considered economics a physical-mathematical science like mechanics". Marchionatti also documents that the Walrasian version of marginalism was immediately questioned by Edgeworth, Marshall and Pareto. They considered mathematics a tool to clarify theoretical reasoning, to provide deductive rigour and consistency, but they also warned that "the fundamental part of a complex real-life problem cannot be grasped in a series of equations" (ibid.: 304).
33 The objective theory of value left equilibrium undetermined, for competitive pricing under constant returns to scale was not enough to define quantities. The problem could be ignored by assuming that demand consisted of the means to survive. If, however, individuals live above mere subsistence levels, a theory of demand becomes crucial: according to Maddison (2005), GDP per capita in Western Europe grew at about 1 per cent a year during the 1820–1870 period, a marked increase with respect to the previous centuries.
34 Keynes explicitly refers to the new resources available thanks to colonization, large food supplies being made available in America and Russia (1920: 22–25).
35 Much of chapter 7 of the General Theory is devoted to the role of, and the damages provoked by, men's instincts and stupidity. Interesting enough, however, in the mid-1930s Keynes seemed to maintain his hardly concealed contempt for the crowds, but dropped the connection between people's behaviour and the disruptive role of government, which creates inflation and prompts hatred towards the entrepreneurial class.
36 Dynamic equilibrium seems almost a sleight of hand in order to accommodate growth as a consequence of increased capital endowments. As convincingly pointed out in a broader context by Holcombe (2007: chapters 2 and 3), the results are far from satisfactory.
37 "L'équilibre économique présente des analogies frappantes avec l'équilibre d'un système mécanique. Quand on connaît bien ce dernier équilibre, on a des idées nettes sur le premier" (Pareto 1897: vol. 2, § 592). Yet, it must also be underscored that Pareto denied that this was a good enough reason to expand the size and the scope of government action. See for instance Pareto (1897: vol. 2, § 672).
38 Keynes himself blamed the politicians – rather than the Bank of England – for the expansionary monetary policy that contributed to the crisis in the 1920s.
39 A milder version is to be found in Hayek (1975), who accepted mathematical modelling as a way of securing logical consistency within a general-equilibrium context. However, Hayek denied its validity for predictive purposes and warned against situations where "a false theory ... will be accepted because it is more 'scientific'", while "a valid explanation ... is rejected because there is no sufficient quantitative evidence for it". In fact, Hayek concluded by saying that "I still doubt whether their search for measurable magnitudes has made significant contributions to our *theoretical* understanding of economic phenomena" (Hayek 1975: 434 and 437). See also Bouillon (2007), who points out that Friedman had an imperfect understanding of the essence of the relation between hypotheses and predictions. This flaw, therefore, makes Friedman's methodological approach fragile even from a Popperian perspective.
40 Despite his efforts and enthusiasm, Pareto eventually realized the difficulties in applying the "experimental method" to economics. Frustration led him to abandon the dismal science and devote his attention to sociology.
41 Although the Austrians argue for an amoral approach to economics, their praxeological vision has clear moral foundations, in that the primacy of the individual over society requires philosophical/moral justifications.
42 In particular, both the mainstream and the Austrian economists claim that economic

policy-making regards the instruments, while politics bears responsibility for defining the goals. Yet, the moral nature of economic analysis has a long tradition, even within the classical camp. See for instance Alvey (1999) and also Campagnolo (2006), who investigate the connections between determinism, hermeneutics and relativism.

43 The *Methodenstreit* dates back to the last decades of the nineteenth century (see, for instance, Bostaph 1994 and Huerta de Soto 1998). On one side stood the advocates of the historical school, according to whom there exist universal laws that apply to society. Such laws can only be discovered by the accumulation and analysis of the data, and can be exploited by the rule maker in order to pursue shared goals and ease social evolution. On the other side stood the advocates of the Austrian school, according to whom society can only be understood by analysing individual behaviour, which unfolds following a limited number of axioms.

44 Marciano (2007) has effectively summed up the current debate on these two different approaches by distinguishing between the value paradigm (economics as a method to maximize wealth, as maintained by Gary Becker) and the exchange paradigm (economics as the study of the institutions that affect exchange, as held by James Buchanan).

3 Time, rationality, cooperation

1 Friedman actually circumvents the danger of falling victim to the whims of the political elites by claiming that "differences about economic policy among disinterested citizens derive predominantly from different predictions about the economic consequences of taking action ... rather than from fundamental differences in basic values" (1953: 5). Friedman's text makes clear that "basic values" means "targets", not moral principles.

2 See Chapter 5 on the existence and the meaning of veils from a constitutional perspective.

3 Chapters 4 and 5 analyse the second pillar: the relation between society and the individual, and thus the role of the social contract.

4 The point was stressed by Hayek, who drew attention to the fact that "since equilibrium is a relationship between actions, and since the actions of one person must necessarily take place successively in time, it is obvious that the passage of time is essential to give the concept of equilibrium any meaning" (1937: 37). In turn, human action is moved by the acquisition of knowledge, which necessarily takes place through time. Thus, in Hayek's view, since mainstream economics does not have a theory explaining the acquisition of knowledge (and is barely aware of the question), classical and neoclassical economics are essentially timeless, and their ambitions to anticipate and predict the future are vain. The reader can refer to Boland (1978) for a mainstream reply to what has become known as the "Hayek problem".

5 See the introductory chapter and Section 1.5 in particular. Of course, psychological patterns also include irrational behaviour. See Section 3.4.3 below.

6 The literature on uncertainty – as opposed to risk and thus the value of the expected-utility criterion – has a long tradition which dates back to Keynes (1921) and Knight (1921). See also Section 5.3.1 in Chapter 5, as well as Basili and Zappia (2010) for a recent critical survey.

7 North (1994: 359–360) has also drawn attention to the time question, but from a different standpoint:

> Time as it relates to economic and societal change is the dimension in which the learning process of human beings shapes the way institutions evolve. That is, the beliefs that individuals, groups, and societies hold which determine choices are a consequence of learning through time.

We find this version slightly confusing, in that it conveys the impression that the future does not contain something really new, but it is simply the period of time where the present unfolds its effects. This definition is satisfactory to describe path-dependence, but becomes powerless when path-dependence breaks apart.

8 Clearly, the shorter the time horizon for the policy-maker, the narrower is the scope for gradualism or trial-and-error. In turn, this implies that policy-making must be razor-sharp and constantly rely on the "perfect model". See also Sections 4.2 and 5.1 in the next two chapters, in which the notions of rule stability and credibility are discussed in greater detail.

9 See for instance Koselleck (1979).

10 Since it was frequently maintained – e.g. by Martin Luther – that the End of the world was imminent, conceiving of long-run plans would have been meaningless, if not arrogant or blasphemous.

11 This juxtaposition is also typical of modern economic thinking, where it has led to the quest for compromises and often ended in contradictions. An example is provided by the so-called "Keynesian Revolution", which tried (unsuccessfully) to combine a "conception of history" with short-run policy-making. See also Asimakopulos (1978) and the references to the earlier literature quoted there.

12 To be fair, Koselleck (1979) noted that during the sixteenth century several Italian authors had already anticipated Westphalia and taken it for granted that man would be the designer of his own future, that the state would be the political framework within which human action would take place, and that the state would be responsible for shaping the future. As will be observed later, this also contributed to raising doubts about the notion of morality, as the notion of "good" and "bad" would no longer depend on an end condition (the Last Judgement), but on state-created contingencies subject to ongoing change. Put differently, the medieval shortening of time implied that all acts would be judged according to a single standard, defined by the end of time. Hence, the universal notion of morality. Instead, the modern emphasis on the acceleration of time implies that human action be evaluated according to the short-term goals set by the social, and is necessarily consequentialist.

13 Mises (1963 [1949]: chapter 1).

14 To complete the picture, it should be noted that the most accredited critics of methodological individualism emphasize that individuals are influenced by social phenomena (e.g. customs and shared beliefs) and that, therefore, in order to understand individual behaviour, one cannot ignore social variables and social interactions (see for instance Hodgson 2004: 16–29). The last advocate of the opposite view – methodological collectivism – was of course Karl Marx, who had followers among political scientists and sociologists, but who met with only isolated success among economists.

   In the end, it seems that it all comes to a terminological misunderstanding caused by the confusion between the nature of the agent (the individual or society, following one's view of political philosophy) on the one hand; and what prompts individual action (genes, categorical imperatives, acquired beliefs, formal and informal rules) on the other. Although the answer on the latter issue is not disputed, the answer to the former question remains open. In our view, it forms the essence of today's debate on the content of methodological individualism and bears important consequences on the role and nature of policy-making. See on this Chapter 4.

15 Until well after Keynes, the standard explanation for irrational behaviour was sheer stupidity, which in fact does not explain much. Today irrationality tends to be explained under two headings. Erratic irrationality is driven by emotions, passions, whims, temper. It is usually short-lived and does not show orderly patterns. On the other hand, systematic irrationally is defined in terms of deontology or of genetic backwardness.

   In the first case (deontology), ideals and values lead the individual to act against his material interest. Policy-making has little to say in this respect, unless deontic instincts are manifestly asocial or anti-social, and therefore clearly harmful to the rest of the community. According to the second set of situations (genetic backwardness), it is maintained that individuals often think according to routines inherited during a long-lasting and very slow evolutionary process. Since in the past two centuries genetic evolution has been much slower than social and technological change, the purpose of policy-making would consist in filling the gap between the behavioural routines motivated by obsolete genetic structures and those matching the current institutional and technological context.

16 We estimate that the most appropriate definition of rationality is "conscious *and* calculated/reasoned", as opposed to "short-sighted behaviour by selfish individuals who do not see the benefits of cooperation". Unfortunately, although the limits of the latter definition are obvious, many authors refer to rational behaviour as sets of "self-interested actions", with no further qualifications; but then develop their explanation of irrational behaviour by emphasizing that even uncontrolled or instinctive action frequently serves the interest of the individual. A typical example of this literature is the widely-quoted book by Frank (1988).

17 To remind the reader, Chapter 2 pointed out that policy-making is validated in that: (*a*) it accomplishes a common/social goal possibly in contrast with the interest of the selfish individual, and (*b*) it fixes a wide range of alleged market failures.

18 Quite rightly, when analysing the notion of rationality Sen (1977: 322–323) observed that:

> It is possible to define a person's interest in such a way that no matter what he does he can be seen to be furthering his own interests in every isolated act of choice ... no matter whether you are a single-minded egoist or a raving altruist or a class conscious militant, you will appear to be maximizing your own utility in this enchanted world of definitions.

See also Zafirovski (2003) and Cowen (2004), who offer further references to a number of terminological issues.

19 As an aside, it could be observed that this claim also applies to masochists and many altruists. In fact, both categories of agents operate in order to enhance their own satisfaction. The peculiar feature of masochists is that their preferences are opposed to those of most other people (certain categories of physically painful experiences increase a masochist's utility). On the other hand, most altruists are peculiar in that their happiness depends on somebody else's utility and is frequently enhanced by the enjoyment of other people's esteem and gratitude. More on this at Section 3.4.3 in this chapter.

20 This is of course the bedrock of paternalism, in the free-market as well as in the socialist versions. The free-market and the socialist versions differ in that only the latter takes into account the notion of social rationality, and therefore compliance with a social welfare function. Put differently, in the socialist version, the individual is rational when he takes into account the strategic consequences of his interaction with the rest of the world and successfully overcomes all his prisoner's dilemmas. By contrast, in the free-market framework, paternalism implies benevolent intervention to ensure that the individual does not make dramatic mistakes.

A third version of paternalism is related to Schmoller's historicism, according to which the social welfare function becomes national(istic). As pointed out in the previous chapter, Schmoller's "young historicist school" came under heavy attack by Carl Menger and died out with his founder and the collapse of Germany's Second Reich.

21 Merit goods include socially-desirable services such as education or health. When "social merit" is the primary criterion, policy-making clearly becomes social(ist), in that the policy-maker pursues outcomes that individuals are not likely to appreciate, either because of their "unacceptable" tastes, or because of their anti-social preferences and lack of "virtue" (e.g. no solidarity).

22 Basu (2000: 37) clarifies the traditional meaning of rational behaviour in the following terms:

> In economics a person is taken to be rational if that person, given his information, chooses the action that maximizes his objective, *whatever that objective happens to be*. So, to describe a person as "rational" is ... simply to say that the person is good at choosing the actions that lead to whatever it is that he or she wishes to maximize (italics in the original).

The economist's way of characterizing the objective is the expected-utility theory. An alternative and less stringent definition of rationality refers to the notion of consistency, which is less vulnerable to circularity, and refers both to the ability to pursue happiness/utility (external or instrumental consistency, which was originally formulated in Hume's *Treatise of Human Nature*) and to one's capacity to order preferences and choose among alternatives (Savage's internal consistency). See for instance Margolis (1982), Sugden (1991) and Basu (2000: 39). This differs from the notion of rationality in the classical world, when the prevailing acceptable principle was virtue. See Aristotle's *Nicomachean Ethics* (I, 7 and 13). On the other hand, our use of the term consciousness corresponds to what Aristotle called "voluntariness" (ibid.: III, 1).

23 For sure, Friedman's claim about common "basic values" – see note 1 in this chapter – can no longer be maintained.

24 Machan goes in the same direction when he claims that "people are indeed the only living beings capable of understanding a moral appeal" (2004: 12).

25 See Barkow *et al.* (1992). The features of perception and categorizations play a key role in explaining economic choice/behaviour. That is precisely why economic analysis must rely on psychology in order to formulate acceptable a prioris. See for instance Cabantous and Hilton (2006) for a review of some well-known situations.

26 An *internal* moral assessment is here defined with reference to a deontic rule followed by the individual. An *external* moral assessment is associated with credibility and reputation, that is with the way a community assesses an individual's behaviour. The internal and external moral standards tend to become the same thing in the impartial spectator, a term coined by Adam Smith who drew from the *Treatise of Human Nature* (2000a [1739] and 2000b [1740]), in which Hume identifies the inner man (2.1.11.9–11) and the common standard (3.3.1.30) as the sources of moral judgement. More on the impartial spectator will be said later in this chapter.

27 As will become apparent in the section and chapters that follow, the distinction between rational and irrational behaviour is actually deceptive, since a significant part of human action is driven by deontic principles. These are usually and rightly considered outside rational behaviour, for deontic principles are rules of conduct that should not be applied ad hoc, whereas rationality implies a case-by-case approach. However, moral standards are also deemed to be outside the irrational sphere, which tends to refer to emotions and passions. Frank's (1988) overall conclusions – it is rational to be irrational – offer an example of the ambiguities generated by this misleading framing of human behaviour.

28 At best, the rationality assumption can accommodate irrational behaviour when the latter is truly accidental and/or short lived, so that it does not affect aggregates systematically. Not unexpectedly, the mainstream approach makes arbitrary statements about the agents' utility functions and considers all deviations from the expected behaviour as the result of irrational elements. The Austrian solution settles for more general claims about what makes a human being happy and what doesn't. In both cases, however, economics becomes a what-if predictive exercise (what would people do if they were all rational?), or an attempt to explain human behaviour by assuming that emotions and moral values play no lasting roles, or cancel out on aggregate.

29 See for instance Gneezy and Rustichini (2000), Cardenas *et al.* (2000), Fehr and List (2004).

30 Gains may be illusory, once the counterparts' reactions are taken into account, so that a second-best solution might be preferable.

31 See Williams (1966) and Dawkins (1976). Of course, these "deviations" also include several phenomena dear to behavioural economists.

32 These refer to the role played by parents, friends, colleagues at work, opinion makers: they all contribute to shaping our deontic principles and more generally, our behaviour.

33 See Sections 6.3.2 and 6.3.3 (Chapter 6).

34 A social contract is an agreement between an individual and an organization serving a set of individuals (Jouvenel 1993 [1945]: chapter 2). It is an "open" contract when there is freedom of exit (and possibly freedom of entry as well). It is a "closed" contract when the contract applies by default (e.g. following birth or residence) and the cost of exit is significant or prohibitive. In general, social-contract theories apply to the closed form (see also Chapter 5).

35 Tocqueville, in writing about the Americans, already made this point almost 200 years ago.

36 See Schlicht (1998), who makes a distinction between clarity (the criterion according to which institutions are selected) and clarification (man's psychological preference for certainties).

37 To complete, it is worth noting that the assumption of bounded rationality differs from that of limited information and knowledge in two respects. First, bounded rationality presumes that the individual knows *ex ante* what information should be acquired and processed; and deliberately neglects the rest. In addition, the strict version also assumes that mistakes can also be made because of uncertainty; but that they cancel out on average.

Both assumptions have been criticized from traditional quarters as well. In order to know which information needs to be acquired or can be discarded, the actor must necessarily be perfectly informed. But then, he would be fully rational. Moreover, there is no reason to believe that the consequences of an uncertain event are evenly distributed with mean equal to zero. If that were actually the case, it would be a matter of risk, not uncertainty. Hence, it seems that bounded rationality applies less to human action than to simulation or teaching techniques.

38 Of course, neither case refers to a situation where A thought the visit to the palace or to the showroom important enough to affect his plans for the day. Had it been so, such visits would have been "marginal", or they would have belonged to a marginal subset of decisions: A consciously decides to allocate his time throughout the day so as to be able to go to the showroom (an explicit destination) and – say – also buy an ice cream at the parlour nearby.

When marginal decisions are involved, free riding is no longer pure, but only partial. Under partial free riding, A free rides on B, since A gives up nothing to compensate B, but A must nevertheless forego the benefits he would have enjoyed had he done something else with the resources he spends – including time – in order to enjoy B's products.

39 This is manifest in the free-market case, where such rights are epitomized by the freedom-from-coercion principle, which includes personal dignity and freedom of contract and presupposes the existence of private property rights. See in particular Section 6.4 in Chapter 6 for a more detailed examination of the relation between scarcity and property rights.

40 Envy and, more generally, the individual notion of fairness do contribute to explaining agents' behaviour. As mentioned in the text, B might be angry at the idea that A systematically enjoys benefits without paying; and B might ultimately decide to stop producing those benefits, as the ultimatum bargaining game proves. This is relevant from an economic standpoint, since it explains human behaviour and accounts for the fact that some goods and services are no longer produced, or for the fact that B is

encouraged to find a way of excluding A. Yet, since envy is about the individual notion of fairness, it should not imply normative reactions. They are justified only when a legitimate notion of *social* fairness is introduced.

41 The partial-equilibrium view is both critical and deceptive. It is critical because it eliminates the problem of comparing the desirability of what is being produced and what has to be given up to allow production. It is deceptive (and wrong) because by doing so it eludes the problem of scarcity.

42 The tones usually get sharper when public opinion considers the producers' surplus (profit), which is perceived as a residual and therefore as the alleged product of exploitation. In this light, Kahneman *et al.* (1986) offer some examples on the perception of fairness and pricing policies under different circumstances. Of course, the equivalence between unjustified surplus and profits is not quite correct, for profits reward entrepreneurship. But in the world of timeless economics, entrepreneurs do not exist. See also our remarks in the previous chapter and those presented later (Chapter 8).

43 Clearly, free rides can be transformed into economic transactions. This is what happens when a positive externality is internalized: e.g. B decides to make A pay for entering the Ferrari showroom. Then, a non-economic action becomes an economic issue. However, when this happens, the surplus has not disappeared – it is just being called another name.

44 In the real world the same applies to merit goods, even if their case is even weaker, since merit goods are generally rival and excludable. Indeed, it is hard to avoid the impression that in the real world paying for the public goods one consumes is just a pretext to justify taxation in general, and has little or nothing to do with the internalization of positive externalities.

45 It may be worth underscoring that according to the Scottish Enlightenment, the impartial spectator does not merely represent the rules of the game typical of a community. In fact, Francis Hutcheson's "unbiassed arbitrators" and Adam Smith's "impartial spectator" reflect the individual's sense of what is right, both because it follows absolute standards and because it is appreciated by the community he belongs to.

46 We ignore the case of "reciprocal altruism" (Trivers 1971), according to which the individual acts altruistically because he expects to be compensated for his good deeds. In our view, these cases do not characterize altruism, but transactions featuring uncertain payback structures. See also West *et al.* (2007) for a survey of the different forms of altruism mentioned in the literature.

47 Of course, this does not rule out that many vain acts tend to be disguised as generosity.

48 Beraldo and Sugden (2010) have recently suggested a simple and yet powerful explanation of why people abandon short-time self-interest and engage in cooperation, even when they know that they can be fooled by their counterparts. They do so, because they know that cooperative societies outperform collective bodies of self-sufficient agents or families. Hence, individuals are genetically engineered to cooperate: evolution has selected the cooperative instinct. This is a very persuasive insight, it helps understand why individuals abandon the myopic version of individual rationality, make the prisoner's dilemma irrelevant, take chances and try to cooperate. Still, this explains cooperation, rather than altruism.

49 See Caplan (2007). The voter's paradox refers to the fact that people vote despite the cost of voting (getting all the necessary information and physically devoting time to go to the ballot box) vastly outweighs the benefit of voting (related to the probability that one's own vote changes the outcome of the elections). The paradox is generally explained by the pleasure one takes in showing his being part of the political community (commitment to the social contract) and in playing the game the whole community plays and recognizes (conformism, possibly opportunistic). That is why the sale and purchase of votes is generally held in contempt, despite its "rationality".

50 Of course, such two adverbs – consciously and willingly – mark the difference between altruistic behaviour and positive externalities.

51 Wilson (1975) calls it *hard-core* altruism, which differs from our concept of *pure* altruism, in that the former is genetic (we are programmed to behave so), whereas the latter is acquired (we consciously decide that something has to be done, no matter what). Following Harsanyi (1955), Sen (1977) made a distinction between "sympathy" (you feel happy to know that somebody else is happy) and "commitment" (you are inclined to act because you believe it is your duty to promote/stop something you think is right/wrong). A different version is "team reasoning" (Bacharach 1999), according to which the individual thinks of himself as a member of a group and identifies what each member should do in the interest of the team: hence, his actions are those which a team manager would prescribe for the benefit of the group.

52 The use of the plural is important. One might have long-run evolutionary processes, according to which "bad" ways of thinking lead to ineffective institutions and/or slow economic growth. Under such circumstances, weak societies are ultimately taken over by stronger groups moulded by "superior" ways of thinking (psychological patterns). By contrast, one can also witness short-run evolutionary processes, whereby "bad" groups might prevail as a result of an ideology which – for instance – justifies violence and cheating.

53 One can surely mention the term "guilt", or refer once again to the role of the external (impartial) spectator, although the Scottish version mentioned earlier might be confusing, for in *The Theory of Moral Sentiments* Smith's impartial spectator includes both an inner deontic drive and a yearning to obtain admiration from the other members of the community. Rather, we prefer to make a distinction between the role of a hypothetical external observer and that of an equally hypothetical inner judge.

    Under spurious altruism, the external observer is conceived of as the representative of the typical individual of the society to which the actor belongs. It reflects what is expected and tolerated, not necessarily what is right or what the letter of the rule prescribes. When present, inner drives are purely evolutionary, i.e. they serve the purpose of enhancing the success of the group, and thus of the gene carried by the individual. By contrast, in the case of pure altruism guilt is not originated by harm (or lack of good) having been done to the victim, but by going against one's nature and having thus offended the inner judge, who is ultimately shaped by the individual's reaction to the prevailing ideological climate. Of course, not all inner judges are the same and, more importantly, they differ according to the historical periods and the political contexts during/within which action unfolds.

54 There is no element of altruism in paying taxes when tax evasion is easily exposed and severely punished.

55 Of course, they can also do both. First they form an enclave, which however melts down over time and gives way to integration.

56 That is how the role of the state or of some transnational authority is perceived in many countries.

57 As pointed out earlier (see notes 45 and 53 in this chapter), the external observer differs from the Smithean impartial spectator.

58 As mentioned in Section 3.4.3, those ingredients reproduce the action of both the inner judge and of the external observer: the perception of generosity/vanity, the role of evolutionary components, the role of ideology. Jones (2006: ix) defines culture as "the pattern of beliefs, habits, and expectations, of values, ideals, and preferences, shared by groups of people, large and small". In other words, *moeurs*.

59 One could argue, however, that the decision to follow habit and tradition is in itself a conscious choice.

4 Institutions

1 The distinction between *imperfect* and *inadequate* information is important. Imperfect information refers to uncertainty and lack of knowledge, as discussed previously. Today this is the handmaiden of entrepreneurship and ultimately progress. By contrast, inadequate information refers to the consequences of the so-called market failures, that is situations in which the system of exchanges fails to deliver desirable outcomes and proper policies are expected to provide suitable solutions. In particular, inadequate information describes a context in which the typical agent acts rationally, but under the influence of distorted signals, which lead him to be "sub-optimally" informed and thus make mistakes. This is what the literature on asymmetric information deals with.

2 According to its best known formulation (Rawls 1971), fairness identifies an ideal situation in which all individuals' surpluses are equalized. As a consequence, fairness would require the more favoured to give away what they acquired because of luck, or because of their having above-average skills, talents or inner motivation. Of course, from this vantage point, redistribution should be on a world scale, rather than on a national scale. One might even wonder whether it should include all living species and not just humans. See also Frank (1988: chapter 8) and Jasay (2002: chapters 9 and 14).

3 Imperfect knowledge stems from three possibilities: (*a*) information exists, but agents do not want to acquire it because it is too expensive, (*b*) information is available, but it is ignored because storage and processing is too expensive, (*c*) information does not exist because the future is partially unknown, the more so the further away the time horizon required to make a rational decision. Of course, should these three requirements cease to be, meaningful choice would no longer exist for a rational individual: either only one appropriate course of action would exist, or all courses of action would lead to the same result.

4 Informal rules are non-codified, founded in habits and hardly enforceable. By contrast, formal rules are characterized by the fact that they are widely known and that violations involve credible sanctions. Katz (2008) surveys the difference between non-legal and legal contract enforcement. The former applies to situations in which the parties successfully renegotiate their contract. The latter applies when one party takes the other to court.

5 See, however Hodgson (1989, 1998), who follows Hayek and North in arguing that the "old/new" divide is far less important than understanding the features of the interaction between institutions and individuals and deriving lessons for institutional design. As a matter of fact, this is also the prevailing view today, according to which the essence of the institutional debate takes bi-directional causality for granted.

6 Of course, this also affects economic growth. For instance, Britton *et al.* (2004) show that bad or poorly enforced formal rules (lack of economic freedom) stifle growth. Slow growth encourages agents to engage in informal and underground activities which in turn conflict with formal institutions and further dampen economic performance.

7 See Section 1.1 in Chapter 1.

8 Constitutional rules will be discussed in the next chapter.

9 There are situations in which optional default rules de facto lose their optional features. The obvious examples are provided by children, handicapped people and senile individuals in a community, for whom opting out is problematic. These are all agents that are deemed unable to make a conscious choice, and thus to accept responsibility for their actions. To illustrate this point, one can imagine the case of schooling, which applies to a class of individuals (young people) who are supposed to be mentally incapable of taking a decision. The inability to decide, and therefore to opt out, transforms the optional rule into a coercive one.

It might also be worth pointing out that nowadays compulsory schooling is however a coercive rule, since it involves a second and rather strong assumption: children are regarded as members of the nation state, rather than of their families; that is why their legislators – not their parents – decide on their behalf, and why parents are subject to sanctions, if they refuse to send their children to school.

10 Of course, enjoying monopoly power does not mean that this power is going to be exercised when the parties wish the state to intervene. On the one hand, the ruler may decide not to enforce his own institutions for lack of resources; on the other hand, he may not enforce institutions created by others, simply because he does not like them. This is often a problem with international arbitration agreements: sometimes the rulers do not recognize them, and do not enforce them. Yet, they do not allow other enforcement agencies to replace the state.

11 Once again, coercive rules do not refer to the presence of violent enforcement, but to situations in which rules cannot be chosen, accepted or rejected.

12 A complex social arrangement is a social structure consisting of the natural units that guarantee the demographic survival of the species. As mentioned earlier, it is widely acknowledged that at least until very recently such natural unit has been the family, broadly understood.

13 "Traditional" legitimacy refers to a situation in which the benchmark is provided by criteria external to human action or to human history. This happens when a king claims to have been appointed or designated by God. Under such circumstances, the religious intermediary obviously plays a critical role. By contrast, "rational" legitimacy applies to moral criteria developed and approved by man, either by rational reasoning (e.g. efficiency or effectiveness), or by experience validated by success (historical relativism).

14 As noted by Nemo (2004: 27), this notion originates from the stoic tradition. See in particular his reference to Cicero's *De Republica* (III, XXII). The philosopher's task is to define these natural traits, while the legal scholar is charged with ensuring that the law is consistent with them.

15 Not surprisingly, the advocates of the man-as-a-social-animal thesis are forced to differentiate men from other mammals according to criteria other than sociability. For instance, Aristotle noted that bees are sociable, but bees are not the same as humans, who are social and political animals. The most frequent answers have been conscious choice and rationality, as recently recalled in Machan (2004). It should be pointed out, however, that there are no such things as *social* consciousness or *social* rationality, for both consciousness and rationality are typical of the individual: the individual chooses and the individual evaluates the costs and benefits associated to choices and contexts. This does not prevent the individual from having opinions about what is (or would be) good for other individuals as well. But even in this case we remain within the realm of subjective speculation and judgement.

16 By doing so, Pufendorf presumably attempted to draw a line between God-given natural instincts and man-discovered natural institutions, thereby suggesting that natural institutions must be compatible with God-given human traits and are ultimately related to the divine order. This would explain why, in his view, (coercive) institutions are not natural, but are nevertheless a moral imperative.

17 Surely, it would be hard to overestimate the role of man within classical philosophy. Still, from the classical – and in particular the Greek – vantage point the critical element remains society, in which an individual realizes his nature of social and political animal. The notion of virtue, which is central to this perspective, serves the purpose of defining the appropriate behaviour of an individual, to fulfil his nature, but also to contribute to the social body.

18 Of course, Hobbes's view on sociability differed from that held by Grotius, Pufendorf and Locke. In Hobbes, legitimacy for the political regime comes from the need to assure survival; in Grotius, from its ability to serve the interest of the universal

community of individuals; in Pufendorf, from its consistency with God-given natural law (to be discovered by the use of reason); and in Locke, from its ability to protect individuals' property rights.

19 See for instance Strayer (1970: chapter 1). Although one may plausibly claim the interaction with family members and friends is also a way of socializing, we shall stick to the Tocquevillian approach, according to which withdrawing into the circle of one's family and friends belongs to "individualism". We shall therefore use the term "society" to define more complex forms of interaction.

20 See also David Hume's *Treatise of Human Nature* (2000b [1740], book 3, part 2), who considers that society is produced by a "convention for the distinction of property, and for the stability of possession" (§ 12).

21 The natural social contract is embedded in the natural traits of the individual: for instance, it might consist in an agreement to fight against a common deadly enemy, since this agreement is consistent with the instinct to survive. The implicit social contract is one that everybody would underwrite if asked and which is therefore enforced by default to save contracting costs. Of course, Locke is perhaps the prime example of this kind of contract. Stein (1980: 2) actually underscores the existence of two separate contracts in Locke: one about the goal to pursue and one about the actor in charge of pursuing it on behalf of the community. In recent decades different versions of the implicit social contract have been put forward by Hayek, Rawls and Buchanan.

22 Today the size of taxation – as opposed to gifts and charity – to finance redistribution seems to suggest that in many countries large minorities and possibly the majority of the population are not sufficiently "naturally social". Consistency would then require that they be regarded as second-rank citizens and, for instance, be denied the right to vote.

23 For instance, Borges and Irlenbusch (2007) have shown that the introduction of compulsory withdrawal clauses in distant selling has generated a substantial increase in exploitative (unfair) behaviour by the buyers (e.g. buying expensive TV sets before an important soccer game and returning them after the match is over).

24 Political science has proposed several taxonomies of the political institutions that have characterized the history of mankind and different interpretations. For instance, Baechler (2002) focuses on contingencies, Bobbitt (2002) suggests an evolutionary mechanism propelled by the advances and requirements of military technology, Darwin (2008) calls attention to the cultural shock (Humanism) that took place in the late fifteenth century.

25 The emphasis on universalism can hardly be overemphasized, for its failure turned out to be a unique European feature, which de facto explained why after the Roman Empire, the European continent never saw imperial rule, other than in purely nominal or administrative terms (the Holy Roman Empire and the Habsburgs, respectively).

26 These terms will be explained in greater detail in the next chapter. To anticipate our presentation, the Gregorian period takes its name from the Pope Gregory VII, who sparked the critical institutional revolution that led to the rise of competing sources of power. The Secular Period includes the centuries during which religion lost its power to confer legitimacy on the political order. The Age of Social Responsibility refers to most of the twentieth century, characterized by the general change of attitude towards the concept of the state: as noted in Hoppe (2001, chapter 2), since approximately the First World War the state is no longer accountable to the monarch or to an elite, but to the "people" and/or its *pro tempore* representatives.

27 The former option was clearly the course of action pursued by the Spanish monarchy (and later on by Louis XIV), who succeeded in stultifying the potential aristocratic threat by transforming aristocrats into nobles, that is, by converting a class of free but powerless individuals into privileged courtiers dependent on the prince's choices and commands, divided by envy and rivalry. An example of the latter course was Venice, where ruling oligarchs ended up regulating the economy, raising the normative

barriers to entry in a large number of industries and even creating a national health service so as to secure people's favour and loyalty – an example that Bismarck followed some four centuries later.

28 For instance, John Law's insight into the possibility of increasing the money supply by adding land and shares to gold and silver as acceptable monetary standards failed to promote growth. The causes were bad economics, since real GDP does not depend on the money supply or on its measurement unit; and the ruler's greed, who soon forced Law to issue paper money with no real collateral (neither metal, nor land, nor company equity).

29 To be fair, although Bacon's and St Thomas's insights could well be considered one of the three cornerstones of Western civilization (together with the fragmentation of power and the notion of individual responsibility), they were soon forgotten a few decades after their death; and an entirely different *Weltanschauung* prevailed for the next two centuries: Faith in human reason was replaced by the doctrine of damnation and abhorrence of the real world, the only hope being the Last Judgement (Delumeau 1983). Those two centuries were characterized by the Black Death, the advance of the Turks, a state of permanent warfare (included the Hundred Years War), turmoil and destruction. Even the worth of knowledge was seriously questioned.

30 North (1994: 361) defines organizations as "groups of individuals bound together by some common purpose to achieve common objectives".

31 From this vantage point, institutions and legislation can perhaps be thought of as path-dependent, although this is not really the notion of path dependence dear to the institutional perspective.

32 See Sowell (1967) for a deeper critical analysis of Veblen's evolutionary vision.

33 To be fair, one cannot actually label post-Veblen old institutionalists such as John Commons or Wesley Mitchell as determinists. It is true, however, that determinism was more or less swept under the rug by appealing to the existence of unpredictable shocks, rather than by acknowledging that what appears to be a path-dependent process *ex post* is hardly one *ex ante*. In particular, professing one's ignorance about the features of the alleged path-dependent process is not the same as recognizing that uncertainty simply makes it impossible to acquire knowledge about the future.

34 For instance, the same themes have been articulated in terms of top-down vs. bottom-up reforms in the literature on development and transition. Chapter 9 will deal explicitly with the economic implications of these approaches.

5 Social contracts and historical rules

1 Revolving-door mechanisms might also play an important role. The more complicated the regulation and the greater the importance of establishing personal stable relations with the civil service, the greater the opportunities in the private sector for those bureaucrats who want to switch to the other side and become an intermediary between the private sector and their former colleagues.

2 Of course, credibility also depends on the characteristics of enforcement, which include straightforwardness and transparency; on the probability of detecting and suing the offender; on the set of sanctions provided for when the rule is violated; on how long it takes to be compensated for the damages suffered.

3 This also applies to common-law countries: see for instance Harnay and Marciano (2007) for an inquiry into the motivations of the judge within a common-law system.

4 See Hoppe (2001), who explains that the rate of time preference necessarily rises as a society becomes more and more democratic. A higher rate of time preference might induce people to construe certain categories of rent-seeking actions (e.g. protectionism), as long as the net benefits are short-term and the net costs long-term (Rizzo 2008: 895–896). This behaviour will also affect the distribution of investment over time, provoke some "malinvestment" and slow down growth.

In a similar vein, Nicita (2007) underscores the importance of what he defines as "*ex ante* transaction costs", i.e. the costs related to the incomplete definition of property rights, which leads to litigation and discourages exchange.

5 Following Hayek (1960), the recent literature on the importance of the rule of law actually focuses more on the features that enhance individual planning, long-term coordination among agents and behavioural predictability, rather than on the actual content of the rules. Put differently, more attention is being devoted to the procedural qualities of the rules, rather than to their foundations. Thus, justice (and the rule of law) is no longer a criterion to make sure that the individual (natural) rights are safeguarded, but that the individual is not discriminated against. The frame of reference is not a moral benchmark, but the other members of the community. For instance, many rule-of-law supporters are happy with regulation as long as it is credible, stable, simple to understand, easy to enforce and applicable to everybody engaging in given activities. Whether the rule is good or bad seems to have a lesser impact on the rule-of-law label. In the end, consequentialism prevails and the main issues of substance are entrusted to popular opinion and current moral standards, thereby short-circuiting the exploration of whether justice and legitimacy should refer to general and everlasting principles, or to mere consensus.

6 Regrettably, the debt to authors like Walter Eucken and Franz Böhm (prominent among the founders of the Freiburg-based Ordoliberal school) is seldom acknowledged. Nor is there much reference to the authors who first emphasized the importance of the connection between rules and economic performance, an intellectual debt that dates back to Adam Smith, if not earlier.

7 Evolutionary in the sense that social interaction is assumed to follow a virtuous process of adaptation, not to be confused with the meaning attributed by the evolutionary school, according to which individuals do not necessarily adjust their behaviour to produce the most desirable social results.

8 The literature makes a difference between the "modern" and the "new" political economy (Boettke *et al.* 2006). The former refers to the revival of the research programme advocated by the Scottish tradition. The latter is a branch of the neoclassical agenda: it assumes rational, utility-maximizing individuals and aims at designing institutions (rules and organizations) that allow to maximize given outcomes.

9 Consistent with our line of reasoning (see Section 4.2 in the previous chapter), we here assume that explicit consensus occurs when the individual overtly agrees to underwrite all the parts of a hypothetical social covenant. Quasi-explicit consensus applies when the social covenant is put into operation by default (tacit consent), but opting out is always possible at no costs.

10 See also McGinnis and Rappaport (2007) for a detailed analysis of the virtues and shortcomings of super-majority voting. Although it is obviously true that qualified majorities provide stability to the rule-making system, one should also be aware of the fact that rule-makers have ways of circumventing super-majority resistance, or softening the constitutional watchdogs. For instance, the incumbent rulers might find it advantageous to act through the appointment of the members of the constitutional court.

11 As a matter of fact, the normative implications of our approach are not negligible, in that they exclude the viability of "rational", efficiency-based or efficiency-enhancing policy-making. Instead, they suggest that those who want to alter the scope of policy-making, or change its nature, act or should act in order to exploit the opportunities to bring about deep institutional changes.

12 See for instance Weingast and Wittman (2006), who characterize (the new) political economy as a technique, rather than as a subject matter: "the theory is based in mathematics (often game theoretic), and the empirics either use sophisticated statistical techniques or involve experiments where money is used as a motivating force in the experiment" (ibid.: 4).

13 See Lewis (2001: chapter 2) for the contradictions typical of all efforts to evaluate results in a context in which natural law or First Principles are excluded.

14 The term was coined by George Santayana in 1937, as quoted in Dougherty (2000: xii).

15 See for instance Hayek (1960), Buchanan and Tullock (1962), Brennan and Buchanan (1985: chapter 2) and – with important qualifications – Jasay (1991: chapter 6).

16 We classify the lack of certainty in three groups. Risk indicates a situation in which the individual knows what might happen and knows the probability distribution of the event. For instance, we know that by tossing a coin there is a 50 per cent head probability and a 50 per cent tail probability. Knightian uncertainty refers to a situation where the range of possible events is known, but their probability distribution is unknown. Future stock prices are an example. Radical uncertainty refers to the lack of knowledge about events (guessing does not count). For instance, we do not know how we shall be producing energy 300 years from now.

17 A different (and equally popular) kind of contract has been conceived in Rawls (1971). Contrary to the classical liberal tradition, however, Rawls posits that the authority is entitled to act by presuming that the individual chooses from behind a veil of ignorance: he does not know what his talents are, has no hope to be the architect of his own future and therefore to achieve his goals by engaging in hard work and entrepreneurial activities.

Despite its name and contrary to Rawls's claim, however, this is not a contract, let alone a fair contract, for in the Rawlsian world the ruler de facto prevents individuals from engaging in social activities unless they accept to behave as if they were ignorant, both about the world to be and about their own abilities. Put differently, Rawls's intellectual experiment is a presumption about individual behaviour formulated by the ruler in order to justify his own discretionary action. Rather than a contract, it looks like a self-serving argument, though a Rawlsian could respond to this criticism by arguing that the approach can only be attacked by those who have broken through the veil of ignorance and therefore have distanced themselves from a fair starting point.

Of course, the problem with the Rawlsian theory is that one's vision of the world cannot be labelled unfair only because it rejects the logical non sequitur whereby fairness necessarily implies blindness and possibly also inaction. It happens that the only rationale for the Rawlsian position is based on the assumption that individual qualities are distributed at random by some superior authority who dispenses his gifts to societies, rather than to individuals. Thus, nobody can object to redistribution, for those talents are in fact social property, not individuals' property. Of course, the counterargument can take different shapes: (*a*) why should intellectual and physical features be redistributed only among human beings and not include animals? (*b*) how do we know that the superior authority gave away gifts randomly in the expectation that we carry out redistribution? (*c*) how do we know that it all comes from a superior authority?

18 Brennan and Buchanan (1985: 55) define this attitude as "quasi-risk aversion".

19 At first sight one might wonder why the constitutional view must go to such lengths to imagine a veil of uncertainty. Yet, there is no other way. For instance, if one maintained that rent-seeking is unacceptable because it is based on coercive norms that restrict the individual's freedom to choose, one should accept the principle of unrestricted personal freedom and give up a claim to an amoral social covenant. Similarly, if one claimed that people should agree on a social contract without knowing where they would end up unless the veil is lifted, one would then fall victim to Rawls's pseudo-contract.

20 See for instance Brennan and Buchanan (1985: 22) and Vanberg (1999).

21 See for instance Hayek (1976: chapter 8).

22 This notion of justice is not entirely new, of course. See for instance Dworkin (1986), who claims that the law is just because it creates a social order. Hence, the moral dimension is the ability to create consensus and eliminate inconsistencies. It seems

that the difference between Dworkin's "interpretive view" and the constitutional view lies in the legal space where consensus is to be reached. According to the former such a space is not restricted and includes both meta- and ordinary rules, whereas according to the latter the emphasis is on the potential conflicts among meta-rules only.

23 Following Locke, the constitutional contractarian perspective explicitly states that consensus can be assumed by default if an individual takes part in social life while having the possibility of opting out (see Brennan and Buchanan 1985: chapter 7). Do they really mean that after having written a registered letter to the president, Prof. Brennan and Prof. Buchanan would feel legitimized to stop paying taxes? We do not think so. Despite Buchanan's very critical attitude towards the role of the state in modern societies, we believe that his failure to opt out is not to due to fear of President Obama's reaction, but rather because he does not really consider it would be consistent with his own constitutional context, which is also the only legitimate context he recognizes.

24 See Jasay (1991), who calls his approach "strict liberalism". Of course, Jasay is neither the father, nor the only advocate of the quasi-minimal state. For instance, Mises was also arguing in the same vein decades ago and Holcombe (2004) has made the case once again in more recent times. However, Mises and Holcombe justify the state as a burden to endure, lest worse situations materialize (chaos or rival bandits fighting for short-term rent-seeking); and express hope, rather than confidence, that the state does not abuse its powers and stays small. On the other hand, Jasay focuses on the allegedly contractual nature of the quasi-minimal state and therefore gives its existence a moral justification, rather than referring to mere expediency.

To complete the argument, it is worth mentioning that the minimal proposal differs from what we define as the quasi-minimal version, in that while the latter does not rule out that the state performs some economic functions, the former aims at restricting the role of the state to the protection of physical integrity (Hobbes) and of private property rights (Locke). Hence, it is actually closer to the views typical of the Secular Period, to be explained in the next section. The minimal proposal, however, will not be further explored in these pages.

25 As a matter of fact, Mill also contemplated other elements. For instance, he maintained that the right to liberty applies only to all those human beings "in the maturity of their faculties". By contrast, coercion can be exercised for the sake of collective utility, or in order to enhance the well-being of "barbarians", as well as "those backward states of society in which the race itself may be considered as in its nonage". (Mill 1977 [1832]: chapter 1).

26 Commons (1924: chapter 2) observed that tampering by the US courts with the actual meaning of private of property already had a distinguished record in the second half of the nineteenth century, when private property was still considered uninfringeable. In particular, he noted that the notion of the right to dispose of resources (goods and services) was replaced with the notion of the right to enjoy the purchasing power generated by the goods and services legitimately possessed. In the United States, the task of translating satisfaction into purchasing power was first entrusted to the legislative body (the Munn Case in 1873) and later to the judiciary (the Minnesota Rate Case in 1890).

27 See also Hamowy (1981 [1961]) and Hoppe (1994) on Hayek and the procedural notion of freedom.

28 See Dewey (1934) and Dougherty (2000: chapters 4 and 7) for a synthetic critical analysis.

29 As Bouillon (2011) has underscored, Jasay's contribution on the foundations of property right is crucial. Following Grotius and Pufendorf, in his *Second Treatise of Government* (chapter V), Locke agrees that natural resources on earth were initially given by God to all mankind in common, rather than to individuals. Locke maintained that man creates private property out of necessity through an act of appropriation (finders

are keepers) as long as (*a*) as a result nobody is made worse off and (*b*) appropriation does not originate wastages. Rothbard's vision of property drops the two provisos, while Jasay makes the essential step by rejecting also the religious origin of common property and thus doing without consequentialism.

30 As a matter of fact, Jasay (2001) claims that his notion of justice is based on that of liberty, and that liberty is rooted in conventions, not in rights. In his vocabulary, however, "convention" means voluntary actions validated by repeated interaction, while "rights" are synonymous with privileges. See also Hohfeld (1923). An alternative option is aired in Lewis (2001: appendix), who identifies a system of natural laws based on a set of traditions shared by different civilizations. Such laws are Beneficence, Duties to the Family, Good Faith, Mercy and Valour.

31 The pure free rider is not really doing anything immoral, for he is not encroaching upon anybody's liberty. If anything, he might be cheating, for he might be consuming against the producer's will, while denying doing so. But of course, if we were able to prove that the individual is actually lying, then excludability could be applied and it would no longer be a public good.

32 It is far from clear what economists understand under the label of "collective good". Nonetheless, it is generally acknowledged that this category identifies excludable goods that are necessary for the existence of social interaction and/or represent shared values (e.g. access to health or education for everybody) that private suppliers fail to offer at the socially desirable conditions. Put differently, their existence depends either on the idea whereby the attainment of a desirable social context is a priority, and/or on the existence of market failures combined with the presence of a social welfare function and the absence of substantial government failures. See also our reference to "merit goods" in Section 3.3.1 (Chapter 3).

33 Of course, this is not the first attempt to characterize the grand rules of social interaction and use such findings to single out specific periods in Western civilization. In contrast with much of the literature, however, we try to describe such rules according to their moral traits, rather than to social tensions. See for instance Unger (1976), who makes a distinction between tribal, aristocratic, liberal and post-liberal societies and gives a sociological account of the evolution of the social order and of the challenges that history presents to social theorizing.

34 See for instance Berman (1983: 4). True enough, the literature refers to many "Wests", e.g. the Hellenistic, the Classical, the Modern. For the sake of simplicity we shall henceforth refer to the West as to the "modern West", that is to a civilization based on the notions of individual responsibility, equal dignity and of advancement by the use of reason, separate from faith (hence, the secular separate from the religious). Some authors also make specific reference to the political dimension, which we acknowledge in the text. For instance, according to Tierney *et al.* (1992: xi):

> There are three major themes whose development and interplay have shaped the distinctive characteristics that set Western civilization apart from the other great historic cultures. They are the growth of a tradition of rational scientific inquiry, the persistence of a tension between Judaeo-Christian religious ideals and social realities, the emergence of constitutional forms of government.

35

> True law, Cicero taught, is right consonant with nature, available to all, constant and eternal ... common to God and man ... The state is nothing more or less than a partnership in law, an assemblage of men associated in consent to law. ... Christianity taught that man is the creature of God, ... brotherhood of man became the brotherhood of man under the Fatherhood of God.
>
> (Dougherty 2000: 13–14)

More generally, as in any societal system, the Western context defines the role of the individual in a community. That involves the definitions of the relevant set of constraints and therefore also the nature and origin of the legitimate rules.

36 Prior to the Gregorian revolution the emperor had the right to the title of Vicar of Christ, while the Pope was some kind of super-bishop (the Vicar of Saint Peter), all other bishops being appointed and de facto controlled by the emperor. The West had to wait until Pope Innocent III (early thirteenth century) for an exclusive papal claim to the supreme title.

37 Indeed, the only reason why the Church had not made its case before the eleventh century was that it could not do without the Emperor's military protection and thus could not risk confrontation.

38 Rather, most efforts were addressed to obtaining legitimacy from the Church authorities and then subdue them. This explains why the divine right to rule was hardly questioned throughout the Gregorian period, while the power of the Church started to decline as of the thirteen century.

39 See also our earlier remarks in Chapter 2, especially in Section 2.2. To be fair, Plato's and Plotinus's loathing for the secular world did not last too long. Material life became the object of appreciation already by Peter Abelard (1079–1142) and, more explicitly, by St Thomas Aquinas (1224–1274).

40 "Authority" refers to the legitimacy of the ruler, which in the Gregorian period was designated by God, as the Church would (or would not) confirm/certify. This notion contrasts with that of "Power", which regards what the ruler can do. In particular, legitimate power defines the instruments and the rules that the authority can issue and enforce in order to pursue its (legitimate) goals.

41 More on this in Chapter 8.

42 Still, the Venetian expansion was conceived as an effort in colonization to acquire the resources to finance the navy and the mercenary army. It had little or nothing to do with an attempt by the oligarchs to prove their right to rule and to eliminate potentially dangerous neighbours before they grew too powerful.

43 The Gregorian time does present us with allegedly constitutional documents, the best known of which are perhaps the Great Charter of León (1017), the Magna Carta (1215), the Golden Bull (1222). All these were, however, concessions made by a weak king to the aristocracy, with very little "social" or "contractual" content. They consisted of a list of freedoms (in fact privileges) that had little to do with the notion of liberty as this term came to be understood in later centuries.

44 Of course, the army had nothing or little to do with the protection of the population. On the contrary, its purpose was to control the territories owned by the ruler – to prevent revolt and enforce taxation, an operational deployment that Colbert refined in the seventeenth century – and to fight against other rulers or would-be rulers. Even when engaged in defensive actions, the Gregorian princes were protecting not their populations, but their own tax-producing territories.

45 See for instance Strayer (1970: 50–52).

46 After all, God was supposed to make his will clear with regard to who was supposed to have the authority, but not to specify the geographical boundaries of authority. This was of course a non-issue until the pre-Gregorian universalistic attitude had some appeal. As pointed out in the text, however, it became a very practical problem once universalism broke down and the figure of the ruler was secularized.

47 It is hard to single out events that could be labelled as dramatic political changes in various parts of Europe, and regard those events as some sort of fundamental institutional shock that marked the beginning of the Secular Period. On a continental scale one could probably identify the moment of deep institutional change in the Westphalia Treaties (1648), which in many ways denoted the end of the religious question (and of the religious wars). With reference to the two leading European countries (England and France), and from a different perspective, some authors would probably single out the end of the seventeenth century (the Glorious Revolution) or the

beginning of the eighteenth (the Utrecht Treaty and Louis XIV's death). But of course, each country has its own history, with its own switching times, as the examples of Catholic Spain and of the Calvinist Netherlands indicate. The difference probably depends on whether one wants to emphasize the accidents that provoked the deep institutional change (Westphalia) or the next great accident (the successful containment of French expansion), where the effects of the former event unfolded and became apparent. For instance, the Glorious Revolution was nothing less than a full-scale and unexpectedly successful invasion of the British Isles, as a consequence of William III's need to prevent England from allying with France, which in turn was about to attack the Netherlands. Religion might have also played a role, as argued in Jardine (2008, chapters 2 and 3). Yet, we do not believe that William invaded England in order to spread the reform across the English Channel.

More important for the argument developed in these pages, however, is to identify the ideas which, after having been conceived over the centuries and debated within a relatively close circle of intellectuals, acquired historical relevance. And to understand why and when they brought about deep and rather quick alterations in the grand rules of the game.

48 One could list several examples of Catholic armies fighting against other Catholic armies, possibly supported by protestant allies – and vice-versa. Irrespective of their religious allegiance, however, they all brought ruin to the regions they marched through or in which they quartered. The religious propensities of the population made no difference: over the 1618–1648 period Central Europe lost about one-third of its inhabitants as a consequence of indiscriminate butcheries and famines brought about by looting and devastation.

49 See Section 1.3 in the introductory chapter.

50 See for instance Kühnel (2001) for an investigation into the many uncertainties and conflicts that characterized the birth of the contractarian state in the late seventeenth century.

51 It is not by accident that as soon as he set foot on English soil, William III hurried to distribute a "declaration" explaining his contract with the English people and his commitment to guaranteeing peace and security, unlike what people feared would happen under James II. Put differently, James II was delegitimized by referring to his failure to comply with the natural order.

52 This concept is of course further developed by Rousseau, who claims in *Du Contrat Social* that if the individual is to obtain his natural goals within a properly-designed social context, it becomes the task of the social elites to define and offer the appropriate social rules and conditions. One should also add, however, that Rousseau's contract is not really a contract, for Rousseau's state is legitimized neither by God, nor by the individual, but rather by an ideal. In particular, *la volonté générale* is neither the protection of individual rights (Locke), nor the expression of the general will (Hobbes). Instead, it defines what is needed in order to ensure that the individual finds and pursues his true nature after having been contaminated by a corrupt environment. Hence, the eighteenth-century attempt to transform the nature of the contract, from one based on securing peace (and possibly property rights) to one based on the accomplishment of an ideal hidden to the normal human being by a veil of moral corruption.

53 In this respect Hobbes was however the only author who had the courage to draw the obvious consequences: not only must an individual necessarily be part of a social contract, but all those who are outside, or who consider themselves outside have to be crushed, both because they have lost or rejected their nature of human being and because by going against their (social) nature, they represent a danger to society.

54 As will emerge from the next section, these "natural" goals were clearly articulated during the Gregorian and Secular historical periods, but not during the Age of Social Responsibility. Nationalism provided a short-lived substitute, with dramatic consequences.

55 It might be worth pointing out that the medieval notion of peace is indeed defined as the absence of war; whereas the secular notion implies an active search for harmony, not unlike what can be perceived when observing today's activities of several national and transnational organizations (governments and agencies).

56 Adam Smith well typifies the doubts of the early economists trying to break away from political economy as a moral science (and a branch of philosophy). In fact, Adam Smith ended up claiming that a free-market system is both morally superior (it stems from virtue and does not violate property rights) and functionally superior (it creates more wealth) to any other system, such as mercantilism.

57 It remains unclear whether ideals (moral standards) are enough to motivate a social contract, as Rousseau would have it. It seems that the answer is in the negative if the social contract has "rational" ambitions, i.e. if it claims a theoretical foundation, as the neo-contractarian theories would maintain. It is also in the negative from a Gregorian perspective, which denies the secular nature of the deal. But the answer might take the opposite sign if irrational elements are taken into account, such as the refusal of individual responsibility, to be discussed shortly.

58 We suggest that the American institutional success had little to do with the very fact of having introduced the Constitution that Americans were expecting. First, because that choice was in fact the result of an imposition upon the 13 colonies by an elite wary of people's emotions and thus of direct democracy. In addition, when the representatives met in Philadelphia they actually had no power to vote a new (federal) constitutional document, but just to amend the Articles of Confederation, a document that reflected well the limited support that the American Revolution enjoyed before the English armies conceded defeat. In addition, at the time it was clear, and the delegates were fully aware, that a popular referendum might have produced embarrassing results: the Constitution was finally approved by ad hoc state conventions, bypassing state congresses that had appointed delegates to Philadelphia. Of course, the above does not mean that it was a "bad" constitution; but merely that it was adopted neither in accordance with people's will, nor in accordance with the very principles it purported to protect.

See also Bennett (2003: chapter 4), according to whom the key to the American success lies in a system that succeeded in keeping the people involved and interested in the world of politics and in believing in productive interaction with authority. Although adherence to the Founding Fathers' rules of the game was rather quickly forgotten, the spirit of the game remained in place for a longer period.

59 If one considers the state welfare system as the symbol of this age, then it is undeniable that important precedents can already be detected several decades earlier. For instance, in Europe demand for a welfare state featured prominently in the manifestos of the 1848 revolutionaries. Napoleon III introduced the first state pension scheme for the elderly, soon to be imitated on a larger scale in Germany by Bismarck. In both cases the origin was not a charitable concern for the poor or the needy, but rather a shortcut to consensus, a move to unify the notions of citizenship, nation and state, ultimately in order to legitimize greater government intervention by the rule-makers, e.g. to meet industry's demand for subsidy and protection (Freeman and Snidal 1982). Precedents of a different nature were typical of the American legal history at the turn of the century, when the courts ruled in order to regulate contracts to protect the needy: "the principle, limited in 1898 to the industries of mining and smelting, was extended in 1916 to apply to all manufacturing industries" (Commons 1924: 63).

60 The American and British experiences are of course different, for neither country went through Westphalia; moreover, the impact of the First World War in the United States was very different from that experienced across the ocean.

61 The notion of exploitation depends on the definition of liberty. If the latter is understood as "absence of coercion", then exploitation and extortion can only occur by means of physical violence (e.g. slavery). On the other hand, if liberty means "access

to a wide-enough range of opportunities" or "right to fairness", then exploitation actually refers to all situations where one of the actors is characterized by deep pockets or unusual greed and the other gets the short end of the stick (Liebermann and Syrquin 1983).

62 See also Unger (1976: chapter 3), who emphasizes the causal link between the rise of the welfare state on one hand, the decline of the rule of law and of individual consciousness on the other.

63 Typical of the third way is the inability to define a social goal, apart from obtaining consensus. This explains why third-way advocates tend to concentrate on two issues. The first consists of finding the best way – i.e. the ideal, constitutionally-guaranteed procedure – to designate those in charge of defining the purpose of state action so as to meet the expectations of a society, possibly providing some protection to the dissenting minorities. The second consists of stopping the rule-makers from making bad (populist) choices in the short run, which might alienate consensus in the long run, possibly leading to revolutionary pressure.

64 The Austrian literature has already discussed at length these matters since its very inception (the *Methodenstreit*). See also Chapter 2 (Section 2.9) and Chapter 3 (Section 3.3.1) in this book.

65 According to social relativism a society does and can change its moral standards over time. A different version of relativism would claim that each individual has and is entitled to its own ethical standard. Of course, this latter version would bring us back to assessing to which extent one can pursue his/her standards when they conflict with somebody else's standards and preferences – an issue which has already been discussed in the previous chapters.

66 The emphasis on the need for *ex ante* explanations is not accidental, as it emphasizes the need to assess the connection between the set of shared preferences and the beliefs (First Principles) that characterize a historical period and policy-making.

67 See "An unpublished manuscript of Leibniz on the allegiance due to sovereign powers", published in Riley (1972: 199–217).

68 This term has been effectively used by Adams (1994: 346) in order to single out those authors who drew attention to the dual origin of individual behaviour: rational self interest dictated by preferences, which however mix with "ideas, values, rules of thumb, urges and misconceptions" when interacting in a social context.

69 According to the atomistic vision, individuals do react to social incentives. Such incentives do not, however, affect the agents' psychological patterns and preferences.

70 Beginning in 1652, *liberum veto* gave each member of the Polish Diet the power to block legislation and paralyse the assembly. As reported in Dunn (1979: 74), recourse to *liberum veto* brought 90 per cent of the Polish Diets to their knees, a particularly fateful experience when the circumstances required the ability to levy substantial funds to raise an army and keep foreign aggressors at bay, e.g. in the late eighteenth century. Of course, it remains to be assessed to what extent the Polish population always identified foreign annexation with oppression.

71 Even when it is required to offer no more than protection services, "either an entity provides such services under compulsion, and is a government, or it does so on a completely voluntary basis, in which case it is part of the free market. There is not third option" (Block 2007: 63).

72 The American case is in several respects unique. It can be considered the only surviving "Gregorian" document, in that it was conceived as a set of principles to protect individual freedom from government abuse. The democratic procedures prescribed by the American constitution were meant to ensure that those principles could not be overturned and, possibly more important, to give them strength and legitimacy through popular representation, without however giving the representatives much discretionary power. It is no secret that Congress initially had very little power and that its representatives did not enjoy much prestige.

In contrast with the American experience, sometimes European Constitutions were just a symbolic effort to mark a change in political regime and give legitimacy to the new rulers (or to the old rulers in new clothes). Sometimes they were a way of portioning power among the various political groups under a (demagogic) cloud of wishful thinking. Not surprisingly, most of the time European constitutions actually present both features.

73 The institutionalists usually refer to behaviour, a term which might however generate some confusion. As the reader might recall from the introductory chapter (Section 1.5), we prefer to make a distinction between psychological patterns and behavioural routines. The former include the way reality is perceived and provide the guidelines along which the individuals' reactions to opportunities available unfold. The latter concern the way individuals actually behave given the biting constraints to which they are subject.

74 See for instance Hodgson (1993).

75 This is indeed Veblen's view, which is not necessarily shared by other evolutionary scholars. They might deplore the way people adapt, but they do not necessarily advocate rule-making as a way of interfering with the choices driven by the evolutionary principles mentioned in the text. As a matter of fact, some actually fall back on the minimal institutional position, whereby policy-making is good whenever it reduces transaction costs without violating the Pareto-optimality conditions (no member of the community must result worse off as a result of the policy measure). The verdict remains ambiguous, however, when the individuals negatively affected by the policy measure are worse off because intervention has reduced or eliminated their rents, especially when the rents have been bought and thus reward past investments.

76 Of course, this does not deny that technological progress might spark new moral debates (e.g. on cloning). But these hardly lead to major shifts in the psychological patterns. Although exceptions are ubiquitous, different attitudes generally reflect differences in opinions, not in First Principles.

77 The explanatory power of a social theory depends on whether the theory is about what rule-makers do, or about what they ought to do. The quasi-minimal contract clearly falls in the latter category. It therefore surrenders all explanatory ambition and should be considered just as a definition of good government and possibly as a benchmark for evaluation. The constitutional contract can be applied for explanatory purposes as long as it accepts democracy as the proper procedure to conceive and enforce the rules. Its "mild" explanatory power is due to the ambiguities of the constitutional school with respect to democracy. Some authors accept it (e.g. Hayek, Buchanan and Vanberg), others qualify their endorsement or have second thoughts (e.g. Hayek 1979: 38–40, who draws a distinction between democracy and "demarchy").

78 Efficient path dependence would suggest that the trend should be declining, but some caution is in order, for path dependence is not necessarily virtuous.

79 Qualifications (*b*) and (*c*) explain why the results of the current efforts to quantify the size of transaction costs might be questionable. See North (1994), according to whom transaction costs account for about 50 per cent of GDP in a modern economy.

6 Legitimacy and efficiency: an introduction to transaction costs and L&E

1 As in the previous chapters, policy-making actually means economic policy-making.

2 Most modern economists would draw on Mises – if not on earlier authors – in order to counteract the critique mentioned in the text. In particular, they would argue that the economist analyses human behaviour within a given institutional environment. While this counterargument might be acceptable within the Austrian tradition, it is much less so within a neoclassical world in which scholarship also aims at shaping "optimal" political institutions and processes. Stated differently, whereas in the

Austrian context institutions continue to be exogenous, they are no longer so in the mainstream agenda.

3 We recall the touchstones of the Ordoliberal system (see also Section 5.2 in the previous chapter), which include firm opposition to rent-seeking, as well as general acceptance of private property rights and of exchange based on market prices, in some cases softened by practical concerns (efficiency and political feasibility) and a general principle of prudence.

In truth, the Ordoliberals seldom make explicit reference to a social contract. Nonetheless, we believe that their cautious position is justified only by relying on some kind of social contract de facto embedded in their idea of good society: consensus, peaceful coexistence, wealth creation with a concern for local interests and suspicion with regard to big business. Of course, it is no accident that the Ordoliberal position has been summarized by two noncommittal expressions – social market economy and social irenic, as in Müller-Armack (1950) – and that these elements are all typical of the Age of Social Responsibility.

4 See Rasmussen and Uyl (2005) for an in-depth analysis of the essence of the neo-Aristotelian approach to liberalism, which is based on the concept of "flourishing" and which presents a very persuasive argument supporting the natural right to individual liberty.

5 Some (including Buchanan 1986: chapter 3) ascribe the constitutional tradition to the so-called "inclusive perspective" of public choice, which is supposed to include the analysis of all political activities that can be framed in terms of exchange. Nonetheless, the reader will have observed that we prefer to think of constitutional economics in Ordoliberal terms (it is about framing the rules of the game) and stick to the traditional, narrower definition of public choice, which relates to the functioning of the legislative and bureaucratic machines and which definitely owes more to Gordon Tullock than to James Buchanan.

6 In Chapter 4 (Section 4.1) we defined "informal rule" a rule that a community expects the individual to comply with. It is not written/formalized and is not accompanied by a violent sanction (e.g. a fine, prison, flogging). Rather, an informal rule is enforced by the people's refusal to cooperate with the rule-breaker.

7 To be fair, the Ordoliberal account assumes the existence of adequate means to constrain the authorities, limit their self-serving behaviour and make them neutral, i.e. free from rent-seeking. In this light, the neutrality of the constrained institutions provides legitimacy. An often quoted example is the complex system of checks and balances typical of the American Constitution.

The free-market camp also offers other views. For instance, the Beckerian perspective would maintain that in a democracy the will and perceptions of the voters will ultimately prevail. Accordingly, as long as democracy is accepted as the best process to gather consensus, the outcome of democratic decision-making ultimately defines an acceptable moral standard. More generally, anything within a sufficiently democratic environment is legitimate. Thus, and not surprisingly, while the Ordoliberal view supports judicial activism, the Beckerian view is much more cautious (see also Calabresi 2005 for the terms of this debate within the American constitutional context). A drastically different view is of course maintained by the public-choice literature, which has pointed out that rule-making is heavily influenced by the legislator's or the judge's personal interests. Thus, talking about legitimacy based on common sense, reasonable value or electoral competition would be wishful thinking at best, possibly a pretext for populism.

Finally, it might be worth pointing out that policy-making according to "contingent politics" has a descriptive counterpart in today's institutional L&E, according to which policy-makers follow some vaguely defined "reasonable value", which clearly draws on Hayek's concerns for public opinion and consensus (see for instance Mercuro and Medema 2006: chapter 4).

8 A typical example of the old-style normative, mainstream approach is the so-called

"old" L&E school, which Posner (1975: 758) identifies with the "application of economics to the antitrust laws".

9 By and large, "well-behaved" has meant that institutions are supposed to operate following the technocrats' wishes. To be fair, the institutional contribution has neither solved the question of legitimacy, nor the problem of defining the perfect institutional context (Libecap 1989a: 3–4). As pointed out in Campagnolo (2010: 6), however, the institutional literature deserves credit for having raised the issue.

10 Manne (1993), Sima (2004) and Rowley (2005) have reminded the profession that the L&E tradition started well before the early 1960s and also before judges and legislators started to worry about optimal anti-trust policies. In fact, from the mid-eighteenth century the connection between law, institutions and economic behaviour was a persistent feature in the work of many authors. And not unlike the current, "new" L&E approach, the causality direction under scrutiny was from law and institutions to economic performance. Nonetheless, there is no doubt that the eighteenth- and nineteenth-century authors were more concerned with grand institutions and policies, rather than with "pragmatic" rule-making and the daily functioning of the judiciary.

11 Of course, Coase (1960) was definitely more cautious when putting forward normative suggestions. Instead he tended to underscore the positive side of the L&E approach; while the Yale L&E view took a nuanced path, with weaker normative ambitions, as Calabresi (1961) shows. Yet, it has been persuasively claimed that Posner's perspective, according to which wealth-maximization is indeed moral, concern for fairness should be the exception, and efficiency is the new criterion for legitimacy, actually makes explicit the original and rather tentative Coasean proposition to the same effect. In particular, Fox (2007: 391) observed that Coase

> dismisses the traditional classical liberal theory of property rights and its related theory of ethics, but he offers nothing to convince his readers that his activist utilitarian theory is superior to the classical liberal theory that he rejects. He offers no well-defined theory of justice.

12 In truth, the economics of transaction costs had already been introduced in the literature by J. Commons (see for instance Cristiano 2009). But it became a distinctive feature of the (new) institutional economics only after Coase (1937), who broke away from the Marshallian theory of the firm. Alchian and Demsetz (1972) tried to bridge the gap between Marshall and Coase by drawing attention to the institutional developments which followed new combinations of technology and transaction costs, and which responded to previously-unknown opportunities for cooperation.

13 Today this view is generally known as the Posnerian L&E approach, which actually owes a great deal to Holmes (1897: 469): "for the rational study of the law the blackletter man be the man of the present, but the man of the future is the man of statistics and the master of economics". Marciano (2007) identifies the normative side of this L&E approach as the "Economic Analysis of Law". This side is much less evident in the argument presented by Coase himself, which forms the basis of positive L&E (or L&E *stricto sensu*). Yet, and in contrast with Marciano, we believe that the ambiguities that have characterized Coase's insights ensure that the difference between Coase and Posner is not that deep, and that the Economic Analysis of Law is indeed compatible with Coase's views.

14 This view is the linchpin of the traditional L&E preference for common-law systems as opposed to civil-law systems, the first being "created" by the judge, the latter by the politician. See for instance Mahoney (2001: 506), who claims that

> there are structural differences between common- and civil-law systems, most notably the greater degree of judicial independence in the former and the lower level of scrutiny of executive action in the latter, that provide governments more scope to alter property and contract rights in civil-law countries,

and concludes that "the association between the common law and growth is a consequence of greater judicial protection of property and contract rights from executive interference" (ibid.: 506). See also Posner (2007: chapter 19). The L&E position in this respect differs from the traditional, Hayekian (1960) standpoint, whereby the superiority of the common-law system is due to its evolutionary nature.

Some caution is in order, though. For instance, the alleged economic superiority of the common-law regime has been questioned by empirical research (Pollin and Vaubourg 2006; Ayyagari *et al.* 2006). The very difference between the two systems is not beyond dispute, either: common law countries are characterized by pervasive statutory legislation, while civil-law judges rely heavily on precedent. In particular, one should observe that once statutes are introduced, precedents are no longer valid, for the meaning and interpretation of adjudication within a given statutory context are no longer the same once the context has changed.

15 In particular, transaction costs include the cost of:

- Identifying the features of the products so as to make them understandable to the counterpart. This category of costs would also include the cost of making potential counterparts aware of an exchange opportunity, e.g. by means of advertising;
- Finding out the counterpart and inspecting the product: A might know what he wants, but does not know who the potential seller B might be, at what conditions B might be willing to sell and whether what B is willing to sell really matches what A is willing to buy. In this case, the transaction costs amount to the value of the time devoted to these tasks, plus accessory costs (especially if an intermediary is hired for that purpose);
- Cooperation and organization (that would eliminate *ex ante* opportunism);
- Negotiating the terms of the contract, possibly with assistance of professionals (e.g. a technical consultant or a lawyer). This can also be regarded as the cost of the contracting between two parties, or of cooperating within the context of broader contractual agreements, such as those generating communal-ownership structures;
- Delivery of the goods and services exchanged;
- Enforcing the contract. This applies both to situations where exchange is not simultaneous (thereby creating openings for *ex post* opportunism) and, more generally, to situations in which at least one party considers the nature of the good obtained/ delivered different from what had been previously agreed upon.

Furthermore, one should also bear in mind that TCs occur with actual, observable transactions as well as with potential, non-finalized transactions. One may wish to buy or sell X, gather information and possibly even start bargaining. But if the parties do not eventually find an agreement, transaction costs have been incurred even if no transaction has taken place.

16 As a matter of fact, the assumption about rationality is not made explicit in Coase (1960). It is nevertheless clearly characterizing his argument, as one can observe from George Stigler's understanding of the Coasean contribution (Fox 2007: 381–383).

It should also be remarked that the Coasean statement whereby the absence of transaction costs makes irrelevant how the judge attributes transaction costs is misleading, if not mistaken. Unless he is in fact a mere policeman (a violent enforcer, as Napoleon had envisaged the role of judges within his civil-code regime), the *judge* – not the assignment of property rights – is irrelevant.

17 Of course, in the monetary case, prices and purchasing power are denominated in the same unit (dollars, euro, etc.). Still, both (relative) prices and purchasing power are real variables, since they are meaningful only when they imply an opportunity cost. For instance, purchasing power Z is always related to the working effort it takes – or it has taken in the past – to acquire the corresponding monetary units. To be precise, this would surely require further refinements in order to take into account capital income from past savings, inheritance, lotteries and luck, possibly the satisfaction

obtained when bequeathing wealth to somebody else. But the idea remains the same: in a monetary economy, an individual trades by comparing the satisfaction acquired from one extra unit of X to the satisfaction surrendered by not consuming other goods or, should the value of his productivity fall relative to the price of his desired consumption bundle, by having to work harder to keep purchasing power constant.

Clearly, the same principle also applies to the labour market, in which the individual decides to sell X (his working efforts) by comparing how much he suffers by labouring to how much he improves his condition with the purchasing power he obtains (his salary in real terms).

18 It might be worth pointing out the classical origin of the TC concept, as one has the impression that the costs relating to the production of the goods and services that meet final demand are "good", while the remaining costs are "bad". The distinction has consequences also from the institutional vantage point, when it is argued that production costs narrowly understood can be minimized through competition and market forces, whereas transaction costs (or some of them) should be monitored and reduced by non-market forces and possibly government authorities. This was indeed Coase's view (1937, 1960).

19 Liggio and Chafuen (2004) are among the notable exceptions to the general view.

20 The political element will not be analysed in these pages. Yet, it is crucial, as noted long ago by Libecap (1989a: 4–5):

> Property rights institutions are determined through the political process, involving either negotiations among immediate group members of lobbying activities at higher levels of government. ... The heart of the contracting problem is devising politically acceptable allocation mechanisms to assign the gains from institutional change while maintaining its production advantages.

21 These are not the only criteria: "ease to understand" and "ease to apply" also play an essential role. But their inclusion at this stage does not change the gist of the argument. See also Chapter 7.

22 Consistent with our earlier argument in Chapter 3 (Sections 3.4.2 and 3.4.3), we define an externality as the result of an action carried out by A, to the extent that such action affects B's utility *and* violates his property rights. When property rights are not violated there are only unintentional effects, which may be desirable or undesirable. Thus, the violation of property rights is critical in transforming an unintentional, undesirable effect into an issue of economic relevance.

By contrast, the commonly accepted L&E notion of externality originates from Buchanan and Stubblebine (1962): it focuses on the difference between private and social welfare (private and social cost) and refrains from fully investigating the role of property rights. In the end, an externality is dangerously close to a "socially-undesirable" effect. Among the many textbooks available, see Mackaay and Rousseau (2008: 8).

23 The issue of recognition has regrettably been neglected in much of the L&E literature. A well-know institutional author rightly pointed out that

> Coase overstates the influence of law. His error lies in his implicit assumption that people can effortlessly learn and enforce their initial legal entitlements. ... The Shasta County evidence indicates that people are aware that the legal system is a relatively costly system of dispute resolution and therefore often choose to turn a deaf ear to it.
>
> Ellickson (1991: 281)

24 In the well-known example of the common pond, the problem of overfishing is not due to the fact that the pond is scarce, for anyone has easy – too easy, in truth – access to the pond. On the contrary, it is provoked by the fact that by not privatizing the pond, access is not restricted. At the end of the day, the pond will still be "abundant",

whereas the appropriated fish will have disappeared. The upshot is that overfishing would not have taken place if the pond had become scarce; and the pond would have become scarce if property rights on the pond had been allowed to develop. As an aside, it is also worth observing that you don't need rules for the development of property rights as long as the Lockean–Rothbardian appropriation principle is accepted.

25 A different situation might emerge when a set of potential claimants *simultaneously* come across a good which cannot meet all the claims to property by the first occupants. Two situations describe this possibility. One is of "purposeful discovery" of the unknown (e.g. the Spanish conquistadores), one is of "artificial shortage" (e.g. a helicopter drops a bushel of wheat to a hungry crowd). In the first case, history shows that property rights on the unknown are agreed upon by the explorers prior to their discovery. In the second case, one may witness a fight to appropriate the content of the bushel. This outcome, however, regards a situation in which the original owner of the good (say, the pilot of the helicopter) gave away his property rights to several potential new owners at the same time. As a result, it is not really a problem of scarcity, but rather of a poorly specified transfer of property rights on a scarce resource.

26 As pointed out in Ridley (1996: chapter 11), the killing was often accompanied by waste (the hunters would take the best cuts and leave the rest of the animal to rot) and ultimately drove some populations to cannibalism.

27 Institutional costs are here defined as what it takes to enforce compliance with a rule that affects social interaction. Exchange is merely one aspect of social interaction, even if it represents the only set of observable interactions the economist is generally interested in.

28 The fact that nowadays property-right enforcement is usually run by state monopolies should not make us forget that defence and police services are not necessarily characterized by static, natural-monopoly structures (i.e. one producer and technical impossibility of competing him away).

29 This also includes the treatment of fugitive slaves, of course. The same would not be true if the slave state is interpreted as a cartel among slave masters. If one slave master had thought it more efficient to sell or grant the slave his freedom, he would have not joined the cartel: the cartel would have been a voluntary agreement, not a state. Thus, the argument according to which inefficiency is generated by the prohibition to trade in liberty is porous: either the ban has teeth, in which case it is not a cartel, but an act of violence by the state authorities; or it has no teeth, in which case the explanation based on the inefficient rule loses its power.

30 Oddly enough, Demsetz does not question the legitimacy of government rule-making activity, which in these cases implies ownership of a forced immigrant from Africa and of a resident's time: permanent and temporary slavery, respectively.

31 De Soto actually seems to argue that it is mainly a problem of formal publicity. If so, it would indeed be a typical transaction-cost problem, since the lack of formal and easily-accessible documents would raise the cost of acquiring the necessary information. One may wonder, however, whether these costs can only be reduced through coercive intervention by the state and/or funding by international aid organizations. It is here upheld that it is mainly a problem of bad protection (unreliable or biased decisions of the courts) and weak enforcement (lengthy and exceedingly expensive judicial procedures), as mentioned in the text.

32 Moreover, and rather unfortunately, the introduction of TCs creates ambiguities or encourages wrong conclusions. For instance, by encouraging the observer to view exchange and opportunity costs as the result of transformation skills (productivity) and transaction costs (the gap separating reality from nirvana), one might wonder about the role of profits – the remuneration for entrepreneurship and risk: for profits are included neither in the cost of transformation, nor in the cost of exchanging. Are they also a nuisance? Similarly, it is not clear where psychological values stand. To

illustrate this point, let us suppose that the manufacturing cost of a piece of furniture is $1,000, but is exchanged at a price of $10,000 because of its historical or emotional content – say, a famous pop star owned it in the past. The standard mainstream reply would be that since $9,000 can be ascribed neither to manufacturing, nor to transacting, it must be the consequence (the cost?) of irrationality (passions, historical craziness). Still, one wonders whether the reader would happily acknowledge that 90 per cent of this transaction falls outside the scope of economic analysis and behaviour.

33 Ownership frequently provides satisfaction per se, as David Hume observed centuries ago (see also Kahneman *et al.* 1990 for a more recent contribution). Nonetheless, for the sake of simplicity, in this section we assume that what one acquires is valuable because it can be consumed or because it can be exchanged directly or indirectly for other goods and services that can be consumed.

34 According to the international-trade terminology, one would then be in a situation in which the international terms of exchange of X are variable, the sign of the change depending on the sign of the deviation from autarky.

35 As pointed out earlier, liberty is here the defined as the right of the individual to prevent other individuals from exercising violence, i.e. carrying out physical aggression or fraudulent behaviour.

36 Fox (2007: 378) also points out at the misleading confusion of the transaction-cost terminology and identifies the costs related to "institutional changes", which in his perspective include those related to changes in policy-making.

37 Legitimacy would be based on the assumption that our societies attribute great value to pecuniary wealth. On this very point many fathers of the L&E approach would agree: Coase, Demsetz, Becker and Posner, for instance.

38 See Barzel (1989: 2) on a similar note, although his focus is on property rights, rather than liberty.

39 Of course, absent liberty, the traditional theory of exchange falls apart.

7 The normative agendas of the L&E approach

1 Barzel (1989: 77) formulates the so-called Coase theorem as follows: "When property rights are well defined and transacting is costless, resources will be used where they are most valued, regardless of which of the transactors assumes liability for his or her effects on the other." Yet, defining the Coase theorem (which was never articulated by Coase, but rather "created" by Stigler (1966)) is a difficult matter, and we shall posit that there is no real theorem, but a tautology, plus some inconclusive normative guidelines for judicial policy-making. Nonetheless, we shall follow the current terminology and use the expressions "Coasean argument" and "Coase theorem" interchangeably.

2 In accordance with the definition suggested in Section 6.4 in the previous chapter, these costs are not mere indirect effects, for they encroach upon the victim's property rights and thus affect his ability and willingness to make use of – and benefit from – the goods and services he owns. This is obvious when A is a producer, as in the Coasean examples; much less so otherwise. For instance, lazy A being awarded a pay rise is likely to make his colleague B angry and envious. Hence the pay rise definitely provokes negative indirect effects. Yet, and contrary to the mainstream view (including Coase), we believe that that does not qualify as an externality.

3 Transaction costs include all the items listed in Section 6.3 in the previous chapter.

4 Some authors have underscored the importance of assigning and enforcing property rights within the Coasean framework. In the light of the argument presented in the previous chapter, however, this emphasis is actually misplaced. First, because unless one rules out homesteading and exchange – which includes the production of goods and services – as the original title to property, all scarce goods and services are always assigned. The context is different when only the state can be a proprietor. But of

course, under such circumstances all exchanges take place among the different branches of government, according to their preferences and bargaining power.

Second, this emphasis is misplaced because weak enforcement does not jeopardize exchange per se, since exchange is the way we call a "give-and-take" mechanism. Instead, the value of what is being exchanged and the range of goods that are worth producing for future trading are affected. This is of course also crucial for welfare: as mentioned earlier, weak enforcement makes durable consumption goods and capital goods (including inventories) all but worthless, and thus stifling entrepreneurship and growth.

5 To be fair, the notion whereby legal principles or previous social arrangements could be waived by the judge for the sake of the general good and prosperity was already known decades earlier, as Coase himself acknowledged.

6 See Zerbe (1998) for an extensive inquiry into the meaning, limits and value of cost–benefit analyses.

7 The Coase theorem does not say that only the economic consequences of the agents' decisions should be taken into account, but that such consequences should be taken into account:

> it is, of course, desirable that the choice between different social arrangements for the solution of economic problems should be carried out in broader terms than this and that the total effect of these arrangements in all spheres of life should be taken into account. As Frank H. Knight has so often emphasized, problems of welfare economics must ultimately dissolve into a study of aesthetics and morals.
>
> (Ibid.: 43)

Nonetheless, it is undeniable that the thrust of Coase's contribution is on the (material) cost–benefit part, and that his reference to moral standards is cursory, it has never been articulated further by the author himself, and has been virtually ignored by most of the Coasean literature.

8 Coase is indeed aware of the possibilities that government abuses its powers, and might not carry out diligent economic analysis at low expense. Similarly, he warns the enthusiast economists that changes in the rules of the game frequently result in significant costs, even when change is for the better. Fox (2007) correctly points out, however, that Coase's caution with respect to government intervention – legislators or judges – is motivated by efficiency concerns, not by the notions of ethics or justice.

9 See Medema and Zerbe (2000) for a survey of the possibilities where the Coase theorem breaks down. Of course, once the perfect-world assumption holds true and endowments effects are ruled out – the price A is willing to pay when buying X is the same as the price he asks when selling X – the Coase theorem is actually a tautology, as mentioned earlier: whenever reality deviates from perfection, the explanation is the existence of deficiencies. In turn, deficiencies are synonymous with positive transaction costs, which in the Coasean world consist of poorly assigned and/or enforced property rights.

10 Not surprisingly, therefore, the traditional line of attack against the Coase theorem insists on its having reduced private property to an exercise in scientism, which actually boils down to adding up monetary flows, with little regard to the damage inflicted upon some of the parties involved. Yet, persuasive as it may appear, this is not entirely fair. Although he does not spend adequate time and space emphasizing the limits of his normative recommendations, Coase (1960) does mention that his economic-efficiency criterion is only one among the elements to be taken into account when assigning property rights. Of course, one may question Coase's view on the object of economic analysis. But that is clearly another matter.

This helps to understand why it is difficult to categorize Coase as a mainstream economist. Coase is well aware that economics cannot be value-free and remains a deductive science where the interaction between human preferences and the rules of the game play a prominent role. But he is not a free-market economist, either, since he rejects the free-market view, according to which (*a*) all violations of property rights run against justice and (*b*) each person justly owns whatever he has acquired from other persons through voluntary exchange; or by combining the resources he owns in order to create something new, which also becomes his own property (see also Rothbard 1982). Coase is not a third-way supporter, either, for he does believe in the virtues of the market and of the price system: his advocacy for government intervention is cautious and qualified. Put differently, and contrary to Calabresi (1968) and Dahlman (1979), Coase's views do not *imply* all-out government action to obtain efficiency.

This last feature is indeed the peculiarity of much of the L&E tradition, which tries to conflate the appeal of the neoclassical approach with the institutional factual features of the real world. As mentioned earlier in the text, and somewhat close to the constructivist perspective, the solution is often times utilitarian. Although Coase does not offer a utilitarian key to operate within what he perceives as a transaction-cost-and-externality context, he is ambiguously open to "reasonable" proposals in that direction.

11 Buchanan and Stubblebine (1962: 383) noticed that Coase's theorem "is applicable only to inter-firm relationships ... because of the incomparability of utility functions". Block (1977) further clarified this point and argued that even if utilities were comparable, the decision-maker still needs a moral criterion to justify his tampering with individual property rights.

12 If good X is for intermediate consumption, the market value of X at the margin is the market price of the final good times the marginal productivity of X. If X is a final-consumption good, then the market value of its marginal use is its price.

13 To be fair, Coase (1960) repeatedly mentions that his whole argument rests on the hypothesis of perfect competition. Nonetheless, the ambiguity remains, in that his reference to perfect competition ensures that all profits (margins) are considered equivalent to value. That makes sense if one assumes that wealth is the sum of all monetary surpluses (profits) and economics is about the production of commodities that are perpetually exchanged and never consumed. However, not only is this last assumption never formulated; but once the argument is extended to the world of final consumption, this potential defensive argument also becomes manifestly weak.

14 "Prohibitively" means that the buyer enjoys a large surplus from consuming X, but does not have the resources required to match the value of the marginal use of X to the seller, which is in turn greater than the market price of X. See Zerbe (1998), who has explained at length the meaning and implications of "psychological ownership" and also Block (1977), who referred to "psychic income". The presence of psychic income may therefore cause a prohibitively large difference between subjective value and market value.

15 Epstein (1989) tries to show that the dilemma between moral deontology and utilitarianism is much less pronounced than commonly understood. It is worth pointing out, however, that Epstein's utilitarian argument is nonetheless developed in the name of economic liberty, and thus never advocates actions that a subjectivist would resent.

16 See also Manne (2005) on the birth of L&E, and on the difficulties this approach met with, both in academia and among lawyers.

17 More generally, North (2002) correctly points out that judicial or technocratic interference with the property rights typically associated with a free society necessarily makes sure that that society is no longer free. One may therefore conclude that a technocratic reading of Coasean economics can easily lead to economic standstill provoked by a high rate of time preference; or to socialism, should the judiciary be supplemented by some benevolent central-planning bureau in charge of the production and distribution of most durable goods.

18 Marciano (2010) aptly underscores that although both Coase and Calabresi emphasize

that the assignment of property rights have important effects on efficiency, they differ in one important point. Coase focuses on the social inefficiencies provoked by externalities, while Calabresi devotes his attention to other forms of market failures, such as monopolies and irrational behaviour.

19 See for instance Rowley (2005: section 4), where the reader can appreciate why the L&E views have been usually associated with downright free-market economics.

20 The constructivist and now dominant view that has characterized much of post-Coasean Chicago brings together Holmes's views on legal scholarship and Posner's attempt to consider the judge as the enforcer of the economic recipes for social efficiency. Such view will be discussed later in this chapter.

21 See for instance Manne (1965) and, more generally, Macey (1998).

22 Williamson usually stops short of normative prescriptions, while Manne uses L&E to demonstrate that normative intervention does more harm than good.

23 By re-assigning property rights, one can discourage productive entrepreneurship, and at the same time involuntarily create incentives for destructive entrepreneurship (rent-seeking activities). More on this in Chapter 8.

24 See Section 6.6 in the previous chapter. Williamson (1979: 239–240) defines as "idiosyncratic" transactions involving expenses that are "transaction-specific (non-marketable)". When contracting the purchase of specialized equipment,

> inasmuch as the value of this capital in other uses is ... smaller than the specialized use for which it has been intended, the supplier is effectively "locked into" the transaction to a significant degree. This is symmetrical. ... The buyer is thus committed to the transaction as well.

25 The culprit is of course the deceptive notion of transaction costs. Not surprisingly, the market/hierarchy dichotomy comes from Coase (1937) and was already detected by G. Stigler, as mentioned in Cristiano (2009). It is a deceiving dichotomy, since all hierarchical agreements aiming at reducing opportunism are in fact market solutions generated by an a priori desire to cooperate, a desire which is technically attainable, but which might face time-related hindrances (uncertainty, limited information).

26 The very term "opportunism" can also be a source of ambiguity, since it actually refers to three different concepts. One is *ex-ante* opportunism, whereby the agent tries to benefit from the positive externalities created by others and refuses to commit himself to sharing the cost of the activity. Free riding clearly belongs to this category. A second notion applies when one agent violates the contract by not cooperating, e.g. when one falls short of the performance/behaviour agreed upon (or reasonably expected) and trusts that he can go scot-free due to the high institutional costs. Moral hazard and shirking are well-known examples. A third class of opportunistic behaviour relates to hold-up situations, i.e. when one party refrains from cooperating in order to acquire bargaining power. Of course, only the second category is relevant for our purposes: the first is a matter of envy, while the third can be solved through articulated forms of exchange or vertical integration (see also Williamson 1983).

27 Posner (1985) makes his case for the wealth-maximization standard by referring to (*a*) the fact it is an easy criterion to use for practical purposes (i.e. it is easy to quantify), (*b*) the presumption that it is an objective measure less vulnerable to subjective interpretation by the judge or the policy-maker, (*c*) the assumption that it is the measure upon which most people would agree. The essence of Posner's pragmatic approach is analysed in detail by Harnay and Marciano (2003).

Parisi (2005: 40) refers to an extended version of the same criterion, which he defines as a functional synthesis. According to this "functional" approach, simulations regarding wealth maximization also take into account how *prima facie* efficient rules interact with the rest of the institutional context. The purpose is to avoid undesirable, indirect consequences.

28 This is precisely the reason why Epstein (1989) declares his allegiance to utilitarianism and rejects the natural-law view.

29 See also Sections 7.3.1 and 7.3.2, below. Of course, the notion of efficiency is in fact itself questionable, for in the L&E context efficiency refers to those actions that minimize the gap between the private and the social cost or, put differently, that ensure that potentially harmful activities are carried out by those who are exposed to the appropriate incentives so that the cost of their actions is fully internalized. It is obvious, however, that the course of action which extends over several time periods may be "optimal" given the present technologies and state of knowledge (or uncertainty), but may be no longer so in the light of tomorrow's knowledge.

30 Since this work is not about definitions and the history of economic ideas, we shall just mention the two most popular versions of socialist constructivism. One is the fascist corporatist vision, which does not deny the principle of private property altogether, but argues in favour of severe restrictions on economic and individual liberties for the sake of the public good to be pursued by a political elite that enforces cooperation through a hierarchically structured society. The other is of course the communist approach, which denies private property and ideally sees the economy led by a central-planning agency pursuing the interest of the working class: wealth is obtained through technocratic efficiency (as opposed to entrepreneurial efforts) and income equality is achieved by considering remuneration a political variable (as opposed to the result of a voluntary agreement between economic agents).

31 The Kaldor–Hicks criterion suggests that when a norm creates winners and losers, then such norm is efficient (welfare enhancing) as long as the winners acquire enough gains to compensate the losers, no matter whether compensation actually takes place. The Kaldor–Hicks criterion in fact suggests that the judge is presented with the technical means to figure out the gains and losses for the "typical individual" and is thereby in a position to set an operational standard, deviations from which are possible, but which must be explained or justified.

Those who oppose this criterion would of course argue that (*a*) the criterion does not specify how much compensation would be required to leave the losers no worse off than before the change in the legal norm, (*b*) at the end, the loser is still worse off as a result of the change, which runs against the very purpose of a social organization (making all its members better off as a consequence of their being part of the community, not exploiting the "small" losers). The opposite view would of course maintain that the first objection is sensible in theory, but that opportunism makes it unacceptable in practice. With regard to the second objection, a Posnerian would argue that in the long run, a more efficient economic system will bring benefits even to those who today seem to be the losers.

32 In contrast with what is frequently maintained, "discovering the law" has little to do with the foundations of the common-law system, which came to life and rapidly spread in England during the twelfth and thirteenth centuries and was based on "writs" (royal statutes), rather than on customary norms (Hogue 1966). It was true that at the time the king was subject to the law, but in the common-law system the law-maker was the king, who had absolute discretionary power, possibly mitigated by his perception of natural-law principles.

33 Of course, moral legitimacy is not an issue, for in this case there is no moral benchmark. Instead, legitimacy comes from the reliability of the default rule and by the capacity of the default rule to meet its consequentialist promises. See for instance Mercuro and Medema (2006: 53–59).

34 In accord with the definition provided by North (1990) and with our earlier references to this term, path-dependence is here defined as a process in which the institutions prevailing at time 0 create a system of incentives for cooperating agreements. In turn, these generate pressure to bring about marginal changes in the institutional context during the following periods.

35 It is not the goal of these pages to offer an in-depth analysis of Epstein's perspective, which presents many interesting and sometimes puzzling aspects. For instance, one may wonder why Epstein insists on underscoring the default nature of his rules if one of those very rules is freedom of contract within a regime of private property rights. One suspects that his proviso would therefore allow for deviations by the authority, not by the individual. If so, the default criterion wobbles. Put differently, either the default rule applies to the individual, but then it is not necessary (for instance, it is logically hard to argue that freedom of contract is the rule, but one or both parties can waive their freedom), or it applies to the authority, but then it is unable to prevent discretion and arbitrariness, since the authority itself decides when opting out is permitted.

36 Attention is also devoted to political feasibility. For instance, when discussing tax systems, Epstein claims that efficiency means reducing the role of government and that this goal is better achieved by a proportional tax system, as opposed to a progressive system, since under the former regime the tax burden would quickly fall on large layers of the population, which would thus resist it more effectively. Of course, if one forgets about populism, a poll tax would be even better and not necessarily "unfair", especially if redistribution is carried out on the expenditure side.

37 As a reminder, the Austrian school is amoral: preferences are exogenous and not subject to any kind of value judgement. By contrast, the neo-Austrian school has normative ambitions and formulates value judgements by adopting the freedom-from-coercion principle as the reference. L. von Mises and M. Rothbard are the main representatives of the two branches, respectively.

38 This is possibly the only point where Beckerian and Posnerian economics diverge. It is also worth pointing out, however, that in the European tradition the role of the judge tends to be taken over by a regulatory agency.

39 In particular, social efficiency includes both compliance with common wisdom (consensus) and the quest for economic growth with the emphasis on production, which is easier to measure.

40 One should take this last statement with caution, though; since the L&E tradition tends to reject the evolutionary view that characterizes the dynamics of customary law (Benson 1991). Instead, the L&E approach insists on the judge's discretionary power to pursue social goals and to refer to precedent as a loose guideline, rather than as a binding constraint. See also Section 7.5 below.

41 See however Cooter (1982), according to whom this need may arise even when transaction costs are zero.

42 If the common law is understood as a contract-enforcement system based on rules filtered by experience and past success, then it is necessarily efficient, as common law represents the judicial counterpart of voluntary exchange. The "limit" of the common law is that it does not address the question of failed coordination. But of course, this is not what the common law is supposed to do, as one can easily discern by recalling Marciano's emphasis on the difference between L&E *stricto sensu* and the economic analysis of law (see Section 6.2 in the previous chapter and Rizzo 1979/1980).

43 See Chapters 1 (Section 1.5) and 3 (Section 3.4).

44 In other occasions, courts are perceived as a devious way to sap someone's activity for a significant amount of time at a considerable cost, with "cost" understood also in terms of reputation. Under such circumstances, the threat of going to court allows the extraction of concessions that would not be conceivable under other circumstances. Of course, this institutional context is hardly amenable to L&E considerations.

45 To complicate matters further, one should also take into account the fact that in many situations the available evidence can be interpreted in different ways, following the different schools of economic thought – not all judges need to be neoclassical devotees. This is even more relevant in the case of econometric expertise, where the data are subject to manipulation and where both the methodology and the

interpretation are often the object of heated debate within the econometricians' community itself.

46 It must however be observed that Manne's and Williamson's views offer a different perspective. Their approach has a much stronger explanatory content, which actually leads them to suggest that the scope for normative intervention or arbitrary decision-making should remain limited. As mentioned earlier, their normative focus aims at reducing institutional costs, while letting exchange cost follow their course.

47 As mentioned in the text, this does not mean that freedom of contract was common: the ruling elites were guilty of all sorts of violations. Nonetheless, the rulers' interference was considered an act of rent-seeking imposed by violence. As Strayer (1970: 100) has pointed out, "well into the seventeenth century the best-organized states were in a sense only federations of counties or provinces, and each unit of the federation adopted orders from the centre to fit its own needs". Sacco (2007) notes that not even Louis XIV had the power to legislate, but just to issue *ordonnances*, which the regional parliaments were free to reject (at least in theory). From this vantage point, judges' activism would have been perceived as a challenge to the ruler, certainly not as an attempt to pursue the collective good, social justice or social efficiency.

48 Somewhat ironically, the very founder of utilitarianism had very harsh words against the common-law system and no faith in judge-made law. Stein (1980: 70) summarizes Jeremy Bentham's (1843) view as follows: "Law is not what the judges say but is rather the expressed will of the legislator, following the principle of utility by maximising happiness. ... The only true law is statute law".

49

> Judges serve for a long time, and when they make mistakes, they have no incentive, not being subject to election, to admit them. In fact, judges often seem to dig in and defend their mistakes as if their reputations depended on it. The result is that judicial decisions tend to be very rigid. This is even truer at the Supreme Court level where ten years can easily go by before any decision gets seriously revisited. The political branches, on the other hand, have every incentive to revisit their mistakes and make corrections.
>
> (Calabresi 2005: 1097)

Similar comments might apply to the judges' incentives to appreciate and elaborate upon the consequences of technological change in terms of optimal (efficient) property-right and liability assignment.

50 This term defines a social structure ruled by an oligarchy of highly qualified technocrats educated at the *École Nationale d'Administration*. The ENA was founded in 1945 by the head of the French Communist Party (Maurice Thorez) and with the approval of Charles de Gaulle, for the purpose of creating a new class of technocrats to occupy key positions in the civil service and state-owned companies, but also ready to accept responsibilities in the private sector.

51 Recent proposals to abolish the ENA should not be taken too seriously, for such proposals are not motivated by the rejection of the regulatory implications of social responsibility. Instead, they tend to be kindled by the elite nature of the *énarques*, which has evolved into some sort of closed oligarchy, thereby stultifying the expectations and ambitions both of the politicians and of the middle bureaucracy. A different but equally revealing example of the all but irresistible drift towards technocratic rule is provided once again by the recent financial crises, which have strengthened those very bureaucrats who were supposed to prevent them by careful monitoring. In this vein, Macey (2008: chapter 7) examines the SEC case in the United States.

52 These terms are borrowed from Greve (2011), with some adaptation. By "consociational" structure we mean a social system based on consensus as defined by large interest groups, each of them focused on the privileges it can attain, while paying less attention to the costs that the privileges awarded to other groups might entail. This is

of course rational for the collective-action reasons that Mancur Olson explained decades ago. But it is also rational if one considers that the consociational game is not played by groups, but by their representatives or leaders. These know that their personal position depends on their perceived performance. Now, perceived performance tends to depend much more on the privileges obtained – which are recognized as leading to immediate benefits – and much less on the privileges obtained by others, the cost of which are less transparent and therefore discounted at a much higher rate. To various degrees, all European societies are consociational. See also Eichengreen (2007) for an extension of this concept to the birth and unfolding of the European Union.

By contrast, a "competitive" structure is one where the state acts as a system that provides pure public goods (e.g. defence) and prevents the individual from being harmed by special interest (e.g. trade barriers). The only example of competitive state is probably the United States as imagined by its Founding Fathers.

53 Current unease with the so-called "Eurocrats" – the "*soi-disant élites*", as Jean-Pierre Chevènement called them – provides some support to this statement and could form the object of predictions for future developments. On the other hand, the role of the European Court of Justice is not questioned (but many Europeans seem to simply ignore its activity).

54 The same holds true for Manne's mistrust of the role of regulation in the market for corporate control and in corporate governance more generally.

55 We define the law of rules as a system where the law is man-made (rules) and the legitimacy of which depends on the acceptance of the procedure through which the rules are formulated. By contrast, in our view the rule of law should refer to a system where the law is sovereign and which draws its legitimacy from a set of undisputed axioms, such as those derived from religion or from the principle of self-ownership. See also our earlier comments in Chapter 5 (Sections 5.2 and 5.3).

56 Two phenomena might trigger the search for radically different ways to look at individual responsibility and thus delegitimize the state as a distributor of apparently-free rents. In the United States, tax pressure is going to increase rapidly in order to finance both the debt issued by the Obama administration and the welfare-state programmes that have been launched in 2010. As the Tea Party movement demonstrates in the US context, this might have a critical impact on public opinion, especially on those low-income layers of the population which had been previously told that such programmes would be financed exclusively by the "rich". In continental Europe, many state-pension systems suffer from severe funding problems, which means that promises won't be kept: in fact, in some countries retirement age has been increased and yearly disbursements to future pensioners have been revised downwards. If widespread, consciousness that old-age needs can no longer be a collective responsibility might lead to dramatic adjustments.

57 It is contradictory if one believes that externalities arise because property rights cannot be assigned/enforced. It is self-explanatory if one believes that stealing is no longer a crime, once the thief is given property rights on what he has taken.

8 Growth and crises reconsidered

1 See for instance Davoine (2009), who reviews the economics of happiness and discusses its normative implications. Once it is measurable, happiness could certainly become an appealing and more comprehensive alternative to GDP and wealth when assessing the desirability of public policies. But for the time being one has the impression that it has little or no operational content and only serves political rhetoric. The latest example is the so-called Stiglitz report (Stiglitz *et al.* 2009) commissioned by President Sarkozy in 2008 in order to point out that his electoral promise to make the French people better off has still held true, as long as one does not look at GDP per capita and the joy of shirking is taken into account.

2 In particular, dynamic equilibrium was the core of the modern neoclassical view, while entrepreneurship – the role of which was originally perceived by Cantillon – represented the essence of the Austrian tradition.

3 The external observer can indeed guess about the individual's expected happiness, as the revealed-preference approach suggests. But he can hardly figure out whether, and to what extent, the individual's actions have brought about the expected results (Kahneman *et al.* 1997), nor can the external observer aspire to make such an individual happy (i.e. virtuous).

4 Hence, one can claim that the germs of growth economics can be traced back to when Bernard Mandeville maintained that by pursuing their own well-being, individuals enhance the welfare of the other members of the community as well. This differs from Adam Smith, who drew on Shaftesbury, Pufendorf and Locke in order to develop a theory of growth based on the morality of spontaneous social cooperation. Thus, Mandeville's growth economics is still firmly within the realm of subjectivism and methodological individualism, whereby Smith's approach is more vulnerable to the (policy-)making of growth.

5 See also Olson (1982), who argued that stability is responsible for increasing rent-seeking, while a shock can destroy the incumbent coalitions and jump-start the economy again. These Olsonian cycles are heavily influenced by the dynamics of rent-seeking pressures and may overlap with – but are intrinsically different from – the better-known business cycles, to be discussed in Section 8.8.

6 According to Moshe Syrquin (private communication), this view was also strongly supported by some international organizations (e.g. the World Bank) in the 1950s, when economic planning on a world scale seemed to be promising and feasible. See also Patinkin (1976), who analyses the debates that took place between the two world wars on the usefulness of national statistics.

7 Indeed, the rule-makers have usually succeeded in acquiring some sort of weak monopoly on the creation of statistics, and have not refrained from using their power to force individuals to disclose information they would not normally disclose to other parties.

8 See however Stevenson and Wolfers (2008), according to whom the so-called "Easterlin paradox" – happiness is independent of purchasing power – was due to inadequate data and poor modelling. In their view, happiness generally rises with GDP, both within and across countries. The correlation becomes statistically weak only for high income levels.

9 See for instance Elmslie (1994). This tradition, however, takes for granted two contested points: first, that the surplus generated by specialization would not be absorbed by an increase in population, and second, that a large enough part of the surplus would be devoted to financing science.

10 Of course, the critical weakness of this approach lies in the fact that in order to assess the optimal investment in technological inputs – scientific research and innovation – one must replace the notion of uncertainty with that of risk, which presents a known probability distribution. This theoretical standpoint has been abandoned, except when describing catching-up phenomena, as in Abramovitz (1986). Nonetheless, the same line of reasoning has surfaced again in the endogenous-growth literature, references to which still abound in most economics textbooks.

11 De Haan *et al.* (2006) and Czeglédi and Kápas (2009) provide appropriate methodological critiques to the standard ways of measuring economic freedom, but confirm the results. In a similar vein, see also Weede (2006) and Headey (2008), who do not deny the importance of market-friendly institutions, but underscore that economic freedom affects growth only indirectly, through education, finance and trade.

However, it is worth pointing out that the convincing results one obtains by looking at economic freedom are much less convincing if one considers the role of "good governance". Good governance seems to characterize developed countries, but fails to explain transition from poverty to affluence (Meisel and Ould Aoudia 2008). These suggest that in developing countries good governance is not enough: it must be reliable, trusted and adapted to the local environment. This train of thought will be further developed in the next chapter.

12 The TFP vision is in fact confusing from an empirical and a methodological standpoint. It coincides with the error term (the residual) of an estimated equation. Thus one needs some imagination to call "productivity" the measure of our ignorance. Furthermore, even if one accepts that aggregate production functions exist, and even if TFP does in fact measure changes in productivity (two big "if's"), within the traditional neoclassical black box "technological change is only observable by its effects on productivity, as measured by such variables as TFP and labour productivity. There are no independent ways of separately measuring changes in technology, economic structure, and productivity" (Lipsey *et al.* 2005: 55).

13 See for instance the survey offered in Castellacci (2007).

14 See for instance the synthesis in Holcombe (2007: 101):

> Schumpeterian entrepreneurship is the engine of economic progress. … The disruptive effect of Schumpeterian entrepreneurship … creates profit opportunities, which opens the role for Kirznerian entrepreneurs to seize them and equilibrate the economy. This Kirznerian entrepreneurship also contributes to economic progress by allowing resources to be employed more efficiently.

15 Attempts to argue the opposite have been ridiculed by reality. The most celebrated example is perhaps Meadows *et al.* (1972).

16 This point was already clearly formulated by Knight in the mid-1930s. Metcalfe articulates it again by concluding that "there can never be an equilibrium in respect of knowledge and, consequently, the development of an economy is unpredictable and open-ended" (2003: 408). The methodological solution suggested by Metcalfe consists in an updated framework to fit sectorial technological trajectories and track interactions.

17 "While even long before the Industrial Revolution small elites had an opulent life style, the average person in 1800 was no better off than his or her ancestors of the Paleolithic on Neolithic" (Clark 2007: 5). In fact, until some two centuries ago the primary goal for the vast majority of the households throughout the world was daily survival (food and shelter). See however Lispey *et al.* (2005: chapter 5), who argue that living standards rose substantially during the pre-Christian world and Stark (2006:42), according to whom "Not only did most Europeans eat far better during the Dark Ages than in Roman times but they were healthier, more energetic, and probably more intelligent".

18 Indeed, "trade is the precursor of politics, not the consequence … Government, law, justice and politics are not only far more recently developed than trade, but they follow where trade leads" (Ridley 1996: 202) – in other words, trade has created the conditions that allowed groups and societies to come to the surface, which in turn required the creation of politics.

19 The role of deductive reasoning should not be underestimated, though. Einstein's relativity theory is probably the most famous example of its importance in modern science.

20 The obvious example refers to medicine.

21 See Robert L. Hotz, "A wandering mind heads straight toward insights", *Wall Street Journal, Science Journal*, 19 June 2009.

22 As the text makes clear, the term "environment" has broader connotation than "institutions". The environment includes the rules of the game, but also common wisdom and attitudes, public opinion, ideology (e.g. *moeurs*, to make the obvious Tocquevillean point). See also Goldstone (2011), who clearly relates the "scientific Enlightenment" of the eighteenth century to the "gradual disengagement with the classical-religious legacy of the prior millennia, and its replacement by a new system

of knowledge acquisition and validation, a replacement that spurred changes in political and economic as well as intellectual life".

23 As a matter of fact, neither the Catholics, nor the Calvinists were tolerant or particularly open towards modern science. In fact, the opposite was much closer to the truth. Nonetheless, the ongoing Spanish and (later) French threats made sure that neither England, nor the Netherlands could risk domestic turmoil. Furthermore, tolerance appeared to be the best way to attract skilled workers and wealth – both necessary to wage and finance war against such overpowering and aggressive opponents.

24 Jardine (2008) provides evidence of intense scientific cooperation (as well as rivalry) between these two countries, notwithstanding the presence of frequent, tense political circumstances. See also Lipsey *et al.* (2005).

25 See Section 8.5.2 below.

26 Neither the West, nor China explicitly opposed individual scientific reasoning and speculation, although the incumbent authorities would always monitor the potential political consequences of such investigations. Islam was different. From the beginning of the second millennium of the Christian era, individual forays into philosophy and natural philosophy were considered all but blasphemous in vast areas of the Islamic world, and therefore discouraged, if not forbidden. That attitude, which many would not consider consistent with the original Koran message, is still popular today (Habib 2008).

27 It might be useful to recall the difference between productive entrepreneurs (or entrepreneurs, unless specified otherwise) and innovators (or engineers – the two terms being here used interchangeably). The former have an intuition on how to organize existing resources and known production processes, and engage in actions of economic value (meet unsatisfied demand). By contrast, innovators transform scientific knowledge into new products and new production processes (including organization).

28 Despite its age, the Cobb–Douglas pattern is still the most popular for computation purposes. But other alternatives are of course available and have been widely made use of.

29 This view owes a great deal to the work by Israel Kirzner, according to whom the entrepreneur is an individual who happens to stumble on a bright intuition, which managers will subsequently transform into economically valuable projects. See also Baumol (1990), who drew on earlier Austrian insights.

30 If anything, pressure to expand the role of policy-making (e.g. regulation) comes from the political arena and with little opposition staged by the entrepreneurs, who do not perceive what they might lose from redistribution. It is no accident that important sections of the modern, West European welfare-state systems were all born in the 1960s, for the financial implications of a pay-as-you-go pension scheme and of a national health scheme financed through ordinary taxation are relatively light only when you have a fairly young and growing population and growth is substantial.

31 When a scientific breakthrough is translated into innovations of economic relevance, it usually stimulates further research and the development of improvements, until that technology is superseded by a different technology and becomes "obsolete". Thus, a technological trajectory identifies the dynamics of productivity related to each technology during its life. By and large, a trajectory is assumed to reproduce a logistic curve: it takes time before the economic potential of a scientific breakthrough is perceived and attracts innovators, while after a number of years innovators are attracted by other opportunities and the contribution of the old technology to the increase in productivity tapers off.

32 It is assumed that in the absence of money printing, public debt should be reimbursed at the future date by running a budget surplus. That requires increasing taxation or reducing expenditure. Either way, this implies a reduction in the household's ability to consume. According to the Ricardian equivalence, the individual perceives right from the moment the government issues new debt that this operation implies a future

reduction in purchasing power. Thus, those who believe in the Ricardian equivalence maintain that there is no difference between financing public consumption through taxation and through debt. From their standpoint, both taxation and debt creation are perceived as a reduction in the purchasing power of individuals.

33 Akerlof and Shiller (2009) recommend that money be pumped in and companies kept alive as long as confidence is restored. Unfortunately, it is less clear why confidence is eventually restored by keeping alive bad companies, denying profitable firm opportunities to expand and perhaps providing good companies incentives to be less careful.

34 Debt-financing is obviously inconsistent with the free-market principles. But this does not necessarily gainsay the possibility that sometimes policy-making intervention changes individuals' attitudes and propensities. Assessing whether this is a good enough reason for the government to encroach upon individual liberty is of course another story (see Chapters 4 and 5 in this book).

35 Surely, rent-seeking is not unique to the present historical period. Nonetheless, whereas in previous centuries the incumbent elites would engage in rent-seeking in order to preserve and expand their power, today rent-seeking can be carried out even by those who do not belong to the elites, but are simply in search of privileges.

36 Some countries outside the Western world offer a different picture, featuring a culture that expects individuals to engage in productive entrepreneurial efforts despite the presence of extensive rent-seeking possibilities. The Japanese experience seems to suggest, however, that the rent-seeking system has ultimately eroded the pre-existing culture, and perhaps drawn Japan closer to Western Europe.

37 For the sake of clarity, we are not arguing that a dictatorial regime necessarily fares better. Rather, we suggest that there have been autocratic systems that are close enough to the first scenario (e.g. Singapore or Taiwan), and autocratic systems that have adopted moral traits typical of the second scenario (e.g. Fascist Italy).

38 Of course, progress also depends on the availability of financial resources, which may originate from government subsidies and from productive entrepreneurs (private companies). It is therefore to be expected that researchers are more likely to carry out their activities in societies that are characterized by large entrepreneurial communities and substantial government expenditure. However, the less the influence of the entrepreneurial element, the more the evolutionary processes governing the development of the research programmes suffer. When government subsidies are substantial, scientists devote their energies to capturing the favour of the policy-makers. As a result, the rent-seeking elements increase, while the error-correction mechanisms weaken and resources tend to be squandered in programmes with relatively modest economic value or initiatives that would have been undertaken all the same.

39 The purpose of subsidizing a project is to enable marginal and extra-marginal projects to see the light. In other words, intervention would be justified when a project is not profitable according to market criteria (it would be extra-marginal), but it would be beneficial according to social criteria. Instead, infra-marginal projects should be out of the picture since they would be viable anyway. As one may expect, however, the decision-maker is encouraged to select and finance infra-marginal projects, i.e. those who can prove to be successful beyond reasonable doubt (Wallsten 2000).

40 It is appropriate to remind the reader that there exists a difference between business cycles and business fluctuations. The former require the definition of a pattern of booms and troughs regularly spaced over time. They affect the world economy or at least a large enough economic region. The latter loosely identifies a situation in which macro-aggregates are unstable. Both definitions may be misleading, though. On the one hand, there are no business cycles: all theories pointing out in this direction have been falsified by reality. On the other, there are no broad-spectrum, business fluctuations other than those induced by external agents (legislators, monetary authorities), which can be more or less persistent according to the adjustment costs imposed by

regulation (Nickell 1986). Therefore, we shall use both terms indifferently in order to identify all non-random changes in aggregate production.

41 When prices are flexible, production may actually increase, as agents might react to unfavourable expectations by increasing their propensity to work, even if at a lower wage rate. The outcome may be declining prices with expanding physical production, which in turn enhances investment.

42 See Keynes (1920, 1926) and also his essay on the "Economic possibilities for our grandchildren", published in 1930, in which he predicts the end of capitalism.

43 In fact, corporatism, or a mild form of central planning, was presented as the ultimate safeguard against future crises. See for instance Rothbard (2000) and Higgs (1997) for the American case during the early years of the Great Depression.

44 If the price change is predictable, the crisis occurs because agents are systematically unable to incorporate those expectations in their decisions, an occurrence that belongs to the second group of crises and will be addressed in the next sub-section.

45 This is not a trivial point. If one accepts the notion of change, one necessarily accepts the notion of uncertainty. The future, therefore, is either a succession of lucky and unlucky events, or luck simply refers to events that do not depend on economic interaction, e.g. the weather. Put differently, would a company qualify for help whenever relative prices change – i.e. virtually every day? And would the size of help change accordingly?

46 The beneficiaries are those whose terms of trade have improved: Whenever there is a change in the terms of trade, there are winners (for whom relative prices have gone up) and losers (for whom prices have gone down).

Closed, highly regulated communities are the prime potential losers, either because of the protectionist policies enforced, or because of the institutional context at large, which may for instance prevent firms from growing and "going global".

47 To be precise, the price change makes some past investment a bad choice. That is why some companies go bust. A favourable behavioural adjustment supplies the necessary resources to create new production capacity. However, lack of vision, of incentives or of institutional flexibility often prevents entrepreneurs from doing so, leading to permanently lower output. Once again, policy-makers have a point in advocating intervention in order to reverse the behavioural crisis. Still, bureaucrats and politicians are no entrepreneurs and they often fail to select winners. In fact, the bureaucratic process all but makes sure that the losers are preferred. As we have seen, in these cases a behavioural adjustment becomes a behavioural crisis.

48 To be fair, in many cases such state authorities lament that they do not have the police powers needed to carry out their assignment. It is a weak line of defence, though. If unable to perform his/her duty, a candidate to the board of directors of the agency should turn down the appointment. If the appointment turns out to be "irresistible", the agency should nevertheless declare publicly that its statement is unreliable. Last but not least, it should be observed that even if in some countries such agencies cannot exercise police powers, they can nonetheless prevent opaque companies from operating. Granting permission is equivalent to certification, which involves the assumption of responsibility.

49 In truth, these educational shortcomings cannot be ascribed only to the state's dominating position. Even when the resources are available and the rules of the game allow, potential free-market supporters have shied away from engaging in large scale educational programmes targeting the new generations. Clearly, some free-market supporters of intellectual entrepreneurship have fallen down on their jobs and failed to provide much needed educational variety.

50 See also Horwitz (2003), who draws on the insights suggested by the public choice, the Austrian and the new institutional approaches in order to emphasize the redistributive and rent-seeking costs of inflation; and Garrison (2006), who shows that today's allegedly "neutral" monetary policies are in fact not neutral at all.

51 See Buchanan (1979: chapter 5).

9 Poverty and transition

1 Although popular and commonly accepted, this definition rules out the possibility that all existing economies are undeveloped. Yet, one may easily imagine situations in which the technology allows higher living standards, but the institutional context generates incentives that prevent agents from exploiting the potential. For example, the price system might distort the allocation of resources, or the rules of the game might thwart productive entrepreneurship. If one considers the manifest advances in technology that occurred during the past decade and the GDP performance of several "developed" Western economies, doubts about the position of these countries with respect to their potential/frontiers seem justified.

2 See however Teitel (1981), who calls attention to the size and role of local R&D activities.

3 More recently, a large empirical literature pioneered by Easterly *et al.* (2004) and recently confirmed by Doucouliagos and Paldam (2009), has supported Bauer's insights by casting serious doubts on the effectiveness of aid. Dovern and Nunnenkamp (2007) are less pessimistic, but only for some specific categories of aid.

4 The literature is not so razor-sharp. In particular, according the so-called "conditional-convergence" hypothesis, all undeveloped countries eventually converge towards a frontier defined by their specific features. For instance, Mankiw *et al.* (1992) draws attention to investment and education, while Gwartney *et al.* (2006) focuses on institutions (economic freedom). We observe, however, that once the frontier becomes country-specific, catching-up is always successful, and the gap can always be explained by institutions (or some other "critical" variable). In contrast with the "conditional-convergence" hypothesis, we maintain that as long as catching-up means chasing and reaching the front runners, failure to adopt suitable institutions, including satisfactory education, is part of the inability to catch up. Thus, there is no conditional catching-up; but merely successful transition or aborted transition.

5 In theory, since the focus is on institutional change, transition may also regard affluent economies, as well as countries in which the new rules of the game are not necessarily intended to promote fast growth. To simplify, however, we shall accept the standard meaning of this term, according to which transition actually means "transition to market". Hence, transition is usually accompanied by promises and hopes for better economic performance and is bound to fail whenever the essence of the market mechanisms is not understood or such mechanisms are simply rejected.

6 By the term "poverty", we shall define economies characterized by a GDP per capita inferior to that of developed countries. Unfortunately, this definition misses all the nuances possibly suggested by courtesy and political correctness, and it also neglects the fact that developed countries include many individuals living in dire conditions, while rich people are surely present in poor countries. Yet, our general definition is preferable for practical purposes, in that it bars all ambiguities regarding catching up: either it takes place or it does not, with no further taxonomic investigation into the different degrees of partiality.

7 See in particular Sections 3.4.3 and 3.4.4.

8 Adamo (2009) examines the historical and epistemic factors that explain why an idea can fail to become "cultural", and thus remains part of only some individuals' psychological patterns.

9 From a different standpoint, one may observe that the prevalence of desires over morality – sometimes defined as the decline of culture – is indeed one of the key worries of the critics of globalization, who do not deny that individuals have values and preferences even in a globalized world, but who underline that people do not have "specific enough" values and preferences, as if national or local differentiation were a

merit good per se. Somewhat ironically, the very advocates of restrained globalization are among the major supporters of political correctness, which is also a way of bridling specific cultural traits and encouraging conformism and opportunism.

More importantly, however, we believe that globalization does not affect culture. Rather, it reflects the consequences of a trait typical of open cultural fabrics – tolerance. It then follows that globalization cannot be a threat to any particular culture. Rather, it is the effect of cultural components (openness and lack of prejudice), combined with new technological opportunities (cheap transport and communication).

10 See our previous discussion in Sections 3.3.1 and 3.3.2. Environments characterized by "individualistic societies" and "no societies" are surely consistent with the radical Austrian approach, according to which culture is not a very useful notion (Menger 1883, Hoppe 1994). Yet, it is hard to mention the rule of law – even in its simplest form (credibility and stability of the rules of the game) – and ignore its origins. As shown in Hansson (2009), over two decades of investigation in this direction have concluded that only religion plays a clearly important role in creating the rule of law. More work is probably required in order to detect eventual additional variables and articulate the mechanisms of interaction.

11 See Paldam and Gundlach (2008) for a recent survey of the literature analysing the direction of causality between growth and institutional change.

12 See Arndt (1987) and Dam (2006) for a more detailed survey of the economics of development during the second part of the twentieth century.

13 For instance, in August 2006 a World Bank agency (IEG) summarized its report on primary education titled "From schooling access to learning outcomes: an unfinished agenda" as follows:

> learning outcomes were *underemphasized* in country programs and Bank support. … Among the projects examined in detail, three quarters included objectives to *improve student enrollments*, but less than one quarter had *learning outcomes* objectives. Over 90 percent of these projects had *improving quality* in their objectives, but until recently this objective has mostly meant providing materials, training, and technical assistance to educational systems rather than ensuring improved student learning (italics in the original).

IEG concludes in its key message that "Despite success with increased primary enrollment, more attention is needed to make sure children are actually learning".

14 Well-known international examples of such wastages are offered by many governmental programmes and institutional agencies.

15 See for instance Lamoreaux and Rosenthal (2005), Pollin and Vaubourg (2006) and also Dam (2006). From a different perspective, Zweigert and Kötz (1998: 67) call attention to the questionable meaning of the traditional classification:

> instead of basing categorizations so much on historical development, legal content or the observable techniques of the rules of law, one should inquire whether countries have the same legal culture, that is, whether its citizens have similar attitudes to law and similar expectations of it.

16 See for instance Mijiyawa (2008). More generally, the Commission on Growth and Development (2008) also emphasizes the crucial role of leadership, which is responsible for garnering consensus and conceiving of virtuous compromises to ensure that good government is consistent with the local traditions and expectations.

17 By "freedom" De Soto refers to political freedom (freedom of movement, of expression, of association), not economic freedom. Though a determined classical liberal, Pejovich (2008: ix) argues in a similar (consequentialist) vein. In his view, one should "not advocate capitalism on philosophical or ideological grounds. … In free societies, those decisions should be made by individuals in accordance with their values and beliefs. My key purpose is to explain why the system has done so well".

18 An exclusive group is one that has a rather stable composition, to which new members can gain access only by discretionary co-opting by the incumbents. For instance, in dictatorial regimes the leader chooses those to be rewarded with powerful and lucrative positions in society. Instead, an open rent-seeking group is one to which new members can gain access without resorting to violence. For example, in a Western democracy that applies to producers that benefit from a tariff against foreign imports or from a highly regulated labour market.

19 To give a more complete account of Tullock's argument, rule-makers can also exploit interest groups in two other ways. They can threaten to deregulate an industry and thus elicit action by those who see their privileges put in jeopardy. Rule-makers can also announce the possible introduction of privileges and then fail to deliver under the pressure of the coalitions that would suffer as a consequence.

20 See Coyne and Leeson (2004) for a different view, according to which the media serve the purpose of making governments accountable, rather than of opening people's eyes to missed opportunities. We believe that accountability surely applies to the developed world, but much less to the poor, who know well about being victim to abuse and violence.

21 Geographical peculiarities are twofold. They may reflect the lack of cultural homogeneity in a given area, so that political fragmentation would mean patchy units characterized by endless bickering over sovereignty, stoked by ethnic or historical justifications. In addition, the origin of trouble may also come from the presence of natural resources, which are bound to be claimed by all the components of the political entity to be dismantled.

22 An exception is provided by situations in which a goal-driven attitude is associated with tolerance – because tolerance poses no threat to the shared goals. In these cases political fragmentation may be feasible and obtain acceptable solutions, possibly leading to some kind of transition.

23 It would be inappropriate to use the expression "cultural change", since it takes time before new behavioural routines generate a culture. But that does not prevent a cultural system from being shattered in a very limited number of years, as witnessed by a number of major revolutions. Anecdotal evidence suggests that something similar also happened within the Soviet bloc in the 1980s, when the import of technology from the West made the "Eastern" elites aware of the fact that communism and central planning were leading to manifest technological backwardness. Apparently, the consequences on personal dispositions and convictions were dramatic: deep and generalized. A similar identity crisis probably characterized the Red Army at the end of the (inglorious) war in Afghanistan.

24 Balcerowicz (2007: 31) uses this expression to describe situations in which "market reforms were linked – objectively and in the public's perception – to some important non-economic goals, like entering the EU or preserving independence (e.g. the Baltics)".

25 See Ialnazov and Nenovsky (2011), who compare the features of a non-cooperative behaviour modelled after the prisoner's dilemma, with those of a cooperative behaviour typical of a stag-hunt game.

26 The "almost" is justified by the remote possibility that the educational system broadly understood (school, family, friends) is already geared – prior to the beginning of transition or in its very early stages – to shaping the new psychological patterns of the young and re-shaping those of the old.

27 As pointed out in the previous chapter (see in particular Section 8.5.3), and contrary to common parlance, the key to growth in difficult times is the ability to mobilize resources (extensive growth). Intensive growth, on the other hand, may produce results in the short run, but it carries in itself the seeds of rent-seeking pressures fed by uncertainty and fears of unemployment.

28 Surely, redistribution does not necessarily imply the existence of centralized

educational systems, let alone with monopoly power. The well-known voucher systems are an example.
29 This probably occurs more easily in large countries, where central control is less effective and more opportunities for educational entrepreneurial attempts are present. India may be a good example of these situations.
30 See Madison's point in Federalist 51.

10 Final remarks on the economic way of thinking

1 The only exception is the consumption of gifts and public goods: they refer to situations in which somebody else has made a sacrifice in our stead.
2 See for instance Stringham and Gonzalez (2009), who summarize and discuss the Austrian view on factual analysis.
3 As pointed out earlier (see for instance Section 5.3.2), natural resources can be thought of as nobody's original property, and thus subject to the rule of first occupancy. But should natural resources be given by God to mankind (collective property), then private property would only be a device the community uses in order to reduce conflict and enhance productivity. In the former context, therefore, encroaching upon private property is always an act of violence. On the other hand, encroachment in the latter environment is legitimate insofar as it reduces tensions, does not undermine stability and enhances social welfare.
4 Spontaneous order and respect for custom and tradition were not warranted. For example, the common-law courts were originally involved only when the interests of the Crown were at stake. Thus, the presence of the "state" in the common-law system was far from marginal. Surely, with the passing of time, common-law courts were referred to even when the monarch was no longer directly involved. But the main principle was upheld: common-law justice was pragmatic, it was based on rules established by a centralized administration and it prevailed because rulings were enforced by a credible and powerful authority.

More generally, the legal environment typical of the Gregorian Centuries, which was characterized by the presence of different competing legal systems, was gradually dismantled as a result of two concurrent phenomena. First, the secular ruler found the existence of legal systems beyond his control barely tolerable. Not only did the independence of such systems threaten to weaken his taxing and regulatory power, but absent a state monopoly on justice, it threatened the very notion of secular authority. Second, as trade relations grew less personal, reputation was less effective as a self-enforcing mechanism. Hence, the threat of punishment inflicted by means of violence became more important than the damage provoked by the loss of standing. As a result, a legal system proposed or monitored by an effective enforcer (the secular ruler) was definitely more appealing than other systems which were possibly more effective and with default rules tailored to the specific needs of the parties involved, but less credible in terms of enforcement. See also Hogue (1966), David and Jauffret-Spinosi (2002), as well as our remarks in Section 7.3.1.
5 The debate on the role and legitimacy of judicial review is typical of the United States. See for instance Bennett and Solum (2011) and Calabresi and Fine (2008), in which the debate between the "original-intent" and the "living Constitution" advocates is analysed in greater detail. See also Napolitano (2004, 2006), who provides convincing evidence of the ease with which the Supreme Court "interprets" the letter and principles of the US Constitution.

In most other countries the problem does not exist, in that constitutions were not considered an instrument to protect the citizen from encroachment by the state, but rather broad definitions of what policy-makers should pursue (the common good) and procedures for renewal through periodic elections and for making the governmental machinery operational.

6 See Hartwell (1995: 197–198), who refers to liberalism in the European, classical-liberal sense.

7 See for instance Bhagwati (2000) and Stiglitz (2002) for two slightly different views within the mainstream (neoclassical) tradition. A more cautious view was suggested by Dembinski (2004) and Cohen (2004), who took an individualistic and a holistic stance, respectively. All such authors would consider themselves free-market advocates (more or less broadly defined).

8 It is worth underscoring that this notion of a priori differs from the Austrian use of the term. Austrian a prioris refer to individual preferences and behaviour (rationality) and serve a positive scope: analysing causal mechanisms. In our context, a prioris serve a normative purpose, in that they establish whether an act is acceptable, i.e. legitimate.

The view proposed in these pages, therefore is neither neoclassical, nor Austrian. As a matter of fact, we question the validity of the rationality assumption, which is rejected even as a necessary simplification, and which is replaced by an appeal to consciousness and therefore to an interdisciplinary approach. Such an interdisciplinary approach is openly rejected by neoclassical and Austrian scholars. The former argue that all social sciences are in the end subject to economic analysis. Thus, they substitute (economic) imperialism for interdisciplinarity. The latter maintain that economics is about rational behaviour, rather than about human behaviour; that preferences are determined before economic action occurs; that no significant feed-back mechanism is in place; and that rationality is a synonym for consistency between preferences and action.

9 As a matter of fact, "economic" freedom (freedom to choose and exchange) was often considered synonymous or highly correlated with "political" freedom (freedom to vote and to express opinions).

10 According to Amartya Sen, the so-called "human capability approach" is the answer to the impossibility of conceiving of welfare economics in the absence of arbitrary decision-making. In particular, the human capability approach aspires to establish "the acceptable priorities between personal liberty and overall desire fulfilment, and ... the information regarding the trade-offs on this that the persons may themselves endorse" (Sen 1999: 364). Thus, compulsory redistribution programmes would be based on the Aristotelian right to "flourish" through active participation in the social context. Of course, by assuming that the individual can only flourish within a society, one has to address the problem of establishing the best society for the flourishing of the individual. The answer was to be offered by king-philosophers in ancient Greece, by elected politicians in modern democracies. As we pointed out earlier, the neo Aristotelian position would draw different conclusions.

11 As the reader may recall from Chapter 2, we defined the neoclassical paradigm as a set of solutions to constrained maximization problems under certainty. Its extended version includes the optimal design of the ideal formal institutional arrangements that make the solution possible.

12 See for instance Pejovich (2008), who effectively exemplifies the conventional classical-liberal position.

References

Abramovitz, M. (1986), "Catching up, forging ahead, and falling behind", *Journal of Economic History*, 46 (2), June: 385–406.

Adamo, S. (2009), "On the social diffusion of sophisticated ideas", *International Journal of Interdisciplinary Social Sciences*, 3 (10): pp. 193–201.

Adams, J. (1994), "Economy as instituted process: change, transformation, and progress", *Journal of Economic Issues*, 28 (2), June: 331–355.

Akerlof, G.A. and Shiller, R.J. (2009), *Animal Spirits*, Princeton and Oxford: Princeton University Press.

Alchian, A.A. (1950), "Uncertainty, evolution and economic theory", *Journal of Political Economy*, 58 (3), June: 211–221.

Alchian, A.A. and Demsetz, H. (1972), "Production, information costs, and economic organization", *American Economic Review*, 62 (5), December: 777–795.

Allsopp, C. and Kierzkowski, H. (1997), "The assessment: economics of transition in Eastern and Central Europe", *Oxford Review of Economic Policy*, 13 (2), Summer: 1–22.

Alvey, J.E. (1999), "A short history of economics as a moral science", *Journal of Markets and Morality*, 2 (1), Spring: 53–73.

Appleby, J. (2004 [1978]), *Economic Thought and Ideology in Seventeenth Century England*, Los Angeles: Figueroa.

Arndt, H. (1987), *Economic Development*, Chicago: University of Chicago Press.

Asimakopulos, A. (1978), "Keynesian economics, equilibrium, and time", *Canadian Journal of Economics*, 11 (supplement), November: S3–S10.

Ayyagari, M., Demirgüç-Kunt, A. and Maksimovic, V. (2006), "What determines protection of property rights?", *World Bank Policy Research Working Paper*, 3940, June.

Azzara, C. (2004), *Le Civiltà del Medioevo*, Bologna: Il Mulino.

Bacharach, M.O.L. (1999), "Interactive team reasoning: a contribution to the theory of co-operation", *Research in Economics*, 53 (2), June: 117–147.

Baechler, J. (2002), *Esquisse d'une Histoire Universelle*, Paris: Fayard.

Balcerowicz, L. (2007), "Institutions and convergence", *Studies and Analyses, Center for Social and Economic Research (CASE)*, 342, March.

Barkow, J.H., Cosmides, L. and Tooby, J. (1992), "Introduction: evolutionary psychology and conceptual integration", in J. Barkow, L. Cosmides and J. Tooby (eds), *The Adapted Mind*, Oxford: Oxford University Press: 3–15.

Barzel, Y. (1989), *Economic Analysis of Property Rights*, Cambridge: Cambridge University Press.

Basili, M. and Zappia, C. (2010), "Ambiguity and uncertainty in Ellsberg and Shackle", *Cambridge Journal of Economics*, 34 (3), May: 449–474.

Basu, K. (2000), *Prelude to Political Economy*, Oxford: Oxford University Press.

Bauer, P.T. (1974), "Foreign aid forever?", *Encounter*, 42: 15–29.

Bauer, P.T. (1991), *The Development Frontier*, London: Harvester Wheatsheaf.

Baumol, W.J. (1990), "Entrepreneurship: productive, unproductive, and destructive", *Journal of Political Economy*, 98 (5), October: 893–921.

Bennett, R.W. (2003), *Talking It Through: Puzzles of American Democracy*, Ithaca and London: Cornell University Press.

Bennett, R.W. and Solum, L.B. (2011), *Constitutional Originalism: A Debate*, Ithaca: Cornell University Press.

Benson, B.L. (1991), "An evolutionary contractarian view of primitive law: the institutions and incentives arising under customary law", *Review of Austrian Economics*, 5 (1), March: 41–65.

Benson, B.L. (1999), "An economic theory of the evolution of governance and the emergence of the state", *Review of Austrian Economics*, 12 (2), June: 131–160.

Bentham, J. (1843), *The Works of Jeremy Bentham*, published under the Superintendence of his Executor, John Bowring, 11 vols. Vol. 5, Edinburgh: William Tait, 1838–1843. Online, available at: http://oll.libertyfund.org/title/1996 (accessed 15 November 2010).

Beraldo, S. and Sugden, R. (2010), "The emergence of reciprocally beneficial cooperation", *ICER Working Papers*, 18.

Berkowitz, D., Pistor, K. and Richard, J.-F. (2003), "Economic development, legality, and the transplant effect", *European Economic Review*, 47 (1), February: 165–195.

Berman, H.J. (1983), *Law and Revolution*, Cambridge, MA: Harvard University Press.

Bhagwati, J. (2000), *The Wind of the Hundred Days*, Cambridge, MA: MIT Press.

Block, W.E. (1977), "Coase and Demsetz on private property rights", *Journal of Libertarian Studies*, 1 (2): 111–115.

Block, W.E. (2007), "Anarchism and minarchism, no rapprochement possible: reply to Tibor Machan", *Journal of Libertarian Studies*, 21 (1), Spring: 61–90.

Bobbitt, P.C. (2002), *The Shield of Achilles: War, Peace and the Course of History*, New York: Knopf.

Boettke, P.J., Coyne, C.J., Davis, J.B., Guala, F., Marciano, A., Runde, J. and Schabas, M. (2006), "Where economics and philosophy meet: review of the Elgar Companion to Economics and Philosophy with responses from the authors", *Economic Journal*, 116, June: F306–F325.

Boland, L.A. (1978), "Time in economics vs. economics in time: the 'Hayek Problem'", *Canadian Journal of Economics*, 11 (2), May: 240–262.

Borges, G. and Irlenbusch, B. (2007), "Fairness crowded out by law: an experimental study on withdrawal rights", *Journal of Institutional and Theoretical Economics*, 163 (1): 84–101.

Bostaph, S. (1994), "The Methodenstreit", in P. Boettke (ed.), *The Elgar Companion to Austrian Economics*, Cheltenham: Edward Elgar: 459–464.

Bouckaert, B. (2007), "The roots of our liberties: on the rise of civil society in the medieval West", *New Perspectives on Political Economy*, 3 (2): 139–184.

Bouillon, H. (2007), "Friedman's methodology of positive economics", *Journal for the New Europe*, 4 (1): 23–32.

Bouillon, H. (2011), *Business Ethics and the Austrian Tradition in Economics*, London: Routledge.

Bowles, S. (2006), "Social preferences and public economics: are good laws a substitute for good citizens?", *Quaderni del Dipartimento di Economia Politica, Università di Siena*, September.

Brabant, J. van (1993), "Lessons from the wholesale transformations in the East", *Comparative Economic Studies*, 35 (4), Winter: 73–102.

Brennan, G. and Buchanan, J.M. (1985), *The Reason of Rules*, Cambridge: Cambridge University Press.

Breton, A. (1996), *Competitive Governments: An Economic Theory of Politics and Public Finance*, Cambridge: Cambridge University Press.

Britton, C.R., Ford, R.K. and Gay, D.E.R. (2004), "Economic freedom, property rights, and the informal underground economy", *Journal of Private Enterprise*, 20: 86–99.

Buchanan, J.M. (1979), *What Should Economists Do?*, Indianapolis: Liberty Fund.

Buchanan, J.M. (1986), *Liberty, Market and State*, New York: New York University Press.

Buchanan, J.M. and Stubblebine, W.C. (1962), "Externality", *Economica*, 29 (116), November: 371–384.

Buchanan, J.M. and Tullock, G. (1962), *The Calculus of Consent*, Ann Arbor: University of Michigan Press.

Buckle, S. (1991), *Natural Law and the Theory of Property*, Oxford: Oxford University Press.

Cabantous, L. and Hilton, D.J. (2006), "De l'aversion à l'ambiguïté aux attitudes face à l'ambiguïté", *Revue Économique*, 57 (2), March: 259–280.

Calabresi, G. (1961), "Some thoughts on risk distribution and the law of torts", *Yale Law Journal*, 70 (4), March: 499–453.

Calabresi, G. (1968), "Transaction costs, resource allocation, and liability rules: a comment", *Journal of Law and Economics*, 11 (1), April: 63–73.

Calabresi, S.G. (2005), "Survey of books related to the law: the originalist and normative case against judicial activism: a reply to Professor Randy Barnett", *Michigan Law Review*, 103: 1080–1098.

Calabresi, S.G. and Fine, L. (2008), "Two cheers for professor Balkin's originalism", *Northwestern Public Law Research Paper*, 8–38.

Campagnolo, G. (2006), *Rothbard et l'École Austro-Américaine dans la Querelle de l'Herméneutique*, Lyon: ENS Éditions.

Campagnolo, G. (2009), "Origins of Menger's thought in French liberal economists", *Review of Austrian Economics*, 22 (1), March: 53–79.

Campagnolo, G. (2010), *Criticism of Classical Political Economy*, Abingdon: Routledge.

Caplan, B. (2007), *The Myth of the Rational Voter*, Princeton and Oxford: Princeton University Press.

Cardenas, J.C., Stranlund, J.K. and Willis, C.E. (2000), "Local environmental control and institutional crowding-out", *World Development*, 28 (10), October: 1719–1733.

Castellacci, F. (2007), "Evolutionary and new growth theories. Are they converging?", *Journal of Economic Surveys*, 21 (3), July: 585–627.

Chirot, D. (1991), "What happened in Eastern Europe in 1989?", in D. Chirot (ed.), *The Crisis of Leninism and the Decline of the Left*, Seattle: University of Washington Press: 3–32.

Clark, G. (2007), *A Farewell to Alms*, Princeton and Oxford: Princeton University Press.

Coase, R.H. (1937), "The nature of the firm", *Economica*, 4 (16), November: 386–405.

Coase, R.H. (1960), "The problem of social cost", *Journal of Law and Economics*, 3, October: 1–44.

Cohen, D. (2004), *La Mondialisation et ses Ennemis*, Paris: Grasset et Fasquelle.

Colombatto, E. (2007), "It was the rule of law. Will it be the rule of judges?", *Revue Économique*, 58 (6), November: 1163–1180.

Commission on Growth and Development (2008), *The Growth Report: Strategies for Sustained Growth and Inclusive Development*, Washington, DC: World Bank.

Commons, J.R. (1924), *Legal Foundations of Capitalism*, New York: The Macmillan Company.

Cooter, R.D. (1982), "The cost of Coase", *Journal of Legal Studies*, 11 (1), January: 1–33.

Cooter, R.D. (1987), "Coase theorem", in J. Eatwell, M. Milgate and P. Newman (eds), *The New Palgrave: A Dictionary of Economics*, London: Macmillan: 457–460.

Cowen, T. (2004), "How do economists think about rationality?", in M. Byron (ed.), *Satisficing and Maximizing: Moral Theorists on Practical Reason*, Cambridge: Cambridge University Press: 213–236.

Cowper, J.M. (ed.) (1975 [1872]), *The Selected Works of Robert Crowley*, Millwood, NY: Kraus Reprint Co.

Coyne, C.J. and Leeson, P.T. (2004), "Read all about it! Understanding the role of media in economic development", *Kyklos*, 57 (1): 21–44.

Cristiano, C. (2009), "Production knowledge: a Marshallian perspective on post-Coasian theories of the firm", *ICER Working Papers*, 11.

Czeglédi, P. and Kapás, J. (2009), *Economic Freedom and Development*, Budapest: Akadémiai Kiadó.

Dahlman, C.J. (1979), "The problem of externality", *Journal of Law and Economics*, 22 (1), April: 141–162.

Dam, K.W. (2006), *The Law-Growth Nexus*, Washington, DC: Brookings Institution Press.

Darwin, J. (2008), *After Tamerlane, the Rise and Fall of Global Empires, 1400–2000*, London: Penguin.

David, R. and Jauffret-Spinosi, C. (2002), *Les Grands Systèmes de Droit Contemporains*, Paris: Dalloz.

Davoine, L. (2009), "L'économie du bonheur: Quel intérêt pour les politiques publiques?", *Revue Économique*, 60 (4), July: 905–926.

Dawkins, C.R. (1976), *The Selfish Gene*, Oxford: Oxford University Press.

De Haan, J., Lundström, S. and Sturm, J.-E. (2006), "Market-oriented institutions and policies and economic growth: a critical survey", *Journal Economic Surveys*, 20 (2), April: 157–191.

Delumeau, J. (1983), *Le Péché et la Peur: La Culpabilisation en Occident (XIII–XVIII siècles)*, Paris: Fayard.

Dembinski, P.H. (2004), "From cracks in the liberal edifice to the rediscovery of the common good", *Journal of Markets and Morality*, 7 (2), Fall: 423–439.

De Soto, H. (2001 [2000]), *The Mystery of Capital*, London: Black Swan Books.

Demsetz, H. (1967), "Toward a theory of property rights", *American Economic Review*, 57 (2), May: 347–359.

Dewey, J. (1934), *A Common Faith*, New Haven: Yale University Press.

Doucouliagos, H. and Paldam, M. (2009), "The aid effectiveness literature: the sad results of 40 years of research", *Journal of Economic Surveys*, 23 (3), July: 433–461.

Dougherty, J.P. (2000), *Western Creed, Western Identity*, Washington, DC: Catholic University of America Press.

Dovern, J. and Nunnenkamp, P. (2007), "Aid and growth accelerations: an alternative approach to assessing the effectiveness of aid", *Kyklos*, 60 (3), August: 359–383.

Dunn, R.S. (1979), *The Age of Religious Wars 1559–1715*, second edition, New York: Norton & Co.

Dworkin, R.M. (1986), *Law's Empire*, Cambridge, MA: Belknap Press.

Easterly, W.R., Levine, R. and Roodman, D.M. (2004), "New data, new doubts: a comment on Burnside and Dollar's 'aid, policies, and growth' (2000)", *American Economic Review*, 94 (3), June: 774–780.

Eichengreen, B.J. (2007), *The European Economy since 1945*, Princeton and Oxford: Princeton University Press.

Ellickson, R.C. (1991), *Order without Law*, Cambridge, MA: Harvard University Press.

Ellman, M.J. (1997), "The political economy of transformation", *Oxford Review of Economic Policy*, 13 (2), Summer: 23–32.

Elmslie, B.T. (1994), "The endogenous nature of technological progress and transfer in Adam Smith's thought", *History of Political Economy*, 26 (4), Winter: 649–663.

Epstein, R.A. (1989), "The utilitarian foundations of natural law", *Harvard Journal of Law and Public Policy*, 12: 713–751.

Epstein, R.A. (1995), *Simple Rules for a Complex World*, Cambridge, MA: Harvard University Press.

Fehr, E. and List, J. (2004), "The hidden costs and returns of incentives: trust and trustworthiness among CEOs", *Journal of the European Economic Association*, 2 (5), September: 743–771.

Fiori, S. (2002), "Alternative visions of change in Douglass North's new institutionalism", *Journal of Economic Issues*, 36 (4): 1025–1043.

Fox, G. (2007), "The real Coase theorems", *Cato Journal*, 27 (3), Fall: 373–396.

Frank, R.H. (1988), *Passions within Reason*, New York and London: W.W. Norton & Company.

Freeman, J.R. and Snidal, D. (1982), "Diffusion, development and democratization: enfranchisement in Western Europe", *Canadian Journal of Political Science*, 15 (2), June: 299–329.

Frey, B. and Stutzer, A. (2002), "What can economists learn from happiness research?", *Journal of Economic Literature*, 490 (2), June: 402–435.

Friedman, M. (1953), "The methodology of positive economics", *Essays in Positive Economics*, Chicago: University of Chicago Press: 3–43.

Garrison, R.W. (2006), "Natural and neutral rates of interest in theory and policy formulation", *Quarterly Journal of Austrian Economics*, 9 (4), Winter: 57–68.

Gneezy, U. and Rustichini, A. (2000), "A fine is a price", *Journal of Legal Studies*, 29 (1), January: 1–17.

Goldstone, J.A. (2011), "The divergence of cultures: enlightenments and conservatism in Europe and the Old World", in D. Porter (ed.), *Comparative Early Modernities*, New York: Palgrave-Macmillan: forthcoming.

Grampp, W.D. (2000), "What did Smith mean by the invisible hand?", *Journal of Political Economy*, 108 (3), June: 441–465.

Greif, A. (2001), "How do self-enforcing institutions endogenously change? Institutional reinforcement and quasi-parameters", *mimeo*, Stanford University.

Greve, M. (2011), *The Structure of the Constitutions*, Cambridge, MA: Harvard University Press.

Gwartney, J.D., Holcombe, R.G. and Lawson, R.A. (2006), "Institutions and the impact of investment on growth", *Kyklos*, 59 (2), April: 255–273.

Habib, S.I. (2008), "Modern science and Islamic essentialism", *Economic and Political Weekly*, 6 September: 55–61.

Hamowy, R. (1981 [1961]), "Hayek's concept of freedom: a critique", in R. Raico, *New Individualist Review*, 1 (1), April: 28–31. Online, available at: http://oll.libertyfund.org/title/2136/195251 (accessed 20 September 2010).

Hansson, G. (2009), "What determines rule of law? An empirical investigation of rival models", *Kyklos*, 62 (3), August: 371–393.

Hardin, G.J. (1968), "The tragedy of the commons", *Science*, 162: 1243–1248.

Harnay, S. and Marciano, A. (2003), *R.A. Posner – L'Analyse Économique du Droit*, Paris: Michalon.

Harnay, S. and Marciano, A. (2007), "Intellectual property rights and judge-made law", in D. Porrini and G.B. Ramello (eds), *Property Rights Dynamics*, London and New York: Routledge: 198–218.

Harsanyi, J.C. (1955), "Cardinal welfare, individualistic ethics, and interpersonal comparisons of utility", *Journal of Political Economy*, 63 (4), August: 309–321.

Hartwell, R.M. (1995), *A History of the Mont Pèlerin Society*, Indianapolis: Liberty Fund.

Hayek, F.A. (1937), "Economics and knowledge", *Economica*, 4 (13), February: 33–54.

Hayek, F.A. (1945), "The use of knowledge in society", *American Economic Review*, 35 (4), September: 519–530.

Hayek, F.A. (1960), *The Constitution of Liberty*, Chicago: University of Chicago Press.

Hayek, FA. (1973), *Law, Legislation and Liberty – Rules and Order*, Chicago: University of Chicago Press.

Hayek, F.A. (1975), "The pretence of knowledge", Nobel Memorial Lecture, *Swedish Journal of Economics*, 77 (4), December: 433–442.

Hayek, F.A. (1976), *Law, Legislation and Liberty – The Mirage of Social Justice*, Chicago: University of Chicago Press.

Hayek, F.A. (1979), *Law, Legislation and Liberty – The Political Order of a Free People*, Chicago: University of Chicago Press.

Headey, D.D. (2008), "The principal components of growth in the less developed countries", *Kyklos*, 61 (4), November: 568–598.

Heckscher, E.F. (1994), *Mercantilism*, New York: Routledge.

Higgs, R. (1987), *Crisis and Leviathan*, New York: Oxford University Press.

Higgs, R. (1997), "Regime uncertainty: why the Great Depression lasted so long and why prosperity resumed after the war", *Independent Review*, 1 (4), Spring: 561–590.

Hodgson, G.M. (1989), "Institutional economic theory: the old versus the new", *Review of Political Economy*, 1 (3), November: 249–269.

Hodgson, G.M. (1993), *Economy as Evolution: Bringing Life back into Economics*, Cambridge: Blackwell Publishers.

Hodgson, G.M. (1998), "The approach of institutional economics", *Journal of Economic Literature*, 36, March 1998: 166–192.

Hodgson, G.M. (2004), *The Evolution of Institutional Economics*, London: Routledge.

Hogue, A.R. (1966), *Origins of the Common Law*, Bloomington: Indiana University Press.

Hohfeld, W.N. (1923), *Fundamental Legal Conceptions as Applied in Judicial Reasoning: And Other Legal Essay*, New Haven: Yale University Press.

Holcombe, R.G. (2004), "Government: unnecessary, but inevitable", *Independent Review*, VIII (2), Winter: 325–342.

Holcombe, R.G. (2007), *Entrepreneurship and Economic Progress*, New York and London: Routledge.

Holcombe, R.G. and Powell, B. (eds) (2008), *Housing America: Building out of a Crisis*, Oakland: Independent Institute.

Holler, M. (2006), "Adam Smith's Model of Man and Some of its Consequences", *Homo Oeconomicus*, 23 (3/4): 467–488.

Holmes, O.W. (1897), "The path of the law", *Harvard Law Review*, 10 (8), March: 457–478.

Hoppe, H.-H. (1994), "F.A. Hayek on government and social evolution: a critique", *Review of Austrian Economics*, 7 (1), March: 67–93.

Hoppe, H.-H. (2001), *Democracy – the God that Failed*, New Brunswick and London: Transaction Publishers.

Horwitz, S.G. (2003), "The costs of inflation revisited", *Review of Austrian Economics*, 16 (1), March: 77–95.

Huerta de Soto, J. (1998), "The ongoing Methodenstreit of the Austrian school", *Journal des Économistes et des Études Humaines*, 8 (1), March: 75–113.

Huerta de Soto, J. (2008), "El pensamiento económico en la antigua Grecia", *Procesos de Mercado: Revista Europea de Economía Política*, V (1), Primavera: 177–188.

Hume, David (2000a [1739]), *Treatise of Human Nature, Books 1 and 2*, edited by David Fate and Mary Norton, Oxford: Oxford University Press.

Hume, David (2000b [1740]), *Treatise of Human Nature, Book 3*, edited by David Fate and Mary Norton, Oxford: Oxford University Press.

Hutcheson, F. (1726), *An Inquiry into the Original of Our Ideas of Beauty and Virtue in Two Treatises*, ed. by Wolfgang Leidhold, published in Indianapolis: Liberty Fund, 2004. Online, available at: http://oll.libertyfund.org/title/858 (accessed 21 November 2010).

Ialnazov, D. and Nenovski, N. (2011), "A game theory interpretation of the Post-Communist Evolution", *Journal of Economic Issues*, XLV (I), March: 1–15.

Infantino, L. (2010), "Hayek and the evolutionary tradition against the Homo Oeconomicus", in W. Butos (ed.), *The Social Science of Hayek's "Sensory Order"*, Advances in Austrian Economics, vol. 13, Bingley: Emerald Group Publishing: 159–177.

Ingrao, B. and Israel, G. (1987), *La Mano Invisibile. L'Equilibrio Economico nella Storia della Scienza*, Bari: Laterza.

Jaffé, W. (1976), "Menger, Jevons and Walras de-homogenized", *Economic Inquiry*, 14 (4), December: 511–534.

James, H. (2009), *The Creation and Destruction of Value*, Cambridge, MA: Harvard University Press.

Jardine, L. (2008), *Going Dutch*, New York: HarperCollins Publishers.

Jasay, A. de (1991), *Choice, Contract, Consent: A Restatement of Liberalism*, London: Institute of Economic Affairs.

Jasay, A. de (2001), "Freedom, 'rights' and rights", *Il Politico*, 198 (3): 369–397.

Jasay, A. de (2002), *Justice and its Surroundings*, Indianapolis: Liberty Fund.

Jones, E.L. (2006), *Cultures Merging*, Princeton: Princeton University Press.

Jouvenel, B. de (1993), *On Power*, Indianapolis: Liberty Fund [Originally published as *Du Pouvoir: Histoire naturelle de sa croissance*, Geneva: Les Éditions du cheval ailé, 1945].

Jowitt, K. (1992), "The Leninist legacy", in I. Banac (ed.), *Eastern Europe in Revolution*, Ithaca: Cornell University Press: 207–224.

Kahneman, D., Knetsch, J.L. and Thaler, R.H. (1986), "Fairness as a constraint on profit seeking: entitlements in the market", *American Economic Review*, 76 (4), September: 728–741.

Kahneman, D., Knetsch, J.L. and Thaler, R.H. (1990), "Experimental tests of the endowment effect and the Coase theorem", *Journal of Political Economy*, 98 (6), December: 1325–1348.

Kahneman, D., Wakker, P.P. and Sarin, R.K. (1997), "Back to Bentham? Explorations of experienced utility", *Quarterly Journal of Economics*, 112 (2): 375–405.

Kasper, W. and Streit, M. (1998): *Institutional Economics. Social Order and Public Policy*, Cheltenham: Edward Elgar for the Locke Institute.

Katz, A.W. (2008), "Contractual enforcement institutions and the structure of information", *Journal of Institutional and Theoretical Economics*, 164 (1), March: 134–154.

Kay, J. (2003), *The Truth about Markets*, London: Penguin Books.

Keynes, J.M. (1920), *The Economic Consequences of the Peace*, New York: Harcourt, Brace and Howe. Online, available at: http://oll.libertyfund.org/title/303 (accessed 8 December 2010).

Keynes, J.M. (1921), *A Treatise on Probability*, London: Macmillan.

Keynes, J.M. (1926), *The End of Laissez-Faire*, London: Hogarth Press.

Keynes, J.M. (1973 [1936]), *The General Theory of Employment, Interest and Money*, London: MacMillan for the Royal Economic Society.

Knight, F.H. (1921), *Risk, Uncertainty and Profit*, Boston: Hart, Schaffner and Mark; Houghton Miffin Co.

Knights, L.C. (1937), *Drama and Society in the Age of Jonson*, London: Chatto and Windows.

Koch, R. and Smith, C. (2006), *Suicide of the West*, London and New York: Continuum.

Koselleck, R. (1979), *Vergangene Zukunft. Zur Semantik Geschichtlicher Zeiten*, Frankfurt aM: Suhrkamp Verlag.

Kühnel, M. (2001), *Das Politische Denken von Christian Thomasius*, Berlin: Duncker & Humblot.

Lachmann, L. (1983), "John Maynard Keynes: a view from an Austrian window", *South African Journal of Economics*, 51(3), September: 369–379.

Lachmann, L. (1986), *The Market as an Economic Process*, Oxford: Basil Blackwell.

Lamoreaux, N. and Rosenthal, J.-L. (2005), "Legal regime and contractual flexibility: a comparison of business's organizational choices in France and the United States during the era of industrialization", *American Law and Economics Review*, 7 (1), Spring: 28–61.

Lange, O.R. (1945–1946), "The scope and method of economics", *Review of Economic Studies*, 13 (1): 19–32.

Langlois, R.N. (1989), "What is wrong with the old institutional economics (and what is still wrong with the new)", *Review of Political Economy*, 1 (3), November: 270–298.

La Porta, R., Lopez-de-Silanes, F., Shleifer, A. and Vishny, R.W. (1997), "Legal determinants of external finance", *Journal of Finance*, 52 (3), July: 1131–1150.

La Porta, R., Lopez-de-Silanes, F., Shleifer, A. and Vishny, R.W. (1998), "Law and finance", *Journal of Political Economy*, 106 (6), December: 1113–1150.

Leoni, B. (1961), *Freedom and the Law*, Princeton: Van Norstrand Company.

Lewis, C.S. (2001 [1944]), *The Abolition of Man*, New York: HarperCollins.

Libecap, G.D. (1989a), *Contracting for Property Rights*, Cambridge: Cambridge University Press.

Libecap, G.D. (1989b), "Distributional issues in contracting for property rights", *Journal of Institutional and Theoretical Economics*, 145 (1): 6–24.

Liebermann, Y. and Syrquin, M. (1983), "On the use and abuse of rights: an economic view", *Journal of Economic Behaviour and Organization*, 4 (1), March: 25–40.

Liggio, L.P. and Chafuen, A.A. (2004), "Cultural and religious foundations of private property", in E. Colombatto (ed.), *The Elgar Companion to the Economics of Property Rights*, Cheltenham: Edward Elgar: 3–47.

Lin, J.Y. (2005), "Viability, economic transition and reflection on neoclassical economics", *Kyklos*, 58 (2), April: 239–264.

Lipsey, R.G., Carlaw, K.I. and Bekar, C.T. (2005), *Economic Transformations*, Oxford: Oxford University Press.

McCloskey, D.N. (1998), *The Rhetoric of Economics*, 2nd edition, Madison: University of Wisconsin Press.

McGinnis, J. and Rappaport, M. (2007), "Majority and supermajority rules: three views of the Capitol", *Texas Law Review*, 85 (5), April: 1115–1183.

Macey, J.R. (1998), "Henry Manne", in P. Newman (ed.), *The New Palgrave Dictionary of Economics and the Law*, London: Macmillan Reference: 609–611.

Macey, J.R. (2008), *Corporate Governance: Promises Kept, Promises Broken*, Princeton: Princeton University Press.

Machan, T.R. (2004), *Putting Humans First*, New York: Rowman & Littlefield Publishers.

Mackaay, E. and Rousseau, S. (2008), *Analyse Économique du Droit*, Paris: Dalloz.

Maddison, A. (2005), "Measuring and interpreting world economic performance 1500–2001", *Review of Income and Wealth*, 51 (1), March: 1–35.

Mahoney, P.G. (2001), "The common law and economic growth: Hayek might be right", *Journal of Legal Studies*, 30: 503–525.

Mankiw, N.G., Romer, D.H. and Weil, D.N. (1992), "A contribution to the empirics of economic growth", *Quarterly Journal of Economics*, 107 (2), May: 407–438.

Manne, H.G. (1965), "Mergers and the market for corporate control", *Journal of Political Economy*, 73 (2), April: 110–120.

Manne, H.G. (1993), *An Intellectual History of the George Mason University School of Law*, Law and Economics Center, George Mason University.

Manne, H.G. (2005), "How law and economics was marketed in a hostile world: a very personal history", in F. Parisi and Ch. Rowley (eds), *The Origins of Law and Economics*, Cheltenham: Edward Elgar for the Locke Institute: 309–327.

Marangos, J. (2005), "A political economy approach to the neoclassical gradualist model of transition", *Journal of Economic Surveys*, 19 (2), April: 263–293.

Marangos, J. (2009), "The evolution of the term 'Washington Consensus'", *Journal of Economic Surveys*, 23 (2), April: 350–384.

Marchionatti, R. (2007), "On the application of mathematics to political economy. The Edgeworth–Walras–Bortkievicz controversy, 1889–1891", *Cambridge Journal of Economics*, 31 (2), March: 291–307.

Marciano, A. (2006), "David Hume's model of man: classical political economy as 'inspired' political economy", *Review of Social Economy*, LXIV, 3, September: 369–386.

Marciano, A. (2007), "Value and exchange in law and economics: Buchanan versus Posner", *Review of Austrian Economics*, 20 (2–3), September: 187–200.

Marciano, A. (2010), "Calabresi, 'law and economics' and the Coase theorem", *ICER Working Papers*, 26.

Margolis, H. (1982), *Selfishness, Altruism, and Rationality*, Chicago and London: University of Chicago Press.

Meadows, D.H., Meadows, D.L., Randers, J. and Behrens, W.W. III (1972), *The Limits to Growth*, New York: Universe Books.

Medema, S.G. and Zerbe, R.O. (2000), "The Coase theorem", in B. Bouckaert and G. de Geest, *Encyclopedia of Law and Economics*, Cheltenham: Edward Elgar: 836–892.

Meisel, N. and Ould Aoudia, J. (2008), "L'insaisissable relation entre 'bonne gouvernance' et développement", *Revue Économique*, 59 (6), November: 1159–1191.

Menger, C. (1883), *Untersuchungen über die Methode der Socialwissenschaften, und der Politischen Oekonomie insbesondere*, Leipzig: Duncker & Humblot.

Mercuro, N. and Medema, S.G. (2006), *Economics and the Law: From Posner to Post-Modernism and Beyond*, Princeton: Princeton University Press.

Metcalfe, J.S. (2003), "Industrial growth and the theory of retardation; precursors of an adaptive evolutionary theory of economic change", *Revue Économique*, 54 (2), March: 407–431.

Mijiyawa, A.G. (2008), "Sustained economic growth: do institutions matter, and which one prevails?", *Cato Journal*, 28 (3), Fall: 385–420.

Milhaupt, C.J. and Pistor, K. (2008), *Law and Capitalism: what Corporate Crises Reveal about Legal Systems and Economic Development around the World*, Chicago: University of Chicago Press.

Mill, J.S. (1879 [1859]), *On Liberty and the Subjection of Women*, New York: Henry Holt and Co. Online, available at: http://oll.libertyfund.org/title/347 (accessed 20 September 2010).

Mill, J.S. (1977 [1832]), "Introductory", in the Collected Works of John Stuart Mill, Vol XVIII – *Essay on Politics and Society*, Part I, ed. John M. Robson, Toronto and London: University of Toronto Press, and Routledge and Kegan Paul. Online, available at: http://oll.libertyfund.org/title/233 (accessed 4 October 2010).

Mises, L. von (1963 [1949]), *Human Action*, San Francisco: Fox and Wilkes, in cooperation with the Foundation for Economic Education.

Misselden, E. (1623), *The Circle of Commerce or the Balance of Trade, in Defence of Free Trade*, London: John Dawson, for Nicholas Bourne.

Müller-Armack, A. (1950), "Soziale Irenik", *Weltwirtschaftliches Archiv*, 64: 181–203.

Napolitano, A.P. (2004), *Constitutional Chaos: What Happens when the Government Breaks its Own Laws*, Nashville: Nelson Current.

Napolitano, A.P. (2006), *Constitution in Exile: How the Federal Government Has Seized Power by Rewriting the Supreme Law of the Land*, Nashville: Nelson Current.

Nemo, P. (2004), *Qu'est-ce que l'Occident?*, Paris: Presses Universitaires de France.

Nicita, A. (2007), "On incomplete property", in D. Porrini and G.B. Ramello (eds), *Property Rights Dynamics*, London and New York: Routledge: 77–90.

Nickell, S.J. (1986), "Dynamic models of labour demand", in O. Ashenfelter and R. Layard (eds), *Handbook of Labour Economics*, vol 1, Amsterdam: North Holland: 473–522.

Norberg, J. (2009), *Financial Fiasco: How America's Infatuation with Homeownership and Easy Money Created the Economic Crisis*, Washington, DC: Cato Institute.

North, D.C. (1990), *Institutions, Institutional Change and Economic Performance*, Cambridge: Cambridge University Press.

North, D.C. (1994), "Economic performance through time", *American Economic Review*, 84 (3), June: 359–368.

North, G.K. (2002), "Undermining property rights: Coase and Becker", *Journal of Libertarian Studies*, 16 (4), Fall: 75–100.

Okun, A.M. (1971), "Should GNP measure social welfare?", *The Brookings Bulletin*, 8 (3), Summer: 4–7.

Olson, M.L. (1982), *The Rise and Decline of Nations*, New Haven and London: Yale University Press.

Opper, S. (2004), "The political economy of privatization: empirical evidence from transition countries", *Kyklos*, 57 (4), November: 559–586.

Paldam, M. and Gundlach, E. (2008), "Two views on institutions and development: the grand transition vs. the primacy of institutions", *Kyklos*, 61 (1), February: 5–100.

Pareto, V. (1897), *Cours d'Économie Politique*, Lausanne: F. Rouge Éditeur.

Parisi, F. (2005), "Methodological debates in law and economics: the changing contours of a discipline", in F. Parisi and Ch. Rowley (eds), *The Origins of Law and Economics*, Cheltenham: Edward Elgar for the Locke Institute: 33–52.

Patinkin, D. (1976), "Keynes and econometrics: on the interaction between the macroeconomic revolutions of the interwar period", *Econometrica*, 44 (6), November: 1091–1123.

Pejovich, S. (1999), "The effect of the interaction of formal and informal institutions on social stability and economic development", *Journal of Markets and Morality*, 2 (2): 164–181.

Pejovich, S. (2008), *Law, Informal Rules and Economic Performance*, Cheltenham: Edward Elgar.

Pelikán, P. (2010), "The government economic agenda in a society of unequally rational individuals", *Kyklos*, 63 (2), May: 231–255.

Poirot, C.S. (1993), "Institutions and economic evolution", *Journal of Economic Issues*, 27 (3), September: 887–907.

Pollin, J.-P. and Vaubourg, A.-G. (2006), "Environnement juridique et systèmes de gouvernance", *Revue Économique*, 57 (4): 919–940.

Pomeranz, K. (2000), *The Great Divergence*, Princeton: Princeton University Press.

Posner, R.A. (1975), "The economic approach to law", *Texas Law Review*, 53, May: 757–782.

Posner, R.A. (1985), "Wealth maximization revisited", *Notre Dame Journal of Law, Ethics and Public Policy*, 2 (1), Fall: 85–106.

Posner, R.A. (2007), *Economic Analysis of Law*, seventh edition, New York: Aspen Publishers.

Rasmussen, D.B. and Uyl, D.J. den (2005), *Norms of Liberty*, University Park: Pennsylvania State University Press.

Rawls, John B. (1971), *A Theory of Justice*, Oxford: Oxford University Press.

Ricossa, S. (1986), *La Fine dell'Economia*, Milano: Sugarco Edizioni.

Ridley, M.W. (1996), *The Origins of Virtue*, London: Penguin Books.

Riley, P. (ed.) (1972), *Leibniz – Political Writings*, Cambridge: Cambridge University Press.

Rizzo, M.J. (1979/1980), "The mirage of efficiency", *Hofstra Law Review*, 8: 641–658.

Rizzo, M.J. (2008), "Justice versus benevolence: a modern Humean view", *Minnesota Journal of Law, Science and Technology*, 9 (2), Spring: 883–898.

Rizzo, M.J. and Whitman, D.G. (2009), "The knowledge problem of new paternalism", *Brigham Young University Law Review*, 4: 905–968.

Robbins, L.C. (1932), *Essay on the Nature and Significance of Economic Science*, London: MacMillan.

Robinson, J.A., Verdier, T. and Torvik, R. (2006), "Political foundations of the resource curse", *Journal of Development Economics*, 79 (2), April: 447–468.

Rosenberg, N. (1994), *Exploring the Black Box*, Cambridge: Cambridge University Press.

Rostow, W.W. (1991), "Eastern Europe and the Soviet Union: a technological time warp", in D. Chirot (ed.), *The Crisis of Leninism and the Decline of the Left*, Seattle: University of Washington Press: 60–73.

Rothbard, M.N. (1982), "Law, property rights and air pollution", *Cato Journal*, 2 (1), Spring: 55–99.

Rothbard, M.N. (1995), *Classical Economics*, Cheltenham: Edward Elgar.

Rothbard, M.N. (2000 [1963]), *America's Great Depression*, Auburn: Ludwig von Mises Institute.

Rowley, C.K. (2005), "An intellectual history of law and economics: 1739–2003", in F. Parisi and Ch. Rowley (eds), *The Origins of Law and Economics*, Cheltenham: Edward Elgar for the Locke Institute: 3–32.

Sacco, R. (2007), *Antropologia Giuridica*, Bologna: Il Mulino.

Say, J.-B. (2006 [1852]), *Cours Complet d'Économie Politique Pratique*, Chestnut Hill: Elibron Classic Series.

Schabas, M. (2005), *The Natural Origins of Economics*, Chicago: University of Chicago Press.

Schlicht, E. (1998), *On Custom in the Economy*, Oxford: Oxford University Press.

Schoeck, H. (1966), *Envy: A Theory of Social Behavior*, New York: Irvington Publisher.

Schumpeter, J.A. (1946), "John Maynard Keynes", *American Economic Review*, 36 (4), September: 495–518.

Sen, A.K. (1977), "A critique of the behavioral foundations of economic theory", *Philosophy and Public Affairs*, 6 (4), Summer: 317–344.

Sen, A.K. (1999), "The possibility of social choice", *American Economic Review*, 89 (3), June: 349–378.

Setterfield, M. (1993), "A model of institutional hysteresis", *Journal of Economic Issues*, 27 (3), September: 755–774.

Shane, S. (2003), *General Theory of Entrepreneurship*, Cheltenham: Edward Elgar.

Sima, J. (2004), "Praxeology as law and economics", *Journal of Libertarian Studies*, 18 (2), Spring: 73–89.

Smith, A. (1982 [1759]), *The Theory of Moral Sentiments*, D.D. Raphael and A.L. Macfie (eds), vol. I of the Glasgow Edition of the Works and Correspondence of Adam Smith, Indianapolis: Liberty Fund. Online, available at: http://oll.libertyfund.org/title/192 (accessed 8 December 2010).

Smith, A. (1981 [1776]), *An Inquiry into the Nature and Causes of the Wealth of Nations*, vol. 1, R.H. Campbell and A.S. Skinner (eds), vol. I and II of the Glasgow Edition of the Works and Correspondence of Adam Smith, Indianapolis: Liberty Fund. Online, available at: http://oll.libertyfund.org/title/220 and title/200 (accessed 8 December 2010).

Smith, A., Wagner, R.E. and Yandle, B. (2010), "A theory of entangled political economy, with application to TARP and NRA", *George Mason University Papers*, Department of Economics, no. 10–22.

Sowell, T. (1967), "The 'evolutionary' economics of Thorstein Veblen", *Oxford Economics Papers*, 19 (2), July: 177–198.

Stark, R. (2006), *The Victory of Reason*, New York: Random House.

Stein, P.G. (1980), *Legal Evolution. The Story of an Idea*, Cambridge: Cambridge University Press.

Stevenson, B. and Wolfers, J. (2008), "Economic growth and subjective well-being: reassessing the Easterlin paradox", *NBER Working Paper Series*, 14282, August.

Stigler, G.J. (1966), *The Theory of Price*, New York: Macmillan.

Stiglitz, J.E. (2002), *Globalization and its Discontents*, New York: W.W. Norton & Company.

Stiglitz, J.E., Sen, A.K. and Fitoussi, J.-P. (2009), *Report by the Commission on the Measurement of Economic Performance and Social Progress*. Online, available at: www.stiglitz-sen-fitoussi.fr/documents/rapport_anglais.pdf.

Stone, L. (1965), *The Crisis of the Aristocracy 1558–1641*, Oxford: Clarendon Press.

Strayer, J.R. (1970), *Medieval Origins of the Modern State*, Princeton: Princeton University Press.

Stringham, E.P. and Gonzalez, R. (2009), "The role of empirical assumptions in economic analysis: on facts and counterfactuals in economic law", *Journal des Économistes et des Études Humaines*, 15 (1), article 2. Online, available at: www.bepress.com/jeeh/vol. 15/iss1/art2.

Sugden, R. (1991), "Rational choice: a survey of contributions from economics and philosophy", *Economic Journal*, 101 (407), July: 751–785.

Tawney, R.H. (1926), *Religion and the Rise of Capitalism*, London: John Murray.

Taylor, J.B. (2009), *Getting Off Track*, Stanford, CA: Hoover Institution Press.

Teitel, R.G. (2000), *Transitional Justice*, Oxford: Oxford University Press.

Teitel, S. (1981), "Towards an understanding of technical change in semi-industrialized countries", *Research Policy*, 10 (2), July: 127–147.

Temin, P. (2006), "The economy of the early Roman empire", *Journal of Economic Perspectives*, 20 (1), Winter: 133–151.

Tierney, B., Kagan, D. and Pearce Williams, L. (eds) (1992), *Great Issues in Western Civilization*, 2 vols, New York: McGraw-Hill.

Tillyard, E.M. (1943), *The Elizabethan World Picture*, London: Chatto & Windus.

Tönnies, F. (2001 [1887]), *Community and Civil Society*, London: Cambridge University Press.

Trivers, R.L. (1971), "The evolution of reciprocal altruism", *Quarterly Review of Biology*, 46 (1), March: 35–57.

Tullock, G. (1967), "The welfare costs of tariffs, monopolies and theft", *Western Economic Journal*, 5: 224–232.

Unger, R.M. (1976), *Law in Modern Society*, New York: Free Press.

Vanberg, V.J. (1999), "Markets and regulation: on the contrast between free-market liberalism and constitutional liberalism", *Constitutional Political Economy*, 10 (3), October: 219–244.

Wallsten, S.J. (2000), "The effects of government-industry R&D programs on private R&D: the case of the Small Business Innovation research program", *Rand Journal of Economics*, 31 (1) Spring: 82–100.

Weede, E. (2006), "Economic freedom and development: new calculations and interpretations", *Cato Journal*, 26 (3), Fall: 511–524.

Weingast, B.R. and Wittman, D.A. (eds) (2006), *The Oxford Handbook of Political Economy*, Oxford: Oxford University Press.

West, S.A., Griffin, A.S and Gardner, A.L. (2007), "Social semantics: altruism, cooperation, mutualism, strong reciprocity and group selection", *Journal of Evolutionary Biology*, 20 (2), March: 415–432.

Wheeler, J. (1601), *A Treatise on Commerce*, Middleburgh: Richard Schilders.

Williams, G.C. (1966), *Adaptation and Natural Selection: A Critique of Some Current Evolutionary Thought*, Princeton: Princeton University Press.

Williamson, O.E. (1979), "Transaction-cost economics: the governance of contractual relations", *Journal of Law and Economics*, 22 (2), October: 233–261.

Williamson, O.E. (1983), "Credible commitments: using hostages to support exchange", *American Economic Review*, 73 (4), September: 519–540.

Wilson, E.O. (1975), *Sociobiology: The New Synthesis*, Cambridge: Harvard University Press.

Wolf, M. (2008), "Keynes offers us the best way to think about the financial crisis", *Financial Times*, 23 December.

Zafirovski, M. (2003), "The rational choice approach to human studies: a re-examination", *Human Studies*, 26 (4), December: 41–66.

Zerbe, R.O. (1998), "Is cost–benefit analysis legal? Three rules", *Journal of Policy Analysis and Management*, 19: 419–456.

Zweigert, K. and Kötz, H. (1998), *An Introduction to Comparative Law*, third edition, Oxford: Oxford University Press and J.C.B. Mohr (Paul Siebeck).

Index

THE TREATMENT

for

HORSES

ENERGY-WORK
FOR BEHAVORIAL, PHYSICAL AND HEALTH RELATED PROBLEMS

THREE WEEKS TO A NEW ANIMAL

by

Alene Sibley

1st Edition

Lucky Spoon Prints
United States of America

THE TREATMENT *for* HORSES

Lucky Spoon Prints
P.O. Box 118
Buzzards Bay, MA 02532

Library of Congress Cataloging-in-Publication Data
Sibley, Alene
The Treatment for Horses – 1st ed.
Energy-Work for Behavioral, Physical and Health Related Problems
Library of Congress Control Number (LCCN): 2002106806

ISBN 0-9719960-0-8

Cover Design and Book Layout by Alan Trugman
Cover Photo by Simona Tarakeviciute
Photographs by Matthew Stemmle and Simona Tarakeviciute
Photo Editing by Tam Halling
Drawings by Arlene Sibley
Printed in the United States of America
1st Edition

acknowledgements

This book is for Matt and because of Matt, with love.

The Treatment is dedicated to the memory of my extraordinary little Morgan friend T'other One, and the teachings of Zachary, Kahlua and Pony. Additionally, I am forever blessed for the healing foundation so selflessly handed to me by Tricia Vigilante, and thank you to Chris Sitwell for giving The Treatment its name.

Tam Halling and my mother Arlene Sibley: the hours you spent helping to make this book a printed reality are more appreciated than you'll ever know.

...and a final extra big, EXTRA SPECIAL THANKS go to the constant inspiration, determination and cooperation (or lack thereof) of Phinneas.

This work is largely inspired by and reliant upon the wisdom and invention of centuries of healing pioneers and scientists— their knowledge has been my guide, and it is through their collective understandings and insights that The Treatment receives its direction.

why energy-work and why The Treatment

Your horse has a problem (or you have a problem with your horse) and you have done everything you can for him. It is likely, however, that you have not. Doing "everything" does not mean exhausting your wallet and your energy and coming up noticeably empty-handed in terms of progress. It means going where you haven't gone before, and most often this will involve drawing on aspects of yourself and your own abilities that you may be unaware are available to you. It will often mean helping yourself to find the answers that are right for your own situation. And how are you supposed to do this? By truly, genuinely, connecting with your horse. This is what your horse wants! Horses are smart and highly sensitive animals—mixing them into the fray of human beings can make for complicated alternatives to their management. Without exception, connecting to your horse and reaching a place of understanding is the *best* way to uncomplicate and help them as individuals, and The Treatment is designed for just this purpose. The Treatment for Horses was developed as a tool to release energetic blocks which manifest in the horse as behavioral issues, physical limitations (such as unsoundness, coat and skin problems, digestive disorders, injuries etc.), or walls hit in training and problems communicating with the horse. It is my contention that every problem is first a problem on the level of energy flow, which is why releasing blocked energy can alter the course of a myriad of problems.

Generally speaking, healing energy-work has been reserved to trained practitioners specializing in any of the numerous modalities offered today: Reiki, Kinergetics, Zero Balancing, Polarity Therapy, Qigong, hands-on healing, etc. Although it can be somewhat non-specific, the use of therapeutic magnets is another popular method for working with body energy.

In discovering and developing the simple three week method of applied energy that I call The Treatment, it has been my pleasure to learn that anyone and everyone can be instantly proficient and effective in treating energy blockages.

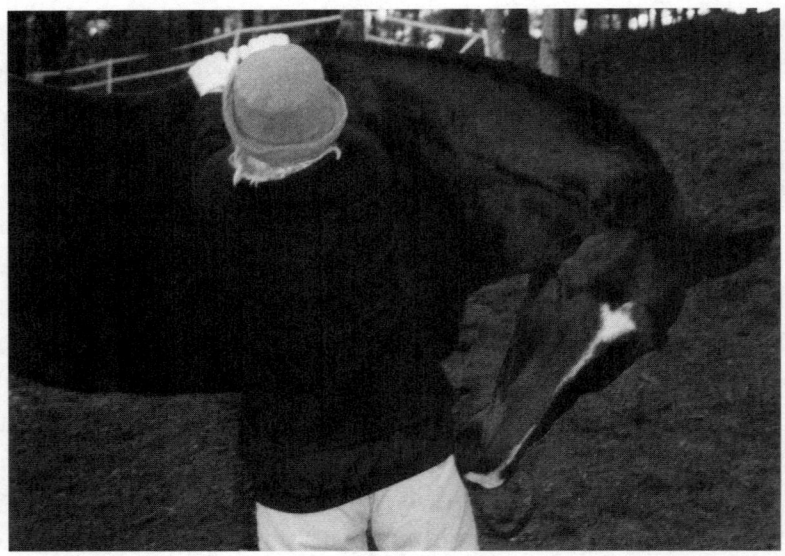

The Treatment is exactly this easy.

the purpose of this book

The Treatment for Horses is an introduction into one's own abilities to bring about healing and transformation, and is to be used as an instrument of discovery. The reason it is offered to the horse owner or horse friend as opposed to only equine healing practitioners is that, to be lastingly effective, The Treatment requires your personal and unique connection to the animal. Bear in mind that your horse is one half of an equation of two living, thinking beings (you being the other half), and as such can be no more than 50% of the current equation of problems in health and behavior. Frankly, the odds are likely that your horse is pretty well blame-free altogether. Have you noticed how some people have the same horse-related troubles over and over, even when they acquire new horses? And have you seen the incident of a "problem" horse—be it in health or behavior—showing instant improvement when switched to a new owner or different location? Whether it was simply a matter of changing from bad hay to good hay, the reason for the primary problem happens on the level of energy and likewise the improvement comes about as a result of an energetic shift. This book is here to teach you how to create just such an energetic shift, by yourself, for the betterment of you and your horse.

The very best relationships are those where growth, spontaneity, and change are welcomed; there is openness for individuality and joy is part of the everyday routine. It is the goal of The Treatment to bring this type of relationship to you and your equine companion. If you are experiencing problems with your horse partner (lameness or other health-related problems, behavioral or training issues, or your own limitations), The Treatment is a bridge to carry you and your horse out of disappointment and into a place of peace and progress. You, as the

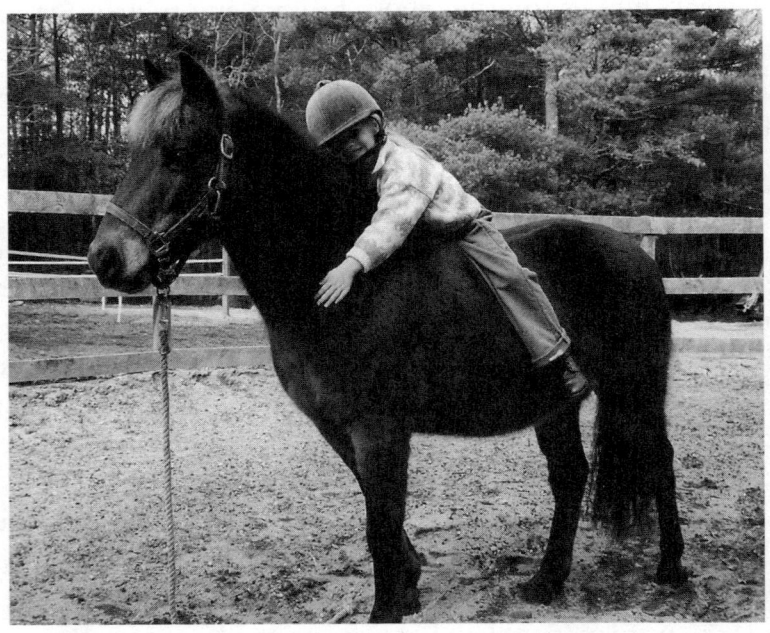

My friend Maggie and her pony Uno show us the very happy and natural connection they share, a type of relating to horses from which adults often feel blocked.

horse-person, will not be unaffected by the work. Nor will you be a simple onlooker to changes occurring within the horse; healing will be coming to you both. If you have no urgent issues with your horse, The Treatment can be the tool to propel you into ever greater possibilities together. Applied with care, commitment and diligence, The Treatment can be subtle or it can be profound, but most importantly it will always be exactly what it is supposed to be for you. Incidentally, you need not worry about causing harm to your horse with The Treatment. If your ultimate Treatment goals are not in the best interest of the animal, you will simply be pulled into a more correct direction.

At all times with The Treatment, enlightenment will be part of the reward. If you have never before experienced enlightenment in connection with horses, you are going to find it to be one of the most satisfying pleasures you were never even looking for. It's like the joy you feel in those fleeting moments of pure connection and flow when riding, only the moments are longer and on a deeper level. Your understanding will go beyond the confusion of asking your horse to conform to your needs and will move into the realm of appreciating who your horse is. The connection you share will begin to deepen and make sense. *This* is the kind of enlightenment I'm talking about, and from there the truest healings can occur.

The point of this work is to rise above diagnosis and analysis to a place where energy alone can arrive at the solution. Hooray! What a relief! You may now stop focusing on "why" a problem exists, "how" the heck to fix it, and all the "whats" and "ifs" that go along as part of the exhausting package. With The Treatment you need to understand nothing other than what you sincerely see to be the ideal outcome. View this as a chance to partake in your own dreams. The only difficult part of The Treatment is maintaining enthusiasm for applying the technique over a three week period, but enthusiasm or not just get out there and do it each day ANYWAY and you will open the doors to the answers. With *that* said, keep in mind that a positive attitude has never hurt any successful endeavor—energy flows more easily from the hands of a smiling person.

The information in this book has been made short, sweet, and easy—reflective of the work itself which is short, sweet, and easy, and will provide you with ample ability for success. As the author, I do not claim to be a master of energy-work or even of The Treatment—it is for each of us to master our own intent and the sincerity we bring to any endeavor, and to remain students of healing opportunities. What I can and do emphatically claim is that The Treatment works. As you practice doing The Treatment with increased focus and compassion, refining your desires as you go, please follow your own instincts and bring a personalized style to the system that is outlined in this book. Just as your horse is *your* horse, The Treatment should be *Your* Treatment.

an introduction

So...CONGRATULATIONS! You hold in your hands the opportunity to become the principal healing-link in the life of the horse you love. Know that you **can** and you **will** overcome the difficulties and limitations experienced in your equine partnership. It takes only minutes a day for three weeks of nominal effort before unmistakable changes begin to take shape for your horse. You alone will be opening the doors to these changes.

Most of the horses kept domestically for pleasure, work, or as our pets harbor at least one "issue." Saddled as they are with our hopes, dreams, and ambitions, they are tied tightly to our expectations. These animals carry the burden of "us" to the very best of their abilities. They work to decipher our all-too human modes of communication while being confined in a man-made environment (however lovingly created). Not surprisingly the horse ends up with growing areas of energy-"disconnection." Such disconnectedness is evident in the relationship with people and with other horses. Tensions within the body can go so far as to manifest into accidents and injuries. What we don't perceive is that at the same time these disconnections are appearing as blocked energy-patterns within the electro-magnetic field of the horse.

Imagine if daily you lived and worked in an environment which caused you some stress and there was no one to whom you could turn for understanding or help. Stress is confusing to the body, and confusion is stressful—it's an insidious and deconstructive loop which isn't usually caught until problems develop on a larger scale. The stress and confusion create energy blocks which create tension which creates energy blocks which create confusion, which creates energy blocks, and so on! When such a cycle is placed into the realm of two beings working and relating closely—as with a horse and human—such ongoing episodes of tension and blockage always form into trouble of one sort or another. Quite often the trouble will multiply upon itself. Fortunately the cycle does not have to spiral out-of-control—this disconnectedness can be nipped in the bud, or reversed.

There are an infinite number of methods being offered today for healing physical problems in the horse: products and veterinarians and therapists, etc. Likewise there is a vast pool of exceptional training systems available for horses, accompanied by all sorts of books and tapes and instructors. You want to get the very most out of whatever avenue you pursue for you and your horse, and you want no more promising half-starts. So, where the *heck* to begin?

You begin with YOURSELF, period.

When we work closely with a horse we infuse the experience, moment to moment, with our own complex psyche. Being such in-tune and adaptable creatures, horses pick up every overt, or subtle, or completely hidden confusion we send their way. *Every* signal is sensed, be it one of fear, worry, lack of confidence, hypochondria, etc. These signals are born in our most tightly-held beliefs about life, and the innocent horse gets swept into these unconscious convictions of ours. Our horse becomes part of our fluctuating emotional ride. Let's say that you feel happiness and self-assurance on the surface, but you are involuntarily sheltering a belief that things may not or cannot go smoothly. That is the very thing your horse will display; things will indeed not go smoothly as he reveals for you your hidden beliefs.

Think for a moment about any of the world's very best and most humane horse trainers and you will see a common denominator; from some innate sense of inner-balance each of these brilliant trainers have an unquestioned belief that the horse will respond well to them. They believe that things will go their way. I don't know *why* they get to have this type of inner-balance, but they do have it. Almost without effort such trainers can find harmony with a horse and maintain it. Confronted with the same horse many of the rest of us would soon face difficulties. How exasperating! What we need here is that very inner-balance and belief in self so that *our truth* can be one which sets our horse free. Imbalance puts horse and rider off-course. In-balance means we can giddy-up along a more positive trail in this life we've chosen for the horse and ourselves. By clearing body-energy blockages, The Treatment clears the way for this type of shift to occur.

There is almost nothing in the world that is easier than The Treatment. It is also one of the most effective undertakings you will ever pursue with your horse. The Treatment starts with your goals and desires and ends by not ending—instead you are deposited onto a journey. In other words, your horse-related goals are used as the incentive to guide yourself onto a path of awareness and *creation* with your horse, leaving behind inattentiveness and *reaction*.

Before beginning The Treatment, read this book from beginning to end. Your level of comprehending the significance of body-energy will be enhanced with the information and will help you understand what you can bring to the work. The Treatment will lead you onward and outward with your own horse, as it has done for me. Let me tell you about Phinneas…

Phinneas, like all horses, just wants to have a good time in life.

in the beginning there was Phinneas

The Treatment for Horses is a product of my years in human and animal body-work, studies with the practical applications of life-energies, and an on-going association with equines—the most relentlessly inspiring of which has been Phinneas. He's a big and tall bay thoroughbred gelding, sweet but not docile, simple but never a fool. In his role as my teacher, this large critter has shown little mercy in getting me to *get it.*

In my past I sometimes displayed those traits that are best avoided when dealing with horses: I could be easily discouraged, often frustrated, and surprisingly impatient with my own progress. I have always been "good with horses," reasonably knowledgeable and consistent, but I was aware of a missing ingredient in my approach. Along came Phinneas, the horse I'd wanted as a pleasure horse who quickly became a "challenge" horse. When I first saw him he was underweight and unloved. Being that I'm smart, I'd made certain to have a pre-purchase exam performed before buying him, and he promptly failed due to a hind-end weakness. So much for smarts—I looked into his eyes, saw a crazy future with this horse, and bought him immediately. I knew we'd be going places together. At the time I hadn't realized that going places would first mean "going within;" how NOT fun that would have sounded. I wanted to be on a horse, not in my head. But I've found that I cannot have the former in a harmonious way if I do not have the latter in a truthful way. Phinneas understood, long before I, that my emotional baggage became his extra baggage, and apparently he wasn't interested in additional burdens. This pleasure horse who I'd supposed should have been oh-so grateful that I'd bought his unsound butt out from under a dubious fate was definitely anything but a pleasure. Phin proceeded to show me exactly how much trouble a horse, living within my desires and domestic boundaries, could be. I spent the greater part of my allotted horse-time dealing with injuries, training faults, behavioral problems, and all sorts of annoying stabling issues. Our many chances for progress were constantly undermined by seemingly outside circumstances. The joy of horses that I yearned for became like a glistening mirage which forever eluded my reach. We went from nail injuries to bite wounds to slips on the ice, from subtle chronic unsoundness to varying acute lamenesses. Peaceful streaks were disrupted in the strangest ways. On one quiet day in the paddock, ambling along the road came an escaped 400-pound pig. I watched powerlessly as my terrified horse went through, not over, the split-rail fence and disappeared into the thick trees. Anything but stick around to face the visiting hog-thing. Later after he'd been salvaged from yonder far-off woods (bathed in mountains of froth, breathing hard, tired and sore from pounding the asphalt roads at a dead gallop) he swiped and ate the tiny glass bottle of Rescue Remedy I'd used to calm him. He stood munching away at my silly little homeopathic ideas even as I was digging into his mouth to try to retrieve the pulverized glass.

And no, he didn't die. He wasn't going to make it that easy on either one of us.

In some way I knew that the ongoing problems and ever-present feeling of pending disasters were my fault and not my horse's, trouble-prone rogue though he seemed to be. Through the vapor of disappointments and set-backs I began to perceive reality: that a horse, first, is subject by no choice of his own to exist within the plans of his owner. No choice! Second to this, the horse's sensitive nature causes him to act as a mirror to those around him; lacking this style of awareness, we people are rarely his mirror in turn. For Phinneas to become sane, sound, and consistently happy (and more than anything I wanted him to be happy), he didn't have to change a thing. *I* did. Then instead of reflecting my scattered energy back at me, he might have a chance for strength, growth, and joy. Was it conceivable that my ability to project problems could even attract stray pigs into my horse's life like a magnet? Maybe. And maybe then it was worth getting the pendulum to swing in the opposite direction, away from pigs and problems. With the assumption that I could change the world if I tried, at least the world of Phinneas and me, I took the energy-work I had been doing for some time with people and began to apply the same principles to my horse. I firmly believe that a horse can know great happiness in his life with people, but love and empathy must be present or the horse is truly left alone to deal with his plight at our hands. There is no reason on Earth to treat these animals with anything other than compassion and understanding—no reason *ever*. The amazing thing is that when you stop forcing agendas and instead seek to find a connection, that simple act of kindness is rewarded by a horse who will lay his trust and his whole world into the palm of your hand. When I first had Phinneas I would have told you I was the most compassionate person in the world, but in fact my capacity to reach understanding and true kindness was severely blocked by my own expectations and self-doubts.

So there I was, having decided to swing that pendulum. Energy shifts cause mental shifts, and I soon found myself contemplating new ideas. Out of all of my friends, I'd thought, were there any on whom I placed the kind of expectations that I placed upon my horse? I certainly never got disappointed at any friends for being who they are, and yet I can say I often felt let down by situations presented by my horse. He was *difficult*. Our relationship was fraught with the kind of neuroses that prevails in so many marriages where the couples forget to be friends, yanking and tugging their partner into their own idea of that person. I was seeing the light. If a friend had been injured, I'd hardly put pressure on them to "get well." I'd simply be supportive. I had to look at the fact that, while I lovingly did all the things required to help my horse be healthy, my personal expectations were so high that I remained inwardly hurt and exhausted by Phinneas' physical troubles. Together we were spiraling into a confused emotional flow which was all about *me*, and not exactly about us.

As I stuck with the development of this new form of energy-work, pathways began to open up for Phinneas and me. Here is what happened in a short time:

During my first weeks with the energy-work and quite by "chance," I stumbled across a nutritionist who changed everything about the way I look at and handle horsefeed. I changed my horse's diet to natural grains with natural supplementing, and within weeks he began to move more soundly—for the *first time* including before I'd bought him. I can say this was nothing short of a miracle.

A new stable for Phinneas became available, and within days of moving him there (where amongst other things he found more freedom and an important equine friend) a persistent wound which had continually developed proud flesh healed over by itself.

I noticed that Phinneas and I were beginning to truly connect. The look in his eyes softened (I hadn't even known how much disillusionment he had been showing before!). We started to have some rides where I almost understood what he was thinking, and meanwhile he became increasingly level-headed about fearful objects on the trail.

Another chance encounter steered me to a clinic where I learned new training techniques which were just right for Phinneas and me, and soon our rides had become even more solid, safe, and consistently fun. Actually *fun*.

This was the beginning of The Treatment.

Besides anything else that he is to me, I have come to see Phinneas as the partner who takes me, my learning, and The Treatment to deeper levels. There are some very forgiving horses out there who will let you get away with a hidden bad mood, but Phinneas has no patience for hypocrisy. He continually insists that I maintain authenticity within myself and in my relationship with him. Be real, he says, or get lost.

"Being real," however, is never so easy as it sounds, because to truly be real means to truly *let go*. This is one of the most important "rules" in The Treatment: you must LET GO OF OUTCOMES. It is absolutely imperative that you allow for the process and the energy to find their own way to results. I will admit that this is, for me, the most difficult of my own suggestions. I am prone to obsess on whatever hinders my animals, particularly lameness— and I mean *obsess*. I cloak my horse in this "concern" of mine, assessing and questioning each movement he makes. Is there improvement or is he worse? Is there more or less swelling? Heat or no heat? No doubt I send damaging laser-beams from my prying eyes directly into the poor horse's tissues. No lameness stands a chance of healing when up against such ongoing negative projection and near-phobic scrutiny! The Treatment has been like a hand reaching into this clouded thinking and leading me out to where I can back off and actually *let go*.

Phinneas's chronic, years-old hind-end weakness has been addressed with The Treatment to great success, but not before he slammed his hip into a tree so hard that he ripped off skin and hair. This accident occurred a mere three days into a three week Treatment (using The Treatment specifically for concentrating on this hind-end unsoundness). Now he displayed *increased* trouble in back. Yeesh! I tell other people to persevere with The Treatment, no matter the obstacles, but this was too much! Yet I kept up the sessions on my limping horse and within days I experienced some important information coming my way by various independent means (book, video, conversation, dream). I began to realize precisely what my horse required from me, and what kinds of changes I needed to make in order for this to happen. Some of it involved just getting up earlier and doing a new kind of ground-training with him. In some way, almost overnight, I knew (unblocked energy!) what my horse needed to gain better use of his body, and it was almost like he was directly telling me. My objectives with my horse were opening up and I became more sincere in my efforts to be there for him. Over the next few days his hip injury healed very quickly, and he seemed to be getting stronger and stronger on his hind legs. His balance improved in all movements. Tensions melted even further away and our work together became infused with a sense of delight.

The moral? If Phin hadn't slammed his hip the way he did, I wouldn't have reached so hard to work with him and, consequently, myself as well. I hadn't exactly gotten what I wanted right away, but I got what I needed. Exactly. And in the end the goal of a sounder horse was achieved.

Today I live in a miracle, because today Phinneas and I swim in that mirage; we have fun. *But what appears as miraculous is simply the natural effect of reconnecting energy.* I find that each time I do The Treatment, my desires become further defined and the truth presents itself more clearly, solidly, and beautifully. Because The Treatment also works like a preventative, injuries and hindrances no longer rule the day. With my new open mind, when something does happen I look to what the language of the incident is trying to say. My relationship with Phinneas, once so peppered with frustration (for both of us), is now marked by constant growth and much gratification.

Unbelievably, my challenge horse has been revealed as the true pleasure he really is.

an overview

With The Treatment, one is working with life energy. I won't overload this text with lengthy explanations of what life energy is understood to be, but I will stress that all matter exists because of energy, and it is energy upon which all of life depends. Energy comes before, and is responsible for, biology, chemistry, cells, molecules, and atoms. It extends from the indivisible quantum level on outward to an all-encompassing universal level. For a quick insight, consider the fact that an atom is composed almost completely of nothing—its emptiness is roughly in proportion to the emptiness of our galactic universe. That's a lot of empty space. Since our bodies are comprised entirely of atoms, we can safely assert that we living and breathing humans and animals are made up primarily of nothingness. So I say thank goodness for energy! It's the glue that binds us, the fuel that runs our motors, and the flow which connects us to everyone, everything, and every bit of healing power into which we might plug our cords. Tapping yourself into life on the energy level makes your possibilities limitless. A good example of this is the phenomenon of "medical miracles" such as spontaneous cancer remission; there is evidence that what seems unexplainable may occur simply as a result of our energetic connections.

The Treatment concentrates on influencing energy as it is manifested along the spinal column. The spine is used as the most easily accessed channel for blocked energies. The principle for uncovering the blocks is similar to that of kinesiology, or muscle-testing. However, in Applied Kinesiology, as an example, a practitioner must understand the relationships between muscles testing "weak" or "strong" and the corresponding organs of the body in order to make a diagnosis and perform treatment. It is the intention of The Treatment to bypass an enormous amount of study and cut right to the chase. Don't worry about knowing anything other than your goals.

In order to bring about results with The Treatment, your own thought-process is employed to expose the blockages along the horse's spine whereby they can be treated. This is achieved through the use of a "wish-list" composed of <u>whatever</u> it is you would like to achieve with your horse, whether it be physical healing, training, behavioral conditioning, etc. It is the wish-list that allows you to do this work without knowing anything about the body. Armed with this list and your desires, the energy blocks and disconnections will appear for you to correct them without you even knowing exactly where they are. Subsequently these corrections will open the doors to the solution. But how?

The powerful influence of your subconscious mind plays a major roll in all aspects of The Treatment, for yourself as well as your horse, and is one reason for the unforced nature in which solutions are obtained. Properly encoding your subconscious by way of the wish-list is like suddenly having a cheerful and invisible army on your side ready to do all the thinking and seeking of answers for you. One of your jobs is to *let it do the work*, and *do not* worry about how it's going about it. Let go. (Remember that is one of the trickiest parts.)

Although you may see improvement with your horse very early-on in the process, the reason for performing The Treatment over a three week period is to firmly establish the new healthy energy patterns and help them be lasting ones. There will be instances where the issue seems unresolved at the end of the three weeks, but don't be discouraged. Stop the sessions after the three weeks are over, as planned; in a short time things will change. Think of it like a raft stuck behind a dam—once the dam is opened it may take the raft some more time to reach its destination, but at least now it's traveling with the currents.

Here we see Maggie, demonstrating how easy it is to work energy along the spine.

Healing energy, once learned, can also be applied directly to facilitate the healing of specific physical issues.

the work

Learning The Treatment is one of the easiest things you will ever do. Don't be overwhelmed by thinking there is a lot of material you must comprehend; your intention and your consistency will matter much more than your knowledge. For your convenience a one page summary of the steps will follow this chapter.

The Treatment consists of two steps: first is the wish-list (from which you will create a mantra, or simple sentence to be repeated frequently), and second is breathwork and the applied energy. The energy-work is to be performed on your horse two times daily for three weeks. If during the three weeks you occasionally miss one session in a day, don't panic, and if your life is such that you are at the barn only once a day, then so be it— **just be sure you *really mean it* when you are doing it!**

Also instill yourself with these most important resources: INCENTIVE (a better horse and a better you), KIND INTENT (base your goals in compassion for the horse), and FOCUSED ATTENTION (stay in the moment for this work to work!). These are key ingredients to empower The Treatment.

Each session takes between 5 and 10 minutes. I recommend that you don't lengthen the sessions; keeping it short will assist in a fresh approach over the three weeks of applying energy. Trust me, it will seem tedious sometimes and you won't always feel connected to the work and its hoped-for results, so don't prolong your time! If you want, get inspired to move elsewhere on the body to play with channeling the energy, like holding your hands over an injury and running energy for a few minutes or more. Energy alone is amazingly healing—and it's literally as easy as breathing.

STEP ONE:
The Wish-list

What is it that you would like to improve or resolve with your horse? No doubt you already know the answer to that question, so it is time for the list.

At the top of a piece of paper write out everything as you would ideally have it with your horse, and be sure to write in the present tense. For example, if your restless horse Jeremy has a vice of kicking down fence boards in order to run off and play in traffic, causing you worry and costing you money in materials and the occasional vet bill, you could write:

> *Jeremy has become completely relaxed in his paddock. He is free of tension, plays nicely with his paddock-mates and looks content. Jeremy is a cheerful horse who loves his time outside and loves his home.*

If your horse is Rex and he's chronically lame from low ringbone, no matter what you and the vets and the farriers try, you might write:

> *Rex is moving soundly, and he is smooth in all of his gaits. Rex now requires only normal horseshoes. He is pain-free and perfect.*

Lastly, your mare Belle is terrified of dogs. Both of you are bored to tears with the arena, but you have grown far too nervous of her phobia to take her out on the trail. Your wish-list sounds something like:

> *Belle is now calm around all dogs—they can bark, run, jump, whatever; she's fine. She and I ride peacefully along the trails. Belle is a composed and trustworthy horse.*

Now look over what you have written and use the list to investigate what is underlying your desires. This is done by searching for the concept words that best describe your ultimate payoffs and will make the most sense to your subconscious mind. Do not get caught up worrying if your desires are right for your horse; assume that they are. It gives you a starting point from which the energy-work itself can lead you in a more correct direction if necessary. As long as you understand yourself to be applying The Treatment for improvement of one sort or another, you're on the right course.

In other words, think with compassion and don't sweat the details.

To illustrate concept words, I'll concentrate on Jeremy:

Jeremy has become completely relaxed in his paddock. He is free of tension, plays nicely with his paddock-mates and looks content. Jeremy is a cheerful horse who loves his time outside and loves his home.

In reviewing my list I see that I want Jeremy to relax. I would like him to be safe, enjoying himself and healthy (since if he stops breaking out, he might stop cutting up his legs and endangering his very life). Additionally I would like to see him content, and even cheery, so maybe happiness is also what I'm looking for. These are the concepts which compute to my real, fundamental goals for my horse:

relaxation
enjoyment
health
contentment
cheerfulness
happiness

As you come up with the concept words, write them down the

middle of the page. Next proceed to the lower part of your paper where you will establish a repetitive command for yourself by boiling your list down to three definitive power words which best "say it all." For Jeremy my command is as follows:

*"Jeremy is **relaxed**, **happy**, and **healthy**—now and always!"*

Nowhere in the sentence do I need to mention paddock or vice, because if he can be those three things (relaxed, happy, and healthy), then it means he's not anxious and breaking out of his paddock. There are any number of ways to express yourself in your command, and there is a very good chance it will feel absolutely corny to you, but carry on! Allow for NO wishy-washiness in your final sentence. Got that? Be assertive. Keep it simple like the above or write it even more emphatically, such as:

"I claim that Jeremy is relaxed, happy, and healthy, right now!"
"I demand that Jeremy be ..."
"I declare Jeremy to be ..."

Whatever best suits you is the way to write it, as this one command is going to accompany you wherever you go for the next three weeks. This isn't about calling on angels or guides or fairies to do the work (although feel free to include whoever and whatever has been spiritually important to you thus far in life). Never get soft and water-down your command—keep it strong and powerful! The Treatment has less to do with faith in magical things outside of ourselves, and everything to do with the fostering of faith in our own personal natures. With the list and continual use of the command, it is your *subconscious mind* that is being spoken to and programmed, and from there you will be able to feel your way into a new reality. Your subconscious mind doesn't recognize niceties like "thank you" and "bless you," etc.; it recognizes belief systems and commands. For three weeks you will say the sentence aloud when you can, repeat it in your

THE WISH-LIST

Jeremy has become completely relaxed in his paddock. He is free of tension, plays with his paddock-mates and looks content. Jeremy is a cheerful horse who loves his time outside and loves his home.

relaxation
enjoyment
health
contentment
cheerfulness
happiness

Jeremy is relaxed, happy, and healthy –
now and always!

mind— THINK IT as often as possible. It is especially important to think it at those inevitable moments of negativity and discouragement when you feel you're getting nowhere with this work (like, while the vet is stitching up Jeremy's leg after another escape one week into beginning The Treatment). At those times declare your sentence with increased emphasis and a smile on your face, and then mentally move on. Pretend yourself to be a confident know-it-all who holds all the answers, even though you don't yet recognize what they are.

You are learning to take the power away from your fears and frustrations and become infused with the power of positive feelings. You will be present in the here and now, with integrity, which is exactly where and how your horse resides.

These new activities may feel strange at first, but as long as they work, who cares? If you keep the process rolling and are serious in your intent, the end results will justify every leap through what may seem a ridiculous new-age hoop. These types of treatments are being used with great success for humans, and it's only fitting that the horses who work so hard for us should profit from our ever-expanding knowledge. When your life opens up to new dimensions with your horse, whatever you did to get there will have been well worth it.

When you have embarked upon your three weeks of energy-work, reread the original wish-list once a day. Repeat the sentence to yourself as often as you like, but *spend no time agonizing about how the goal will be reached*. Did you hear me? LET GO! This is the very important process of redrawing the blueprint of your thoughts and how they relate to your horse—set your concerns free and all that you need to know will emerge as you unblock the pathways.

STEP TWO:
The Energy

In order to repair energetic blocks from the spine outward, the blocks must be brought to the surface—it's like having a sunken treasure bob to the top of murky water where you can grab it quickly and easily, only in this case the treasure is something you will never actually see.

To expose energy blocks we use our thoughts (as they have been formed on the wish-list). Thoughts are influential in everything we do and our thoughts and feelings have an immediate effect on anyone we come in contact with. This includes animals, in particular the horse who is built to register the tiniest traces of information. This is why the use of visualization techniques in the riding arena has gained such wide acceptance as a routine training exercise. Try riding for two minutes while repeating the word "no" over and over in your mind, then try another two minutes while saying "yes, yes, yes." The difference in your horse's cooperation and body-willingness will be unmistakable.

Prove-it (the sugar test demonstration)

If you are altogether new to the idea of working with body energies, and if the concept of energy blockage is foreign to you, I suggest trying the following exercise to illustrate how rapidly the body manifests alterations upon its energetic currents.

Stand facing a friend and have the friend hold one arm straight out to their side with the palm facing down toward the floor. Place your hand on their wrist and apply steady downward pressure onto their arm while the friend resists by pushing upward. Neither one of you should apply so much force that it's a fight; you're only doing this to establish available strength. Now take a one moment break and then place some sugar onto the friend's tongue (table sugar, or a piece of chocolate or other candy).

Immediately apply downward pressure again to the friend's out-wardly-held arm as the friend resists by pushing up. The sugar has been in contact with his or her system for only a second or two, but you'll find that your friend has effectively just lost most of the strength displayed only a moment before. While the overall sustainable energy wasn't noticeably depleted by the introduction of sugar, their body was reacting to an energy block (particularly in relation to the thymus gland). *Try this same exercise on a friend by first applying the downward pressure to their arm and then simply thinking the word sugar.* Unless your friend has a body designed for powerful sugar assimilation, they will most likely be notably weaker at the unheard suggestion. THAT is a block being brought to the surface, and it has even at that moment been made present in the spine. Many sensitive and trained energy-workers would be able to detect the weakness in the spine at this point, but The Treatment has been designed to allow anybody to make the corrections with very little knowl-edge of even how they are being made.

With The Treatment, repeating the sessions daily for three weeks strengthens and further supports the corrections made each time while also ensuring that you deliver the healing ener-gy to the correct points. It's sort of like making a hundred attempts to tap a golf ball into a nearby hole; even if you've never held a golf club in your life—heck, even if you're *blindfolded*—it's a good bet that several balls are going to drop right where you want them to go.

WARNING: BE ON THE LOOKOUT FOR THESE BAD-GUYS
In applying the energy, the two most common areas of failure are *distraction* and *worry*. They are like poison to The Treatment. Distraction can quickly lead to agitation with the process, which can lead right into quitting. While I would emphasize the importance of attention, let me also say that there is no need to be excessively interested in the redundant

Performing the sugar test.

proceedings of moving energy along the spine—just be as mentally and peacefully present as possible. When I catch my mind wandering during a session, I try to imagine myself as Winnie the Pooh (odd but true!) working on a pot of honey (my horse's spine is the honey). A character like Winnie the Pooh is utterly complacent and in-the-moment, and to model myself after such gentle focus is always unexpectedly helpful and grounding.

The other problem is that of worry. Worry translates into distrust and fear. It is the part of you which will discount every step of The Treatment and laughs at you for trying such an unconventional experiment—it freezes up the subconscious and does not allow for intuition. It is a nagging voice which, when listened to, builds on itself. Worry will skillfully undermine your ability to forge ahead with purpose. As with distraction, it can lead rapidly to quitting. When I begin three weeks of The Treatment I make a pact with myself to see it through to the end no matter what. I keep this in mind as I do my best to ignore the nagging voice and continue to run my energy like a good Winnie the Pooh would.

Be sincere in your efforts and put in the time (which, as you remember, does not have to be a lot of actual time). You will find yourself increasingly proficient in running healing energies and the work you do will be more effective in a shorter period.

PRODUCING THE ENERGY FLOW

It is time to proceed onto the generating of energy and getting comfortable with channeling it through your hands. This is not hard to do! It is a skill available to absolutely everyone, but keep in mind that we all have different levels of observation. Some people feel a profound shift within themselves when beginning this work while others are aware of a depth of sensation in their hands that extends into the animal they work with. Still, there are plenty of people who are unsure if they feel anything at all, so be patient with yourself. Don't forget that what you really need on your side is plenty of your primary INCENTIVE, kind INTENT, and focused ATTENTION. These components will take your work farther, and be more effective, than a keen awareness can do alone. No two people are alike and no two energy experiences will be felt or understood in quite the same way. Do not worry about the hows and the whys, remember? Just get out there and do it to the best of your abilities, and then do it again and do it again. In a very short time you will notice a tingling in your hands and fingers, and when all is said and done you WILL attain results. This book has been written because The Treatment works—follow the plan and you will see and feel the difference for yourself.

Before you begin, one off-hand suggestion I can make for the purpose of strengthening and intensifying your energy-work is to **drink water**. If you are not in the habit of consuming a lot of water now, please try it for the three weeks of The Treatment. Water is of the utmost importance *anyway*, but is even more so when working with healing energies. Your own cells will be responding to the energy-work, and released impurities should be given smooth sailing out of the body. Moreover, water is an energy conductor so will give you more of what you need to efficiently run energy through your body. So drink up, okay? Okay.

The method for quickly producing a high energetic vibration in your hands combines rhythmic breathing and very simple visualizing. Practice a few times in the beginning before you place your hands on the horse so that the breathing comes naturally to you. The rhythmic breathing will stop feeling awkward once you are doing the sessions regularly. Note that you *cannot* do this work without maintaining the rhythmic breaths—the breathing is vital to running energy properly so don't shortcut around it. Be sure to find a rhythm that suits you.

Some suggestions are as follows:

Have a count for which you are intaking breath and then exhaling; this count can be compared to the steady beating of a drum. The intake of breath is to be rapid and strong, not prolonged. Upon exhalation you expel the breath all the way out to empty the lungs entirely. My personal favorite is a rapid in-breath to the count of 2 beats, and an out-breath to the count of 3 beats. The breaths should be fast but not so fast as to cause hyperventilation. Your rhythm will soon become automatic, so you won't always feel like you need to count.

It is ESSENTIAL that on each out-breath you empty the lungs all the way. This ensures that on your next inhalation you are introducing completely new air into your lungs, and thus new energy. Push out a bit harder on that very last bit of air from your lungs, like a final "whoosh."

The function of this style of breathing is to establish a strong current for the running of energies through your body. Your mind and body recognize the breath's ability to open these energy channels, so you need not over-think about what you are doing.

Think of your hands as the power tools in using The Treatment, and your breathing as the source of electricity.

Keeping hands relaxed, hold palms facing each other and place your fingertips together gently (as in prayer but cupped so that only the fingertips are touching). Begin your breathing, allowing for your consistent rhythm to develop—shorter inhale, longer, stronger exhale.

As you breathe you will focus on bringing energy into your hands and fingertips. This is done by feel and visualization, and

As you commence with the breathwork, hold hands relaxed to feel
energy flowing.

is another area where you need to determine for yourself what is comfortable. My suggestions are:

1) With each quick in-breath, visualize the energy pulled inward from the crown of your head and flooding your entire body. On the out-breath gather all that energy and push it down your arms and out of your hands and fingertips.

2) With each quick in-breath, visualize energy as it is pulled upward through the soles of your feet, all the way to the top of your head. On the out-breath, push the energy down your arms and out of your hands and fingertips.

3) With each quick in-breath, pull energy in through all of your pores to gather into your lung area. On the out-breath, push the energy from your lungs into your arms and out of your hands and fingertips.

It's as easy as your imagination. If it's helpful to you, add any imagery you like; give color to the entering energy, picture yourself in a beautiful setting, etc. This is not necessary, but for many people it's useful to add such mental pictures. As you begin to sense the energy running down your arms, concentrate on the feeling in your palms and fingertips. It may only be a slight sensation, but most likely you will detect some tingling in your hands, or a sparkly-feeling. This is the sensation you will be going for when you place your hands on your horse's spine. The spine is where we want our influence to be felt. The spinal cord controls *every single* function within the body through the system of nerves connected to the cord—it is the entire body's link to the brain and, presumably, beyond. When one steps into the connected realm of energy, it's conceivable that one leaves behind understood limits. The notion that body energies can be applied for the purpose of healing is perhaps intimidating to some, or it may seem ridiculous and eccentric, but only because of its relative newness to the western world. The most natural facts are often seen as far-fetched when they haven't yet achieved the status of "common knowledge." Ah well, let's never forget that the world was flat for a very, very long time.

All right, ready? Get set: you may now begin sessions on the horse. Each individual session should last no more than 5 or 10 minutes.

I often work the energy while my horse is preoccupied with eating hay, doing whatever is necessary to gain his happiness and cooperation. Most often the horse will appear to ignore the proceedings, although some are interested in helping in their own way. If your horse needs to be held by someone else and fed grain from a bucket just to feel safe and relaxed, do it. More training can come later. And if for some reason he cannot be touched along his spine, keep him distracted (food is by far the best entertainment) while holding your hands over and as close as possible to the spine while envisioning the energy flowing outward from your hands and into the spine from however much distance is required.

To start, place your hands anywhere on your horse and repeat your power-sentence (from the bottom of your wish-list) several times. Say it, whisper it, think it; whatever works for you. Shouting positive affirmations at the top of your lungs in the middle of a busy barn is not required, luckily, but don't skip this tiny, preparatory step. As with sugar on the tongue, by stating the sentence while connected physically with the horse, spinal energetic blocks to the very concepts within your sentence will be exposed so that you may treat them. This is why your own connection to the horse and the goals is so important. The blending of both of your energies and unconscious selves has a lot to do with the outstanding issues and also with the ensuing solutions. No one else can do this for you because it is about you. The horse you have and the issues you are contending with are no accident.

Immediately upon finishing reciting your sentence ("*Jeremy is relaxed, happy and healthy—now and always!*"), begin rhythmic breathing and running the energy down your arms and into your hands. If you have familiarized yourself with the breathing and running of energy by practicing a few times, there is no reason to spend a great deal of time before the session with building up your energetic vibrations. Jump right in and start work along the spine as follows:

With each placement of your hands, you will do three repetitions of your rhythmic breaths while pushing the energy outward from your hands. For example, put your hands in the first position on the horse (to be explained) and breathe in and out (1), in and out (2), in and out (3), then move to the next spot. That was three repetitions.

After each set of reps, move down the spine to the very next position over from where your hands were just placed and repeat the reps. You will do this the entire length of the spine and down the tailbone. With each hand position, picture the energy traveling from your hands and into the horse's vertebrae and spinal cord. Think about this energy soaking down into the horse's spinal canal, which is the tube created by the arches of the vertebrae through which the spinal cord runs. Have an understanding of the horse's structure so that your mental image will make sense. The spinal cord lies well below the topline of your horse.

As illustrated on the next four pages, you will begin at the first

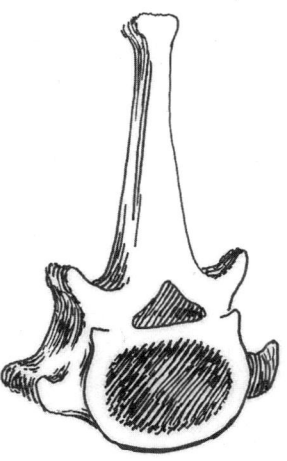

One example of an equine vertebra. The dark circle represents the
area through which the spinal cord runs. The spinous process is the
tall segment at top.

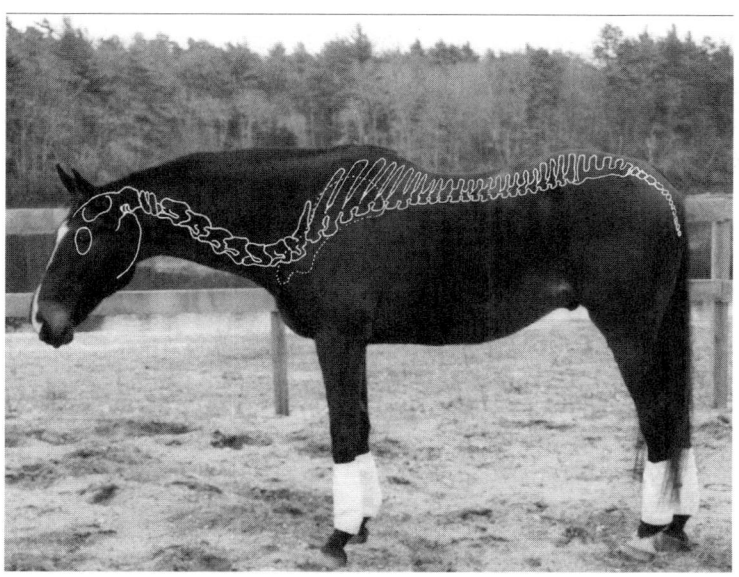

To have a clear mental picture for directing your energy work,
understand the shape of the horse's spine.

cervical vertebra just below the poll with one hand on each side of the horse's neck (sandwiching him between your hands). The cervical vertebral column of the horse does not follow the top of the neckline, but rather curves as a gentle 's' through the neck beginning from the atlas (at the skull) to where it attaches to the thoracic (chest) vertebrae. You will want to keep this 's-curve' in mind as you work so that your hands remain sandwiching the vertebrae. When you approach the scapula (shoulder blade) the spinous process changes significantly as you move onto the thoracic vertebrae. The spinous process is the top segment of the vertebra that points toward the topline of the horse. (This is what can be felt as the bumps of the backbone.) The spinous process of each equine cervical vertebra is quite short, but as you move along into the back these processes can be long, in particular those directly behind the scapula which make up the withers. You need know this only to have a mental picture for more proficiently running energies from your hands and into the horse's body. At the shoulder you will position your hands somewhat inward toward the spine as it grows up behind the shoulder blades, then your hands will move upward onto the withers and begin working side-by-side, no longer sandwiching the spine. It does not matter at any point on which side of the horse you stand.

When you reach the tail, step behind the horse (obviously only if your horse is safe behind, otherwise stand to the side). Holding your hands over the tailbone, complete your final sets down the tail.

As closure to a session you will grasp the tail in two places—one hand toward the end of the tail bone and one hand about halfway up the tail toward the dock—and pull outward and downward gently while imagining your energy moving up along the spinal cord all the way to the horse's head. If your horse doesn't like his tail being handled, improvise with a lighter,

The dots follow the direction of the equine cervical vertebrae.
Remember 3 in- and 3 out-breaths at each spot.

Traveling along the vertebrae, step by step.

If your horse is not standing this quietly, just improvise; ie, if he's eating hay from the ground, hold your hands from above his neck instead. If he moves, move with him.

At the shoulder, hands angle inward toward where the vertebrae connect beneath the scapula.

Now moving upward to follow changes in vertebrae shape as they grow up into the withers.

Hands are now placed side-by-side to continue work along the backbone.

Shifting position to send energy into the tailbone.
You're almost done!

almost make-believe version of pulling his tail (and start handling his tail as much as possible at other times to get him over the problem). Keep a steady and always gentle pull on the tail and try to feel a stretching along the horse's spine. What may happen is nothing at all, or you may be aware of resistance or a blockage (all of which will seem like it's just your imagination). Continue with the rhythmic breathing and mentally reach your energy up through the spine and into the blockage. After the first week you may become aware of a lengthening sensation, and trust me, the horse is feeling it too. By the third week you might notice your horse pulling gently forward as if to help the stretching. Sometimes a horse will shake and bones will click. Or nothing will happen but do it anyway and keep the time short, between ten and twenty seconds on the tail-pull. Then stop.

Tah dah! You did The Treatment, and that's all there is to it.

Now keep it up for three weeks, twice a day, all the while coaching yourself NOT to question progress concerning your goal. Do not give up, do not give up, do not give up! Stay the course, and *do* repeat your power sentence often so that your subconscious mind can find its way to manifesting a better reality.

When you embark upon The Treatment, resolve at the beginning to see the sessions through for the whole three weeks. Read your wish-list but let go of outcomes, and remind yourself to get out there and just do it. Simply put, if you do the work, **it works**, so: *just do it.*

The time invested in The Treatment will open you to wisdom where once you had questions, you will have solutions to problems, but mainly, you will have a new relationship with your horse. Your perspective will be greatly changed, be it through a physical healing, reversal in behavioral problems, progress under saddle, or enlightenment within yourself which gives you *real* understanding, peace, and connectedness with your horse. The change will be so natural as to be almost anti-climactic, but it is no less real and profound for its gentle integration.

Closed-mindedness abounds in the horse world as elsewhere, and there exists an overabundance of very strong and very conflicting opinions. Free yourself by making your own mind the one that is opened, providing entry for the answers that are right for you. There will be no turning back to the limitations of the past as you and your horse trek into the beginning of newly acquired feelings, healings, and dealings together.

We conclude with the gentle, awsome tail pull. Maggie is included here as yet another reminder of how happy we should all strive to feel and be around our horses. That smile is what it's all about.

A grateful Treatment recipient.

summary of The Treatment

The Treatment For Horses is to be performed daily for three weeks. Resolve at the outset to see this work through for the entire three weeks !!!

(Don't forget your primary *incentive*, kind *intent*, and focused *attention*) and…**drink water**

THE WISH-LIST
(your desires, concept-words, and command):
- Read your original wish-list each day
- If you like, read it MANY times throughout the day.
- Repeat your power-sentence, or mantra, whenever you think of it throughout the day. Out loud is great, in your head is fine.

THE ENERGY-WORK (twice per day):
Remember that DISTRACTION and WORRY are like *poison* to the process.
- Hold your hands on your horse as you repeat the command three times.
- Follow with rhythmic breathing to work the energy down through your hands, doing 3 reps of breathing at each hand-placement. Sandwich your hands on the vertebrae at the back of the skull and move along from one spot to the next. At the withers your hands move to work side-by-side, onward to the end of the tail-bone. Picture the vertebrae as you go!
- Standing at the tail, conclude the session with gently pulling outward and downward on the tail while concentrating on sending a final stream of energy upward along the spinal canal toward the head. Use your imagination to envision the horse's spine stretching as you do this.

AND THAT'S IT!

now for the fun part: what to expect

Results from your work with The Treatment will come about in any number of ways, usually unpredictable and more often than not will take a different form than you might have guessed at the outset. The results can manifest at any time during the three weeks of sessions or within one to two months following. Normally, however, you can expect to understand change on some level as your three weeks draws to a close.

Let's pretend that you have decided to perform The Treatment on a mare you have owned for two years. The mare has proven herself to be unmanageable in the ring—tense, easily spooked, and prone to rearing. You have already sought professional training, a new saddle, longeing before the ride, equine massage, and pulled your hair out with one hand while you prayed with the other, but your horse continues to be a danger to you and herself as soon as you mount. What might you expect from The Treatment? (Note that, while modified here, the following examples are gathered from actual experiences).

■ A purely spontaneous change in attitude occurs where you and your mare begin to communicate on a deeper level. Her fears and tension literally evaporate along with your own, and your rides together become increasingly pleasurable.

■ An awakening of sorts occurs within yourself and you learn to apply your influence to your horse in a different way—this shift of your personal understanding can come about gently or it can be quite intense. You may find something specifically wrong with your own riding that is causing problems. Or you might end up seeing a problem within your own personal life (outside of the barn) and seek a solution—harbored tensions suddenly begin to dissipate and you and your mare are free to move forward. Your rides improve considerably and your schooling together will finally advance.

■ Often The Treatment brings an answer to you that will seem obvious, but to which previously you had not been alert. This is a payoff for working with your subconscious—it awakens you to existing answers. For instance, you hear something about feeding which makes you aware that your mare is getting far too much grain and protein for the type of work she is doing. A change in her diet begins to moderate her personality under saddle. Meanwhile you find yourself accepting your mare's individual character—you learn to work *with* her as opposed to *in spite of* her.

■ An outward modification of your reality can happen, one which you weren't looking for. You'd been happy with your current neighborhood stabling situation, but suddenly you are offered a stall in a wonderful barn across town. It has pastures and the switch onto grass and extensive turnout creates a happier and more responsive horse overnight. Or perhaps your trusted old farrier retires, and the new farrier tells you your mare's hooves need to be allowed more of a spread. By widening her shoes, your horse's feet stop pinching and your rides improve.

■ You become more open to hear clues from the world, and in those clues are planted the seeds to the solution. These can come to you in any number of ways:

> You are handed a book which gives you an idea of a direction to take with your mare.

> A conversation is overheard about a saddle-fitter. When you find him, he ends up correcting a poor fit in your saddle which hadn't been caught previously and was causing your horse serious discomfort.

You see an ad for an upcoming clinic and you sign up; subsequently the amazing trainer helps you get to the root of the problem and you and your mare progress into sane riding.

What happens as a result of The Treatment is the synchronicity of attunement. Your subconscious is busy adjusting to new directives, and your horse's energy is rewired for healing; blocks are released and solutions are able to present themselves. If a horse suffers from azoturia (chronically tying-up), the unblocking process may actually allow the horse's body to repair its own chemistry, or the unblocking will awaken the owner to feeding or training issues which contribute to the tying-up, or perhaps one day by fluke a veterinarian walks into the barn who has had luck using an unconventional therapy for horses with this condition. And etc., etc., etc.

But really, why would thinking happy thoughts and putting your hands on the horse do anything at all? To accept this, you are being asked to trust in a relatively unexplored science. When you do the breathing and running of energy through your body, you begin to resonate at a higher vibration. Your hands—already channeled to handle the majority of life's creative tasks—are the easiest site to run this energy through in a concentrated manner. Conveniently, it is a natural response of other cellular bodies to link upward to that vibration. By putting your hands and attention on a subject, their own energy and cells respond to the higher vibration and work to raise up to that level. In this case, as a "healer" you were not responsible for building the doorway, but you assisted in opening the door. With The Treatment a little properly-applied attention goes a long way, much farther than all the fretting and thinking and researching at which most of us are already so skilled. By reprogramming the subconscious and your feelings, your approach to life and your horse shifts in such a way that changes can happen automatically. "Lucky" people always believe in their good fortune and on some level "unlucky" people always accept their misfortune—both were preprogrammed mentally for what seems their lot in life. If the "unlucky" ones only knew that they could just change their mind!

When doing energy-work of this sort on another living being, count on the fact that as the animal changes *you yourself will not go unchanged.* The Treatment will be a discovery of self through your horse, and of horse through yourself. At the outset you will look mainly to what you want to achieve, but soon you will let go of how you think it "should be" or "should happen." By exposing your wishes and worries and LEARNING TO DISCARD ALL EXPECTATIONS, you might find that what emerges is more of a horse than you ever knew you had. Harmony and peace accompany your results. Your horse will become your friend and you will be a genuine friend to your horse. Problems will continue to surface, but with energetic empowerment those problems will not rule your equine experience in the same way.

in conclusion

I commend you for having chosen The Treatment for your horse. This new approach places huge potentials into your very own hands. The Treatment has a domino-type effect, in that any Treatment work you do with the horse will continue to build on itself. Over time the body and mind (of you and your horse) will get stronger and more in-tune, your understanding of your horse's needs will sharpen, and many future problems will be avoided altogether. Horses teach us about tension like almost nothing else can—tightness within ourselves (mental or physical) translates into tightness within the horse, and vice-versa. To release tension on *any* level is to open up to life on that level. Creating this release through energy is a more lasting change because it reaches from the most minute aspects of ourselves on outward to the most far-reaching. Any time you find yourself feeling stuck in an issue with your horse, begin again with three weeks of The Treatment. Since The Treatment will have led you and the horse out of stagnancy and onto a pathway of progressiveness and increased wisdom, you won't find yourself needing to do sessions very often.

Once energy-work is learned it will stick with you forever, getting stronger with regular practice. Use it to support and accelerate any conventional means of treatment. Of course, laying open your horse's capacity for joy and grace will be the most profound reward of all.

final thoughts

When working your way out of perceived problems, the benefits of keeping a simple log book or journal can be substantial. Consider jotting down impressions of your horse's improvements or setbacks in a notepad every day or two. Be to-the-point and objective or go all-out and write down every feeling you have in connection to your horse. Try not to read back over the notes for at least a week or more. When you do finally read your log, you'll find useful insight; it's like a quick ticket out of the muck of your own thoughts and fears into a place where you can see your progress and developments more clearly.

The Treatment may be used for any animal, and even applied personally for yourself. Be creative. Having practiced with The Treatment, be aware that you now own a tool that is accessible to you wherever you go. Energy work is powerful and versatile; for acute situations like injuries you can move beyond the spinal work as described in this book. Use your breathwork and by placing your hands, run energy into cuts, bruises, sprains, aches and injuries of all kinds, in animals and in people. Calm a high-strung horse by running gentle energy into the cranial area before a ride. Etc., etc.

Open up—start reading more books on horses, those with an intelligent and humane angle; whatever jumps out at you from the shelves. Go to natural horsemanship clinics. Watch some lessons taught by instructors who care how horses think. Wherever horses seem truly happy is where to look! One important suggestion is to explore the work of trainer Pat Parelli. He has created what I believe to be the most thorough and workable home-study courses for training horses, as well as having the most comprehensively trained instructors offering clinics across the U.S. and beyond. Find his information on the web at www.parelli.com. Regardless, whoever feels genuinely right to you is right for you—studying other people's compassion, techniques and opinions is a handy way to define your own perspectives. Your personal vision, your own methods and your particular horse-associated character will emerge more strongly as you mingle with the growing amount of information available to you. Not only is there more information nowadays, but it's getting smarter than ever before. The horse world is increasingly leaning toward holistic healthcare, natural methods of management in feed and housing, balanced riding, and NATURAL horsemanship. Finally! These methods work faster, are far simpler and cheaper in the long run, and are more effective than anything else we've been doing thus far. Try it and you will see. So many people are now putting the concern and welfare of the horse at the forefront of horse ownership and use, it's like one massive evolutionary movement. And it is catching on rapidly. If that many more of us strive for better and better ways to help our horses to live happily amongst us, then we too become the teachers. Kindness and fairness to the horse; what a powerful concept.

about the author

Alene has been involved with bodywork on animals and people since 1990. She continues to explore both the tactile advantages of deep-tissue work upon the physical structure as well as the unlimited range of healing offered when working directly with body energies. She resides on Cape Cod.

NOTES

NOTES